Trust Ownership and the Future of News

Trust Ownership and the Future of News

Media Moguls and White Knights

Gavin Ellis

palgrave
macmillan

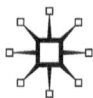

First published 2014 by
PALGRAVE MACMILLAN

Palgrave Macmillan in the UK is an imprint of Macmillan Publishers Limited, registered in England, company number 785998, of Houndmills, Basingstoke, Hampshire RG21 6XS.

Palgrave Macmillan in the US is a division of St Martin's Press LLC, 175 Fifth Avenue, New York, NY 10010.

Palgrave Macmillan is the global academic imprint of the above companies and has companies and representatives throughout the world.

Palgrave® and Macmillan® are registered trademarks in the United States, the United Kingdom, Europe and other countries.

ISBN 978–1–137–36943–7

This book is printed on paper suitable for recycling and made from fully managed and sustained forest sources. Logging, pulping and manufacturing processes are expected to conform to the environmental regulations of the country of origin.

A catalogue record for this book is available from the British Library.

A catalog record for this book is available from the Library of Congress.

To Jenny Lynch, an accomplished journalist and editor who is also my beloved wife

Contents

Figures and Tables

Figures

Tables

Acknowledgements

This book owes much to the many people who gave freely of their time to talk to me in the course of my research. I am particularly indebted to those connected with the three trustee-owned newspapers that are at the core of the study – *The Guardian, Irish Times* and *Tampa Bay Times*. *Trust Ownership and the Future of News* had its genesis in a doctoral thesis, and I am indebted to Dr Joe Atkinson and Dr Geoffrey Kemp of the University of Auckland for their guidance and advice on the initial research. I wish also to thank Felicity Plester and Chris Penfold at Palgrave Macmillan for their encouragement and assistance, together with their associate Francis Arumugam and his colleagues at Integra who handled the pre-production of the book. The cover is the work of my former colleague, *New Zealand Herald* cartoonist Rod Emmerson, who has shown that there is expression in a splash of printer's ink as well as in his award-winning cartoons.

I am grateful to the following publishers and journals for permission to reproduce passages in the book. Chapter 2: Princeton University Press for permission to reproduce the extract from *Republic.com 2.0* by Cass R Sunstein © Princeton University Press; Sage Publications for the extract from Les Hinton's article in *British Journalism Review*; and Cambridge University Press for the extract from the essay "Political Communication Systems and Democratic Values" by Michael Gurevitch and Jay Blumler in *Democracy and Mass Media: A Collection of Essays*. Chapter 3: University of Illinois Press for permission to reproduce the extract from *Four Theories of the Press: The Authoritarian, Libertarian, Social Responsibility, and Soviet Communist Concepts of What the Press Should Be and Do* © 1956, 1984 by Mary Derieg, Andrew W Siebert, Theodore Peterson and Wilbur Schramm. Chapter 4: The Day Publishing Company for the extract from Gregory Stone's history of *The Day*; Beacon Press for the extract from *The New Media Monopoly* by Ben Bagdikian © 2004 by Ben Bagdikian; and the *Globe and Mail* for the extract from its edition of 2 January 1999. Chapter 8: the *Vermont Law Review* for the extract from Richard Schmalbeck's essay "Financing the American Newspaper in the Twenty-first Century". Full citations for these and other works on which the author has drawn can be found in the bibliography.

Finally, I wish to thank my wife, friends and colleagues for their encouragement in bringing this work to publication.

Part I
Journalism in Crisis

1
Why We Need Public Interest Journalism

There is absolutely nothing wrong with profit. The issue for today's news media organisations is the purpose to which profit is put. If it is siphoned off as dividends to investors it is lost to journalism. If it is employed to make the media organisation self-sustaining, journalism can be the beneficiary. In an age of marginal viability, the former no longer makes much sense and the latter is a necessity.

It is necessary because, as the late C. Edwin Baker noted, a country is democratic only to the extent that its media, as well as elections, are structurally egalitarian and politically salient. And democratically significant journalism is under threat.

Baker's summation of the importance of the media, contained in the opening pages of *Media Concentration and Democracy*, was penned shortly before the 2007 Global Financial Crisis. If media ownership at that point struggled to be "structurally egalitarian", the economic maelstrom into which the world was subsequently propelled appeared to be the final straw. The future of commercial news media ownership – egalitarian or otherwise – was being called into question by plummeting revenue and mountainous debt.

It was not, however, the final straw. In the following years, news corporations tottered on. However, the integrity and even morality of the media was tested to the limit in phone hacking and sex scandals in the United Kingdom, financial collapses in North America and "big business" interference in Australia. In South Africa the integrity of government became the issue as repressive laws were placed in the way of news media attempting to be "politically salient".

The end may not be nigh but news media, in the English-speaking world at least, are headed for a cathartic moment. It may result in what economist Joseph Schumpeter called "creative destruction" – the need to replace old products and services with new ones – that will reform and renew the way the public receives information. Or it may fail to do so in a way that meets Baker's prerequisite for a democracy and leave, instead, a democratic deficit.

His definition is no less resonant now than it was in 2007: ownership and governance remain central to the survival of democratically significant news media, that is, media willing to provide information that citizens *need* to know, and able to distribute it to sufficient numbers of citizens to make the information broadly relevant.

It is time to ask whether the form of corporate ownership that both sustained and benefitted from news operations in the second half of the 20th century will do justice to this democratically significant journalism in the 21st century. Entertainment-driven media and specialist financial newspapers will continue to find friends on Wall Street and in the City of London but increasingly the former are diverging from traditional views of journalism and, in particular, its civic purposes. Serious mainstream journalism can no longer rely on the financial support that was forthcoming in the halcyon days when news-based print and (to a lesser extent) broadcasting had monopolies on advertising space or time and when rivers of gold flowed into dividend accounts.

In the days when media companies delivered double-digit annual profit growth it would have been heresy to suggest that "the news" was not a business. Purists determined to preserve the separation of church and state might suggest that the business was advertising but, in fact, that would not exist but for the news content that sat alongside. Now the advertising is migrating to digital platforms where that symbiotic relationship with news is no longer deemed necessary. It is a step too far to suggest the corporate world has no business in serious journalism but it is important to consider whether alternative forms of ownership and, certainly, governance are needed to counter a growing civic deficit in the traditional business model. Large questions hang over the future of that business model and of the structure of the industry.

It would be easy, but not altogether appropriate, to let technological determinism dictate both the form of this book and the nature of the news industry in future. Certainly, many scholars have an understandable focus on the massive impact that digital platforms have had on traditional mainstream media, but a longer view will recognise that the distribution of news has been a process that began evolving before Phidippides was dispatched to inform Athens of victory over the Persians at Marathon. And while invention has precipitated changes in the method and scale of delivery, it has not fundamentally altered the purposes of news dissemination. There is something enduring about what society makes of information.

Journalism and, in many respects, media enterprises have been formalised for at least 150 years. Today there is broad acceptance of the institutional nature of the press, both as an element of the political landscape and in its internal structures and practices. Therefore the subject is examined here in its institutional context. While opinions differ on the relationship between journalists and the political establishment (see, for example,

Bennett & Livingston 2003, 359–362; Davis 2003, 669–690), there is little doubt that the relationship is systematised. Hallin and Mancini's *Comparing Media Systems* and its predecessor *Four Theories of the Press* both attest to the development of the news media as political institutions within particular social settings (Hallin & Mancini 2004, 14). Likewise, the structures and practices of journalism have become institutionalised, along with the values and ethics to which professional journalists subscribe (Brighton & Foy 2007; Kovach & Rosenstiel 2001; Sparrow 2006). The nurturing of these institutional values and practices in the face of mounting external pressures is central to the argument made in this book that different – more altruistic – forms of governance will be necessary to sustain democratically significant journalism.

The *Shorter Oxford Dictionary* has seven definitions of institutions but Scruton (2007, 332–334) sums up for us the important characteristics of these bodies, as they are perceived within sociology and political science, and which may be found within journalism and the news media:

- They contain members but are not identical with any member.
- They have independent agency – the faculty of action – and may have rights and obligations that do not belong to individual members.
- They may endure beyond the life of any member and have a history that is not simply the history of its members.
- They manifest their existence through the intentional acts of their members, whose intentions they form and govern.
- They may be autonomous, or not.

Scruton sees autonomy in two distinct senses: as self-governing and answerable to no external constraints other than law; and as a body that *requires* its institutional arrangement to fulfil functions that could not be discharged any other way. News media organisations qualify on both counts although subject, of course, to the caveat that they are *influenced* by external political, economic and social agencies.

Likewise, Barley and Tolbert (1997, 93–94) could have been writing directly about the news media when they described institutions as organisations (and the individuals within them) that are suspended in a web of values, norms, rules, beliefs and taken-for-granted assumptions that define their view of the world. These are characteristics of a newsroom familiar to any journalist.

Some scholars make the case for placing the media within the ranks of major political institutions rather than simply acknowledging influential linkages between two autonomous fields (Cook 1998, 2006, and Sparrow 1999 among others). To delve too far into such arguments risks adding unnecessary complexity: the following chapters will demonstrate both the autonomous institutionalised nature of the press and the way in which its structural and cultural institutional elements have been impacted by both internal and external pressures. They will show that the obligations, values and codes that in many ways define the institution of journalism have been threatened and demonstrate how governance structures can be bound – morally and legally – to protect them.

The principal focus will be on mainstream print media because their future is most at risk. A symptom of their predicament is the fact that the concept of "mainstream" is no longer as clear-cut as it was even a decade ago. Cook's more recent contribution notes that the media landscape has become "messier" due to the declining power of mass media and the growth of autonomous Internet-based outlets, and is more circumspect in ascribing homogeneity and complementarity across media organisations because he acknowledges more players, greater diversity and more permeable institutional walls (2006, 165). The walls have not, however, come tumbling down and, for our purposes, it is still possible to define "mainstream" as media that continue to have a generalised distribution of news, comment and analysis to significantly sized audiences and which continue to follow established institutional practices and exert political influence.

It is important, however, to acknowledge that many traditional outlets have, under profit-driven commercial ownership, swerved towards entertainment and away from information that helps the audience to function as citizens. Hence, profit-driven companies under pressure to deliver shareholder dividends do threaten the institutionalised qualities and values of journalism. Alternative forms of ownership and governance based on a concept of trusteeship of journalistic ideals are now urgently needed to protect both the values and political significance of mainstream media.

Here we hit another definitional issue: what are journalistic ideals? Predictably, there are differing opinions and it may be useful to group them in order to find points of agreement and to distil the essence of what it is about journalism that needs to be protected and fostered. Opinion falls broadly into four camps that I have labelled traditionalists, restructuralists, reductionists and individualists.

Traditionalists believe that the social responsibility model articulated in 1947 by the United States Hutchins Commission continues to hold sway. Restructuralists advocate structural change and set their norms accordingly. Reductionists recognise changes to the media landscape in a digital age, and place journalists in a more narrowly defined role within a broad informational mix. Individualists believe that if media structures have not satisfied journalism's democratic imperatives, the need can be met by granting autonomy to socially responsible individual journalists. Each approach takes some account of current realities, but generally does so to identify deficiencies that will be overcome if a particular theoretical position is taken. Each requires a more detailed examination.

The traditionalist view places the informed citizen at the centre of democracy and journalism as its servant. At the core of its journalistic ideals is the proposition, expressed by American editors in 1912, that "freedom from all obligations except that of fidelity to the public interest is vital" (Friend & Singer 2007, 5). While recognising that changing market circumstances affect its application, the traditionalist position does not concede that the normative role of the media should be compromised for the sake of expedience. Rather, it acknowledges that some conditions make the ideal harder to attain (Patterson 2003). It is a theory seen by some as the best defence against negative effects of ownership. Soderlund and Hildebrandt (2005, 137–150), for example, argue that adherence to the doctrine (with its parallel requirement of editorial autonomy) could protect the Canadian press from the interventionist tendencies of major chain owners. In so saying, they reflect views expressed by two enquiries into Canadian press ownership, neither of which was under any illusion about the dimensions of the lofty heights to be scaled. The Davey Committee in 1970 described newsrooms as "bone yards of broken dreams" while the Kent Commission in 1981 added that there were now "fewer dreams to be broken" (Canadian Royal Commission on Newspapers 1981, 218).

A subset of the traditionalist view (what I will term the New Traditionalists) is the basis of civic or public journalism that seeks to reinvest citizens with democratic participation through journalism that is attuned to the community's civic needs and desires (Fallows 1997; Sparrow 1999). It is a standpoint at odds with interpretations of objectivity held by some mainstream media, because of its forms of advocacy engagement with the public but it is, nonetheless, consistent with the Hutchins Commission's ideals. A further example of New Traditionalism is Gans' theory of "multiperspectival" news (2003), which is the embodiment of the Hutchins Commission's pluralistic ideals.

The value preferences of the restructuralists suggest, perhaps self-evidently, that complex democracies require complex media ideals. The complexity is derived in part from their equal emphasis on structure and its effects on practice. Both Baker and Curran, for example, develop ideal-type ownership structures which they believe more capable of delivering journalistic ideals in a pluralistic democratic society, but which require enormous restructuring and re-regulation. Baker's vision of an ideal press is for "separate media entities, with each entity focused on, and preferably controlled and maybe owned by, one of the various groups making up the polity" (1998, 343–344) and for widely dispersed ownership (2007, 163–189). Curran envisages a broadcasting-based "working model of a democratic media system" with a core public service television sector, supplemented by a ring of four peripheral sectors, which he admits embodies a "complex set of requirements" (2002, 240–247). His model envisaged a civic media sector supporting activist organisations, a social market sector embodying minority media supported by the state, a professional media sector under the control of professional communicators utilising state-supported non-commercial structures, and a private sector operating on a commercial basis but with constraints to prevent subversion of the other sectors. His view of the significance of media structures is reinforced by his collaborative study with Iyengar, Lund and Salovaara-Moring of media models in the United Kingdom, United States, Finland and Denmark. It found that a public service model provided a greater amount of democratically significant programming than entertainment-centred, market-driven media (2009, 22). Baker's solution is for a "structurally mixed system ... with different economic bases and different goals for different portions of the press" facilitated by "intelligent and properly oriented structuring of the media" by means of government regulation (2002, 283–284). There is recognition among the restructuralists that the structural change they envisage will redefine journalistic norms to embrace an express pluralistic ideal, and redefine the relationship between journalist and government.

While Baker and Curran meet complexity with complexity, reductionists such as Zaller (2003) see it as a reason to reduce expectations and accept the value of journalists producing "burglar alarm news" to satisfy citizens' desire to be informed in moments of need. This viewpoint, drawn from a re-examination of the role of the citizen by Schudson in 1998, is that the scope and detail of government activity has grown to the point where no citizen can hope to be informed across its range, and the role of the journalist should therefore be confined to those aspects of policy and administration that meet the civic needs of "monitorial" rather than "informed" citizens (Graber 2003a; Zaller 2003). If the notion of the "informed citizen" has been over-stated, and Schudson is not alone in thinking so (Carpini 2000) then, by extension, the role of the press must also have been exaggerated. The reductionist argument accepts what Zaller calls "the Full News standard" in elite publications like the *New York Times*, but applies a different standard for "ordinary people". The "burglar alarm" standard calls attention to matters requiring urgent attention and does so in "noisy and excited tones" (Zaller 2003, 122). The reductionist approach finds support for the need to redefine the role of the media in line with a pragmatic re-evaluation of citizens' democratic activity (Graber 2003b), but its ready acceptance of aspects of tabloid journalism and imprecise explanations of democratic theory have rightly drawn criticism (Bennett 2003; Patterson 2003; Strömbäck 2005). It is an approach that, in the name of pragmatism, replaces the aspirational dimension of journalistic ideals with resigned acceptance.

The individualist model, taken from Merrill's *Existential Journalism* (1977) and applied by Singer (2006), also recognises extensive information flows in a complex society. However, this model takes a fundamentally different approach from that of the reductionists and structuralists, while embracing the traditionalist principle of social responsibility. It holds that, as "anyone can disseminate his or her views instantly and globally with a few keystrokes", the role of journalists has changed and the structures within which they worked are no longer the means by which that role should be defined (Friend & Singer 2007; Singer 2006). It may also be seen as an individualised reaction to the homogenisation of news and loss of identity by the journalist. Under this approach, normative practices are pivotal in identifying journalists as professionals (and thereby differentiating them from other "information providers") but the onus is placed on individuals to adhere to these practices and to accept the level of social responsibility that the model identifies as a key component of journalistic professionalism. Singer's "socially responsible existentialist" is not oxymoronic but an attempt to rationalise the dilemma faced by journalists in an exploding media galaxy: if an ever-expanding range of information options is destabilising traditional media structures, journalists have only themselves to rely upon to apply the professionalism necessary to discharge their social responsibility to the public. Kovach and Rosenstiel (2001) arrive at the same point. The nine elements of journalism that they articulate place the onus on the individual journalist (2001, 12–13).

Table 1.1 demonstrates how each of the perspectives on journalistic values and their delivery shares common elements, but each school has a different way of shuffling the pack and dealing different cards.

Each approach is, in fact, seeking a means to the same end – a socially responsible media equipped to, as Dahl puts it, "improve citizens' capacities to engage intelligently in political life" (2000, 187). The traditionalist ideals should remain the gold standard to which news media aspire but the financial and professional deterioration of traditional media organisations cannot be ignored. Nevertheless, journalism is capable of more positive contributions than the reductionist view suggests but requires a more robust and substantial infrastructure than individualists envisage if it is to achieve its democratic function. A variant of the restructuralist approach best suits the needs of civic society and within this framework lies the potential for extending the role of trustee governance.

That form of governance aims not only to protect and promote the ideals but also the professionalism of journalism. Journalists are guided by the organisation in which they work. In turn, the organisation is guided by a combination of heritage, industry-wide approaches and public expectation. This amalgam creates the standards and guidelines under which reporters and editors operate. Just as shared practices contribute to the defining characteristics of an institution, so too, do shared desires. Hence journalistic ideals, viewed from any of the standpoints set out above, contribute to the news media's institutional character. Common institutional settings can be applied nationally and, in key respects, across all of the countries studied here.

10

Table 1.1 Four approaches to journalistic ideals

Approach	Ideals
Traditionalist	• A truthful, comprehensive and intelligent account of the day's events in a context that gives them meaning. • A forum for the exchange of comment and criticism. • A means of projecting the opinions and attitudes of the groups in the society to one another. • A method of presenting and clarifying goals and values of society. • A way of reaching every member of the society by the currents of information, thought and feeling which the press supplies, expressed as "full access to the day's intelligence". • Acknowledgement of market forces. *Source*: Hutchins Commission 1947
Structuralist	• An account not only of major events but also the issues and problems that give rise to them. • A balanced form of journalism and a forum for debate open to different opinions. • A watchdog role achieved by mediating the investigative resources within a free society (e.g. whistleblowers, dissenting elite members, critical researchers). • A structurally mixed media system, with different economic bases and different goals for different portions of the press. • A role for government in the "intelligent and properly oriented structuring" of the media, creating a mixed system, and providing it with adequate support. *Sources*: Baker 2002, Curran 2007
Reductionist	• A "Full News Standard" (along traditionalist lines) governing elite media that provide sober, detailed and comprehensive coverage of public affairs to allow citizens to form opinions about the full range of important issues independent of government recommendations. • A modified standard to meet the needs of monitorial citizens "who scan (rather than read) the informational environment in a way so that they may be alerted on a very wide variety of issues for a very wide variety of ends and may be mobilised around those issues in a variety of ways", recognising that the obligations of public life should be "dispatched with efficiency". • Coverage that is intensely focused, dramatic and entertaining, with "ample opportunity" for opposing views. *Source*: Zaller 2003

Individualist	• A journalist makes a personal choice to uphold the public trust.
	• Complete autonomy is conferred on individual journalists who create their own standards and choose, act and decide on the basis of personal integrity and responsibility.
	• A subjective approach that considers alternative courses of action before commitment to one of those courses reflecting the honestly held views of the journalist.
	• Resides editorial decision-making in the hands of each journalist, who must consider the consequences of his or her actions.
	• A response to what is seen as loss of freedom and integrity within highly institutionalised "corporate" journalism.

Sources: Merrill 1977, Singer 2006

There is widespread use of industry-wide standards within the English-speaking world. Each publication has its own characteristics but operates within a general framework, even when transformed into a publication-specific code. Codified principles vary in both form and detail, but there are clear similarities in the ethical expectations of the organisations that have created them. Table 1.2 illustrates this conjunction.

Journalism operates on numerous related planes – technological, cultural, constitutional and commercial – that may be stable or volatile, crystal clear or ambiguous. It also exists in a number of different institutional environments:

• Political: the institutional setting, national and supranational that determines the political importance that should be attached to the news media
• Professional: the normative work practices that create a context within which journalistic performance can be understood and assessed
• Practical: the organisational structures and practices that define news media entities and their development.

The institutional settings with which we are concerned here are those that influence – or are influenced by – ownership. At times it is necessary to step outside the field of journalism to find appropriate elements – for example to institution-related theory of the firm, and to path dependency – that help to explain media business practice. Generally, however, the discussion of journalism itself takes place here within the framework of shared practices in news production and against a background of homogeneity that Cook might again have revisited had he lived. Falling newsroom staff numbers (already declining when the recession that began in late 2007 brought even

Table 1.2   Common principles in Anglo-American journalism

	UK Press Complaints Com.	National Union Journalists UK	Irish Press Council	New York Times	Los Angeles Times	Associated Press (U.S.)	Brit. Columbia Press Council	Canadian Newspaper Ass.	Australian Press Council	MEAA*** (Australia)	New Zealand Press Council	EPMU*** (NZ)
Accuracy	•	•	•	•	•	•	•	•	•	•	•	•
Attribution		•	•	•						•		
Balance		•	•	•					•	•	•	•
Children	•		•		•	•					•	
Confidentiality	•	•	•	•	•	•	•		•	•	•	•
Interest conflict	•	•	•	•	•	•	•	•		•		•
Correction	•	•	•	•	•	•	•	•	•		•	•
Discrimination*	•	•	•					•	•		•	•
Fabrication**		•		•	•	•				•		
Fairness		•	•	•	•	•			•	•	•	•
Grief/shock	•	•	•						•	•	•	•
Harassment	•		•	•								
Identification	•			•	•	•	•			•		•
Privacy	•	•	•	•		•	•	•	•	•	•	•
Right of reply	•			•	•	•	•	•	•	•	•	
Sex victims	•				•	•	•					
Subterfuge	•	•	•	•	•		•		•	•	•	
Treating				•	•	•						•

*Includes communal tension; **Includes plagiarism; ***Media, Entertainment & Arts Alliance, Engineering, Printing & Manufacturing Union.

more savage cuts) have led media outlets to practice a follow-my-leader approach to what they cover, adopt similar ways of doing more with less, and utilise increasing amounts of "news-on-a-plate" provided by public and private sector media management or public relations teams.

Gans' preface to a 25th anniversary edition of his widely cited study *Deciding What's News* (2004/1979) notes that the media landscape as a whole has changed since the first edition but the organisations that he had studied "have remained virtually unchanged". He doubts that a restudy would produce significantly different conclusions to those he reached in 1979. Among those conclusions was the propensity for news organisations to "routinise" the journalistic task, produce "journalistic efficiencies" and publish similar news. A quarter of a century earlier, Gans noted that there were imped-iments to journalists changing the way they practised their craft. Those impediments – audience reduction, increased external pressure, higher costs, organisational (management) obstacles and the "competitive bind" requir-ing virtually identical news offering – now appear remarkably prescient (2004, 288–289).

Gans' highly institutionalised view of news practices and structures (much of which accords with my own experience as a daily newspaper editor in New Zealand) has lost none of its validity over time, recessional effects notwithstanding. News media outlets continue to display significant professional, structural, procedural and cultural similarities.

Numerous scholars (Baker, Bollinger, Cook, Curran, Gans, Norris, Patterson, Schudson, Sunstein and Tuchman among others) have described the journalistic function, each imbuing it with a particular emphasis or dimension that takes it beyond the simple social responsibility model espoused by the Hutchins Commission in 1947, and almost all finding large gaps between what Schultz calls the ambition and reality of journal-ism (1998, 45). There is a question over whether this gap has developed or has always existed. Habermas (1996) takes the view that journalism's contribution to the public sphere began well but deteriorated over time. Other historical perspectives such as those by Schudson (1978, 2005), Kaplan (2002, 2006) and Starr (2004) suggest an evolutionary process that at no stage produced a perfect specimen. A third alternative, which might be called New Jerusalem Journalism, is less concerned with the past than with the future. Zelizer, drawing on Cook's judgement of journalism critiques (1998, 173), explains it thus: "Driven by a concern for the ideal and the optimum, political science developed a wide-ranging litany of tools by which to trans-form journalism's actual state into a more perfect enterprise" (2004, 149). Ideological fashion and socio-economic change have facilitated the peri-odic redefining of shortcomings and what the "perfect enterprise" should be. Curran, echoing a belief shared with others, says that the traditional the-ory of the role of the media now seems "so pious, so fossilised" (2007, 34). It is, he says, disconnected from an understanding of the working of con-temporary democracy and its emphasis on social groups, political parties, civil society, ideology and globalisation. To this should be added commer-cialisation, which Hallin and Mancini describe as "the most powerful source for homogenisation of media systems" (2004, 273). Curran also believes tra-ditional theory is narrowly focused on serious political journalism, which is a diminishing component of market-driven, entertainment-oriented mod-ern media (Cook 2006, 116–117; Hamilton 2004, 238–241; Underwood 1993, 56–57). In parallel, Baker contends that journalistic theory cannot be divorced from the economic structure, legal rules and governmental actions that affect its implementation, nor from the effect of budget cuts that affect professional practices – deficiencies he often lays at the feet of media owners that detract from a fulfilment of the democratic promise (2002, 282–284).

Baker's contention is our starting point. A large majority of journalists have not lost sight of their responsibilities to citizens or of their commitment to journalistic codes and values. However, they acknowledge the reducing autonomy of journalism as an institution and increasing difficulty in discharging its obligations. If the dominant forms of news media organisation are failing to fulfil their broader fiduciary obligations – by reducing the ability of journalists to fulfil their democratic function – are there ways of re-ordering the institutional foundations to provide structures more likely to meet the desired needs?

It is unnecessary to retrace in detail the footsteps of Curran, Baker and other distinguished scholars who have addressed the negative impact of corporate ownership and conglomeration on journalism and its contribution to democracy. As already stated, the focus here is on a form of ownership that has received relatively little attention – private sector trustee governance.

There is nothing particularly novel about trusts or, indeed, the presence of trusts in the media business. However, the majority of trusts in that industry, as we shall see in the following chapters, serve the interests of specific owners. Only a handful are bound to the protection and promotion of significant journalism through the ownership of newspapers that they hold in trust. That handful includes three newspapers that are the subject of case studies in this book – *The Guardian*, the *Irish Times* and the *Tampa Bay Times* (formerly the *St Petersburg Times*). They were chosen as case studies because they are the largest and most influential publications held under this particular form of private sector ownership. No other newspapers operating under trust governance match their scale of operation or influence. There are, however, a number of "hybrids" with some of the characteristics of this trio that also will be encountered in the book. Altruistic trusteeship – that serves a social purpose rather than preserving and enhancing the fortunes of individuals – also exists outside print media. The governing bodies of public service broadcasting operations act as trustees even when not formally constituted as trusts, as do many news agencies and investigative journalism start-ups described later.

One of the desired outcomes of the book is that it will provide a governance game plan for those wishing to establish new digital ventures to fill gaps in the media's service to democracy. Any plan should identify obstacles to be avoided and for that reason it will explore not only the positive attributes of trusts but past failings. However, like all good game players, we need to know the game rules and to study how past and present players employ winning and losing gambits. Much of the book is devoted to a study of the development of this news game.

The first of three parts explores the state of the news media and reasons why an alternative approach to ownership and governance is not only desirable but also necessary. Part II is devoted to an examination of trusts from their origins within the news industry to their history and institutional structure within the present media landscape. The final part draws on an aspect of path dependency theory called bricolage to piece together the governance road map that should inform the establishment of new media ownership structures.

"Bricolage" is a term that can be found in disciplines ranging from the visual arts and music to anthropology and information technology. It has a number of applied meanings but will be used here in the context used by Lanzara in a discussion on institution building (1998). He drew on Levi-Strauss' introduction of the term to anthropology in *The Savage Mind* (1962), in which second-hand materials are used to create new structures and functions. Lanzara notes that institutions – even those that serve new purposes – are seldom created from scratch but are the outcome of the recombination and reshuffling of pre-existing available components or other institutional components (1998, 26–27). He believes that bricolage may be the only way to build and innovate in volatile environments. Nothing is more volatile, surely, than the world in which our news media exists.

2
Journalism's Crisis

In 2005 the Canadian-based media conglomerate CanWest had newspaper and broadcasting interests in seven countries. It boasted revenue in Canadian dollars in excess of $3 billion and assets of more than $5 billion. Five years later it was bankrupt, its assets were dispersed and it was ignominiously reduced to a shell company called 2737469 Canada Inc. CanWest was a dramatic example of the evolutionary trajectory of media companies and the largest to take Darwinian theory to its terminal conclusion in the turbulent aftermath of the Global Financial Crisis.

Others tottered on the brink of extinction but survived. Across the border, the owners of both of Chicago's metropolitan newspapers – the giant Tribune Company and the smaller Sun-Times Media – filed for bankruptcy within four months of each other, with the former then restructured and the latter sold. In Britain, *The Independent* was sold for £1 to a Russian entrepreneur after the London newspaper's Irish owner hit a brick wall of debt. The effects of high debt were also felt in Australasia, where billions of dollars were wiped off the value of newspaper-owning companies.

These were not, however, innocent victims of wider economic woes. They conformed to a pattern that began to take form years before Western banks introduced the term "sub-prime" to everyday speech. The financial crisis simply accelerated processes that were already underway.

The United States is the leading media market and for years its news media companies were high earners. In 2005 (a year in which the US media castigated oil companies for making 10 per cent "windfall profits" following petrol price increases) profit margins in American media companies fell a modest 1.5 points to an average of slightly less than 20 per cent. However, disaster struck in the wake of the international recession. The average operating margin for the publicly reporting companies, which represented about 40 per cent of the nation's daily newspaper circulation, was estimated in 2010 to be around 5.6 per cent.[1] Two years later it was hovering around 6 per cent but assorted special charges reduced iconic companies like the

New York Times Company, McClatchy and the Washington Post Company to break-even or worse.

Globally, newspaper advertising revenues fell by 22 per cent between the onset of the financial crisis in 2008 and 2012. The international print industry organisation WAN-IFRA found the five-year fall was driven principally by newspaper advertising declines in the United States; a 42 per cent fall over that period accounted (in monetary terms) for nearly three-quarters of the global loss in newspaper advertising.[2] Employment in the industry told a similar story: a US Bureau of Labor Statistics survey showed the total number of people employed by newspaper publishers declined from a 1990 peak of 457,000[3] to 230,730 in May 2012 – the same number as were employed in January 1947 – while a 2013 estimate by the Pew Center put the number of professionals employed in US newsrooms below 40,000 for the first time since the census began in 1978.

Such numbers indicate the parlous state of most newspaper companies at the end of the first decade of the 21st century – and the newspapers of Canada, Britain and Australasia fared little better than their American counterparts – but it represents only the latest addition to two decades in which the newspaper industry's business model was progressively undermined. The industry itself lays blame generally on a combination of periodic economic recession and sustained migration of audiences and advertising to the Internet. Both *are* factors in the malaise but underlying these effects is a deeper internal problem: a business formula that was fundamentally flawed.

Common forms of ownership shaped an institutional approach to business strategy in the newspaper industry and gave rise to common responses to a rising tide of challenges that, in turn, led to predictably similar impacts in enterprises where journalism is but one ingredient of the "product". It suggests a need for mechanisms to protect what Jones calls "serious news, the iron core of information that is at the centre of a functioning democracy" (2009, 1).

It is unnecessary to reiterate the doom scenarios for a dying press beyond noting that the worst case is that the death of the paper edition of the *New York Times* is nigh. In *Epic 2014,* an online film made in 2004 by Robin Sloan and Matt Thompson, the Grey Lady in a print dress was predicted to disappear in 2014. The more optimistic view is that newspapers will struggle on until 2043 (Meyer 2004). However, the concern should not be with the predicted demise of the ink-on-paper edition but with the possible death of the type of serious journalism for which the printed page has become an idealised metaphor. The difference was recognised by the Knight Commission, which stated that, from the standpoint of public need, the challenge was not to preserve any particular medium but to "promote the traditional public service functions of journalism" (2009, 27).

The accelerated decline in the economic well-being of traditional media companies has led to newsroom cuts and less time and space devoted to "serious journalism". A Pew Research Center/Project for Excellence in Journalism survey of US journalists published in March 2008 noted that 55 per cent of journalists at national news organisations cited a financial or economic concern as the most important problem facing journalism, up from just 30 per cent in 2004. The centre's *State of the News Media Report 2013* found that more than 30 per cent of Americans had stopped using a news source because it no longer met their needs and 60 per cent of that number did so because they felt stories were no longer complete. If these trends are extrapolated, the notional endpoint is a world in which professional journalism has been supplanted by citizen journalism, unmediated access to original sources via the Internet, wholesale online chatter, entertainment and discontent.

Professional journalism and its normative values are vulnerable if the future is bound up in a digital matrix of online social networks, information exchange, Google groups and so-called Digital Democracy that has the appearance of access but which is, in fact, a form of information control in which the vested interests of political, bureaucratic and corporate elites determine what the public has a right to know. The future is made more tenuous by the use – particularly among young adults – of digital media not as a substitute for "print journalism" but as a substitute for serious news of any sort. A Pew Center report in March 2010 indicated that only 35 per cent of Americans aged 18–29 followed the news "all or most of the time".[4]

For news media companies the combination of these three factors – a flawed business model, general economic recession and shifting patterns of media usage – have converged to mimic that rare weather phenomenon that occurs when a trio of significant meteorological events converge at sea: the perfect storm. Examination of the factors will provide insight into the areas where protective governance is needed to preserve journalistic quality and delivery but, first, we need to retrace some history.

The corporate history of newspapers since the Second World War can be divided into five phases: growth, consolidation, destabilisation, danger and crisis. While there are variations in timescale and detail within the Anglo-American markets, the patterns of development generally follow these phases and the business model that grew around corporate newspaper ownership is as consistent across the markets as are the journalistic norms that bind the six countries together. Inevitably, the flaws in the model are equally consistent.[5]

Growth phase

The four decades following the Second World War were golden years for Anglo-American newspapers. After the lifting of wartime newsprint rationing, daily circulations rose steadily and the wholesale disappearance of afternoon newspapers (as television began its own rise) was offset by increases in the number and circulation of morning editions. In the United States, total daily circulation rose from 41 million in 1940 to 63 million in 1974 and it stayed above 60 million for almost 30 years. In Britain, overall daily circulation that had stood at 17.8 million before the war rose to 28.6 million in 1947 and stayed above 20 million until 1998. Canada showed a similar pattern, with total daily circulation surging from 2.2 million in 1940 to 3.3 million in 1950 and peaking at 5.7 million in 1989. Australia's metropolitan/national dailies grew steadily from a 1940 total of less than 1.5 million to more than 3.5 million by the mid-1970s. Regional dailies experienced a significant setback in the late 1960s but they, too, rose steadily to peak in the 1980s at more than 650,000. In New Zealand, combined daily circulations that stood at 785,000 in 1957 had reached almost a million copies a day by the mid-1960s and peaked at 1.06 million in 1985. Historical circulation figures for Ireland are unavailable. In 1956 the combined circulations of the three Dublin morning newspapers (*Irish Independent, Irish Press, Irish Times*) was 351,235 and rose only marginally (to 369,534) by 1979 as the Celtic Tiger had yet to roar.

Advertising revenue displayed similar upward paths. If there was a downturn, recovery occurred within two years and the upward trend continued. Newspaper Association of America statistics show that between 1950 and 2000 print advertising revenue in the United States increased from $US2 billion to $US48.7 billion. The monopoly status that newspapers held in many cities enhanced this position. Over time, the composition of advertising revenue changed. The proportion of revenue derived from display advertising dropped and reliance on classified advertising grew. Picard (2002b, 30–31) observes that this shift in the United States changed the business model. In 1950 classified advertising represented 18 per cent of US revenue but rose to 40 per cent by 2000. Classifieds – notably car sales, employment and real estate–were economically sensitive and contributed to the periodic dips and recoveries in profit (although these ripples were nothing compared to the Internet-induced classified collapse in the first decade of the 21st century).

Similar patterns in newspaper advertising growth were seen elsewhere. For example, national and regional newspaper advertising growth in the United Kingdom also was initially relatively modest – between 1960 and 1970 annual growth averaged 7 per cent – but accelerated rapidly, growing 18-fold between 1969 and 1999 to reach £4.4 billion.

Concentration phase

The upward trajectory had two benefits: profits were enhanced and the monthly cash flow provided enviable liquidity that began to attract the attention of potential shareholders. There had been various ownership structures in the Anglo-American markets, including family-owned concerns, private companies with unrelated shareholders, a small number of trusts and share market listed companies that had newspapers among their assets. Their assets ranged from single titles to significant groups such as the Hearst Corporation, although many continued to be strongly influenced by the interests of founder families and few had widely held shares. In 1977 the Royal Commission on the Press noted that only one group in the United Kingdom, Reed International (owner of the Mirror newspapers), was widely held. However, the United States, which had led the revenue growth path, was to demonstrate how the newfound value of newspaper companies could be translated into growth and reward through the stock exchange.

The rapid growth in commercial value began to change the US ownership landscape in the mid-1960s for two reasons: to unlock some of that value for existing owners, and to avoid heavy death duties. In the early 1960s the US Inland Revenue Service (IRS) saw the growing affluence of newspaper companies and sought to reflect this by changing the formula used to calculate newspaper owners' assets for gift and estate duties (Neiva 1996, 26–27). One concern among family groups over these changes was that the death of one member could necessitate a sale to cover estate costs. In 1963, Dow Jones (publisher of the *Wall Street Journal*) became the first newspaper company in America to be listed on the stock exchange in order that its owners, the Bancroft family, could realise some of its growing value while family members retained a majority of shares. The following year the Chandler family followed suit and listed the Times Mirror Company (publisher of the *Los Angeles Times*) while retaining a substantial shareholding (*ibid.*, 32–33). In order to retain control – while benefiting from initial public offerings and subsequent rises in market capitalisation – some families created two-tier share structures that conferred special voting rights. These structures are discussed in Chapter 6.

The third company in the United States to seek share market listing was Gannett but the reasoning behind the Gannett Company's decision to float in 1967 was different: that company had already embarked on an aggressive acquisition strategy (see Chapter 5) and issuing public stock provided both new capital and tax advantages to the company at a time in which there were willing sellers.

The incentive for families to sell to groups like Gannett was given impetus by the change to IRS estate duty appraisals but was also enhanced by the offering of part-payment in shares, which gave tax advantages not available in cash sales (*ibid.*, 33). Gannett gave the American newspaper industry a model that others were quick to follow: stock exchange listing provided capital and tax advantages that facilitated acquisitions that provided a bigger share of a bright and growing market.

In 1930 there were almost 2000 daily newspapers in the United States and only 16 per cent of them were held in chain ownership. The number of independently owned titles began to diminish as rapidly as the fortunes of the industry grew. By the 1990s, 77 per cent of the nation's newspapers had been consolidated into a diminishing number of increasingly powerful groups as bigger fish ate them.

Stock exchanges began to see newspapers as "good business", particularly when their assets were in monopoly markets and were able to withstand the cyclical effects of economically sensitive advertising like real estate and employment. Gannett provided a perfect example. Spectacular growth was fuelled by the acquisition between 1970 and 1989 of 69 daily newspapers, 16 television stations, 29 radio stations and an outdoor advertising business with 45,000 billboards in the United States and Canada. Between 1967 and 1987 the company had an uninterrupted pattern of growth (Neuharth 1989, 180):

- Annual revenue rose from $US186 million to $US3.1 billion.
- Annual profit increased from $US14 million to $US319 million.
- The company experienced 80 uninterrupted quarters of earnings gains.
- Shareholder dividends increased 20 times in 20 years.
- The value of 100 shares purchased in 1967 increased, with stock splits, from $US2700 to $US74,588.
- Within five years of stock exchange listing, Gannett stock was selling at twice the average Standard & Poor price-earnings ratio.

Gannett smoothed out its earnings by investing in plant and staff during periods of growth and cost-cutting in lean years. In so doing the company satisfied what Meyer describes as the financial analysts' "lust for predictability" (1995, 42). This earnings management provided a further model for other owners to follow but also created an unfortunate pattern of fluctuation in editorial resources and the amount of space devoted to editorial content.

In his autobiography, Gannett's former CEO, Al Neuharth, set out the strategy he employed to convince analysts that his recently listed company was worthy of their endorsement. It is the blueprint for relations between media companies and analysts throughout the Anglo-American financial markets. Analysts, he said, did not want to know how many journalism prizes had been won or the quality of editors and journalists. The bottom line was paramount: "Gannett was a dependable profit machine in good times and bad" (1989, 178).

Media companies in the other markets saw the advantages of acquisition, but not always as the buyer. In Britain, where the number of newspaper-owning companies dropped from 490 in 1961 to 220 in 1977, international conglomerates – many with significant interests outside the news media – began buying newspapers. Between 1969 and 1986 nine multinationals bought 200 newspapers and, as Curran notes, exposed titles to influence from the financial and industrial sectors because of conflicts of interest (Curran & Seaton 1997, 82).

In Canada 75 per cent of newspapers were chain-owned by 1980. This percentage of chain ownership was matched in New Zealand by 1985, while by 1989 Rupert Murdoch's News Limited controlled 70 per cent of Australia's metropolitan daily circulation.

For newspaper owners and investors these were heady times, encapsulated in a contemporary study of newspaper proprietors by Nicholas Coleridge, the London managing director of the Condé Nast magazine chain. He described the 1980s as "the greatest scramble for newspaper assets ever known", noting that the prices paid were unprecedented because buyers recognised that newspapers were in many cases one of the few remaining monopolies. Many family-owned newspapers in single-newspaper towns were run conservatively and their owners were satisfied with modest returns. Corporate owners set about raising returns by increasing cover prices and advertising rates and profits grew accordingly (Coleridge 1994, 21).

It was a feeding frenzy and none was more rapacious than Rupert Murdoch. He took News Limited from Australia to the United Kingdom and the United States, beginning with his purchase of the *News of the World* in 1968 and culminating by 1990 in his entry into both markets with direct-to-home satellite broadcasting – having collected the *New York Post*, *The Times*, *The Sun* and 20th Century Fox along the way. It was at this point that the effects of over-eating began to be felt, in a portent of what would become widespread almost two decades later.

Destabilising phase

In 1990 Murdoch's News Corporation, which had been propelled skyward by huge bank loans, ran out of fuel and stalled. Banks would no longer add to his company's $US7.6 billion debt and News Corporation (which changed its name from News Limited in 1979) found itself on the brink of foreclosure.

The empire was saved only after a masterful effort by Murdoch who negotiated with 146 banks to reschedule the debt, perhaps relying on the belief that the debt level was so high the banks could not afford to let News Corporation fail (Greenslade 2004, 559). However, Murdoch also enacted a clearly explained recovery strategy that included share issues, significant sale of assets, cost cutting, restructuring and a commitment to a diversified entertainment industry profile. Within a year profit had risen by 315 per cent and the company's share price had quadrupled from a low in January 1991 of $A2.65.[6]

There were four lessons in the near-disaster:

- Leveraged acquisitions must be kept within manageable limits.
- Divestiture may be a strategic necessity.
- Transparency in governance and strategic management reassures lenders.
- The share market rewards profit.

The lessons may have influenced the future activities of News Corporation but they were not universally acknowledged or followed by others. Indeed, debt-funded acquisition became a regular occurrence.

By the early 1990s the transnational conglomerates (Atlantic Richfield, Lonrho, Reed International, Thomson and Trafalgar House) had sold their UK papers, and not always to august buyers: Reed International's Mirror Group was sold to Robert Maxwell (whose embezzling was discovered after his death), the *Daily Telegraph* to the Hollinger Group (whose chief executive, Conrad Black was later jailed on fraud charges although these were partly overturned on appeal) and the *Express* newspapers to Richard Desmond (owner of a pornography empire). This phase also coincided with other notable changes in the newspaper environment.

US daily newspaper circulation in 1993 dipped below 60 million for the first time in 30 years and marked the beginning of a year-on-year decline that continued unabated and which began to accelerate in 2004.

The American newspaper industry had been relying on basic circulation sales figures for decades and had painted pictures of a strong industry. However, there had been signs of decline well before 1993. The proportion of the population reading daily newspapers dropped from 78 per cent in 1960 to less than 40 per cent by the year 2000 (Meyer 2004, 16).[7] There was a similar trend in Britain, with the proportion of the public reading a newspaper dropping from 85–90 per cent in the mid-1960s (Tunstall 1996, 223) to 45 per cent in 2006.[8]

In circulation terms, the first decade of the 21st century was a picture of decline across most Anglo-American markets. While some major metropolitan dailies (nationals in the case of the United Kingdom) enjoyed occasional lifts in circulation, the general trend has been downward. The exceptions have been Ireland, which experienced later circulation gains on the back of the Celtic Tiger economic boom, and South Africa, where the emancipation of the Black majority in the post-Apartheid era led to a burgeoning in newspaper readership (see Table 2.1).

In order to offset these declines, and to meet the demands of shareholders, newspaper-owning companies capitalised on their unique position in print advertising: many advertisers were hostage to what was often the only daily newspaper in town because they sold products or services that could not be advertised as efficiently in other media. Supermarkets and department stores were particularly vulnerable because of the multi-item nature of their display advertising. Newspapers continued to increase their advertising charges even though they delivered fewer potential customers, creating a service gap that would return to haunt them as alternative media became available.

Most of the Anglo-American countries suffered revenue downturns in the economic shocks that followed the 9/11 attacks in 2001 but quickly recovered. With the exception of the United States (which had experienced an unusually high increase in advertising revenue across all media in the

Table 2.1   Relative 21st century decline: Circulation trends

	USA	Canada	UK	Ireland	Australia	NZ	S. Africa
2000	55,773	5,167	18,609	574	3,083	777	1,118
2001	55,578	5,185	18,297	588	No data	764	1,169
2002	55,186	5,005	18,349	591	No data	745	1,137
2003	55,185	4,930	17,450	772	2,582	739	1,286
2004	54,626	4,911	16,679	742	2,563	739	1,408
2005	53,345	4,799	16,571	758	2,555	729	1,504
2006	52,329	4,573	16,133	800	2,531	721	1,628
2007	50,742	4,699	15,482	797	2,513	711	1,672
2008	48,597	4,295	14,995	833	2,484	653	1,681
Change '00–'08	−12.86%	−16.88%	−19.42%	+45.12%	−19.43%	−15.96%	+50.35%

Source: WAN/IFRA World Press Trends.

millennium year), all countries had print advertising revenue in 2005 that was well ahead of 2000. In Ireland revenue increased by 55 per cent (circulation up 32 per cent) over the period, in Australia by 49 per cent (circulation down 17 per cent),[9] in New Zealand by 39 per cent (circulation down 6.6 per cent), in Canada by almost 32 per cent (circulation down 7.1 per cent) and in the United Kingdom by 17.5 per cent (circulation down 9.3 per cent). In the United States newspaper advertising revenue fell 3.8 per cent (circulation down 4.4 per cent) over the period that had included the one-off effects of that high millennium year income, although between 2002 and 2005 it increased by 7.5 per cent.

Shirky notes that American newspapers had been in a market governed by supply rather than demand and were able to overcharge and under-serve.[10] Figure 2.1 – which combines the circulation totals and newspaper advertising revenue totals of the United States, the United Kingdom, Canada, Australia, Ireland and New Zealand – show clearly that the decline in circulation and rise in revenue created the growing service gap that was common across the Anglo-American press. Only Ireland could claim to have a reasonable correlation between circulation and advertising revenue when the country's cumulative inflation rate of 18 per cent between 2000 and 2005 is factored into the increase.

As circulations declined, newspaper managements turned increasingly to the use of readership figures, rather than circulation, as a measure of audience reach, employing a myriad of statistical permutations such as audience and section segmentation to persuade advertisers that print reached their target markets. However, analysis shows that, on overall readership, the Anglo-American press did not close the service gap (Picard 2003, 130).[11] At best, readership flatlined between 2005 and 2008, as Figure 2.2 illustrates.

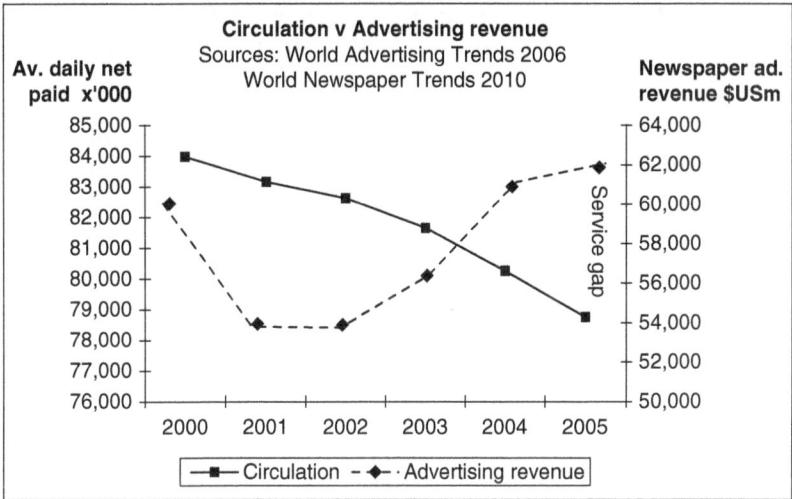

Figure 2.1 Six-country aggregation of circulation and advertising revenue

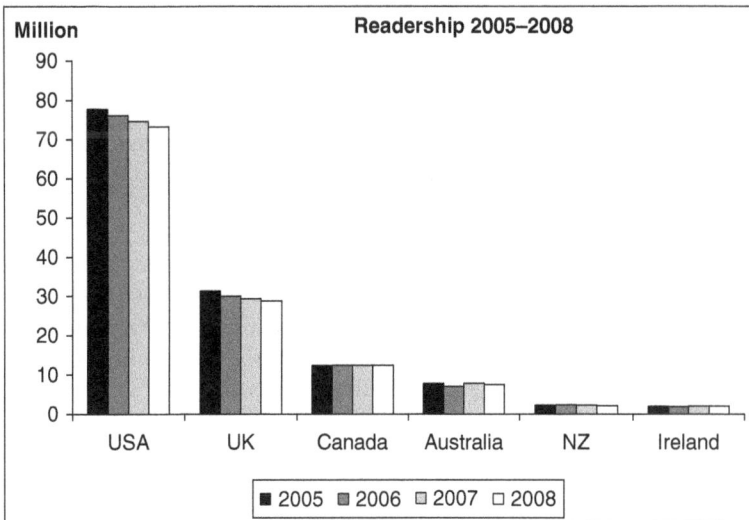

Figure 2.2 Declining or flat readership
Sources: Newspaper Association of America (USA), National Readership Survey (UK), NADbank (Canada), Roy Morgan (Aust./NZ), Joint National Survey (Ireland).

Newspaper managers could not have been blind to the growing service gap although they did little to reflect it in their pricing policies. They would also have seen, over time, the declining share of the advertising spend that was going to newspapers. In the United States the percentage declined from

36.9 per cent to 28.9 per cent between 1996 and 2005. The pattern was repeated elsewhere: the United Kingdom down from 40.4 per cent to 35.5 per cent, Canada from 40 per cent to 35.1 per cent, Australia from 41.7 per cent to 38.7 per cent and New Zealand from 41.2 per cent to 38.8 per cent. Only Ireland's newspapers fared reasonably well: a 60.6 per cent share in 1996, two-thirds of the market in 2001 and back down to 59.2 per cent in 2005.[12]

Danger phase

To give an impression of growth, newspaper groups continued to "up-size" by taking over other groups whose revenue could be added to their own. However, the industry was by now in what might be termed third-stage acquisition. The first stage had been the buying of single newspapers by companies only a little larger than themselves. The second stage was the acquisition of one relatively small group by another of roughly similar size. The tertiary phase that now presented itself was one in which few independent titles of any worth remained on the market and individual groups had grown in size on the back of the prosperity of the 1970s and 1980s, leaving only relatively large organisations as the most likely acquisition targets. The erosion of foreign media ownership rules in a period of neoliberal market reform also meant that news media groups could look beyond their own shores. However, these offshore acquisitions also were on a group scale.

The news media groups were operating in mature markets and saw little choice but to acquire the existing revenue streams of other groups rather than to invest in elusive organic market growth. They trusted that size would bring with it a form of protection (Gershon 2006, 213).

These mergers and acquisitions took place during a period when media stock prices were high and this was reflected in the multiples demanded for the sale of "lucrative" businesses. Companies failed to heed the debt lesson presented by News Corporation's near-collapse in 1990. While Rupert Murdoch attracted criticism over the amount his group paid for Dow Jones in 2007, News Corporation had the financial strength and diverse revenue streams to sustain the high-priced purchase.[13] The purchase of Dow Jones – $US5 billion for an asset with operating income of $US100 million – is an extreme case, but it indicates the manner in which media companies discounted the relevance of revenue multiples in determining the prices they were prepared to pay to increase the size of their businesses. In so doing, those without diversified profit bases made themselves vulnerable.

Conservative debt-to-equity ratios gave way to highly leveraged regimes in which the servicing of debt and the maintenance of profit levels became a difficult juggling act that had a greater sense of urgency than Neuharth's revenue/cost management of the 1970s and 1980s. In fact, groups were building increasingly high debt mountains as they sought to use acquisition as a substitute for organic growth. The buying spree reached its zenith in 2006–2007,

$M   **Media group debt**

4000
3500
3000
2500
2000
1500
1000
500
0

Daily Mail & General Trust ($US5.7bn)
Independent News & Media ($US4bn)
Trinity Mirror Group ($US3.4bn)
McClatchy ($US4.1bn)
New York Times Co. ($US3.5bn)
Canwest ($US7bn)
Torstar ($US1.9bn)
Fairfax ($US7bn)
APN News & Media ($US2.6bn)
Guardian Media Group ($US1bn)
Irish Times ($US0.2bn)

□ 2005 □ 2006 ▣ 2007 ▣ 2008 ■ 2009

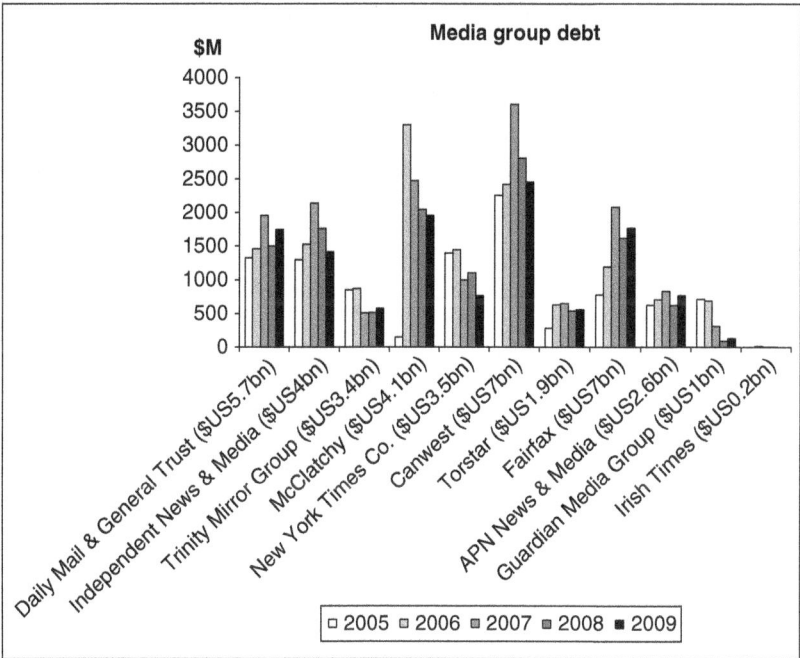

Figure 2.3 High debt burdens
Source: Group assets in 2009 shown in brackets (DMGT assets 2007); INM Group 2009 figures as at 30 June; Trinity Mirror Group 2009 as at 25 October; CanWest 2009 as at 30 November; Torstar 2009 as at 30 September; APN News & Media 2009 as at 30 June; currencies converted to $US at mid-market rates on 1 December in relevant year.

on the eve of the credit crisis. Figure 2.3 is a graph of media group debt levels that resembles the Manhattan skyline.

These were not isolated excesses by one or two groups: there was an almost boilerplate institutional response to the newspaper industry's declining economic indicators. The common strategy was to buy groups similar to their own (or be bought) and to acquire digital (Internet) properties irrespective of the inability to apply traditional due diligence to their sales forecasts. The Jordan, Edmiston Group reported that, led by the online media and marketing services sectors, mergers and acquisitions for the US media and information industries reached record highs in 2007 with 838 transactions and nearly $110 billion in value for the year – up 32 per cent and 79 per cent, respectively, over 2006 levels. The scale of the newspaper company mergers and acquisitions can be judged by the fact that while the number of sales dropped by almost 40 per cent to 45 transactions, the combined value rose by over a third – from $US10.3 billion to $US13.8 billion. In Britain, PriceWaterhouseCoopers reported that the media sector's M&A activity hit a record level in 2007. The publishing portion was substantially boosted by the Canadian Thomson Corporation's acquisition of the Reuters News Agency for $US17.2 billion, which accounted for more than half the total value of media acquisitions that year. In Australia in 2007, Fairfax completed its $A9 billion merger with Rural Press while, in New Zealand, Ironbridge (an Australian-based private equity company) paid $NZ741 million for radio and television broadcaster MediaWorks. That year, Independent News and Media – the group led by Sir Anthony O'Reilly – made an unsuccessful bid for the remaining shares in the trans-Tasman group APN News & Media, in which it had a 39.2 per cent holding. The bid valued the company, which publishes New Zealand's largest daily newspaper (the *New Zealand Herald*), at $A2.97 billion.

Such mergers and acquisitions added materially to annual operating accounts.[14] For example, in 2006 the total revenue of the Australian Fairfax group was $A1.9 billion and only two years later – after its merger with Rural Press – revenue had increased to $A2.9 billion. Thomson's revenue in the year before its merger with Reuters was $US11.7 billion and a year later had risen to almost $US13 billion.

The emphasis on growth and the bottom line (Baker 2007, 28–29) was enhanced by the widespread practice of "incentivising" senior executives against profits. Bonuses were based on profit margins and year-on-year growth – both of which encouraged expansion and rigorous cost-containment. A component of the annual bonus was often given in share options, which provided an added incentive for executives to impress analysts and keep the share market happy. In effect, encouraging rises in stock prices and preaching the industry's bright future put extra money in the executives' pockets.

In 2007 the chief executives[15] of prominent newspaper-owning companies had significant share options or incentive shares that were exercisable at varying times and under varying conditions. These options or incentive shares were often in addition to existing holdings in an organisation's ordinary shares and, while share prices remained high, these men and women could display significant paper wealth.[16]

Then it came time to pay the price for flawed strategies. Financial institutions that had begun to look unstable late in 2007 began to tumble in 2008 as a liquidity crisis in the American financial sector deepened and infected other countries. The effect on the newspaper industry was threefold: it lost the ability to refinance its debt, advertising and circulation dropped and its share prices plummeted.

Crisis phase

High debt burdens left these companies ill-prepared to weather the recession and their newspaper subsidiaries in even more dire straits. It is one of the perversities of commercial life that acquired companies can be made to bear the cost of being bought. The common practice had been to burden the balance sheets of acquired subsidiaries with the debt generated for the purchase. As a result, newspaper subsidiaries that may have been marginally profitable in an operating sense were plunged into large deficits by the requirement that they carry the debt on their books.

The adverse impact in 2009 exceeded the effects of the economic downturn that followed the bursting of the dot.com bubble in 2000, which had in turn been compounded in 2001 by the September 11 terrorist attacks in New York and Washington. The 9/11 aftermath had been savage: US newspaper advertising revenue fell by 9 per cent in 2001, Ireland's by 9.3 per cent, Australia's by 11.8 per cent (2000–2002), Canada's by 3 per cent and the UK's by 2.3 per cent (although national revenue dropped by 8.4 per cent). New Zealand newspapers had shown a modest 1.6 per cent gain overall but the country's largest newspaper, the *New Zealand Herald*, suffered a three per cent drop. However, where there had been rapid recovery from that downturn, there was to be no similar bounce-back from the Global Financial Crisis.

In the United States newspaper advertising revenue dropped 45 per cent between 2007 and 2011 – from $US49.9 billion to $US27 billion. In the United Kingdom press advertising dropped by 31 per cent and in Ireland by an alarming 85 per cent. In New Zealand advertising revenue was down by 24 per cent and in Australia, where high world mineral prices had shielded the economy from the worst of the Global Financial Crisis, by 17 per cent. In Canada, total print revenue dropped by 23 per cent. In South Africa the newspaper advertising market has been highly volatile, peaking at $US1230 million in 2006 before rising and falling in a range between $US834 million (2009) and $US910 million (2011).

Circulation fared no better and even the earlier newspaper sales trend-beaters, Ireland and South Africa, went into decline (see Table 2.2).

As a result, companies took desperate measures and instituted widespread cost-cutting that had immediate effects on staffing levels. In Britain, the National Union of Journalists (NUJ) estimates that more than 1500 journalists lost their jobs on local newspapers between May 2008 and May 2009.[17]

Table 2.2 Circulation decline

Year	USA	Canada	UK	Ireland	Australia	NZ	South Africa
2008	48,597	4,295	15,062	833	2,508	653	1,681
2009	46,278	4,117	14,009	767	2,482	632	1,596
2010	44,412	No data	14,965	700	2,482	633	1,596
2011	44,421	3,844	13,504	625	2,444	618	1,514
Change '08–'11	−8.6%	−10.5%	−10.3%	−24.9%	−2.5%	−5.3%	−9.9%

Source: WAN/IFRA World Press Trends.

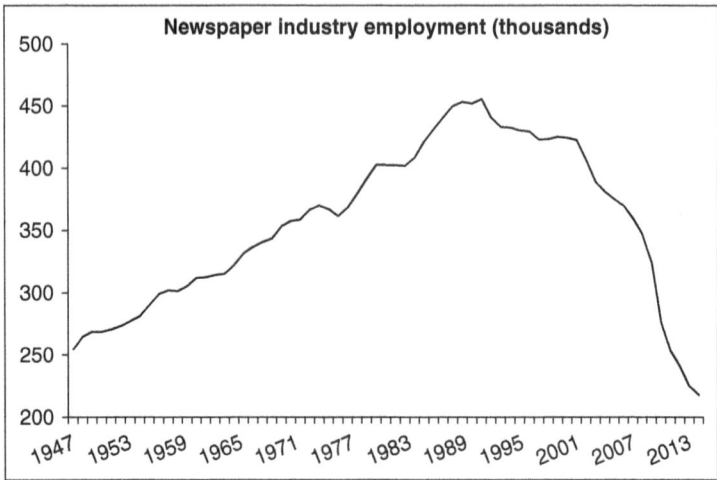

Figure 2.4   US newspaper industry employment decline
Source: US Bureau of Labor Statistics.

The rate of decline in US newspaper employment gained alarming momentum in 2008. Figure 2.4 illustrates the apogee and perigee of total American newspaper employment which, in 2013, was at its lowest level since the Second World War. The annual census of newspaper news staffing conducted by the American Society of News Editors indicates that the US journalistic workforce shrank by more than a quarter between 2007 and 2012. Estimates for 2013 by the Pew Center put the total number of US newsroom employees below 40,000.

In Australia, the journalists' union Media Entertainment and Arts Alliance estimated that between 2001 and 2008 the number of full-time journalists declined by 13 per cent across all Australian media to about 7500.[18] Numbers continued to decline and in 2012 the largest newspaper publishers, Fairfax Media and News Corporation, embarked on major programmes that would reduce their total staffing by more than 3000 – about 800 of the job losses in editorial departments.

In a number of cases, reductions were not enough and in the United States and Britain, newspaper closures began. In 2003 there were 1165 regional and local newspaper titles in the United Kingdom and a decade later the total had fallen to 1054. In London, the *Evening Standard* and *The Independent* titles were sold to Russian oligarch Alexander Lebedev for nominal sums.[19] In the United States the ominously named newspaperdeathwatch.com reported that, between 2007 and 2013, 12 metropolitan newspapers, including the *Rocky Mountain News* and *Cincinnati Post*, were closed. More than 100 American newspapers reduced the number of days on which they published and the *Christian Science Monitor*, which is discussed in Chapter 5, moved its weekday print edition online in 2009 and printed only a weekly magazine.[20] Where once newspapers had been sold for ever-increasing sums, the trend turned the other way. The *Philadelphia Enquirer* and *Daily News*, which had been bought for $US560 million in 2006, were sold four years later for $US149 million – to creditors who were owed $US360 million – and again in 2012 for $US55 million. In 2012, 84 daily newspapers were sold in 25 transactions worth $642.83 million, according to Dirks, Van Essen & Murray, a leading newspaper mergers and acquisition firm that reported a decade earlier that 38 daily newspapers had changed hands that year in deals totalling nearly $1.2 billion.

The debt position of some companies sent them over the brink into bankruptcy, as noted at the beginning of the chapter. The largest collapse in the US newspaper market was that of the Tribune Company, which had been subject to a 2007 buyout, led by real estate investor Sam Zell, that was so highly leveraged that creditors in subsequent bankruptcy proceedings alleged "fraudulent conveyance". The $US8.2 billion buyout was, they alleged, so debt-burdened that the company was insolvent from the beginning. The Tribune Company, which owns the *Los Angeles Times* and *Chicago Tribune* as well as television stations, filed for Chapter 11 protection in December 2008. It emerged from bankruptcy four years later and its newspapers (which, according to *Forbes* magazine, had lost a third of their value in a year) were reported to be for sale.

In all, five major US newspaper companies filed for Chapter 11 bankruptcy protection between December 2008 and April 2009, among them the *Chicago Tribune's* competitor, Sun-Times Media, which was hit by a huge tax liability as a consequence of its purchase of the *Chicago Sun-Times* from Hollinger International in the aftermath of the jailing of that group's chairman, Conrad Black, on fraud charges.

Some had a relatively short period in protection. In January 2010, the parent company of MediaNews (publisher of the *Denver Post* – direct competitor of the *Rocky Mountain News* which had closed in 2009 – and 53 other daily newspapers across the United States) filed for Chapter 11 protection with liabilities close to $US1 billion. It emerged from protection two months later after relinquishing 89 per cent of its ownership to lenders.

The chapter began with the demise of CanWest Global Communications, which stands as an object lesson on the consequences of overly geared acquisitions. For several years most of the group's income had been used to service debt and in March 2009 it failed to make an interest payment of $US30.4 million but secured a series of extensions while it sought to restructure its liabilities of more than $US3.5 billion. In October 2009 it filed for creditor protection and began to sell down assets such as the TEN Network in Australia (it had sold its New Zealand television and radio assets in 2007).

In 2010 its publishing division (which owned the nationally distributed *National Post* and ten metropolitan dailies) was sold to Postmedia Network for approximately $US1 billion and its broadcasting interests to Shaw Communications for $US1.9 billion.

There were other consequences to the downturn in the newspaper market: in February 2010 the second largest newsprint manufacturer in North America, White Birch Paper Company, filed for bankruptcy protection in Quebec – citing a decline in newspaper demand.

Some avoided bankruptcy. In Britain, regional newspaper publisher Johnston Press restructured its £485 million debt in August 2009 only days before its loan covenants were due to be tested. In 2013 it reported its first increase in operating profit in seven years after major cost and debt reduction and the relaunch of 183 of its titles. In Ireland, Independent News & Media was unable to repay bonds in May 2009 and received extensions but five months later was forced into an equity swap with bondholders, which reduced the shareholding of Sir Anthony O'Reilly, who had retired as chief executive in May. A rival Irish businessman, Denis O'Brien, built up a holding that surpassed the O'Reilly family's interests and engineered a board rout in 2012.

Root causes

There is no doubt that the Global Financial Crisis and resultant recession created extraordinary circumstances but the newspaper companies with parents listed on the stock exchange were predisposed to infection. They succumbed to the flaws in their business model.

A. J. Liebling said that the function of the press in society was to inform but its role was to make money (1964, 6). Nevertheless, when *The Press* was first published in 1961, newspapers were able to sustain the reportorial function because, even allowing for his belief that they would spend no more on the journalistic function than was absolutely necessary, proprietors were under less pressure to deliver large profits. Consider the environment in which they were operating: although circulation and advertising revenue were on upward trajectories, many were in multiple newspaper markets that demanded a competitive level of reinvestment in their publications and it was a labour-intensive industry that traditionally produced modest profit margins. Ownership of a newspaper (or even a group of newspapers) carried with it a sense of community engagement and this was also an industry that had yet to fire the imagination of the stock market. Forty years later it had changed almost beyond recognition.

By the closing of the first decade of the new millennium, the newspaper industry had reached a low point because, fundamentally, it had lost sight of the functional side of Liebling's equation in its quest to fulfil its role as money-maker. Its ownership structure had changed to one primarily based on publicly traded shares held by investors attracted by years of profit margins that exceeded Fortune 500 and FTSE averages. Then, spurred on by market expectations, companies had their judgement clouded by a self-induced belief that they must expand or die. Incaution was fed by ready access to credit, by a culture of management incentives and bonuses, and by a sense of legitimacy instilled by mergers and acquisitions across the media sector. However, market expectation and economic reality were separated by a widening gulf. The notion of newspapers generating sufficiently large profits to sustain both handsome dividends (for a large shareholder base) and debt servicing fell into that chasm.

The newspaper industry reached a point where it was faced with the following irreversible conditions:

- The Internet had broken its traditional advertising monopolies.
- Benefits such as de-manning and productivity improvement that had accrued from editorial computerisation that began in the US in the 1970s had been fully depreciated.
- Circulation declines could not be substantially redressed and cover price increases became counter-productive.
- The ability to extract costs became progressively more difficult and damaging.

Newspaper executives have not been blind to these developments but the business model under which they all operated has been incapable of overcoming the effects. Without comparable alternative revenue sources (and they have proven elusive), newspapers cannot continue to provide above-average profit margins and highly attractive year-on-year growth. They cannot service high debt levels to sustain growth-through-acquisition in markets that are, in any case, already concentrated to levels that risk regulatory intervention. In short, the future is one of contraction rather than expansion, which suggests that the attraction of newspapers as commercial investments will also decline. That is not to say that newspapers are finished but, rather, that the scale and structure are likely to change. Media companies will need to diversify (say, into entertainment media) to remain attractive to the share market and newspapers are likely to become, at best, minor parts of their portfolios. Those companies in which families continue to hold sway through two-tier voting systems will face mounting demands from public shareholders for voting parity which could push the enterprises towards more profitable business. Investor pressure may lead to divestiture of newspaper titles or further closures. And in the midst of these structural changes, professional print-standard journalism is under immense pressure – caught between budget cuts and the Internet.

Journalism's future

Professional journalism has always had its own flaws and some would argue that commercial news media have never satisfactorily discharged their functions in the service of democracy. McChesney and Scott (2004, 7) argue that, in the American context at least, failure by the commercial press to meet those obligations is now mainstream media theory and that the notion of a press that has served the ends of democracy has been illusory. Numerous texts suggest newspapers were in trouble well before the dawn of the Internet and, when the Internet arrived, journalism itself was in a "fullblown crisis" involving what McChesney and Scott describe as the "near total elision of public service priorities by commercial imperatives" (*ibid.*, 2), a generalised view that nonetheless pays too little attention to the integrity of many journalists and some fine examples of their craft.

The crisis manifested itself not only in the direct effects of editorial budget cuts but also in a rising public antipathy towards the news media that gained full expression during the British Leveson Inquiry. Surveys of public attitudes towards journalists show that in the United States, Canada, the United Kingdom, Australia and New Zealand the public rank journalists low on the trust scale. The Pew Center for Research on People and the Press showed perceptions of believability in US newspapers dropped from 80 per cent in 1985 to 59 per cent in 2002 while in 2005 only 28 per cent had "a great deal" or "quite a lot" of confidence in newspapers. A survey of trust levels by the *British Journalism Review* found that of the 23 groups covered in the survey, journalists had performed the most poorly, with almost half the respondents having little or no trust in journalists on "up-market" newspapers while 83 per cent had little or no trust in journalists on "red-top" (tabloid) national titles. Furthermore, trust levels had declined by about 20 per cent over a five-year period but that decline did not include red-top reporters, "whose reputation was so low that it could hardly sink any further" (Barnett 2008). Angus Reid Global Scan surveys in 2003 and 2006 indicated that less than half of the Canadian population trusted journalists. *Reader's Digest* surveys in Australia and New Zealand between 2000 and 2008 indicated similar levels of trust in both countries, which consistently placed journalists in the bottom third of surveyed professions. In the 2012 New Zealand survey, journalists were ranked in 34th place, three ahead of sex workers and five ahead of door-to-door salesmen.

There is no single source for the malaise that confronts journalism. It is possible, however, that its roots can be traced to changes in the way news has been conceptualised – not by audiences but by those who purvey it. The advent of commercial television led to news being treated as entertainment (Postman 1986), and the stock market listing of news media companies – bringing with it a business ethos driven by the bottom line – led to its corporatisation. The news came to be regarded by media executives as a "product" no different from the other commodities with which investors were familiar. News media, which had previously been set apart from other businesses by their "fourth estate" status, became integrated into the business world, culminating in mass consolidation and absorption in some cases into conglomerates with wide-ranging interests. Group owners, often removed from the cities in which they had news media outlets, were less constrained by local community pressure in adopting policies and practices. These approaches occurred in parallel with a decline in civic engagement (Putnam 2000). Consequently, by the time the Internet began to challenge traditional media, the intrinsic worth of news had already been devalued and the survival of traditional journalism as a significant social force was under threat.

News as entertainment did not begin with commercial television. The lurid details of crimes and misdemeanours that filled the pages of the 19th-century *News of the World* and *New York Herald* were designed to entertain and titillate their readers. Later, with the emergence of news feature sections and supplements in quality newspapers came recognition that even "serious" publications could entertain as well as inform. Television, however, brought a fundamental change in thinking about what "the news" was and how it should be presented to audiences. News became part of a programme mix: vying with comedy and quiz shows, crime dramas and "dramatised" history. It was given a prime time place in the programme schedule that may have emphasised its importance but also placed strong pressure on its journalists to perform. As Postman says, "a news show, to put it plainly, is a format for entertainment, not for education, reflection or catharsis" (*ibid.*, 87–88).[21] And it worked. Television advertising revenue in 1981 represented 62 per cent of the newspaper spend in the United Kingdom and 58.5 per cent in the United States.[22] In both countries a decade later the figures had risen by 10 percentage points.[23]

The response, over time, was to recognise that newspapers could not beat television so they should join it. There were the obvious moves – where regulation allowed – of buying television stations but there was also a more subtle and corrosive development. Newspapers began to treat news as entertainment and to mimic the devices that were television's stock-in-trade (see, for example, Stepp 1990). Stories began to reflect the shorter, simpler construction of television news with lower levels of detail, qualification and explanation. Story angles, while always designed to engage the reader, began to titillate and entertain. Wherever possible, stories were personalised (the way television brings the all-important visual element to a story that otherwise "lacks pictures") and framed in ways that readers would "enjoy". What had been primarily a textual medium also became more visual, with significant increases in the use of photographs and graphic elements. Page design became more modular: where once the vertical column had characterised newspapers, now a square or horizontal box (a subliminal reminder of the television screen) became a characteristic of many newspapers. Political journalism moved from the formal discourse of debate coverage and policy analysis to a form that had parallels with entertainment such as sport, game shows and, at times, soap opera. It became spectacle and combat rather than representation and government. In order to entertain, political journalists had to lower the level of esteem in which politicians were held. Context and reasoned analysis became less common as political journalists strove for effect. As a result, political stories assumed less importance to the audience but they were not alone. Adding entertainment to the news generally diminished the perceived importance and credibility of the information and if news became less relevant so, too, did the media that distributed it. Newspapers contemplating more graphical designs – as a response to claims young readers were more visually oriented – risked losing some of their previous gravitas if they adopted the approach or some of their advertisers if they did not.

Advertisers, who exerted a strong influence over commercial television schedules, began to influence the structure of the newspaper. Technical constraints often limited the size of the main news section of newspapers (the prime location for advertising) and publishers had to find ways of attracting advertising to other sections. Lifestyle and special interest sections proliferated and attracted advertising. Advertising grew because such sections were popular with readers and advertisers. New Zealand reader research provides an example. News Works NZ (formerly the Newspaper Advertising Bureau) reported in June 2013 that 1.249 million people (out of a total population of 3.8 million over ten years of age) read at least one newspaper lifestyle section a week. The Nielsen Consumer & Media Insights survey (Q2 2012–Q1 2013) quoted by the bureau found 78 per cent of lifestyle section readers decide where to purchase goods and services using their daily newspaper. These sections proliferated as ownership aggregation and conglomerate control increased. Their inclusion in publications was consistent with conglomerates' revenue expectation and their familiarity with entertainment and consumer goods. Newspapers' sky boxes or promotional panels at the top of the front page highlighted specialist sections ahead of the news and reinforced the entertainment/consumer focus.

This consumer focus became increasingly prevalent and, as the power within news media organisations shifted from editors to business managers, it was reinforced in both overt and subliminal ways. News media companies either established or expanded marketing departments that applied the same market research techniques to news as had been used in consumer goods and services. The audience segmentation in this research correlated with advertising demographics and, inevitably, any data that led to editorial change to meet a perceived reader need also benefited advertisers. Shultz, citing Australian examples, notes that strategies to provide more high-quality journalism "barely figured" in marketing plans (Shultz 1998) but marketing and advertising departments were deeply involved in the creation of new sections of the newspaper. Marketing departments were at the forefront of treating the news as a commodity, "normalising" news content so that it could be regarded in the same way as the other consumer goods with which they were familiar. They were aided by managers who no longer referred to the newspaper as a "publication" but as a "product" or a "brand". It signalled the downgrading, in the minds of managers, of the journalistic ethos that had previously ranked above or outside business considerations.

Turning the news into a commodity not only characterised it as a familiar commercial object but also, by suggesting that news was no longer "special", gave the appearance of a reduced sense of obligation to meet certain public needs and civic responsibilities. In parallel with this terminological change and marketing focus, there was an administrative shift in many media companies that drew editorial departments into the same management practices as commercial departments including performance monitoring – management "tools" such as Key Performance Indicators (KPIs), 360-degree assessments and "performance" bonuses – and the creation of detailed budgets that, by costing coverage of unspecified news events, attempted to predict the unpredictable. Attempts were made to "benchmark" journalistic performance because, as the World Association of Newspapers noted in 2002, editors needed to "demonstrate the quality, value and efficiency of their resources".[24] Many journalists saw these moves as the removal of some of the symbolic practices that set them apart from "the business side". When combined with the cuts to editorial budgets and resources that became a familiar consequence of company takeovers and of economic downturns, the impact on journalistic autonomy became manifest (Underwood 1995).

Commoditisation, trivialisation and conglomeration became recurrent themes in media criticism. Not only did the effects of the phenomena alarm academics but also the general public displayed a growing antipathy towards the media and towards journalists (Downie & Kaiser 2002, 28). There was a decline in reader and viewer loyalty that was reflected in both newspaper circulation and television audience ratings. Any sense of foreboding on the part of owners was ameliorated, however, by continuing increases in overall advertising revenue, the trend that, as has been noted, fuelled investor expectations of high margins and double-digit year-on-year growth. The benefits of higher revenue were taken to the bottom line rather than investment in journalism. The net result was that, by the time significant Internet services made their appearance in the latter part of the 1990s, the delivery of traditional journalism was already in trouble.

The impact of the Internet on newspaper advertising – particularly classified listings – is well documented. The revenue decline was damaging, but it also occurred in parallel with a growing public belief that informational needs could be met entirely by the Internet and it would be "free".[25]

The Internet holds out two basic democratic promises. The first is access to a cornucopia of knowledge. The second is the creation of a non-commercial information common within which citizens can freely exchange that knowledge and form opinion. There is little doubt that, with 252 million Internet domain names registered by 2013 (according to Internet manager VeriSign), the first promise has been met. Some would say it has been over-subscribed. The second promise, however, may be seen as a glass half full or half empty. The issue is not the quantity of material being placed on the World Wide Web but its nature, quality and distribution.

The optimistic view is one of empowerment. A report by the Aspen Institute's Forum on Communications and Society in 2007 said the Internet "represents a direct challenge to the primacy of market-based production with a new model of 'social production'". It reported that 47 per cent of Americans who used the Internet felt empowered by it and listed politics, healthcare, commerce, creative arts and blogs as areas where the Web had engendered a sense of involvement and choice.[26] And the sense of direct participation has grown over time. A national survey by the Pew Internet and American Life Project in 2012 found 41 per cent of all adults regarded themselves as "local news participators" by engaging in online activities such as emailing story links, posting news on social media and contributing to news sites.

The pessimists see the Internet as being overwhelmingly colonised by commerce, which has applied proprietary principles to create an "anti-commons" in which the individual's voice and civic empowerment has been subsumed. The non-profit sector through which citizens organise themselves for collective efforts shows no greater "share of market" in the new medium than it did in traditional media, buried under commercial content (Chester & Larson 2005; Hunter 2003). Even the pessimists, however, acknowledge that the Internet has already met some of the promise.

The overwhelming success of the Internet has been in the creation of a new class of consumer – the Web browser – whose online behaviour fashioned the tools that have aided information retrieval.[27] Sunstein coined the phrase "the Daily Me" to explain an environment in which Internet users could construct for themselves an information diet that included only those things in which the individual was interested. Note the use of the phrase "information diet", not "news diet": under Sunstein's scenario there is the capacity to avoid news altogether. He added that, in many respects, the communications market was moving rapidly in the direction of the vision:

> The market for news, entertainment and information has finally been perfected. Consumers are able to see exactly what they want. When the power to filter is unlimited, people can decide in advance and with perfect accuracy, what they will and will not encounter. They can design something very much like a communications universe of their own choosing.

And if they have trouble designing it, it can be designed for them, again with perfect accuracy.

(Sunstein 2007, 3)

This filtering function, facilitated by an array of ever-more-intuitive search engines in the hands of ever-more-powerful services like Google and Yahoo, replaces one of the core mediation roles of the journalist – deciding what is interesting. And if users are disinclined to create their own Daily Me, aggregation sites pull together material such as news and weblogs for like-minded people. Filtered content opens the way for citizens effortlessly to scrutinise sites such as legislative and judicial bodies, government ministries, political parties, civic organisations, monitoring bodies, lobby groups, academic institutions and news organisations. Online social networks and weblogs give individuals a "voice" by allowing them to post unmediated content, even if the emergence of a formal civic commons is problematic.

In March 2013 Facebook estimated it had 1.11 billion active monthly users, while Twitter had almost 555 million registered accounts. In June 2013, two of the largest blog accommodation sites, Tumblr and Wordpress, hosted 115 million and 67 million blogs respectively. By sheer contributor numbers alone the digital environment would, therefore, appear to be a "democratised" medium, a view reinforced by the rise of citizen or participatory journalism. Citizen journalism should not be seen simply as amateurs trying their hand at reporting. It is a broader-based process through which audiences become stakeholders in the news, a process that Boczkowski describes as "news as conversation" (2005, 186). Participation takes many forms and engagement is both within and beyond the boundaries of traditional news organisations, some of which have embraced citizen journalism as a way to re-engage with the community.

Bowman and Willis identify eight categories of participatory journalism but only three involve original source reporting. The remainder either critique or augment existing material (2003, 33–36). By these means, Bowman and Willis say, the Internet community (and other media) "appropriates the stories, retells them, comments on them, adds additional information or overlooked angles, and reworks them as part of a broad-based web of ideas and information" (*ibid.*, 60). Implicit in their description, however, is the interaction between traditional media and "participatory journalists" in a relationship that can be variously characterised as synergistic, symbiotic or parasitic. Those traditional media outlets that have embraced the concept believe that, in so doing, they have improved their journalism and grown closer to the communities they serve. The synergies that combine the relative strengths of press and public produce journalism that neither entity could deliver unaided. The phenomenon is, according to one enthusiast, "fundamentally altering the nature of journalism in this new century".[28] A symbiotic relationship recognises the fact that traditional media provide much of the feedstock to which non-traditional participants add their own ingredients and perspectives. A pejorative version of this view is that "participatory journalists" simply feed off the work of professionals, a reaction common among journalists who resent others intruding on their territory. Citizen journalism has, indeed, intruded on that territory in some of the functions it fulfils and has changed the power relationship between press and public. It is aided and abetted by the providers of search engines who capitalise on what may have been one of the great strategic errors of media history – the decision by newspapers in the 1990s to put free content on open websites.

In a lead-up to News Corporation's policy shift towards "paywalls" on its news websites in 2009, the then chief executive of Dow Jones (and former executive chairman of News International), Les Hinton, acknowledged the error of placing free and unprotected news content on the Web, which played into the hands of "the digital vampires of the internet age". In a colourful article in *British Journalism Review*[29] he left no doubt about who was eating the news media's lunch:

> Search engines sucked the lifeblood out of the newspaper industry, nourishing themselves of the journalism we spent hundreds of millions to produce. This juicy, free information gave Google's fangs a great place to bite. Google's search algorithm had something to find – something valuable, something free. It wasn't just Google which was dining at our expense, threatening to make newspapers road-kill along what we once called the information superhighway. Bloggers of all types were grateful for the opportunity to cash in on the expertise and expense that went into the news process. Readers also showed no concern for the economics of the news business. When the price is zero, demand can tend toward the infinite.
>
> (Hinton 2009)

The Internet provides the audience with extensive access to information, the ability to retrieve and manipulate it and wide dissemination – all of the things that journalists have for more than a century regarded as their stock-in-trade.

Are we, therefore, at that critical juncture where citizens have overcome the impediments that have stood in the way of their producing material to rival the output of professional reporters and are able to counteract the effects of mainstream media decline?

There are numerous potential "suppliers" on the Internet. Some organisations have, in fact, come to resemble traditional media, employing trained journalists and observing journalistic norms and ethics. An example is the commentary website talkingpointsmemo.com, whose founder Joshua Marshall received a George Polk Award in February 2008 for legal reporting. It carries advertising, utilises public fund-raising and has a paid staff of 28 (including a five-person Washington bureau launched in 2010).[30] It has six associated websites and a high level of reader contribution. Huffingtonpost.com in the main aggregates the work of other media but also hosts thousands of bloggers who make unpaid contributions to the site. However, it has a similar structure to traditional media organisations and a newsroom employing professional journalists. It had a staff of about 100 when it was acquired by Web portal AOL in February 2011 and this number grew to nearly 500 by mid-2012, according to the Nieman Media Lab.

There are other "independent public interest" news sites that rely heavily on professionals and it is difficult to define their output as "citizen" journalism. They might more accurately be described as non-profit news organisations. The Pew Research Center in 2014 identified 204 digital non-profit news outlets, ranging from national to hyperlocal, that had been launched in the United States since 1987, three-quarters of them with paid full-time staff.

Some Web-based news organisations seek to fill gaps left by the shrinkage of traditional coverage. MinnPost.com was established in 2008 following retrenchments at the two newspapers serving Minneapolis-St Paul. According to its 2012 report it has a full-time staff of 19 and 39 freelance contributors. VoiceofSanDiego.com was created in 2005 following dissatisfaction with local coverage and employs a full-time staff of nine journalists. San Francisco boasted not one but two online responses to perceived deficiencies in the city's newspaper. The San Francisco Appeal was launched in March 2009 as a for-profit online-only rival to the *San Francisco Chronicle*, which had been particularly hard hit by high Internet usage in the city that is home to the classified advertising website craigslist.com. In 2010 a donor-supported website called The Bay Citizen began operation but merged three years later with the Center for Investigative Reporting – an organisation that predated the Internet – to create a 47-strong investigative team that CIR boasts is the largest in the United States.

The Center for Investigative Reporting was the beginning of a new form of philanthropy-funded journalism (examined in Chapter 8) in which investigative projects are undertaken in partnership with mainstream media. It is a model exemplified by ProPublica.org, which was established by Paul Steiger, a former managing editor of the *Wall Street Journal,* and Stephen Engelberg, a former managing editor of *The Oregonian* and former investigative editor of the *New York Times*, with significant philanthropic funding.[30] Other specialist groups, however, hope to be self-sustaining rather than rely on philanthropic support. GlobalPost, for example, was established in 2009 to provide an alternative to what was seen as a shrinking coverage of international events. It has a network of correspondents in 50 countries and has partnership agreements to supply foreign news to the *New York Daily*

News and CBS News as well as to its own advertising-supported website and subscription premium service.

A third alternative model for investigative journalism is university-based. The Schuster Institute for Investigative Journalism was launched in 2004 by Brandeis University "to help fill the void in high-quality public interest and investigative journalism – and to counter the increasing corporate control of what Americans read, see, and hear". Charles Lewis, a former investigative journalist with *60 Minutes* who helped to pioneer the concept of specialist investigative entities when he set up the Center for Public Integrity in 1989 (also discussed in Chapter 8), established the Investigative Reporting Workshop at the American University in Washington DC in 2008.

University-based operations are not limited to the United States. The Bureau of Investigative Journalism, which emulates ProPublica, was established in the United Kingdom and has been based at City University since 2010. The Australian Centre for Independent Journalism, whose establishment in 1990 predated the current crisis in the media industry, is a not-for-profit operation based in the Faculty of Arts and Social Sciences at the University of Technology, Sydney.

These operations lie at the high end of what Bruns describes as "an emerging new media ecosystem – a network of ideas" (2008, 94). Below these sites are those that have professional editors who process material supplied by public contributors (such as South Korea's OhMyNews.com) and those with a more egalitarian outlook in which contributors also act as editors in citizen cooperatives (Indymedia.org). At the other end are idiosyncratic "bloggers", who may have their own blogs or who contribute to social media sites such as Facebook and Twitter, registering opinions and comments. Social media has enabled ordinary citizens, who may not be regular "bloggers", to contribute often graphic eyewitness accounts of news events such as the Asian Tsunami of 2004, Cyclone Katrina in 2005, the "Arab Spring", the 2011 Japanese earthquake and the Syrian conflict.

Bruns also identifies a form of citizen participation that he calls "gatewatching", a shift away from the publishing of noteworthy information to the "*publicising* of whatever relevant content is available anywhere on the Web (and beyond) and a subsequent evaluation of such material". It is a function that its proponents believe can "limit or eliminate the need for journalistically trained staff" (Bruns 2005, 2). Others go further and claim that the list of contestable activities is so wide-ranging that the question "who is a journalist?" could be met with the answer "everyone" (Friend & Singer 2007, 35–42).

Does this level of direct information retrieval and creation, in fact, allow society to forego the services of professional journalists? Gurevitch and Blumler (1990, 25–26) provide a useful checklist of what the public require of professional journalism and its institutions. It deserves repeating because it encapsulates the functions that will need support and protection in the future:

- Surveillance of the socio-political environment, reporting developments likely to impinge, positively or negatively, on the welfare of citizens
- Meaningful agenda-setting, identifying the key issues of the day, including the forces that have formed and may resolve them
- Platforms for an intelligible and illuminating advocacy by politicians and spokespersons of other causes and interest groups
- Dialogue across a diverse range of views, as well as between power holders (actual and prospective) and mass publics
- Mechanisms for holding officials to account for how they have exercised power
- Incentives for citizens to learn, choose, and become involved, rather than merely to follow and kibitz over the political process
- A principled resistance to the efforts of forces outside the media to subvert their independence, integrity, and ability to serve the audience
- A sense of respect for the audience member, as potentially concerned and able to make sense of his or her political environment.

The press is capable of meeting these needs because it has been granted, or has appropriated, the status needed to meet them. It has access to information, the ability to interpret and evaluate it and the means by which it can be disseminated to a broad and attentive audience. The effect over time has been the accrual of economic and political status that amplifies its power to the point where none of the functions identified by Gurevitch and Blumler is beyond its reach. The key to its power is critical mass.

This critical mass is what differentiates it from the Internet communities that are said to challenge mainstream news media. It can be explained, first, by analogy. Imagine each member of the public as a feather and each journalist as an ounce of lead. Many feathers are required to fill a large, fluffy one-tonne bag; far fewer units of lead are needed to form a one-tonne block. Both weigh the same but, when thrown, the impact of the former is far less than that of the latter. The greater impact of the press is due to its density – a concentration of resource, content, audience and influence. It is this mass that allows it to assert its power and independence. The Internet, by contrast, has a dispersed structure and multiplicity of "sole traders" whose "weight" is minimal unless they are able to attract the attention of mainstream media outlets.

Political organisations, government and public bureaucracy are complex organisms. The interrelationship between the three institutions compounds the complexity and an overlay of their interrelationship with the private sector adds another twist. Together they stand on contested ground, not least in the management of information where political and bureaucratic machines may vie – albeit sometimes in subtle ways – to present the dominant message (Peters 1981, 74). Complexity and contestation make "surveillance of the socio-political environment" difficult enough for professional journalists but they have the advantage of institutionalised access to the actors in each arm of public administration. Individual citizens may gain access to isolated pieces of information but their ability to *maintain* "surveillance" is limited by (i) a lack of accreditation and access, (ii) a lack of resources, (iii) a likely lack of institutional knowledge and analytical ability, and (iv) a narrow range of interests. Public oversight is generally limited to appraising the information that those involved in public administration – or their specialist communication advisors – decide to place in the public domain. These factors also seriously inhibit the ability of private citizens to identify issues, set agendas and hold officials to account – functions also hampered by the nature and volume of user-generated content on the Internet.

Only a small proportion of user-generated content could be described as "journalism". Wright, drawing on Walter Ong's linguistic theories, characterises a large proportion of the textual material produced by individual Internet users as "talk" rather than "writing". The difference between these oral and literate cultures is important. Ong states that oral traditions are "additive rather than subordinative, aggregative rather than analytic, empathetic and participatory rather than objectively distanced, and situational rather than abstract". Hence, large amounts of Internet content are inherently subjective. Contributions that follow a literate culture are more likely to achieve a level of objectivity (Wright 2007, 232–234)but the dominant citizen contributions have been talk – what Friend and Singer describe as "a joyous – and raucous – celebration of free speech" (2007, 116).

Ironically, this celebration of free speech is an impediment to citizens' matching of the press's role as a platform for advocacy and dialogue, let alone balanced reportage. The Internet is Babelopolis, a seemingly endless landscape of tower blocks whose occupants fight to be heard above an overwhelmingly discordant noise. Some inhabitants group together in particular towers to share their common interests but even their collective voices lack the strength to be heard throughout Babelopolis. A measure of order is provided by services that collect and redistribute selected residents' views but inhabitants are able to restrict themselves to only that which they *wish* to hear. And the noise continues around them.

Fragmentation and the tendency for Internet users to interact with those who share the same interests – what Sunstein describes as "echo chambers of their own design" (2007, 6) – is an impediment to realising the democratic potential of the Web. Equally injurious is the failure of the Web to achieve the same simultaneous "reach" as nightly television news or daily mass circulation newspapers. The risk is that common views, or a "national consensus", will be eroded. There is no mechanism by which a majority of citizens can be expected to have accessed the same body of information on the Internet within a short timeframe. Indeed, it has been argued that Internet users do not constitute an "audience" because the medium is a multipurpose technology loaded with a broad range of communication functions that does not denote the sharing of a common text (Liebes 2005). While such a claim should not be taken too far – individual websites do have audiences that share common texts – it is recognition of the Internet's diverse purposes and emphasises the atomised nature of the World Wide Web. It is this atomisation that denies online contributors the critical mass necessary to create – and, more importantly, demonstrate – the broad-based public opinion that is capable of swaying government policy. Where Internet contributors disclose wrongdoing by politicians or government officials, their role is catalytic: their claims generally lack strength until acted upon by mainstream media who may subject the allegations to further scrutiny. Lessig (2004) claims, for example, that bloggers led mainstream media to revisit a previously unchallenged report of Senator Trent Lott's comments supporting segregationist politician Strom Thurmond, which led to Lott's resignation as Republican Senate Leader in 2002. The impact of revelations by Wikileaks, then Edward Snowden, owed as much to partnerships with British, German and American newspapers as to the disclosures themselves.

The press' imprimatur is important as it is seen to invest reports with the benefits of professional standards that the Internet may lack because of its almost literal acceptance of the belief that the truth will emerge in the marketplace of ideas. Bruns' view of citizen journalism, for example, relies heavily on an assumption that the checks and balances inherent in journalistic norms will be provided by the scrutiny of many users – "the power of eyeballs"– who have the ability to correct mistakes. He likens the process to that of open-source software that is progressively debugged by users (Bruns 2008). The difference is that mainstream journalism applies its tests *before* publication while Bruns' model sees it applied *after* publication. It is, at best, a haphazard approach to fairness and accuracy and one which political elites and officials are apt to discount. Their attitude also is likely to be coloured by the general profile of bloggers that indicates they are likely to operate alone, create weblogs as a vehicle for self-expression and self-empowerment and reflect their own subjective (often intimate) perspectives on matters of current personal interest. This assessment is based on a longitudinal content analysis of blogs in 2003–2004. The analysis of 203 randomly selected blogs also found that 70 per cent take the form of personal journals in which authors "report on their lives and inner thoughts and feelings" (Herring et al. 2004).

Subjectivity, the assumption that the Internet is "self-correcting", and the ability to hide behind anonymity all contribute to the widely held view that individual contributions are without consequence. It stands in contrast

to the accountability implicit in requirements placed on professional journalists by their peers, by employers, by regulators and by civil law. This
difference is important. A select number of blog contributors may enjoy
a positive reputation based on "a synthesis of consistency, accuracy, and
frequent comparison by the reader" (Bowman & Willis 2003, 48), but this
standing does not necessarily reflect adherence to the tenets of journalism.
Certainly it does not require an upfront commitment to accuracy and objectivity, particularly as the distinction between fact and opinion in blogs is
invariably blurred and publish-first-then-refine is the rule. Reputation may
be an incentive for contributors to apply a consistent approach to their
work but they are under no obligation to so. Blood, among others, proposed a blog code of ethics in 2002 (*The Weblog Handbook* quoted in Friend
& Singer 2007) but the blogger community takes an existentialist view that
each contributor should apply his or her own ethical standards to content.
Professional journalists employed in traditional institutions are subject to
non-negotiable disciplines that lie at the core of public confidence in their
endeavours. In the absence of tight regulation or censorship of the Internet,
it is difficult to imagine how bloggers and social network contributors collectively would be bound by a similar regime and enjoy widespread public
confidence.

The individualised nature of user content is a celebration of free expression but it is also an open invitation, as Gurevitch & Blumler put it, "merely
to follow and kibitz over the political process". The *direct* contribution of
blog content to political education, choice and involvement in established
democracies is, at best, inconsistent and inconclusive (Cook 2005; Jenkins
2006; Livingstone 2005). The majority of political blogs are a form of (usually partisan) political expression rather than participation and may be, on
domestic politics at least, an echo chamber of what appears in mainstream
media (Wallsten 2005). They may be less read than has been thought, command little trust and may have "failed miserably" when they tried to shape
political outcomes (Drezner & Farrell 2008). They are an emerging form of
expression and their eventual impact should not be under-estimated. But it is
not journalism. Rosen claims that "When the people formerly known as the
audience employ the press tools they have in their possession to inform one
another, *that's* citizen journalism."[31] In fact, few do employ the "press tools"
that determine the qualities of professional journalism. The most likely outcome for these citizen commentators is that they will provide an "alternative
press" in which minority views are emphasised and celebrated. They are
what Wolfe calls "the new pamphleteers".[32]

This should not be taken as a dismissal of the worth of user content or of
the belief that it can improve professional journalism. It has the potential to
influence professional journalism and, in some areas, sit comfortably alongside it. Participatory media, as Blood (2003, 62) describes user content, can
perform at least four functions to the benefit of journalism:

- Alerting journalists to issues and events that have been unreported or under-reported
- Providing eyewitness accounts and perspectives that can be included in mainstream reports
- Providing journalists with a gauge of public opinion on a given issue
- Auditing the work of professional journalists and mainstream media for deficiencies and mistakes, exposure of which promotes redress.

However, citizen participation is not a replacement for professional journalism. The Internet, or other forms of digital delivery such as eReaders and tablet computers, may well ultimately replace the ink-on-paper daily edition of a newspaper but they will not obviate the need for either professionals or the institutional structures that underpin the richness of Liebling's deceptively simple functional description of the press. If professional journalism does, indeed, have a use-by date it will not be because non-journalists on the Web have provided a substitute for it. Rather it will disappear because it has been denied the material support necessary for its survival as an institution. Will that be allowed to happen? The answer almost certainly is that the importance of journalism to democracy – an ideal that grows in scholarly appreciation in inverse proportion to the erosion of the traditional media's capacity to serve it – will lead to some form of intercession to prevent its demise. The price of that intercession, however, may be structural change and a demand that journalism lives up to the ideals that began to erode long before Sir Timothy Berners-Lee created the World Wide Web in 1990.

3
Media under Scrutiny

Two books highly critical of press ownership appeared on either side of the Atlantic as nations were about to emerge from the First World War. Almost a century later their content leaves modern readers with a curious sense of déjà vu. There is nothing new about claims of journalistic or institutional failure and the belief that the news media is rushing headlong toward a precipice. A survey of the intervening years reveals a recurring inability or unwillingness to find enduring solutions. The inevitable conclusion is that significant structural change in private news media governance will require extraordinary action by extraordinary people.

During the final year of the First World War, Hilaire Belloc wrote an essay extolling the virtues of small and struggling independent journals in the United Kingdom. These independent publishers were contrasted with the "Capitalist (or Official) Press" controlled by "a tiny oligarchy" that was irresponsible, deceitful and working hand-in-glove with Establishment politicians. A year later, Upton Sinclair warned of the connection between US newspapers and "big business" in *The Brass Check: A Study of American Journalism*. The title referred to a token purchased in brothels for paying prostitutes. It was a metaphor for journalists prostituting their craft on behalf of newspaper owners. Self-published by the author, the first edition of 23,000 copies sold out in two weeks. A pamphlet enclosed in the second edition stated that a further 30,000 orders had been received and arrangement made to print a total of 185,000 copies. He stated that the "Empire of Business" controlled journalism through ownership of the newspapers, ownership of the owners, advertising subsidies to the press and "direct bribery". It was, he maintained, a form of control "more absolute than any monopoly in any other industry" (1919, 241) and, as part of the antidote, recommended a widely distributed non-commercial weekly chronicle of news that contained neither advertising nor comment.

Sinclair and Belloc approached the issue from different philosophical standpoints. The former was an outspoken socialist who believed that America's institutions (including the press) had been corrupted in the class struggle (Becker 1959). The latter was a distributionist who believed that large property holding should be discouraged and that Britain should be a nation of small property owners (Epstein et al. 2007). Sinclair used salacious detail and muckraking journalistic style to build a picture of a corrupt press beholding to big business; Belloc relied on the normative benefits of pluralism and perils of power elites to mount his argument.

Both were writing at a time when newspaper owners such as William Randolph Hearst in the United States and Lord Northcliffe in Britain wielded immense power and a propensity to interfere in politics (Jenkins 1986; Nasaw 2003). It is unsurprising, therefore, that critics detected in the mainstream media grave shortcomings that stemmed directly and indirectly from ownership. In 1924 Nelson Antrim Crawford wrote in a matter-of-fact manner about "those who maintain that the press is essentially and consciously corrupt", noting that they sought solutions not from within journalism but from changes to the nature of ownership. Crawford discussed both endowed and government ownership as possible solutions to the shortcomings of corporate ownership, rejecting the first because it would be hostage to vested interests and the latter because it would promote propaganda (Crawford 1969 [1924]). In 1928, *The Economist* – which had, itself, been the subject of a partial takeover that year – concluded a survey of British press ownership by saying that "little in the development of the Press combines to admire and much to regret". The newspaper stated that the political mood swings of two of the largest newspaper owners (Lord Rothermere and the Berry Family) "tend...to give colour to the belief that democracy is 'up against' a solidly hostile 'Capitalist Press,' and undoubtedly weakens the influence of the newspaper as a factor in the formation of right opinion".[1]

In the 1930s, amalgamations and closures – a result of both the Great Depression and fierce circulation battles – altered the press landscape. In 1936 British journalist Hamilton Fyfe wrote acerbically of the "social risk" of Britain's national press being dominated by "very rich men"[2] while two years later Wickham Steed, noting that in New York the number of "responsible morning newspapers has now been reduced to two by failures and amalgamations", warned that similar forces were at work in Britain, where ownership of newspapers had become concentrated in fewer hands and significant publications had been "absorbed".[3] Steed's book coincided with the release of a report by Political and Economic Planning (PEP) on the British press, as a result of which he revised some of his manuscript.[4] The PEP report described the national press as an oligarchy and catalogued "progressive consolidation of ownership" since 1900. While acknowledging that national dailies remained competitive in spite of attempts by the Harmsworth group (founded by Northcliffe, who was Alfred Harmsworth before being elevated to the peerage) to consolidate its hold on the British press, the PEP report noted the major groups had developed non-competitive strategies in the provincial press. It found that the industry was run largely for profit and sometimes "by the pursuit of very high rates of profit" (1938, 255). Nevertheless, its criticisms were both measured and qualified. For example, while stating that the commercial nature of the press was in conflict with its "social functions of enlightenment", it accepted that newspapers had to be driven by popular tastes if they were expected to be read and by competitive practices to boost circulation and advertising revenue (255–257). The report was an early attempt to set out the "broader social responsibilities" of the mainstream media (259–263), a subject to which we will return later in this chapter. However, its efforts were marred by qualifications, concessions and no small measure of class bias that extended to a statement that one could not expect a working-class family to act as if they had the advantages of education and opportunity. It accepted that accuracy could fall victim to the competitive need for haste and that the popular press could not be expected to perform the same social functions as quality dailies, and – in what could only be a sign of the times – stated that "in a world living uncomfortably close to the edge of strife...it may be dangerous to print fully, or even at all, reports that are unquestionably news, and certainly true" (259).

The report's recommendations recognised the dangers of the consolidation of press power but the authors displayed a marked aversion to state intervention as a solution. While they had some novel suggestions related to non-commercial ownership structures, there was a somewhat fatalistic tone to their conclusions: "Unless it can be made profitable once more to start new national newspapers, the number in existence must be expected slowly to decline through amalgamations and suspensions."

In the 1930s, American critics were similarly concerned by consolidation of the market, although the United States did not have the national newspapers that characterised British media and which bore the brunt of criticism. Concern in the United States was with the growth of local newspaper monopolies, self-serving collective actions by newspaper proprietors through the American Newspaper Publishers' Association, and the gulf between popular ballot-box support for Franklin D. Roosevelt and publisher opposition to his New Deal. Lee (1939) calculated that the number of centres in which there were competing dailies was dropping at a rate of 10 per cent a year and there were 1249 cities with "admitted newspaper monopolies". He had doubts about the level of real competition in many of the 209 cities that had more than one newspaper in 1938. Coupled with this concern over the low level of competition was a widely held belief that newspapers were more interested in furthering the interests of their owners and advertising clients than in fulfilling a social function. In short, the role inherent in First Amendment protection was not being fulfilled because, as Dewey (2004) put it, "the newspaper business is a business". Sinclair's view of a press in thrall to big business was a theme continued through the 1930s, heightened by the birth of a militant journalists' union, the American Newspaper Guild, which likened the attitudes of publishers to those of the big business union-busters.

President Franklin D. Roosevelt issued a challenge to publishers to examine their own houses. In response, the *St Louis Post-Dispatch* – whose publisher Joseph Pulitzer II had, in fact, supported Roosevelt's New Deal – in 1938 instituted a symposium on freedom of the press. It did not challenge ownership rights but did produce one of the more enduring statements about the pre-war American press. Political scientist Charles Beard wrote: "Freedom of the press means the right to be just or unjust, partisan or non-partisan, true or false, in news columns or editorial columns."[5] It was a statement that encapsulated not so much the virtues of the First Amendment as deep cynicism about the state of America's newspapers.

The decade culminated in actor-director Orson Welles paraphrasing the popular public perception of the megalomaniac media mogul in *Citizen Kane*. The film screened in 1941, only to be effectively "buried" for years in an ironic display of the power of the man it sought to portray – William Randolph Hearst (Nasaw 2003, 564–574).

The Second World War brought censorship as well as newsprint rationing and other controls that served to diminish the exercise of power by media owners, although censorship was stricter in Britain than in the United States, where opinion was not constrained. It did not end scholarly concern although the focus shifted to audience effects. The Frankfurt School, exiled temporarily to the United States from Germany in 1933, expressed its neo-Marxist opposition to capitalism and the private ownership of media. The essays of Adorno and Horkheimer were not, however, translated into English until 30 years later and their influence on contemporary discourse was limited. Nevertheless, their development of mass culture theory and critical theory was to gain considerable influence with the translation of *The Culture Industry: Enlightenment as Mass Deception* in 1972 and with the work of second-generation Frankfurt School scholar, Jürgen Habermas.

German-speaking Paul Lazarsfeld was, however, partly influenced by Adorno and Horkheimer in his audience research and his attitude to corporate ownership of mass media (Jensen 2002, 282). Lazarsfeld addressed the issue of cross-ownership of newspapers and radio in 1942 but, true to his empiricist bent, declined to judge whether the majority ownership of a quarter of the nation's radio stations by newspaper companies was, in fact, bad. He believed that the Federal Communications Commission (which had been conducting hearings into cross-ownership)[6] would have no evidence against newspaper-owned stations as a group but added that public opinion – from which he carefully disengaged himself – might favour a separation of ownership simply because "the newspaper industry should be checked and that here is a constitutional way to do it" (Lazarsfeld 1942, 42). In an essay co-authored with Robert Merton in 1948, Lazarsfeld blamed "the present organisation of business ownership and control" of the mass media for both maintenance of the social and cultural status quo and suppression of the agencies of change. Consistent with his audience research, however, he did not ascribe great social power to the media, believing it was confined to "peripheral social concerns" (Lazarsfeld & Merton 2009 [1948]).

In addition to worries about cross-ownership, concern continued to be expressed during the war years at the ongoing reduction in the number of newspapers in the United States. Villard (1944, 3–18) reported that "no less than 104 dailies died or were amalgamated between September 30, 1941 and March 31, 1943". He noted that in 159 large towns or cities with more than one newspaper, ownership was nonetheless vested in "one man or one group" and maintained that "every successful publisher is beset by the temptation to increase his power and to make sure of financial profit by eliminating competitors". The war itself sheeted home the power of propaganda that had been foreshadowed by Lippmann (1922) and Lasswell (1927) in the inter-war years which, mixed with newspaper consolidation and rising cross-media ownership in America,[7] presented both politicians and scholars with rising concerns over the post-war communications order.

The founder of *Time* and *Life* magazines, Henry Luce, foresaw post-war problems for the media industry and in 1944 set up a scholarly commission (Harold Lasswell, author of *Propaganda Techniques in the First World War*, was a member) to undertake an independent enquiry into the press. The Hutchins Commission was to have far-reaching effects on journalistic norms but none on ownership issues. It issued its final report in 1947, by which time the press had also become a matter of renewed political concern in Britain. In addition to its general report, the Hutchins Commission published a series of monographs, among them *Freedom of the Press: A Framework of Principle* by the Emeritus Professor of Philosophy at Harvard, William Hocking, who was one of its members. Hocking's work discussed the philosophical basis of free expression and the impediments it faced in modern society.[8] He articulated a dilemma: the right of an entrepreneur in the American marketplace to fashion a large business empire that created a "more or less unitary editorial policy" which led to a "speculative net loss" to the community in the free flow of ideas. The commission believed freedom of the press was in danger on three main fronts related to ownership:

- Its development "has greatly decreased the proportion of the people who can express their opinions and ideas through the press".
- "the few who are able to use the machinery of the press as an instrument of mass communication have not provided a service adequate to the needs of the society".
- "those who direct the machinery of the press have engaged from time to time in practices which the society condemns and which, if continued, it will inevitably undertake to regulate or control".

The solution, adopted in the commission's general report, was not a system to guarantee plurality – although it remonstrated against the consolidation of the newspaper market – but one that advocated social responsibilities for the press. The commission felt that existing anti-trust laws were sufficient to prevent over-concentration but suggested those powers be used sparingly. It believed media should "accept the responsibilities of common carriers of information and discussion" which would limit the ability of editors to block access and recommended an agency to monitor press performance. Recommendations that might limit the power of owners fell on deaf ears. Altschull notes that many of its criticisms and recommendations were poorly received (1984, 181). He does, however, credit the Hutchins Commission with popularising the "social responsibility thesis" that, within a decade, became a mantra for US journalists. It acknowledged both a positive role for the press in the economy and government and an increased responsibility in relation to both the quantity and quality of information provided to citizens.

As the United States moved into the Cold War and McCarthyism, criticism of corporate America waned and pre-war ownership criticism by socialists like George Seldes[9] fell out of favour. The "Golden Age" of television was beginning and "limited effects" research cast the media as a relatively benign presence. The pro-business post-war attitude was summed up by Siebert in an essay that formed part of the highly-influential *Four Theories of the Press* in 1956.[10] After stating that the press must have its foundations in private enterprise, he went on to express a view that saw few dangers in corporate ownership:

> A press characterised by bigness, fewness, and costliness in effect holds freedom of the press in trust for the whole population. Media operators and owners are denied the right to publish what pleases themselves. Free expression being a moral right, they are obligated to make sure that all significant viewpoints of the citizenry are represented.
>
> (Siebert 1963, 101)

Social responsibility was a convenient antidote that did not impinge upon the commercial "rights" of American business and Siebert's *Four Theories* collaborator Wilbur Schramm later added to this commercial model by suggesting that the public (as audiences) had power over owners in determining media content by dint of popularity (1960, 648–660). Their research, and that of the majority of social scientists in the field, was functionalist. The media were not only seen as cogs in a larger machine but were ideologically situated within the political and geopolitical forces of the time.

While the United States began the post-war era renewing the American (commercial) Dream and holding back the "red tide" of communism, Britain's new Labour government was intent on developing a new economic order. The left wing of the Labour Party, in particular, harboured deeply entrenched resentment of the "Tory Press" that they felt had kept them from power and saw an opportunity to recalibrate the scales. Their antipathy was encapsulated in a remit to the party conference in 1947 which demanded a Labour propaganda campaign to refute "the pernicious, persistent and poisonous press campaign of the Capitalist Press". The Labour government established a Royal Commission on the Press under the chairmanship of Sir David Ross at the urging of the National Union of Journalists, Labour MP Aneurin Bevan (who, in 1948, described Britain's newspapers as "the most prostituted press in the world") and former Beaverbrook journalist-turned-MP Michael Foot. The Royal Commission was the first of three to be convened over the next three decades, supplemented by other enquiries.[11] Two commissions (1949, 1977) were established with wide mandates under the aegis of Labour governments while the 1962 commission, with a narrow economic remit, was established by a Conservative government following closure of a major newspaper plant in Scotland. Collectively, the three Royal Commission reports provide a comprehensive summary of major media issues in the prelude to what might be termed the modern communications era, and an enduring dilemma acknowledged in the third report: that freedom of the press is incompatible with its ownership by capitalists on the one hand or with intervention by government to secure the public interest on the other (1977, 10). The three reports are marked by a common concern over the potential effects of media concentration; by a desire to prevent further aggregation; and by spectacular failure to achieve that desire. The common ground is demonstrated by Table 3.1.

Between the release of the first two reports 17 daily and Sunday newspapers, plus numerous weeklies, ceased publication and those that remained were in fewer hands. One London newspaper publisher acquired two national papers and a raft of magazines in a single purchase.[12] The 1962 commission acknowledged that its predecessor's faith in the Monopolies and Restrictive Practices Act had been misplaced, hence its recommendation that a special Press Amalgamation Court be set up. Instead, the Wilson government strengthened requirements for referral to the Monopolies and Mergers Commission – which approved all six applications it received up to the convening of the third Royal Commission. Many purchases were not referred for approval. Government acquiescence, in the interest of preserving titles, was no more evident than in the uncontested sale of *The Sun* to Rupert Murdoch in 1969 and the *Daily Mirror,* the *Sunday Mirror* and *The People* to the Reed Group the following year (Tunstall 1996, 383). Similarly, the 1962 commission's desire to see divestiture of controlling interests in television contract companies failed to materialise. Legislation passed in 1964 to allow revocation of licences controlled by newspaper companies had not been invoked by the time the third commission examined the matter. And that commission's desire to see tighter controls almost immediately fell victim to the Thatcher government elected in 1979 and its determination to let the market rule.

After Thatcher's fall, the government of John Major steered clear of ownership issues but sponsored an enquiry into privacy led by Sir David Calcutt.

Table 3.1 Common themes in British Royal Commissions on the Press

	1949 (Labour)	1962 (Conservative)	1977 (Labour)
Commission origins	Press concentration, rising commercialism and anti-Labour bias	Economic effects generally, arising from closures and consolidation	Economic factors, editorial standards, consolidation (following closure of two left-leaning dailies) and anti-Labour bias
Ownership	Present degree of concentration did not call for action but any further concentration was undesirable. The case against chain ownership was overstated; it was not necessarily undesirable, although there were circumstances in which it could become so.	The extent of concentration had increased substantially since 1949, with the top three dailies and Sundays accounting for 63% of circulation. There were potential political and social influences from chain ownership, which remained matters of serious concern. Present laws provided no protection from potential dangers of amalgamation.	There was no a priori reason to believe that newspapers in chain ownership were worse than independents but the potential for centralised control of opinion existed. Consolidation had not reached the stage where the public interest had been damaged. It would be "regrettable" if large companies were allowed to grow "much further" and there were grounds for inhibiting further concentration.
Cross-ownership	[Broadcasting was fully state-owned and cross-ownership was not an issue]	It was contrary to the public interest for television contracting companies (which enjoy statutory monopolies) to be controlled by newspaper companies.	Did not believe cross-holdings should be prohibited but felt measures to prevent newspaper control of broadcast entities should be strengthened

Table 3.1 (Continued)

	1949 (Labour)	1962 (Conservative)	1977 (Labour)
Political bias	Partisanship was present in all newspapers to one degree or another but less pronounced in the provincial press. Partisanship was distinguished from excessive bias. Shortcomings were not peculiar to newspapers in any particular form of ownership.	National press tended to the right but freely criticised Conservative governments and views of the left were "not insignificantly expressed". There was a considerable range of opinion in the national press but less than in 1949. Press influence was "not as great as suggested".	A gap had been created by the demise of left-leaning newspapers. There was "consistently higher" support for the Conservatives than for Labour. However, the evidence did not suggest that the balance against Labour in either the national or provincial press was strong.
Ownership effects	The number of national newspapers was not so small as to prejudice either free expression or the accurate presentation of news.	There was a potential danger that the variety of opinion may be stifled and a danger of loss of local character through chain ownership. Neither situation had been proven.	Fewer companies would lead to a loss of diversity of voices and a large number of newspapers in the hands of one owner presented the potential for widespread damage if he acted irresponsibly. Concern over provincial monopolies and chains.
Remedies	Present degree of press concentration did not call for action. Commission did not recommend breaking up existing concentrations but relied on Monopolies and Restricted Practices Act to limit consolidation. Recommended ownership disclosure and formation of a General Council of the Press to maintain standards.	Recommended reconstitution of the General Council of the Press with more lay members, right to hear complaints and monitor ownership issues. Recommended a Press Amalgamation Court to rule on mergers and acquisitions. TV contracts controlled by newspapers should be terminated.	Recommended tighter provisions in monopolies and merger laws, with lower thresholds for referral. Suggested Press Charter guaranteeing editorial freedom for editors and journalists. Recommended stronger measures to prevent press control of television companies.

It recommended the establishment of the self-regulating Press Complaints Commission, which the industry duly set up. Calcutt examined the operations of the PCC 18 months after its establishment and concluded it was inadequate and a statutory body was required. That was a step too far for the Conservative government but 20 years later another Conservative leadership would be faced with precisely the same challenge.

In the United States, the Federal Communications Commission (FCC), roused from the inertia it had displayed over cross-ownership regulation in the 1950s and 1960s, moved in 1975 to limit newspaper involvement in broadcasting in the same market. While it forced divestiture in 16 specific "egregious" cases, the commission's rules did not have any significant effect on major media companies. A study completed after implementation of the FCC rules found that "significant common ownership" of newspapers and broadcasting remained in markets with populations over 100,000, and a quarter of the newspapers in markets of more than 500,000 had television affiliations.[13].

In Canada, mergers and closures over two decades led in 1969 to the formation of the Special Senate Committee on Mass Media (The Davey Committee). The Davey Committee commissioned significant research including a qualitative and quantitative study of public attitudes towards the mass media involving a national random sample of 2254 participants. Like its British and American counterparts, the Davey Committee's report in 1970 expressed grave concerns over press consolidation and chain ownership. It recommended the establishment of a Press Ownership Review Board with one basic guideline: "*all* transactions that increase concentration of ownership in the mass media are undesirable and contrary to the public interest – unless shown to be otherwise" (1970, 1/71). In keeping with its transatlantic counterparts, it was largely ignored by the government of the day although a number of provincial quasi-press councils with limited scope were set up, largely at the behest of publishers as defensive moves to forestall possible action by Ottawa (Jackson 1999).

In Australia the number of owners of newspapers in state capitals dropped from 12 in 1951 to 3 in 1981[14] but the federal government did not carry out a formal enquiry into newspaper ownership until 1991, although it instituted Royal Commissions into Wireless (1927), Television (1953–1954) and FM Broadcasting (1973–1974). The Liberal-led Victorian State government, however, established a committee under the chairmanship of Sir John Norris to examine newspaper ownership in 1980. The Norris Inquiry recommended a tribunal to curb ownership concentration but the new Labor state government did not act on its recommendations and consolidation continued during its term (Schultz 1998, 91). A parliamentary select committee inquiry into print media in 1992 – occasioned by an attempted takeover of the Fairfax stable of newspapers – according to a recent commentator, "lies unstudied and forgotten in the parliamentary library".[15]

In New Zealand, newspaper proprietors were able to fend off official scrutiny and even scholarship on media ownership was sparse until the 1980s. The 1986 report of the Royal Commission of Inquiry into Broadcasting and Related Telecommunications in New Zealand fared no better than other official media inquiries. It was ignored by the Labour government, which embarked on a market-driven, highly commercialised restructuring of the sector.

India, following independence in 1948, instituted a number of constitutional enquiries including a Press Commission. The commission, which sat from 1952 to 1954, decided that newspapers and magazines should be vested primarily in Indian hands. The government did not believe the problem of existing foreign ownership was significant and therefore did not order any divestitures. It did, however, decree that future publications should be predominantly Indian-owned and foreign-owned media not permitted to publish there. It also recommended a statutory press regulator to protect press freedom and maintain standards, which led to the establishment of the Indian Press Council in 1966. A second Press Commission in 1982 had some influence on media codes of ethics but little notice was taken of its recommendations on separation of the press from other business interests, a newspaper development council to foster expansion of local media and trust boards to sit between management and editors.

In South Africa under apartheid the news media were subjected to repressive controls, some of which the government from time to time sought to legitimise by commissions of enquiry. In 1956 the Commission of Enquiry in Regard to Undesirable Publications (the Cronje Commission) recommended registration of all publications and the sale of magazines only from authorised kiosks. The recommendations were not adopted by the National Government but the report informed the Publications and Entertainment Act 1963 that gave the Minister of the Interior the power to ban publications. Commissions of enquiry became almost permanent fixtures and were, Gerald Shaw notes in a history of the *Cape Times*, held over the press like a sword of Damocles (1999, 169). The van Zyl commission was appointed in 1950 and eventually reported in 1964, and threats of statutory control forced the media to establish their own disciplinary body to forestall a government watchdog.[16] Nevertheless, for the following two decades – and a further commission of enquiry (the Steyn Commission in the 1980s) – the National Government maintained the threat through statutory control legislation passed in the 1970s but not enacted. And it had many other repressive laws used to persecute and prosecute "unfriendly" media.

With the notable exception of South Africa (and to a lesser extent India),[17] large media companies in the English-speaking world were virtually impervious to both official enquiry and oversight, deflecting criticism and prevaricating over solutions to identified problems in both constitution and content. Two obliquely related factors precipitated a re-examination of ownership and the performance of media as this millennium entered its second decade but there is every indication that news media companies will, again, successfully employ tried and true tactics to avoid any state interference in what they have long regarded as *their business* rather than a public good.

The obliquely related factors that brought matters to the surface again are convergence – the drawing together of all news media in a digital embrace – and the ability to eavesdrop on the digital environment.

In 2003 the Labour government in Britain had passed the Communications Act. Primarily designed to empower a new regulatory body for the digital age (the Office of Communications or Ofcom) it also imposed a series of tests on proposed media mergers and acquisitions. In 2007 the House of Lords Select Committee on Communications, chaired by former Thatcher government minister Lord Fowler, began an enquiry into ownership that examined, among other factors, the functions of Ofcom. It took evidence from 63 witnesses and met 16 groups in the United States, including news organisations and regulators. Its report the following year contained a raft of recommendations including limitations on the tests Ofcom could apply to mergers, a lifting of a number of news media ownership and market restrictions and a broader spread of public service broadcaster funding. The Labour government of Gordon Brown acknowledged the validity of a number of recommendations but said, politely, that it would develop its own policy in those areas where its Communications Act was not performing to its expectations.

The committee's report had begun by agreeing with a comment by Rupert Murdoch (during its meeting with him in New York) that the state of the news media was "fairly chaotic" (House of Lords 2008, 6). Murdoch made the remark four months after the Press Complaints Commission appeared to have closed an ugly chapter by clearing the *News of the World* in a royal phone-hacking scandal that had sent the newspaper's "royal editor" and a private investigator to jail. The News Corporation chairman had no inkling of just how chaotic his world was to become, nor of the way events would reopen – in an unprecedented manner – issues of media power and regulation.

Investigations by *The Guardian*, supported by the *New York Times*, revealed the royal phone-hacking scandal was the tip of an iceberg. Those investigations progressively revealed more and more of the iceberg – to the point where the Conservative–Liberal coalition had no option but to order an inquiry "into the culture, practices and ethics of the press". Among the tasks set the Leveson Inquiry was an examination of aspects of ownership and its regulation. Numerous witnesses attested to the widely held view that there were institutionalised malfunctions – a "sub-culture" – in sections of the press that had adversely affected both attitudes and conduct. Lord Leveson was particularly interested in media ownership as a form of power – and devoted considerable energy to an examination of the overly close relationship that proprietors and their editors had with politicians – but was also charged with considering issues of plurality. He heard from advocates of ownership caps and structural remedies that would limit market share. Others advocated behavioural remedies such as requirements to invest in content, to make space available for alternative viewpoints and to establish independent editorial boards.

The main thrust of his report, of course, was to recommend statutory controls on the *behaviour* of the press. However, he acknowledged that "the culture or tone of an organisation is set by or at the top" (2012, 731). He also noted the importance (and shortcomings) of internal governance in media organisations. Leveson, however, stopped short of any finite recommendations on ownership, opting instead to defer to the existing regulator, Ofcom, and recommending periodic government reviews on the state of media plurality. The aftermath of his report mirrored that of the Royal Commissions – intensive lobbying and negotiation by media organisations to minimise or negate impact on their business.

The second decade of the millennium also ushered in a string of enquiries in other countries. Central to much of this activity were issues of cross-media ownership, concentration and the effects of convergence. None, however, dealt directly with the nature of ownership and its effectiveness in ensuring the continuing delivery of public interest journalism.

In the United States the quadrennial enquiry by the FCC into media ownership reported in 2010 but devoted itself entirely to matters of market domination. The review became bogged down in partisan in-fighting among commissioners that put hearings at least two years behind schedule. While broadcasting in the United States is subject to such regular review by the FCC, the First Amendment makes regulation of the newspaper market problematic.

The Australian Government Convergence Review in 2012 also limited itself to considering the effectiveness of existing rules on market domination and cross-media ownership of television, radio and newspapers in single markets. Australia has one of the developed world's most concentrated newspaper ownership models, according to the Finkelstein Inquiry into media and media regulation which, also in 2012, made a detailed analysis of the structure of that country's media and its importance in a democracy. It stopped short of recommending structural change and was devoted primarily to issues of accountability. Both reports became mired in a struggle between media organisations who wished to maintain the status quo and a Labor government beset by internal power plays[18] that led Stephen Conroy, who had championed a programme of regulatory reform, to resign his Cabinet position.

The New Zealand Law Commission (an independent, government-funded body charged with reviewing areas of the law that need updating, reforming or developing) conducted a regulatory review of media "in the digital age" and its March 2013 report had the benefit of input from the British and Australian inquiries. It called for "a news media that is responsible, independent, and genuinely accountable to the public on whose trust they depend" but limited itself to oversight of content and the consequences of convergence. Its call for a single regulator for news content was well signalled and its recommendation in favour of self-regulation rather than statutory control met with initial approval of media companies but was later rejected in favour of the status quo. The government also opted for the status quo – self-regulation for the Press Council and Online Media Standards Authority[19] and statutory control of radio and television by the Broadcasting Tribunal.

The end of apartheid did not remove the sword of Damocles. The news media in South Africa has had a new politically motivated blade suspended over its head in the form of recommendations to government from the ruling African National Congress party (ANC). The ANC recommended a parliamentary inquiry into media ownership and the need for a charter to increase Black empowerment in the media, the establishment of a Media Appeals Tribunal (an independent statutory body that would sit above self-regulatory mechanisms) and mechanisms to counter what a 2010 ANC discussion paper called "anti-competitive behaviours".[20] However, after ANC Vice President Kgalema Motlanthe met the National Editor's Forum in late 2010 the South African press tightened its self-regulatory regime to stave off government intervention.

Ireland, it seemed, had been too preoccupied by its economic crisis and the need to reform its financial sector to cast its eye over the news media. In any case, the country appeared to be well served by a press council and press ombudsman system that began operating in 2008.

Downing Street had been forced to institute the Leveson Inquiry in the face of mounting revelations of wrongdoing by a section of the British press. One might have thought that the government of Canadian Prime Minister Stephen Harper would have been similarly moved to enquire into the state of the news media in that country. CanWest had collapsed, the Hollinger newspaper empire that included the *National Times* had been torn apart by the imprisonment of its chairman Conrad Black (Lord Black of Crossharbour) in the United States, the national news agency Canada Press had to be rescued from failure (see Chapter 8) and the major surviving media organisations – citing financial hardship – were campaigning for regulatory relief. Yet, in spite of campaigns for media reform by organisations such as OpenMedia.ca, the Conservative (and, to some, neoliberal) Canadian government appears content to rely on its regulator, the Canadian Radio-Television and Telecommunications Commission (CRTC), to maintain electronic communication licences and for newspapers to be ruled by market forces.

Journalistic standards and ethics have been common themes in attempts over the past century to bring to heel what is perceived to be a wayward news media system. Concentration of ownership has also perturbed politicians afraid of aggregation of press power. Governments have met with limited success in instituting or encouraging systems to monitor standards. Licensing of scarce radio spectrum gave control over ownership of radio and television stations (until distorted by boundless digital capacity) but politicians have been spectacularly unsuccessful in fundamentally altering the ownership and commercial characteristics of the press. Why? Fundamentally, they have been afraid. There is a symbiotic relationship between politicians and the press that works – give or take the occasional fit of hiccups – for both parties and which is upset at the politicians' peril.

Press proprietors can react with breathtaking arrogance. When the Australian parliamentary select committee investigating the Fairfax takeover bid in 1992 asked the country's richest man (and Australian Consolidated Press proprietor) Kerry Packer whether he thought Parliament had no right to enquire into the print media, he replied: "Yes, I am saying exactly that. I do not think under the Constitution you have the right to do it." His treatment of Australia's elected representatives was said to be "so contemptuous as to be embarrassing" (Barry 2007, 478–480).

Proprietors' campaigns during media enquiries – both before commissions and through the columns of their newspapers – have been powerful deterrents to significant change. Greenslade, for example, chronicles the way in which newspaper owners have "seen off the challenge to their positions of power" (2004, 49). When confronted by adverse commission recommendations, they have persuaded governments to ignore potential impediments such as the suggestion by the 1962 Royal Commission of a Press Amalgamation Court to oversee takeovers (*ibid.*, 146). Even if proprietors have been pushed into self-regulation to forestall intervention, politicians have been content to allow them to do it on their own terms.

When slighted, the press can react with startling vindictiveness and force. In Australia, Labor Prime Minister Gough Whitlam was subjected to open hostility at the hands of the Murdoch press, according to Murdoch because his policies had failed or, according to Whitlam, because the government had blocked a mining deal (Tuccille 1989, 38). Whitlam was controversially dismissed by Governor-General Sir John Kerr amid a constitutional crisis in 1975 that brought the conservative opposition to power. In Britain, John Major endured five years of adverse treatment across an even broader front because Murdoch, Lord Rothermere and Conrad Black – the principal Fleet Street proprietors – believed he was undermining Thatcherite values. Major beat off a leadership challenge in 1995 despite widespread press calls for change and was subsequently reported as saying he would "get the millionaire press" (Greenslade 2004, 620). Murdoch swung his support behind Blair and the Labour Party in the 1997 election and sealed the Conservative Party's fate. Such shows of power have not been lost on politicians.

Hence, when the Australian Labor-led government attempted to implement recommendations suggested by the Convergence and Finkelstein reports, media hostility was immediate. An editorial on 12 March 2013 in the *Advertiser* (Adelaide) stated:

> Make no mistake. These media "reforms", to use the term both loosely and wrongly, have nothing to do with ensuring higher standards of media conduct and greater diversity of views. They are about one thing and one thing only – spite... One thing the PM should reflect on is that more than two-thirds of Australians don't trust her Government to run the country – and probably wouldn't trust it to run their newspapers and news websites either.

The campaign was successful. The proposals fell in disarray – watered down, amended and finally smothered in June 2013 when, as already noted, Julia Gillard was replaced as prime minister by previous incumbent Kevin Rudd, who was immediately preoccupied by an impending general election in which he elicited no more media support than had his immediate predecessor. The Labor government was defeated at the polls.

In Britain in mid-2013 a Mori poll had the Conservative Party trailing Labour. Prime Minister David Cameron would have been all too mindful of the need to maintain press support in spite of the fact that an election is not due until 2015. It was hardly surprising, therefore, that he tried to reach an accommodation with the press over calls for media reform following the Leveson Report. The Media Standards Trust, tracking the progress of negotiations, found six different versions of a Royal Charter since that alternative to legislated media reform was mooted in December 2012. By early 2014 the industry had exhausted its rights of legal appeal against a charter but, in spite of threats by Prime Minister David Cameron of more direct controls, the largest newspaper companies continued to push for self-regulation.

Press freedom and its constitutional guarantees have often been cited as reasons for a light-handed approach to media reform. Legislative controls are seen as harking back to the licensing regime against which Milton railed in *Areopagitica* in 1644. That certainly is a valid stance as far as editorial content is concerned. It is less obvious why governments have been reluctant to interfere in the commercial activities of media companies, even when to do so would be beneficial in terms of pluralism and the avoidance of concentrated ownership. Tunstall provided an overview of the power of the British national press in 1996 that pointed to a paradox – a series of policies that had the opposite effect to that which appeared to have been intended. Hence a monopolies policy that should have prevented concentration of power actually worked to increase it, just as self-regulation that should have protected the public actually protected the press (1996, 379). The paradox can be explained only by the press exercising informal power, particularly in the preservation of its commercial interests and structures.

The history set out here suggests that the flurry of enquiries in the past three years are unlikely to lead to structural reform of the industry that reduces the power of existing interests and promotes the media egalitarianism that Baker said was essential to a democracy. However, a further paradox may be the catalyst to change. Just as market forces have, in the past, maintained the power and influence of the press they may now lead to changes in structure and governance. That change will not be driven by political will or policy creation but by force of circumstance.

Media companies in the late 20th and early 21st century were large consumers of capital in pursuit of an acquisition-equals-growth strategy. Before the Global Financial Crisis there was no shortage of investors to provide that capital. Post-crisis the picture is different: investors see newspapers in particular as sunset industries and have reconciled themselves to the fact that past levels of profit/dividend are unlikely to return. Structures and governance designed to control and manage large newspaper enterprises may no longer meet the needs of operations reduced in scale and scope. Listed companies have only one purpose – to provide a return to investors. If the returns are insufficient to provide a reasonable return to those investors the only options are winding up or transformation.

Already, some companies have ceased operation while others have diversified away from the news business. There remain, however, a large number of news media enterprises that, although no longer able to sustain the siphoning off of net revenue in dividends to investors, are capable of being self-sustaining. These newspapers (in particular) could benefit from a different form of ownership and governance dedicated to the preservation of the type of journalism they have come to represent. Their traditional medium – ink on newsprint – may not survive but their journalism can continue to inform through other means of dissemination. Beyond these publications lie the digital start-ups that seek also to sustain public interest journalism and which desire more enduring forms of ownership and governance as they prove their survivability.

The remainder of this book explores one such form of ownership – the trust. It is by no means unknown in the newspaper business but the requirement of selfless altruism that is needed for an enterprise that seeks above all else to sustain its journalism is a rarity. The trust offers significant benefits but it is not an instant fix for the problems confronting the news business. The following chapters explore the development and pitfalls of trusteeship, their application to the news industry and the possibilities they present for the survival of the sort of journalism to which decades of official enquiry has aspired.

Part II
The Trust Models

4
Genesis of Media Trusts

The aptly named Yorkshire Conservative Newspaper Company, publisher of the *Yorkshire Post* and *Yorkshire Evening Post,* had a clause in its articles of association that allowed it to refuse to register any share transfer if the potential owner did not have conservative opinions. The Liverpool Daily Post and Echo Ltd, for its part, had articles of association that ensured that the liberal outlook of the *Liverpool Daily Post* would be maintained. These are examples (commendable or otherwise) of the use of trustee principles by newspaper owners. The 1949 Report of the Royal Commission on the Press described two undertakings operated under a deed of trust, and three with articles containing provisions for the appointment of trustees with power to restrict the transfer of control. They illustrated the principal types of trusteeship to be found across the history of modern news media. They also displayed the core element of trust law – protection in one form or another. Not the least of those forms has been the protection of the editor against undue influence. Such mechanisms have been employed to shield editors and to guide their editorial policies but, sometimes, there have been fatal chinks in that armour.

An examination of the use of trust mechanisms in the ownership and control of newspapers since the early 20th century shows why they cannot be simply assumed to benefit the public interest. The motivation for establishing media trusts has ranged from the unalloyed altruism exemplified outside the news media by the Wellcome Trust health research foundation described in the final chapter, through attempts to exert power (often from beyond the grave), to cynical misuse for personal gain. Public-spirited schemes are not guaranteed survival, and selfish schemes can endure in spite of their obvious shortcomings. Strong personalities have an undoubted part to play. At the same time, the history of media trust ownership and trustee governance identifies the components from which public interest media trusts may be created and some of the traps to be avoided. That is the purpose of this chapter and our tour begins in the United Kingdom.

Britain

In 1949, the oldest newspaper trust in Britain was the Daily News Trust (established 1911). In its evidence to the Royal Commission, it described its ownership as "voluntary agreements of owners to limit their own sovereignty in the public interest" (1949, 24). The Royal Commission, after enumerating the types of trust instrument it had found in its enquiry, expanded the definition:

> The objects of these arrangements are one or all of the following: to prevent the control of the undertaking from falling into unsuitable hands, to perpetuate the character and policy of a paper, to avoid the crippling effects of death duties, and to ensure, through the limitation or the ploughing back of profits, the preservation or expansion of the undertaking.
>
> (*ibid.*, 24)

The public interest objective claimed by the Daily News Trust was absent from the commission's definition. Rather, it saw trust arrangements in "business as usual" terms, although it did accept that the articles of one publication (*The Economist*) specifically protected the independence of the editor. The wide-ranging recommendations of the commission's report did not include the use of trusts as a solution to the "growth of monopolistic tendencies in the control of the press".[1] While some witnesses saw trusts as a means of drawing newspapers away from the negative effects of commercialism, the Royal Commission did not agree. It stated that trusts did not necessarily remove a newspaper from ordinary commercial ownership, and did not necessarily protect the editor or produce higher-quality publications. It did, however, acknowledge that a trust could be "a valuable means of preserving quality where quality already exists" and expressed the hope that the number of newspapers "so protected" would grow (*ibid.*, 156–158).

The Royal Commission was correct in determining that a trust was not (and is not) a universal cure for the illnesses that afflict the news media. It is not a panacea, because like the human body, the news business is complex and sometimes mysterious. We can liken the trust to a medicine – it may have limited curative properties, compete against other medical products, be wrongly prescribed, be misused, but may sometimes restore the patient to health. Its effectiveness depends not only on its pharmacological properties but also on the use to which it is put.

In 1959, a British research organisation, Political and Economic Planning (PEP), produced a report, *The Work of Newspaper Trusts*,[2] which investigated three ownership trusts identified in the Royal Commission's report – the Daily News Trust, Scott Trust and Observer Trust. In each of these ownership trusts, principled journalism was the aim that trustees were to support and facilitate. Even if the provisions of their trust deed did not legally bind them, they had a strong moral obligation to follow the spirit and intention of the trust founder's wishes.

However, the report began by noting that while trusts had been touted in Britain as a means of preserving integrity and ordering future conduct of a newspaper, they raised many more problems. The report then set out to determine whether or not trusts helped "toward a better Press" in the United Kingdom.

Only one of these ownership trusts – the Scott Trust – survives today. The Daily News Trust sold its newspaper interests to the Daily Mail & General Trust in 1960 and the *News Chronicle* was subsequently closed. *The Observer*, run by a trust set up by the Astor family in 1945, went through a turbulent change of ownership before being added to the Scott Trust's Guardian Media Group in 1993 following allegation of editorial interference by its then owner, Roland 'Tiny' Rowland. The Scott Trust is studied in detail later but some provisions in the now-defunct ownership trusts are worthy of note as their genesis differed from that of the survivor, and their trust deeds contain provisions that were not replicated by the Scott Trust.

The Daily News Trust was owner of the *Daily News* and acquired *The Chronicle*. The two newspapers were later merged to become the *News Chronicle* in 1930. The first newspaper ownership trust in Britain, it was formed in 1911 by chocolate magnate George Cadbury after he had bought out his fellow *Daily News* shareholders to ensure the loss-making newspaper survived. The trust deed allowed for profits (if any) to be given to charity or staff members, but did not set out the founder's purpose in forming the trust, nor his preferred editorial stance. To have done so would have bound trustees. Instead, Cadbury (who was a Quaker) set them out in non-binding memoranda and authorised the trustees "to follow their own conscientious convictions [for] circumstances change, but the spirit of Christ's teachings is unchangeable". He further wrote:

> I desire, in forming the Daily News Trust that it may be of service in bringing the ethical teaching of Jesus Christ to bear upon National Questions, and in promoting National Righteousness; for example, that Arbitration should take the place of War, and that the spirit of the Sermon on the Mount – especially of the Beatitudes – should take the place of Imperialism and the military spirit...Much of current philanthropic effort is directed to remedying the more superficial evils. I earnestly desire that the Daily News Trust may be of service in assisting those who seek to remove their underlying causes.
>
> (Owen 1964, 442)

Three editors came and went shortly after Cadbury bought the *Daily News*. In each case, the reason was disagreement over editorial policy. The editor at the time the trust was created, A. G. Gardiner, "gradually acquired complete editorial control" during his 18-year tenure, but had to endure letters of criticism from Cadbury's wife that invoked her husband's name. He was forced from the editorship in 1918 as circulation fell and his editorial stances on David Lloyd George (a friend and political ally of Cadbury) and the Treaty of Versailles were at odds with Cadbury's views. Cadbury's son was by then general manager of the company (Boyd-Barrett et al. 1977, 288). The liberal views held by Cadbury continued to be reflected in the newspapers of the Daily News Trust until the *News Chronicle's* demise in 1960 after five years of heavy losses. Greenslade describes the *News Chronicle* at the time of its closure by the new owners, the Daily Mail & General Trust, as "unsmart, inefficient, non-hip, elderly" (*ibid.*, 102).

The Observer Trust deed also gave trustees the power to prescribe the general policy to be adopted by the newspaper and it also had religious overtones. It was strongly Protestant in several of its provisions. No person could become or remain a trustee who was not of the Protestant religion, a term to be interpreted "in the widest and most liberal sense". Directors, managing director, editor and business manager were to be Protestants. It further allowed them to appoint directors responsible for the business operations of its trading company, and required their approval before an editor could be dismissed.

Like George Cadbury, the trust founder, Viscount Astor, used memoranda attached to the deed to set out his views on the relationship between trustees and editors, and the direction he wanted the newspaper to take. For example, in 1945 a memorandum stated:

- The purpose of the *Observer* should be "to reflect and guide public opinion in the ways of good citizenship" – and to pay its way.

  The editor will naturally desire to keep in touch with the proprietors to retain their confidence. The character and quality of a newspaper are the concern and responsibility of the editor. He should be a person with independent views and the trustees should not play for safety by appointing someone who will be neutral. The editor must not feel himself in the hands of a committee, whether of the trustees or the directors. He should have the full and independent right of running the newspaper. He should not be neutral on controversies, nor tied to one political party. He should be responsible for everything printed in the newspaper (except advertisements) and for the appointment of editorial staff. If there is a lack of confidence on major policy the editor and proprietors should part company. On occasional or minor differences the editor should decide.[3]

- Contact between the editor and the proprietors or trustees is especially desirable before a general election or highly critical national issue.

In 1949, the trustees themselves added a further memorandum that they said expressed the commercial purposes of the trust that had been omitted by Lord Astor in his 1945 addendum. The purposes, they said, were:

- To ensure the continuity of the character of the *Observer*, and to enable it to achieve excellence and the greatest possible success within its defined character.
- To extend the service to the community, which it is hoped the *Observer* will do by starting new publications or aiding by investment existing publications which aim at the same ideals.
- To help raise the standards of British journalism by whatever educational means seem appropriate.
- To perform purely charitable acts, chiefly within the world of journalism.

One could speculate that the memoranda were in fact designed to give the editor (and effective co-owner), the viscount's son David Astor, institutionalised freedom of action when he took the editorship from *The Observer*'s wartime substitute. Whether that was the case or not, two things are apparent: his editorship was consistent with the emphasis on responsibility and public spirit in the memoranda; and the clauses provide a worthwhile template that other newspaper ownership trusts could usefully employ, particularly by inclusion in a trust deed to make them binding.

It would be naïve to think that such clauses would give an editor complete protection. The case of the *Daily News* editor, A. G. Gardiner (and countless examples from non-trust newspapers), proves that in the event of a serious policy disagreement, there could be only one outcome – the trustees would prevail, and the editor would resign or be dismissed. Viscount Astor was being no more than realistic when he wrote about the role of the editor in his 1945 memorandum, but implicit in the memorandum is the need for trustees to use their judgement. An occasional or minor disagreement was not seen as grounds to "part company", so the inference is that the use of their "nuclear option" should be a weapon of last resort. It is also apparent from the manner in which the memoranda were written that the members of the Observer Trust were expected to follow the memoranda's directions irrespective of their legal status. In observing that trustees were "morally bound by the spirit and intention" of the memoranda, the PEP Report acknowledged the strength of documents that clearly were not intended to be seen as mere afterthoughts and "are probably of more practical effect than any legally framed document could be" (p. 144). It is important to also note that the 1945 memorandum bound not only the trustees. It was a clear message to the editor of *The Observer* on how he should operate. It did not appear, however, to allow for the possibility that a woman could edit the newspaper.

Newspapers did not have to be in the hands of trustees to be bound by such instruments. Deeds of trust adopted by, or in some cases imposed on owners often embodied similar moral obligations, but their principal purpose was to restrain the owners from certain activities. For example, in 1942 the purchasers of the Birmingham Post & Mail Company were required by the executors of the estate of the late owner, Sir Charles Hyde,[4] to enter into a deed of trust designed to ensure that, for the following 21 years, the company

> shall carry on the newspaper substantially on the same lines and with substantially the same policies as pursued by Sir Charles Hyde, and in particular: (i) provide a full impartial news service with only such comment as is fair and free from bias; (ii) preserve the independence and local character of the newspapers and their freedom from control by any political party or trade association or any London newspapers or any combine or syndicate of newspapers.

Hyde has been described as a regional newspaper proprietor who "represented the kind of sturdy independence, the incorrigible, sometimes eccentric individuality which condemned metropolitan values and whose papers reflected their pride in local achievements and an intimate involvement in local affairs" (Scott 1968, 178). His contempt for the press barons of Fleet Street was summed up in his reaction to news that Lord Rothermere (owner of the *Daily Mail*) was planning to launch his *Evening World* newspaper in Birmingham to challenge "an old family property" – "Tell Lord Rothermere that, far from being a decayed old family property, the papers are owned by a young bachelor who will fight him until his blood's white if he comes to Birmingham" (*ibid.*, 179).

Rothermere turned his sights elsewhere and found similar attitudes. He became embroiled in a prolonged newspaper war in Bristol that led to the creation by prominent citizens of a new newspaper, the *Bristol Evening Post*, to compensate for the loss of independent titles. It ended in a "deal" between his interests and those of the local competitor. A new company was formed, in which the Rothermere interests held a majority of shares, but which was governed by a trust deed guaranteeing that the *Evening Post* had independence under its own board of management. In 1939, a transfer of shares returned a majority of control to the local interests (Royal Commission Report 1949, 23). The PEP Report states that in 1947, the directors reinforced the provisions of the deed of trust by passing a resolution, stating the company policy of the *Bristol Evening Post*, which the report recognised was taken directly from the will of Adolph Ochs, proprietor of the *New York Times* (to which we will return). The Bristol directors felt it also summed up their approach to company policy. The resolution had no legal status, but the directors told the PEP that they felt bound by it and expected editors to follow its provisions (PEP Report 1959:148). The resolution stated the company's purpose was:

- To perpetuate the *Bristol Evening Post* as an institution charged with a high public duty and to maintain the *Bristol Evening Post* as an independent newspaper, entirely fearless, free from ulterior influences and unselfishly devoted to the public welfare without regard to individual advantage or ambition, the claims of party politics, or the voice of religious or personal prejudice or predilection;
- To reflect the best informed thought of the country, honest in every line, more than fair and courteous to those who may sincerely differ from its views;
- To present, without recognising friend or foe, the news of the day – "all the news that it is fit to print" – and to present it impartially, reflecting all shades of opinion;
- To conform to the highest standards of business ethics in its business departments, and to treat all persons associated or connected with any of the departments of the *Bristol Evening Post* organisation with justice and generosity.

The *Bristol Post* (as it became) later was absorbed into Northcliffe Media, the regional arm of the Daily Mail & General Trust. In 2012 ownership was transferred to Local World, a company that bought the assets of Northcliffe Media and another regional publisher, Iliffe News & Media. The deed by this time had been consigned to history.

Other newspaper companies used trust provisions in their articles simply to keep the business in the family. Many of these newspapers at the time were owned by private family companies in which the transfer of shares was restricted, for example to keep ownership within a family. The News of the World Ltd, for example, was held principally by two branches of the Carr family and its articles required shares to be offered first to existing shareholders. When one branch of the family put its shares up for sale in 1968, the other major family interest was not in a position to buy. A share-buying tussle ensued between Czech immigrant Robert Maxwell and a young Australian upstart called Rupert Murdoch. The brash antipodean prevailed and ultimately gained full control, only to close the *News of the World* in 2011 in an apparent act of contrition over the phone-hacking scandal that had engulfed the 168-year-old newspaper.

The PEP Report also examined the articles of association of *The Economist*, *The Times* and *The Spectator*, which each had provisions that imposed trust-like requirements on their owners that were designed to ensure continuity of the character and traditions of the publications.[5] The report noted that only *The Economist* had formal safeguards for the editor. It also questioned, somewhat rhetorically, whether there was a discernable difference between publications with such provisions and those that did not have them (*ibid.*, 153–154).

The Economist acquired trust provisions in 1860 on the death of its founder James Wilson, whose estate was held in trust for his widow and six daughters. His executor, and arguably the newspaper's most renowned editor, was Walter Bagehot. He was also a trustee, but his co-trustees gave him a free hand (Edwards 1993, 256) until his death in 1877 when his Scottish-based successor, George Wilson (brother of the founder), began what has been characterised as an "interventionist regime". He was aided and abetted by some of the daughters, who joined "Uncle George" in discussions over the appointment of editors and aspects of *The Economist* editorial policy. James Wilson's offspring had a long association with the newspaper. The last daughter did not die until 1933, and the daughters were referred to as the "dear old ladies" by Francis Hirst, an editor dismissed by the trustees – "in an entirely civilised manner" – during the First World War for expressing pacifist views (*ibid.*, 542).

In spite of the periodic appearances of the "dear old ladies" at *The Economist*'s offices, and a sometimes active role by their trustees in the pursuit of laissez-faire policies, the hold on ownership was less than tenacious. There was no resistance in 1928 to a proposal by then-editor Walter Layton that the newspaper be sold to a number of investors including Financial Newspaper Proprietors Ltd, which over time metamorphosed into the current major shareholder, Pearson (publisher of the Financial Times).[6] Layton later wrote: "A family trust... is not an instrument well fitted for the management of an important journal of opinion. With every decade that passes its members get more scattered and out of touch with the paper and with one another" (*ibid.*, 617). His observation was prophetic, not for *The Economist* and its new owners but, as we shall see, for a number of other prestigious newspapers.

As part of the ownership change, Layton demanded and received built-in guarantes of editorial independence. He had, on his appointment as editor in 1921, signed a contract that required him to "obey and comply with all lawful orders and directions given to him from time to time by the proprietors" while being free to do whatever he considered "*bona fide* and to the best of his judgement conducive to the interests of the proprietors" (*ibid.*, 610). The articles of the new company formed in 1928 contained provisions for the appointment of *independent* trustees who had the following powers:

- The right to veto the appointment or dismissal of any editor – but the editor was to have sole responsibility for the policy of the paper so long as he remained in that position
- The right to veto the transfer of voting shares in the new company
- The right to be represented on the board of directors.

Layton experienced attempts by the first chairman of directors, Henry Strakosch, to interfere in the policy of the newspaper and to remove Article 105 in the company constitution that gave the editor what he described as "dictatorial powers". There is no evidence that Layton asked the independent trustees to fight the battle on his behalf. Instead, he dealt with Strakosch's criticism of his editorship by issuing a withering rebuttal that ensured that, thereafter, *Economist* editors were protected by unchallengeable guidelines set out in his defence (*ibid.*, 731–741):

> It is thus clear that when the constitution was drawn up, the public was intended to understand that the Board would not function as a body to control policy as is normal with an ordinary newspaper, but the ultimate responsibility would rest with independent trustees functioning through an editor in whom they had confidence. I venture to think that these provisions have achieved their object and that it would be detrimental to the paper if they were whittled away... I am opposed to the simple deletion of Article 105, because I think that however smoothly things may work in the immediate future, it will mean that ultimately it may be taken for granted that normal Board-room control over policy may be legitimately exercised. Indeed it seems likely that sooner or later it will be so exercised unless a particularly strong-minded editor refuses to take instructions and shelters himself behind the Trustees.
>
> (*ibid.*, 739)[7]

Layton's successor, Geoffrey Crowther, suggested in correspondence that the role of *The Economist's* trustees was a benign one: "the business (which normally consists only of approving the occasional stock transfers) is conducted entirely by correspondence, and so far as I know nothing has arisen in the 24 years that the present company has been in existence that has occasioned any argument". Later, trustees began the practice of meeting annually with the editor. The remarkably stable shareholding in the private company has contributed to a benign relationship between editor and trustees, although the possibility in the late 1980s of Rupert Murdoch's News Limited becoming a significant shareholder in the *Financial Times* raised the prospect of the trustee shield being raised to protect the editor by opposing the transfer of shares. The News Limited foray into the *Financial Times* petered out (*ibid.*, 622–623).

The same could not be said of Murdoch's designs on *The Times*, and although the PEP Report was written over 20 years before his purchase of the venerable title, it stated categorically that the editor of *The Times*, "far from having his independence guaranteed, is on paper entirely in the hands of the Chief Proprietors who are specifically empowered by the Articles of Association to control editorial policy" (1959, 151). The articles did, however, provide for a committee of notables with power to veto share transfers that were incompatible with "maintaining the best traditions and political independence of *The Times* and national rather than personal interests, and eliminating as far as reasonably possible questions of personal ambition and commercial profit". The PEP Report asked, perhaps prophetically and certainly with some disdain, whether a foreigner could tell that *The Times* was covered by trust provisions.[8]

Control of *The Times* had passed to John (later Lord) Astor in 1922 in a partnership with John Walter III, a descendent of the newspaper's renowned 19th-century proprietor and editor of the same name. When Geoffrey Dawson assumed the editorship (for the second time) in December of that year he preceded acceptance of the appointment with a lengthy memorandum, in which he stated that any editor worth his salt would require a "free hand" and added: "The power of the Proprietors is exercised properly by the appointment and dismissal of the Editor, not by interfering with his work or doing it themselves" (*ibid.*, 779). Astor and his partner agreed with the sentiment, but this was always understood to mean that the policies of the editor were in broad agreement with the views of the proprietors, or did not at least, conflict with them (*ibid.*, 784). It was, perhaps, their familiarity with Dawson's policy direction that led them to see no inconsistency between their acceptance of the memorandum (together with subsequent statements that the editor had a "free hand") and their inclusion in the articles of association of the proprietary control over policy that the PEP Report derided.

The proprietors were in fact, more concerned about stability of ownership and the preservation of *The Times* as a national institution than the relationship with the editor. There had also been irritating challenges to the power of the Chief Proprietor (the Walter family) by factions of minor shareholders through much of the 19th century (*ibid.*, 786) and the stewardship by Lord Northcliffe had been eccentric, even before the press baron's descent into madness in France in June 1922 and his death two months later. Initially, Astor and John Walter III considered placing their shares in the hands of ten "governors", "referees" or "trustees" who would each hold a parcel of shares in trust, and none could be transferred without the agreement of a majority of holders. However, there were legal impediments to this arrangement, and instead an article was included in The Times Holding Company's constitution in 1924 to provide for the formation of the committee of notables to safeguard the future transfer of shares. The committee was to comprise the Lord Chief Justice, the Warden of All Souls College (Oxford), the president of the Royal Society, the president of the Institute of Chartered Accountants in England and Wales and the Governor of the Bank of England. The article said, in part:

> the Committee, in coming to their decision, shall have regard to the importance of (a) maintaining the best traditions and political independence of *The Times* newspaper, and national rather than personal

interests, and (b) eliminating as far as reasonably possible questions of personal ambition or personal profit.

It was to be more than 40 years before the committee had a serious role to play. In the 1960s, the economic burden of *The Times* was too great for the Astor family to sustain, and both merger and sale were considered. The Canadian newspaper owner Lord Thomson made a successful offer in 1966 to purchase *The Times*, and the committee of notables raised no objections after the Monopolies Commission approved the sale.[9] Thomson replaced the committee of notables with four independent directors who sat on the main Times Holdings board. He agreed to run the newspaper for at least 21 years, with a guarantee of editorial independence (Greenslade 2004, 200). The editorial guarantee was honoured (Evans 1983, 127; Shawcross 1992, 222), but the 21-year tenure pledge disintegrated when Thomson lost patience with unions that resisted direct editorial computer input and photocomposition (Melvern 1986, 75–76). Industrial action closed *The Times* and the *Sunday Times* for a year, and Lord Thomson of Fleet put his London titles up for sale in 1981.

The successful suitor was Rupert Murdoch, who negotiated new terms of ownership. He avoided referral to the Monopolies Commission with the assistance of the Thatcher government and a loophole that allowed the sale of unprofitable companies to proceed without referral. The government turned a blind eye to the fact that, although *The Times* was losing money, its stablemate, the *Sunday Times*, was profitable. The bid was approved by a *Times* vetting committee that included the independent directors and the editors of *The Times* and the *Sunday Times*. Murdoch had given guarantees of editorial independence, and undertook to create a Court of Appeal role for the independent directors (whose number he proposed to increase from four to six) in any dispute between proprietor and editor. The negotiation process was documented by Harold Evans (1983, 2009). Although his views need to be seen in the light of his antipathy towards Murdoch following his forced resignation as editor of *The Times*, he suggests Murdoch made sufficient concessions and undertakings to convince the vetting committee that editorial independence was safeguarded and that the independent directors had an effective trustee role. Murdoch agreed that:

- *The Times* and *Sunday Times* would remain in their own company which had its own board of directors and would not simply become a subsidiary of News International.
- National (independent) directors would be appointed for three years and could "suggest" their successors – although Murdoch would have a power of veto on appointments.
- The number of national directors would be increased from four to six, with the additional directors nominated by Murdoch.

- The appointment and removal of editors would require the approval of the board and a majority of the national directors.
- Editors would have discretion within agreed budgets, which could be reviewed every six months.
- Editors would have sole right to give instructions to editorial staff.
- Editors would have sole control of the selection and balance of news and opinion (Murdoch reserved the right to discuss politics with editors but he agreed they would have the final say).
- The character of *The Times* as a paper of record and of the *Sunday Times* as an investigative newspaper would be maintained.

The first attempted breach of the agreement was over the retention of the newspapers in a separate corporate entity. Less than a year after buying the newspapers, an attempt was made to take the titles under the News International umbrella. The chairman of Times Newspapers at the time, Sir Denis Hamilton, describes the episode in his 1989 autobiography, in which he states that the managing director of Times Newspapers, Gerald Long, and a News International executive, Richard Searby, had attempted to amend the Times Newspapers articles of association in Murdoch's absence. At that point, Hamilton resigned and Long and Searby attempted unsuccessfully to put through the proposal via the company's executive board.

> The national directors had not been consulted, there was a public outcry, Rees-Mogg [William Rees-Mogg was an editor of *The Times*] made a public protest and, together with my resignation, this put Murdoch in a very bad light, forcing him to reconsider. To his embarrassment and shame, his executive board's decision had to be rescinded, leading ultimately to Gerry Long's own departure. (1989, 183)

In the most celebrated test – a challenge to the protective shield around the editor – the guarantees and the power of the national directors again were found to be more apparent than real. In March 1982, Evans (who had moved from the editorship of the *Sunday Times* to *The Times*) was forced by Murdoch to resign. His departure followed months in which Murdoch had adroitly circumvented the spirit, if not the letter, of the agreement. Evans' dismissal was neither debated nor sanctioned beforehand by the board of directors or, particularly, by the national directors who under the articles held the prerogative to decide the editor's fate.

The episode demonstrated the frailties of both editorial independence and of apparent trust-like safeguards written into the constitutions of corporate entities whose real purpose is to satisfy their principal private shareholders. Murdoch was able to:

- Circumvent guarantees of editorial independence by limiting his definition of interference to formal instruction

- Subject Evans to continuing telephone calls and memoranda outlining his views and wishes in terms that carried an expectation of compliance
- Influence editorial content by refusing to set a formal budget (in spite of undertakings to do so), thus requiring the editor to seek approval for assignments involving significant expenditure
- Appoint national directors who were sympathetic to his views
- Appoint and dismiss editors of *The Times* and the *Sunday Times* with impunity.

Andrew Neil (editor of the *Sunday Times* 1983–1994) claimed in his autobiography (1996, 38) that he was under no illusions about safeguards when he accepted Murdoch's offer to edit the Sunday title, describing the national directors as "an inadequate, paper-thin shield" in whom he would place no faith if his job were in jeopardy.

In a more contemporary setting and in another hemisphere, the Bancroft family members justified the sale of Dow Jones and the *Wall Street Journal* by placing their faith in similar safeguards only to find – as we shall see – that, once again, they were paper-thin and inadequate.

Committees of notables were not unique to *The Times*. The PEP Report noted that, at *The Spectator*, any attempt to gain more than 49 per cent of control would trigger the formation of a committee whose members were to include the chairmen of the London County Council and the Headmasters' Conference, plus the presidents of the Royal Society, Royal Historical Society, Law Society and Institute of Chartered Accountants. They were required to "have regard to the importance of: (a) maintaining the best traditions and political independence of the *Spectator*, and national rather than personal interests; and (b) eliminating as far as reasonably possible, questions of personal or commercial profit". These provisions did not prevent a succession of sales of the magazine or the new owners each pursuing their own brand of conservatism. It had four owners between 1967 and 1988, when it passed into the hands of its present proprietors, the group that also owns the *Daily Telegraph*.

The presence of public figures on a trust could be as much an impediment as a protection. The PEP Report suggested that the more a trustee was a person with public standing with definite views on public affairs, the more difficult it was to avoid expressing those views to an editor and seeking to influence editorial policy. Such attempts to influence decision-making could undermine the editor whose independence they were charged with protecting. On the other hand, an errant editor could use the trustee bulwark to delay or even prevent legitimate dismissal by giving an editor "a chance to fight a long delaying action even against his own trustees" (*ibid.*, 153).

The PEP Report was under no illusions about the effectiveness of the various arrangements it had examined. It found that the existence of a trust "does not in itself, however necessarily ensure greater editorial independence and importance", or automatically convert a newspaper from a commercial to a non-commercial concern, or imbue it with qualities that it had not previously possessed. A trust could in fact, merely substitute one owner for another and the newspaper could still be required to make profits, or to direct profits to causes nominated by trustees (*ibid.*, 151).

Its conclusions (*ibid.*, 156–158) contain a number of observations and cautions:

- Existing trusts had been formed around existing newspapers. While it was possible, with sufficient financial backing, to create a new newspaper with trust provisions, this would not guarantee its success, quality or character.
- The successful operation of a trust depended on establishing the right context in the form of the trust, on the selection of sound trustees and the appointment of suitable staff. A great deal depended on the choice of the first trustees and the arrangements made for their replacement.
- Too precise a definition of a trust's aims or ideals could be harmful if circumstances changed. The best trusts may be those where the objects laid down are "quite vague".
- There is no way of controlling the future conduct of a newspaper by legal arrangements, whether as trusts or in any other form. The tradition of a newspaper, the calibre of the people running it and its reputation would govern its future.

United States

Britain did not, however, hold a monopoly on trusts. Forms of trustee ownership of newspapers began to appear on both sides of the Atlantic in the mid-19th century, and as in Britain, American trusts and trustee articles were to serve a variety of purposes – with equally varying degrees of success. Undoubtedly successful was the *Deseret News*, established under a trust deed by the Church of Christ of Latter Day Saints (Mormons) in Salt Lake City in 1850. The title was not a misprint: it was derived from the Mormons' early name for what became the state of Utah. It continues to be published and is owned by a for-profit subsidiary of the church. In 2013 it had a daily print circulation of more than 100,000 copies and was listed among the top 25 digital newspapers in the United States.

Trustee ownership of religiously affiliated and funded American newspapers (most of them with small circulations among adherents), was relatively common in the late 19th and early 20th century. The most successful was the *Christian Science Monitor* that was established in only 100 days in 1908 at the direction of Mary Baker Eddy, founder of the Church of Christ, Scientist. A three-member board of trustees had been established to run the Christian Science Publishing Society ten years before the *Monitor* was launched, because the existing statutory limits on the earnings of a church interfered with the proper running of the business (Peel 1977, 417). In 1908,

Mrs Eddy was the subject of concerted attacks in newspapers owned by Joseph Pulitzer.[10] Coincidentally, a parishioner wrote to her suggesting a newspaper whose purpose would be to "present the news constructively rather than sensationally and would put 'principle before dividends' " (*ibid.*, 309). Two months later, she ordered the creation of the *Christian Science Monitor* – her letter to the directors stated "This must be done without fail" – and stated:

> It will be the mission to the *Monitor* to publish the real news of the world in a clean wholesome manner devoid of the sensational methods employed by so many newspapers. There will be no exploitation or illustration of vice or crime but the aim of the editors will be to issue a paper which will be welcomed in every home where purity and refinement are cherished ideals. (quoted in Lee 1947, 185)

Although it was nominally overseen by the publishing company trustees, the *Monitor's* policy and destiny were actively guided by Mrs Eddy. The first sheet of the editorial page was sent to her home each day "for her information" (*ibid.*, 497), but she understood that it was first and foremost a newspaper and not a church publication.[11] The sole concession she made to its origins was a requirement for the publication of a single religious article each day. Apart from that single religious article which continues to be published each day, the newspaper follows non-denominational, non-partisan journalistic principles. After Eddy's death, the board of directors of the church assumed oversight over the newspaper's editorials and editorial cartoons, and continues to do so. The directors appoint the editor, but do not have a record of interfering in the newspaper's content. The *Monitor* maintains staff writers in eight countries as well as eight cities around the United States. It operates a significant Washington bureau, and employs an extensive international network of non-staff correspondents. As we saw in Chapter 2, journalism's "perfect storm" has exerted extraordinary pressures, and at the time of its centennial in 2008 the *Monitor* announced that it would replace its weekday newspaper with an enhanced news website and publish only a weekly magazine. Throughout most of its existence, the newspaper, which continues to be owned by the Christian Science Publishing Society, has been subsidised by the church ($US12.1 million in 2009 and down to $US4.5 million in 2012). The digital strategy aims to have the publication self-sufficient by 2017.

The longevity of the *Monitor* is unusual. The vast majority of such church-affiliated daily newspapers established before the Second World War could not sustain their losses, and many failed after a small number of issues. Similarly, worker-affiliated newspapers (often with union or worker ownership) struggled financially in the years leading up to the Second World War. *The Call* was published by the Workingman's Cooperative Publishing Association under the oversight of a 15-member editorial board composed of tailors, butchers and mechanics. It was regarded as a "powerful influence" with a credible circulation of 28,000 in 1908. However, the revocation of mail privileges during the First World War,[12] and a refusal to reinstate them after the Armistice, led to its closure in 1923 (Lee 1947, 191–192). The Communist Party's *Daily Worker* was published in New York from 1924 until after the Hungarian Uprising in 1956, and a succession of small-circulation dailies followed until the 1990s when publication was abandoned.

Trust structures have been used to allow employees to obtain equity in the newspapers for which they worked. In 1926 the *Kansas City Star* and *Times* were sold to employees for $US11 million, more than three-quarters of which was by way of a mortgage. Despite predictions of failure, the mortgage was repaid two years ahead of schedule (in 1939). Under the terms of the trust deed, employees gave other employees or the company the right to purchase their shareholdings when association with the organisation ceased, thus guaranteeing continued employee ownership. However, in 1977 the company agreed to sell its interests to the McClatchy chain. In 1937, the *Milwaukee Journal* (now the *Journal Sentinel*) created an employee stock trust, modelled on the *Kansas City Star* agreement, under which workers received a 25 per cent stake in the company. A public share issue was made in 2003, but it included a staff equity incentive plan, discounted staff purchase scheme and other mechanisms including special voting rights to maintain employee participation in the ownership of Journal Communications Inc.

A small number of proprietors bequeathed their interests to establish either non-profit newspapers for the benefit of the community, or to provide funds for public projects. Dunlap (2004) says in an appraisal of these non-profit enterprises that the best arrangements "value community responsibility, commitment to local ownership, and a passion for quality journalism". One of them, the *Tampa Bay Times* (formerly the *St Petersburg Times*), is owned by the Poynter Institute (where Dunlap is president and a trustee) and is the subject of a comparative study in chapters 6 and 7. Another example of non-profit newspaper structure and split-interest governance is provided by *The Day* of New London (Connecticut). The will of Theodore Bodenwein, the publisher of *The Day* from 1891 until his death in 1939, vested the company's assets in a trust that paid nine-tenths of the dividends to his wife and two children, and the remainder to the Bodenwein Public Benevolent Foundation. Following the death of the last of the trio (in 1978) the trust's annual proceeds were to be distributed through the benevolent foundation to the Connecticut communities in which *The Day* circulated. The first article of the will set out the newspaper's continuing purpose:

I have devoted nearly all my life to building up a newspaper in New London which should become a recognized institution in the community, a leading factor in the growth, development, and improvement of the city and vicinity and the happiness and prosperity of the people.

I believe a newspaper should be more than a business enterprise. It should also be the champion and protector of the public interest and defender of the people's rights. I am not unmindful that I owe the success of The Day in large degree to the confidence and support of the people of Eastern Connecticut, and I believe the profits of the large business I have created with their help should, except for the provisions I have made for my dear wife and for my children, be returned to the community...

The will provided for the appointment of five trustees, two of whom were to be employees of newspapers published by the trust. It charged them with publishing *The Day* (and other media), and clearly proscribed their ability to sell the company. Grounds for sale were limited to (a) ceasing to publish a newspaper in New London, Connecticut, or (b) failing to pay in each of any two successive calendar years the sum of $25,000 to the benevolent trust. This provision has guaranteed that the company has remained in the trust's hands.

Bodenwein also set out how he expected the trustees to run the company. His prescription might be described as a model of newspaper commercial governance, although he made no demands relating to editorial quality beyond the sentiment expressed in the will's first article:

To hold said stock; to manage and operate by means thereof a newspaper to be published in New London, Connecticut, hereinafter referred to as *"The Day"*, and morning or Sunday newspapers, or both, should the growth in the field or competition warrant it: to so manage said newspaper or newspapers as to provide liberal compensation and various forms of assistance and rewards, such as insurance, bonuses, and pensions, to its employees; to pay sufficient salaries to assure a high type of executives and skilled writers and workmen; to make provision for providing in the course of time a new building to house the paper and such other tenants as they consider it desirable to provide space for, such building to be distinctive in character, a credit to the City architecturally, and an evidence of a farsighted policy; to constantly improve and maintain the mechanical plant used for publishing the paper; to maintain reasonable reserves for all of the above and for unforeseen contingencies, including taxes; said provisions as to compensation, assistance, and rewards to employees, salaries to executives, the erection of a building, and the maintenance of reserves are to be in every respect at the discretion of said trustees...

The Day Trust has not, however, gone unchallenged. In 1984, it faced court action brought by the Inland Revenue Service (IRS), which had rejected its claim to be treated as a split-interest trust, able to operate a commercial newspaper while supporting the charitable Bodenwein Public Benevolent Foundation. The tax service argued, unsuccessfully, that the charitable ends of the foundation were compromised in order to perpetuate a family business and to operate it at an advantage over its competitors due to the foundation's tax exemption.[13] Nevertheless, Stone (2000, 440–443) notes that the IRS lawyers accurately pointed to its vulnerabilities:

> The stewards of the trust could, and actually did at times, take advantage of the arrangement to reward themselves. Executives could take care of relatives and feather their own nests unfettered by the usual restraints of a stockholding company. Watchdogs occasionally appeared nevertheless to check some of impulses... The importance of guarding against abuses from self-interest presents one of the greatest tests to the future generations of trustees, directors and managers. Yet the Bodenwein will at least still provides a clear direction, and enjoys the force of law for any member of the public, employee, or member of the board to invoke, in the Probate Court if necessary.

In other words, the trust does not have explicit covenants to prevent personal gain or nepotism, but must rely on the general fiduciary requirements of trusteeship and on recourse to law. The IRS lawyers had assumed the worst of trustees, and Stone regards their performance generally in a better light. He acknowledges that the trustees looked after themselves and brought relatives onto the newspaper's payroll. However, he adds that they also did everything that Bodenwein told them to do, including paying employees liberally, maintaining and expanding the plant and trying "to run a newspaper that was more than just another business".

In fact, no members of Bodenwein or The Day trustees' families have been employed or otherwise compensated by the company since the mid-1980s. After the last of Bodenwein's children died in 1979, any "excess profits" were returned to the community. *The Day* is not a large newspaper – it has a daily and Sunday readership of about 100,000 – but the trust has enabled the Bodenwein Foundation to distribute more than $US10.6 million within the newspaper's 20-town circulation region in the form of grants to non-profit agencies, performing arts groups and other charitable organisations. It is one of the largest philanthropic organisations in Eastern Connecticut.

The Day was described by the *New York Times* in 1998 as "New London's feisty newspaper" after the paper stood up to pressure over stories it had written linking a local casino to organised crime. The story acknowledged that the newspaper "prides itself on its autonomy and willingness to uncover facts, regardless of how unpopular they may prove with major advertisers or subscribers" (Rierden 1998).

However, its altruistic aims have not created a newsroom nirvana and, like other publications, it has been hit by economic downturns. An analysis of non-commercial journalism by Stepp in 2004 noted that the newspaper had reduced staff by early retirements, cut the size of its newshole (the space devoted to editorial content) by 5 per cent and begun charging for obituaries that contained more than basic information. However, Stepp highlights two fundamental differences between *The Day* and its commercial counterparts: the company accepted profits that were half (or less than half) those of other newspapers, and when *The Day* missed its budget, had offered "profit forgiveness" rather than forcing further cuts. Such attitudes could not, however survive the effects of worldwide recession. In 2008, the company began forced layoffs and instituted a pay freeze that was due to expire in July 2009. Three months before expiry, and faced with a $US2 million revenue shortfall, the company extended the moratorium until July 2010, made further staff cuts and forced employees to take unpaid leave. The cuts were not as drastic as in many newsrooms: the number of full-time equivalents dropped from 66 to 57 between 2001 and 2012.[14] The Bodenwein Public Benevolent Foundation continued, however, to make grants ($US50,000 in August 2009) rather than risk triggering the sale provision of the trust deed.

Bodenwein's legacy has been positive – *The Day* continues as an independent company and provided a template that others have followed. The publisher of Alabama's *Anniston Star* (weekday circulation 19,068 in 2012) established a foundation in 2002 that would receive all the shares in Consolidated Publishing, the company that owns the newspaper, and provide funding for journalism education. Publisher H. Brandt Ayers' stated object in establishing the foundation was to maintain the independence of the family-owned newspaper after the death of its owner. The *Anniston Star* established a strong reputation as a liberal newspaper during the Civil Rights Movement when it advocated racial integration in Alabama schools. It, too, was hit by recession. In November 2008, the newspaper laid off 15 staff and in June 2009 instituted 10 per cent across-the-board pay cuts. In 2012 it discontinued its Monday print edition but maintained its commitment to train interns from the University of Alabama.

Intentions, however, may not always be fulfilled when, for example, circumstances change. F. G. Bonfils, publisher of the *Denver Post*, announced in 1927 that he would leave $US20 million to a foundation in his name "for the betterment of mankind". When he died five years later, the estate realised only $US10 million – left largely to the foundation – but the bequest was further eroded by litigation (Lee 1947, 196–197).

Altruism is no guarantee that the placement of newspaper ownership in the hands of a foundation or trust will, in the long run, produce either good journalism or journals dedicated solely to the service of the communities in which they circulate. In 1935, *Time* magazine lauded the announcement by Frank E. Gannett, owner of a small group of newspapers headquartered in upstate New York, of a new foundation into which he would place his company's voting shares in order to maintain their independence in perpetuity. The company had two classes of shares: voting shares that had been held entirely by Gannett and non-voting preferred shares held by family members and some company executives that attracted generous dividends.

Time described him thus: "Antithesis of the late hated Chain Publisher Frank Munsey, Frank Gannett gives his editor a free hand, signs his name to anything he asks them to publish in conflict with the papers' policies." Decades later, Bagdikian offered a biting summation of the empire that grew from Gannett's beneficence and the group's acquisition policies recounted in Chapter 2:

> The largest and most aggressive newspaper chain in the United States was not so different from other corporate media giants. It was neither the best nor the worst. But Gannett Company, Inc., is an outstanding contemporary performer of the ancient rite of creating self-serving myths, of committing acts of greed and exploitation but describing them through its own machinery as heroic epics. In real life, Gannett has violated laws, doctrines of free enterprise, and journalistic ideals of truthfulness. But its official proclamations are a modern exercise, with appropriate Madison Avenue gloss, of the ancient privilege of the storyteller – transforming the shrieks of private sins into hymns of public virtue.
>
> (Bagdikian 2004, 178)

Much of the activity that led to this indictment of the Gannett Company took place after its founder's death in 1957, but he sowed the seeds of acquisition and the creation of monopoly markets that were to be the hallmark of the group. The ownership structure of the company and the governance of his foundation did nothing to ameliorate the corporate activities of a group whose aggregation of newspaper assets became a model that others followed and from whose lead "the acquisition trail had become a superhighway ... " (Neiva 1996, 37). It also developed a reputation for business executives exerting financial pressure that led to the resignation of editors, and a disdain for editorial independence that led to the adoption in 1991 of a corporate head office formula for determining the content goals of each newspaper in the group (Overholser 2001, 177).

Frank Gannett appointed 11 directors, most of them former Gannett executives, who were to serve for life and appoint their own successors. In 1936, he transferred the majority of his voting stock to the foundation, but there was no doubt that for the remainder of his life he controlled the company's direction. He hand-picked his successor, Paul Miller, who served a ten-year apprenticeship before becoming president on Gannett's death. Miller and *his* successor, Allen Neuharth, led the company's acquisition strategy, which included the decision in 1967 to publicly list the company to finance its purchases. The conversion of both voting shares and non-voting preferred shares to common stock in the listed company[15] diluted the foundation's theoretical power (which had, in any case, been deferential in relation to company activities) and, in any event, the chief executive enjoyed the support of company directors who gave him considerable operational latitude. Neuharth's rapacious acquisition strategy and the profit focus that was examined in Chapter 2 saw the company become the largest newspaper group in the United States by the time he retired in 1989, and his corporate legacy was an ongoing reputation for driving out competition (Friedman 1998, 327) and putting profit before journalistic quality (Gissler 1997, 42).

However, the group's financial success had another downside that was closer to home. The US Tax Reform Act of 1986 tightened the requirements on foundations for tax exempt status, notably the need to pay out a sum at least equivalent to 5 per cent of their assets each year. The Gannett Foundation's dividends from the company represented only approximately 3 per cent of the asset value, and its tax status was therefore in jeopardy. In 1990, the trustees approved the sale of some or all of the shares. The company's initial offer to buy back the foundation's block of shares for about $US523 million was rejected, but a subsequent offer of $US670 million was accepted and the foundation severed its ties with the empire Frank E. Gannett had sought to maintain beyond the grave. When it announced the sale, the Gannett Foundation stated that proceeds would be used to acquire assets that paid a higher income.

The history of the Frank E. Gannett Foundation and its group of newspapers furnishes several lessons. The first lesson is that in the absence of binding trust deed provisions, there are no guarantees that editorial independence and quality will be maintained beyond the active lifetime of the trust's creator. The second lesson is that a forceful chief executive returning good dividends to the beneficial owners of shares is likely to be given a free hand to exploit market opportunities unless there are binding constraints (such as limits on debt/equity ratios and voting rights dilution). The third lesson is that the desire of a benefactor for the retention of newspaper assets may not prevail in the face of unforeseen circumstances, such as legislative or regulatory change, or hard-to-resist market opportunities.

Only a small number of endowment trusts envisioned the bequest as trusteeship of a public service. The majority were designed to protect family assets for the benefit of family members.

The Hearst family is an example of this. For many years, William Randolph Hearst resisted the pleas from his lawyers that he should draft a will. Finally, in 1947 at the age of 84, he signed a will that would create a series of trusts. One benefitted his estranged wife, the Hearst Family Trust benefited his five sons and their heirs, and there were two "charitable" trusts (Nasaw 2003, 584–585). In 1950, he drew up a further secret trust that would have granted control of the Hearst empire to his mistress, Marion Davies. However, after his death in 1951 she relinquished voting rights on her shares, and over time the Hearst Family Trust became the sole owner of the Hearst Corporation. There were also other significant examples of family-based trusts involving several of the world's great newspapers. They are discussed in detail in the next chapter.

Canada

Legislative change has had a significant impact on trust ownership of newspapers in Canada, where Ontario's Charitable Gifts Act prohibits charitable bodies from holding more than 10 per cent of the equity in a business carried on for gain or profit. The Act, which has passed through several iterations, first became provincial law in 1949. Its immediate – retrospective – effect was to thwart the wishes of the recently deceased Joseph E. Atkinson, who had established the Atkinson Charitable Foundation in the expectation that it would inherit his controlling interest in the *Toronto Star*. Atkinson had harboured strong views on the role of the newspaper in a democratic society and is credited with strongly influencing Canadian social policy implemented by the Liberal government led by William Lyon Mackenzie King (prime minister 1935–1948). The trustees would be bound to administer the foundation in accordance with his stated beliefs which, although not codified in the deed of gift, had been well documented elsewhere and were summarised by his successors (which became known as the Atkinson Principles), and to use profits from the company for a variety of philanthropic purposes. The Foundation would also retain ownership of the newspaper. Atkinson died in 1948, and while the official reason for the new law was the removal of unfair advantage over commercial owners, there were suspicions that it was retribution for his opposition to the provincial government and to curtail the perpetuation of his liberal views. The longevity of the legislation would suggest the official reason was more credible.

Nonetheless, its passage into law in 1949, which had been opposed by the *Toronto Star* in its editorial columns, gave the Atkinson Foundation seven years to put the business under private control (Kesterton 1984, 87–88). The trustees were faced with a dilemma – the law was clear, but so too were Atkinson's instructions that the *Star* would be run by those "familiar with the doctrines and beliefs which I have promoted in the past", and that publication of the newspaper would be conducted "for the benefit of the public in the continued frank and full dissemination of news and opinion". The trustees (drawn from the Atkinson family and senior employees) sought and were granted court approval for a novel solution. They purchased the company as individuals, but bound themselves to trust provisions that preserved Atkinson's intentions. A Voting Trust was formed that bound together the shareholders who collectively raised $CA25.5 million to purchase shares in what became Torstar Corporation. Today, seven groups representing the descendants of the original five buyers form the Voting Trust that controls 98 per cent of the voting shares in the corporation, with restrictions on their sale to ensure the Trust retains control. Non-voting B shares (20 per cent of which are held by the "A" shareholders) are freely traded on the Toronto Stock Exchange. The deed forming the Voting Trust stated that its purpose was "to ensure that control of the *Toronto Star* newspaper would be maintained by persons who would continue to honour the doctrines and beliefs of Joseph E. Atkinson". Since the corporation was formed in 1958, Torstar has become a diversified group, but the Toronto Star subsidiary continues to be separately operated, according to the Atkinson Principles which stand for:

- A strong, united and independent Canada.
- Social justice.
- Individual and civil liberties.
- Community and civic engagement.
- The rights of working people.
- The necessary role of government (when the private sector and market forces are insufficient).

Ultimate responsibility for ensuring observation of the principles lies with the Voting Trust, but day-to-day responsibility is delegated to the newspaper's chief executive and to its publisher. It should be noted that editorial independence is not included among the six principles although, at the court hearing which granted approval of the Voting Trust ownership structure, the shareholders did pledge to uphold principles of liberalism, independence and a free flow of information. There is, however, at least one recorded instance of Torstar executives interfering in editorial decision-making. The 1981 Canadian Royal Commission on Newspapers (the Kent Commission) was highly critical of Torstar, which had acquired most of the larger weekly newspapers in Toronto that it did not already own. The Commission stated, pejoratively, that "Torstar is a conglomerate" and was critical of its ownership of multiple titles (*ibid.*, 240).

In 1985, the group entered into a $CA220 million share swap with Southam Inc., then the second largest newspaper publisher in Canada. It was a protective move, as Southam had become a takeover target. The agreement – Torstar acquired a 23 per cent interest in Southam, which acquired about 30 per cent of Torstar's non-voting shares – amounted to a partial merger and raised concern over concentration of ownership, even though the protective screen around the *Toronto Star* was maintained through the Voting Trust's control of Torstar's voting shares. Under the agreement, the two groups agreed not to seek further shares in each other for ten years. However, five years later the share alliance was terminated in the face of legal challenges to the arrangement, and Torstar sold its Southam holding. In 1998, Torstar attempted to buy Sun Media, which owned newspapers in Ontario and Alberta, but was outbid. The failure to capitalise on its Southam shareholding, and a series of blunders that led to the failure of the Sun Media bid, were seen by critics as fundamental failings of the Voting Trust structure. A (rival) *Globe & Mail* analysis of the Sun Media failure stated that Torstar had erred in its overall business strategy and that its corporate structure was to blame:

> Indeed, some critics now question whether they [the families that inherited the business] have become so preoccupied with social principles that their attention to the core business of newspapers has slipped, thereby allowing more focused, aggressive and politically conservative competitors to reshape the newspaper business.
>
> (*Globe & Mail* 2 January 1999)

The *Toronto Star* itself is generally above criticism of its corporate owner. The Kent Commission applauded the newspaper's decision to become the first Canadian newspaper to appoint a public editor, a person to whom members of the public can complain about the practices of the newspaper and seek published redress. In 2006, the Canadian Standing Senate Committee on Transport and Communications report on the Canadian media[16] suggested other newspapers should follow the *Star's* example. In 2000, the newspaper formed a community editorial board in response to claims that it did not accurately reflect the issues and concerns of particular communities in the Greater Toronto Area. Membership of the 12-strong board changes each year, to ensure that over time each of the ethnic and territorial communities in the conurbation is represented. Six hundred people applied for the 12 positions in 2003 (Russell 2006, 224). The board meets monthly with the newspaper's editorial staff, and members write opinion articles reflecting the views of their particular communities that may be critical of the newspaper. It is also apparent that the Atkinson Principles remain the guiding standard in the newspaper's editorial department. In the same *Globe & Mail* article that criticised adherence to the principles, Torstar director Nelson Thall described them as "like a cult – the belief in the principles keeps us together" and, in a profile by Marco Ursi published in 2006, one of the publication's most outspoken columnists, Antonia Zerbisias, stated (in an affirmative way), that they were "tattooed on my ass". The *Toronto Star* remains Canada's largest daily newspaper with an average weekday circulation in 2012 of 346,000 and 474,000 on Saturday. It continues to follow a "liberal with a small l" editorial policy that is a legacy of Joseph Atkinson's stewardship of the newspaper.

South Africa

Mining has been a vital part of the South African economy since a diamond was discovered in Hopetown in 1867. The companies that grew from the extraction of precious minerals developed tentacles that spread throughout South African society. One of these tentacles was wrapped around the

English-language press in which mining interests were the biggest investors but a trust arrangement kept that tentacle stretched.

The Argus Group, which became the country's largest newspaper owner, was controlled by Central Mines and Rand Mines Group. Known as the Corner House Group, it later became Central Mining and Investment Corporation. For the first half of the 20th century all Argus Group directors were drawn from Central and another mining-related organisation, Johannesburg Consolidated Investments (JCI), that also had a shareholding. Both had a staunchly pro-British outlook.

In 1931 there were fears of a takeover of Central by French investors which, if successful, could lead to a shift of support to Afrikaner interests in which the newspapers of the Argus Group would be vitally important. The mining company decided to vest its voting shares in the press group in an Argus Voting Trust that was created to ensure that control remained in the hands of Anglophiles. In fact, until 1948 there were only two trustees – Sir Reginald Holland and John Martin. Both were chairmen of Central Mining and were the architects of the Voting Trust. In 1943 they set out what they saw as its purpose. There was a commendable adherence to maintaining "an honest, responsible standard of journalism" and pursuit of company policies that balanced journalistic esteem and financial strength. Two provisions, however, were designed specifically to tie trustees to a pro-British stance: assistance in the development of the country as a member of the British Commonwealth; and furthering the cause of racial co-operation and the welfare of the non-White population.[17]

The Argus Voting Trust was a classic example of a newspaper trust in the sense that it combined journalistic aspirations and maintenance of control. While Holland and Martin were alive it worked as intended and was effectively the sole policy-controlling body of the Argus Group. The Van Zyl Commission of Enquiry into the Press concluded that the two men had virtually complete control over Argus newspapers. (Potter 1975, 56–57). However, Holland died in 1948 and Martin a year later. Their deaths were further evidence of the roles that strong personalities can play in the administration of newspaper trusts.

Holland and Martin had held considerable sway within Central Mining and during their lifetimes no-one was prepared to challenge the notion of ownership without control. They had instilled the belief that the Argus Group must be seen to operate at arm's length from the mining interests. With their passing questions were raised, particularly about the effect on a sale of the mining company's shares – which could leave control but not ownership of the Argus Group in the hands of the previous owners. The trust's future was further called into question when JCI increased its shareholding in the Argus Group. Until Holland's death JCI had been unaware of the trust's existence and, when it was made aware, did not want growing influence in the newspaper group encumbered by that stranglehold. Potter (*ibid.*, 58–59) says the trustees tried to persuade the mining companies to accept a trust arrangement similar to *The Times* or *The Guardian* but were unsuccessful. However, they did persuade Central and JCI – in exchange for being released from the provisions of the trust – to reduce their holdings in the Argus Group by selling to sympathetic buyers. These new investors then handed the voting rights to the trust, which remained a strong voice in the Argus Group.

There were further significant changes. Following reconstitution of the trust's rights, all trustees were appointed from within the Argus Group and the group's board of directors – after 1961 made up of four representatives from within the Argus Group and two from each of the mining companies – was chaired by an Argus Voting trustee. This was also a period of consolidation in the mining industry and Central Mining and JCI both came under the control of the Anglo American Corporation, which acquired their combined shares in the Argus Group. Anglo American was content to allow the Argus Group to be seen to operate at a distance from the largest conglomerate in South Africa but the Voting Trust was little more than a figurehead. Anglo American's chairman, Harry Oppenheimer, claimed on more than one occasion that his group did not "interfere" in editorial policy, although others claimed he did not need to interfere because the newspapers followed policies helpful to the conglomerate (Innes 1984, 204–205).

Nevertheless, the Argus Group newspapers stood against the apartheid policies and repression that reached its height during the State of Emergency from 1985 to 1989. A former executive director for corporate affairs of Anglo American, Michael Spicer, recalls that the corporation felt it needed to hold the media asset during the apartheid years – "it felt very strongly on the importance of a free press" – but that need receded as South Africa moved towards full democracy. Anglo American decided to sell its holding in the Argus Group to Dublin-based Independent News & Media in 1994. By that stage, the Argus Voting Trust was little more than a fragment of media history – as was the Argus Group itself when the Irish company took full ownership and changed its name to Independent News & Media South Africa (INMSA).[18]

The Argus Voting Trust was by no means the only example of news media trusteeship in South Africa. The country had a regulatory structure that gave rise to extremely complex ownership arrangements and a number of self-serving shareholding trusts existed that do not warrant examination here. However, it was also a form of governance that played an important part in the rise of the alternative press.

A prime example is provided by *Grassroots*, a community publishing project that began in 1980 as a newsletter[19] containing community news for the disenfranchised peoples of the Western Cape whose needs were not being met by the mainstream media. It eschewed what it saw as capitalist values in the commercial press and committed itself to a form of journalism aimed at being understood by the poorly educated masses. It was managed and controlled by a board of trustees – consisting of community leaders, community workers, academics and journalists – established after the Writers Association of South Africa (WASA) sought help in establishing the newsletter. The resulting trust was independent of WASA and constituted an editorial board but it did not control the content of the publication, which it wished to leave in the hands of community groups. In a case study of the newsletter, Johnson (1991, 191–206) says *Grassroots* found itself at a publishing frontier that involved "a painstakingly democratic production cycle" that began with a news-gathering meeting to which all workers and community organisations were invited to send representatives.

Unsurprisingly, the newsletter – closely identified with the "coloured" or mixed race population – incurred the displeasure of the apartheid regime, which subjected the alternative press to banning, harassment and prosecution. *Grassroots* was twice banned between 1980 and 1984 but continued to play a role in encouraging community responses to government pressure and developing community projects. Its existence became precarious during the State of Emergency when censorship and confiscation were rife. The last issue appeared in 1989.

Australia and New Zealand

Australasia presents little of significance in the history of newspaper trusts. Family trusts (and trust-like structures to administer small narrow-interest publications), have existed over the course of the newspaper publishing history of Australia and New Zealand, but trustee-type governance in major enterprises has been limited to the administration of the respective national news agencies (Australian Associated Press and the now-defunct New Zealand Press Association) and public broadcasting. These entities, are discussed in Chapter 8.

Trustee-type governance may have been expected in the Labour Party/trade union newspapers that were established in both countries. They were in fact registered as businesses, with allotted share capital, boards of directors and – importantly, given their financial performance – limited liability. The most prominent newspaper of this type in Australia was the *Labor Daily*, the sole metropolitan survivor of a plan to establish Australian Labor Party (ALP) newspapers in each state capital. Started in 1922, it was used by New South Wales premier J. T. (Jack) Lang to further his political aims. After changing its name to the *Daily News* in 1938, it was sold to Frank Packer's *Daily Telegraph* in June 1941, and closed the following month.

Trustee governance of a major daily newspaper could have become a reality, had the ALP's plans for the resurrection of its dream of a newspaper chain to counter the "capitalist press" been put into action. The concept had been debated in labour movement circles since the 1890s, but gained momentum with the publication of A. E. Mander's *Public Enemy The Press* in 1944 (Mayer 1964, 251). In 1961, the ALP federal conference endorsed a proposal for an Australian Newspaper Commission, modelled on the Australian Broadcasting Commission, to publish newspapers in parallel with the ABC's radio and television services (Walker 1980, 231). When the Labor Party came to power after a long period in opposition, the proposal was advanced further, after the creation of a Department of the Media by the Whitlam government. A 1975 paper released by the department advocated the establishment of the newspaper commission. It also advocated a Royal Commission on the media, a voluntary press council, legislation to restrict ownership of electronic media by newspapers, newspaper licensing similar to broadcasting licences and the establishment of a government-funded university-based media research unit. O'Malley describes the press reaction as "violent" (1987, 95) and while a voluntary press council was formed to pre-empt federal regulation, the newspaper commission was never established.

New Zealand's experience with Labour Party/trade union newspapers was similar to that in Australia. Titles came and went (see Scholefield 1958, 40–43), culminating in the *Southern Cross*, a Wellington-based daily published from 1946 to 1951, that had the capital structure and governance of a standard commercial enterprise.

There were early, short-lived examples of cooperative ownership in the New Zealand colonial press. *The Colonist* and the *New Zealand Spectator* for example, were each established in the 1840s by groups of Wellington settlers. *The Colonist* was short-lived, but *The Spectator* enjoyed a longer life-span. It was initially administered by a "committee of half a dozen of the principle gentlemen in the settlement" elected at half-yearly meetings (Hocken 1902, quoted in Day 1990, 38–39). After two years, however, the arrangement began to break down and ownership was eventually vested in the editor, Robert Stokes (*ibid.*, 41). Collective ownership was to become a feature of the daily press in New Zealand, but it would take the form of shareholding arrangements and commercial enterprise.

Lessons from history

This brief historical overview suggests newspaper proprietors have seen trust ownership and operation as a means of preserving their legacies, when conventional forms of ownership offered insufficient guarantees for the continuation of the culture they had created. It also suggests that legal status, without an ongoing commitment by trustees, shareholders and executives to the ideals of the founder, may not invest those principles with the longevity that he or she envisaged. It also recognises the legal and political environment in which a newspaper is published may affect not only the fortunes of a newspaper-owning trust but also its very existence, as the executors of Joseph Atkinson's estate discovered. And it adds weight to the PEP's conclusion that a trust may make a good newspaper better but it will not make a serious broadsheet out of a red-top tabloid. From the examples in this chapter, we can distil a number of potential issues in the trust system that could confront present-day and future trustees if they do not possess the mechanisms – and the will – to avoid them.

While a founder is alive, the trust and its publications are hostage to his or her wishes. Cadbury (and his wife) continued to exert a pervasive influence over the *Daily News*, as did Mrs Eddy over the *Christian Science Monitor*. A strong-willed founder is also predisposed to leave detailed instructions to ensure that influence is as strong in death as it was in life. As the PEP Report concluded, to be effective, trust deeds and articles must strike a balance between the detail necessary to provide the intended protections and the latitude that provides room for effective action over time. That has not always been the case. Lord Astor, for example, left the *Observer* trustees with little discretion and the restrictions on their appointment (a provision also present in the appointment of national directors at Times Newspapers) predisposed them to certain courses of action dictated by their backgrounds or stations in life.

Even founders who have been mindful of such matters have created problems for their trustees by leaving detailed codicils and memoranda which, although they do not have the force of law, are treated as such. Both the *Daily News* trustees and the *Observer* trustees treated memoranda not as suggestions but as instructions. Even where such instruments are absent, trustees have felt a need to perpetuate the founder's will in some way. Joseph Atkinson's last testament stated only that he wished his editorial policies and the independence of the *Toronto Star* to continue after his death, but faced with the challenge of establishing their own legality, the Torstar Voting Trust went further and drew from his statements and writings the set of principles to which they bound themselves before an Ontario judge.

Trustees, however, may not be in full control of their founders' legacies. There are numerous instances where shareholders (e.g. Rupert Murdoch at Times Newspapers), family members (e.g. the Astors at *The Times* and *The Observer*) and strong-willed executives (e.g. Bagehot and Layton at *The Economist*) have asserted themselves in ways that have usurped or marginalised trustees. Trustees may, for example, be characterised as an unutilised "court of last resort", or be overlooked in an act-first-and-seek-approval-later stratagem. George Layton at *The Economist* regarded the trustees as a somewhat quaint institution, while News International (in spite of the initial undertakings given before the sale of Times Newspapers) tried to work around them. An example was the debacle that ensued when the parent company attempted to subsume Times Newspapers. On more than one occasion, Rupert Murdoch has used pillars of society, acting as trustees to prevent excessive use of power, as a lever in the purchase of prestigious newspapers. It was a necessary device in winning government approval for the purchase of Times Newspapers, and was repeated when News Corporation bought Dow Jones from the Bancroft family (discussed in the next chapter). In neither case did it prevent (for better or worse) intrusion into editorial departments or the removal of an editor within a year of purchase. Without a strong commitment to their use as effective "public representatives", and the power to assert themselves when *they* deem it necessary rather than at the 11th hour or too late, such trustees (by whatever name) may be no more than hollow effigies towed into place to impress an audience, or modern-day Trojan horses.

In circumstances where trustees co-exist with owners (often in tiered shareholding arrangements), the trust mechanisms that were established to ensure continuity of ownership may be only as good as the resolve of present owners to continue to hold their shares. The determination to retain independent ownership of the *Bristol Evening Post*, *Kansas City Star*, South Africa's Argus Group and Reuters news agency (see Chapter 8) changed over time, and circumstances led the foundation that was the beneficiary of Frank E. Gannett's estate to divest itself of Gannett shares.

History also demonstrates that the relationship between trustees and editors is complex. Trustees have usually been given powers over the appointment of editors, although proprietors may be seen to exercise even greater influence over appointments, and the wording of such provisions in trust instruments requires careful drafting if trustees are to prevail. Once appointed, editors are as bound as trustees by trust provisions, articles of association and memoranda. The duties may be explicitly stated, as was the case with the Birmingham Post & Mail Company, the *Bristol Evening Post*, the *Christian Science Monitor* and the *Toronto Star*, or in cases such as *The Economist* and *The Times* (under Lord Astor) editors may be guaranteed the independence to set editorial policies and "govern alone". Complete editorial independence has proven a problem for trustees who felt editorial policies had diverged from an established ethos. A trust deed that too tightly enshrines the rights of an editor may leave no alternative but to exercise a reserve power to dismiss an editor who directly challenges the trustees, as editors of the *Daily News* and *The Economist* found to their cost. At the other end of the scale, guarantees of editorial independence may be narrowly interpreted by a proprietor or a trust, thus nullifying them. Rupert Murdoch (and Lady Cadbury before him) did not issue formal directives to the editors of *The Times* and *Sunday Times*, and was able to claim that he did not interfere – but informal influence was both direct and effective while below the national directors' radar. The Leveson Inquiry's conclusions (2012, 1432) included the observation that Murdoch's editors knew [and by implication followed] his opinions and wishes "without having to ask". Editorial budget allocation, as Harold Evans found, was an effective form of proprietorial control, which because of its operational nature was deemed to be beyond trustee oversight.[20] Experience shows there is a pecking order – trustees prevail over editors in a terminal disagreement over editorial policy, and proprietors prevail over both trustees and editors in such circumstances.

Trusts outlined in this chapter have at times been subject to unfortunate effects of family involvement. Family trusts are discussed in detail in the next chapter but we have already seen some of the effects. William Randolph Hearst's will was pre-destined to cause conflict, and illustrates the folly of creating multiple trusts – to provide legacies to groups with little in common – that can affect the operations of the enterprise. The appointment of family members as trustees carries with it risk. James Wilson was well served at *The Economist* by his son-in-law Walter Bagehot, but following the latter's death, the Wilson daughters and the geographically remote but nonetheless interventionist "Uncle George" (Wilson's brother) interfered with the smooth operation of the newspaper.

However, it is not all bad. History has provided evidence of the positive outcomes of trust ownership and trustee governance. We have seen, for example, how public-spirited aims can be embodied in commercial enterprises by embracing trustee-like obligations, as was the case with Torstar in relation to the *Toronto Star*. That newspaper also illustrates how selected publications within a media group can be operated under trustee-like governance while other parts of the enterprise function as normal commercial enterprises.

Financially, there are some benefits to be gained from trustee governance. Altruistic trusts have the capacity to accept financial performance that would be unacceptable in publicly listed companies, as operations at *The Day* demonstrate, while direct or indirect subsidies may be a welcome addition to revenue. Such has been the case with the *Christian Science Monitor* over its lifetime and, as will be seen in later chapters, has been the lifebelt of *The Guardian*. A more benevolent attitude to financial performance should not, however, be seen as a signal that trust-governed newspapers are immune to marketplace realities. Trust-run newspapers have, like their listed company-owned counterparts, been subjected to severe cost-cutting during recession. The difference, however, is that cuts are made in ways that are calculated to do least damage to the journalistic core to which trustees are bound.

These lessons point to the need for considerable care in the crafting of trust documents. While no trust deed is likely to be ultimately immune from concerted action to undermine or undo it, it will be more robust if heed is given to the following:

- Trust deeds must strike a balance between direction and flexibility and recognise that trustees are likely to feel bound by "helpful" memoranda and codicils. Trusts can be compromised by a founder who attempts to "direct from the grave", by dictating the appointment of inappropriate trustees or binding them to restrictive covenants.

- A trust that coexists with a shareholding "proprietor" may need explicit independent powers to avoid being usurped, circumvented, ignored or turned to the "proprietor's" interests.
- The relationship between trustees, "proprietors" and editors is finely balanced, and specifications on how it is to be managed must, on one hand, preserve the journalistic principles that are the institution's foundation and, on the other, prevent any of the parties from assuming unbridled power.
- Flexibility is the key to both the governance and operation of a trust that will endure beyond a generation, and be able to apply the altruistic principles that differentiate it from a profit-driven publicly listed or private company.

An examination of present-day structures will enable us to judge how many of these lessons have been taken to heart.

5
Keeping It in the Family

There is nothing unusual about families owning companies. Founding families have control over more than half of America's public corporations and huge international companies like Walmart, Samsung and India's Tata Group. Many of these families use legal devices to retain control of their enterprises after their ownership has been diluted by public share offerings – media-owning dynasties among them.

This chapter examines contemporary newspaper companies on both sides of the Atlantic where family involvement stretched back several generations, and in which trust structures have played a part in the retention (or loss) of control. These examples are by no means the full sweep of family trusts in the news business. Many families, the Hearst, Pulitzer,[1] Scripps and Chandler clans among them, retained trusts to consolidate and manage their investments. However, our focus will be on the Ochs-Sulzbergers and the *New York Times*, the Grahams and the *Washington Post*, the Bancrofts and the *Wall Street Journal*, and the Harmsworths and Britain's *Daily Mail*. The Murdoch Family Trust also will be acknowledged but not dealt with in detail, because its media interests have yet to move beyond the control of its founder, Rupert Murdoch.[2] These families have been chosen because their interests include nationally significant publications, and each illustrates an important aspect of trust development or operation. First, however, we will consider some of the dynamics of the "family firm".

There is a growing body of research on family firms, much of it based on agency theory and comparisons with companies that have non-family shareholding and management structures. One body of research is an extension of the view that agency costs are minimised in owner-operated firms (Jensen & Meckling 1976), and that family ownership can bring unique positive attributes to the conduct of business (Pearson et al. 2008). Other research suggests that family relationships can complicate and negatively impact business activity (Schulze et al. 2002). A number of generalised findings have a bearing on the conduct of the family trusts examined in this chapter.

Family businesses have been defined as those whose policy and direction are subject to significant influence by one or more family units, with that influence exercised through ownership and, sometimes, family participation in management (Davis 1983, 47). They are characterised by three interacting elements: the family unit, individual family members and the business itself. Habbershon et al. describe the family business as a "metasystem" in which the controlling family represents the history, traditions and life cycle of the family; the individual family member embodies the interests, skills and life stage of the participating family owners or managers; while the business unit is the entity in which strategies and structures are used to create wealth (2003, 454–455). These researchers believe the systemic influences generated by the interaction of these three subsystems "create an idiosyncratic pool of resources and capabilities... [that] have deeply embedded defining characteristics that we refer to as the 'family factor'... " (*ibid.*, 460). Davis regards this "family paradigm", in which the sentient elements of "family" (attributes such as loyalty ties and trust) interact with the business unit to produce behaviour that is unique to the family firm. It is likely, for example, that family businesses are "predominantly consensus-sensitive". He believes that the family paradigm is particularly strong in early generations of the business, and derives from the character of the founder (1983, 52). It is a further characteristic of family firms that they are more likely to be dominated by a strong individual (such as the founder) who is unwilling to cede control to others (Daily & Dollinger 1992, 133) and who, consequently, has a deep and lasting impact on the business.

Family characteristics transcend national boundaries. In 2012, *Harvard Business Review* conducted a study of 149 publicly listed family-controlled companies in the United States, Canada, France, Spain, Portugal, Italy and Mexico (Kachaner et al. 2012, 102–106). It identifies seven common business approaches by these family firms, many of which were focussed on resilience rather than performance, which set them apart from other corporations.[3]

Social capital theory has been applied to the family firm in an attempt to understand the "familiness" that it possesses. Broadly, the networks of entrenched and dense social ties that bind a family can be transferred to the business, imbuing it with a form of social capital that Pearson et al. believe "is unique in family firms, because it is often embedded in the family's history" (2008, 957). Dyer and Whetten see this social capital extending beyond the internal workings of the company to the firm's external actions. Their study of firms in the Standard & Poor 500 over a ten-year period suggests that family firms are more likely to be socially responsible than firms without family involvement: "likely due, in part, to the fact that families see their image and reputation as inextricably connected to the firms they own, and therefore will be unwilling to damage those reputations through irresponsible actions on the part of their firms" (2006, 797–798).

Family firms play significant roles in many economies but their dominance diminishes as capital markets develop (Bhattacharya & Ravikumar 2001, 188). This may explain why so many companies in Asia continue to be under family control. The factors that lead to the sale of a family firm vary according to economic structure and financial climate, but, although sale of the family firm is not inevitable, the pressure to sell is greater in sophisticated capital markets where family members can achieve greater utility by "cashing up" than by continuing to operate the business. Bhattacharya and Ravikumar assume that although a family cares about bequeathing *wealth* to the next generation, it does not care whether this wealth is bequeathed in the form of an ongoing business, or in the form of proceeds from its sale (*ibid.*, 190). This assumption is tempered by the enduring sense of identity that some families derive from their enterprises, and by the experience of some of the families examined in this chapter. It cannot, however, be dismissed, because experience suggests that eventually, every family will have its price.

Nonetheless, the 2012 Harvard study showed that family firms do have positive attributes, particularly during financial downturns when frugality, debt-adversity, diversity and employee loyalty help to weather the storm. So what other advantages might we find in the family firm?

Family firms have the advantage of integrated decision-making and control that minimise the agency costs that would otherwise be associated with monitoring and bonding (Jensen & Meckling 1976, 312). Such owners make operating decisions that maximise the benefits that fall to them, and therefore there is a greater incentive to seek out new endeavours such as innovative profit-making projects (*ibid.*, 313) – although we should note that the reference was not made in relation to publishing enterprises. These advantages can be matched in other forms of ownership – through appropriate management structures and incentive bonuses – but there are a number of attributes that are unique to family involvement in business.

Established patterns of interaction and involvement provide families with internal networks that can be transferred to the family business (Pearson et al. 2008, 957) and also have a unique reservoir of social capital that can guide the family firm in ways that non-family enterprises would find difficult to establish and maintain. This social capital provides the family firm with a sense of trust, obligation, stability and interdependence (*ibid.*, 959–961), and contributes to a belief in commitment and stewardship that enables those family firms that exhibit such traits to be strategically flexible (Zahra et al. 2008, 1039–1040). Family firms, in short, may be based on what Lansberg calls "shared dreams" or "a collective vision of the future that inspires family members to engage in the hard work of planning, and to do whatever is necessary to maintain their collaboration and achieve their goal" (1999, 75).

"Shared dreams" may well have their beginnings in the vision of a company founder, whose influence in family firms can pass through generations.

Eddleston (2008) argues that "a founder who is a transformational leader is able to establish a common purpose, identity, and shared sense of destiny among family members that help to create positive family cultures that embody commitment, stewardship, and strategic flexibility". She adds that a family firm is inextricably tied to the founder, because he or she establishes the initial decisions about the firm's purpose, structure, strategy and operating methods. Founder influence can persist well into the life of a firm (Nelson 2003, 722) and the founder becomes a role model for both family members and employees. That is certainly the case in many of the family-owned newspapers that are examined here and in Chapter 6.

Family control can, of course, have its downside. While many researchers acknowledge the *potential* benefits that can accrue from family ownership, there are cautions and qualifications aplenty. For example, Schulze et al. recognise that the altruism that is common in family groups can be displayed in family firms without negative consequences, but there are dangers in putting the family first. Family altruism and owner control combine, they say, to increase the need for formal governance but decrease its use. This decreases the family firm's ability to compete in the market (2002, 256).

A prime example is found in dual-stock arrangements (in which families retain the voting shares but make non-voting shares available to the public), that create a "wedge" between family and non-family interests. Villalonga and Amit conducted a survey of 210 founder or family-controlled firms in the United States and found that 80 per cent used investment vehicles to administer their shares (two-thirds of which employed trust structures). They acknowledge the benefits of using trusts to secure professional advice for heirs, to avoid the delays and costs associated with the probate process in wills and to secure certain tax advantages. However, trusts also enable the separation between voting and cash flow rights and the authors found clear evidence of the use of this "wedge" to ensure control stayed with the families (*ibid.*, 3069–3072). As will be seen in the following newspaper examples, public stockholders are not always satisfied with an arrangement that provides dividends but no control over the company's fortunes.

Yet the greatest weakness of family firms may lie in the transition from one generation to the next. An *Economist* article in 2004[4] stated that family firms combined "all the tensions of family life with all the strains of business life", and added that "at no moment do both sorts of stress combine so forcefully as at that of generational change". It quoted from a J. P. Morgan Private Bank survey of 47 family firms, all of them second-generation or beyond, that found that 52 per cent expected to be family-owned and family-managed in a generation's time, but found from other research that in reality, only one-third of firms make a successful transition from one generation to the next. It noted that family firms were frequently "more riven with intrigue and visceral hatreds than a medieval court" and compared founders and professional managers with medieval monarchs and courtiers. It suggested that the addition of family rivalries made the perfect recipe for a Shakespearean drama.

Sibling rivalry and the growth in family size with each succeeding generation require a daunting level of control and diplomacy. Lansberg notes that in companies that extend over four generations, it is not uncommon to find more than 100 cousins, each holding a small fraction of the company. In many respects, the family firm then takes on the characteristics of a publicly traded firm, but he says the family enterprise often does not have clear boundaries between management and ownership that are a characteristic of most publicly traded companies, and this adds to the complexity of decision-making (1999, 142). It also requires great care in the structuring of cousin consortiums if the potentially destructive effect of unequal distribution of children among siblings is to be avoided. Lansberg, who explores various permutations of the problem at the "cousin stage", says this unequal distribution poses a fundamental problem for shareholding parents: whether to maintain a distribution of stock directly to their own offspring – and thus create a situation whether some cousins will hold more stock than others – or to reallocate shares so that each of the cousins controls an equal amount of stock. The resolution of the dilemma, he says, depends on the degree of trust that exists between the various branches (*ibid.*, 143).

Inheritance carries its own risks. Bloom and Van Reenen cite the "Carnegie Effect", named after the philanthropist Andrew Carnegie, who identified one of the dangers in the promise of considerable inherited wealth: it tends to deaden the talents and energies of the intended beneficiary. They identify primogeniture as a major risk and find that while companies that selected chief executives from among all family members were no worse managed than other companies, the same was not true when the first-born had a right of succession. They find that a combination of family ownership and primogeniture family management "significantly damages company performance" and suggest several causes: the absence of an ability-based selection process, the Carnegie Effect and the likelihood that such a form of succession suggests the persistence of "old-fashioned" management techniques. Their findings were drawn from a survey of more than 700 mid-size manufacturers in Britain, France, Germany and the United States, and an associated paper (Dorgan et al. 2006) noted that the prevalence of family-owned companies run by eldest sons in France and the United Kingdom appeared to account for "a sizeable portion" of the gap in the effectiveness of management between those countries and the United States and Germany.[5] They believe that primogeniture may be a disincentive for the first-born to acquire the skills and knowledge that would be sought in a broader selection process.

Each of these researchers tempers the discussion of systemic weaknesses by acknowledging that family firms (even those that survive over successive generations) have positive attributes, but optimum family involvement requires sound judgement – too little or too much involvement in the family firm can be detrimental (Chrisman et al. 2008, 944). The involvement of independent (non-family) directors who successfully perform their governance functions can help to resolve a number of potential weaknesses (DeMott 2008, 861).

There are parallels between family firms and media trusts. The frailties found in the former can manifest themselves in the latter when a media cooperative or trust grows and matures. However, the parallels are even closer when the family firm is a newspaper publisher and trusts are used to maintain control. The newspaper dynasties that survived into the 21st century demonstrate that responses to generalised family firm traits are varied, and – importantly – that the trust "weapon" they have in common can be a double-edged sword.

The Ochs Sulzberger family and the New York Times Company

The extended family that descends from Adolph S. Ochs, the *Chattanooga Times* publisher who gained control of the bankrupt *New-York Times* in 1896 (the newspaper's name was originally hyphenated), exemplifies much of what is good and bad in newspaper-owning family trusts. It represents the finest qualities of stewardship, the dangers presented by the "cousins" generation and the imbalance of two-tiered stock issues.

The history of the family that has become synonymous with one of the world's great newspapers has been extensively documented by Tifft and Jones (1999), running from Ochs' birth to German immigrant parents on the eve of the American Civil War, to the appointment of his great-grandson, Arthur Ochs Sulzberger Jr., as chairman and publisher in 1998. The family history is a curious combination of loyalty and competition overshadowed by the trust, established under Ochs' bequest, that charged his heirs to maintain the *New York Times* "free from ulterior influence and unselfishly devoted to the public welfare" (*ibid.*, 165).

Ochs had secured the financial well-being of the company (he allowed it to ride out the Depression better than many of its contemporaries by ploughing back most of the profits) and established a strong editorial ethos in the *New York Times*. An early innovation was the removal of the hyphen between *New* and *York*.

On his death in 1935, Ochs bequeathed his controlling interest in the New York Times Company to his only child, Iphigene, with the shares held in the newly created Ochs Trust. On her death, the trust would dissolve and her shareholding in the company was to be equally divided among the four children of her marriage to Arthur Sulzberger.[6] She lived a long life and before her death in 1990, the family, under the leadership of her only son, Arthur Ochs "Punch" Sulzberger, moved to create a share structure that firmly cemented its control of the company, and a trust structure that guaranteed family ownership of the *New York Times* for many years to come.

The New York Times Company that Adolph Ochs left behind had an unusual ownership structure, and the division of shares among his grandchildren was a potential time bomb when the time came for them to bequeath their holdings. The common stock of the company (largely held by the family) did not pay dividends until 1957 – income for family members was derived from the dividend-paying preferred stock they held. In that year the complex and unwieldy share arrangement was changed, and in a move that we have seen is not uncommon in family firms, two classes of common stock were created: Class A non-voting shares and Class B voting shares. Tax law meant that Adolph Ochs' four grandchildren would receive their shares tax-free when Iphigene died, but estate duties would be incurred when they themselves died. The purpose of the restructuring was to provide a means by which the family could pay future death duties by selling Class A non-voting shares (*ibid.*, 322).

The structure worked without difficulties until the 1980s, a period in which, as we saw in Chapter 2, family-owned newspapers were being sold to corporate buyers at an increasing rate. In 1980, an insurance company owner began to buy Class A shares and announced he would seek up to 30 per cent of the stock (*ibid.*, 586–587). He eventually accumulated 5.2 per cent of the stock before being persuaded to sell his holding. Had he been able to persuade dissident family members to sell Class A shares he may have been able to reach his target, although it is highly doubtful that he would have been able to secure any of the controlling Class B shares. The family had, however, maintained a united front. Nevertheless, to avoid tempting fate, the family took two steps that created the ownership structure that governs the New York Times Company today.

In 1986, the family arranged the recapitalisation of the company, and created a new Class B voting share that absorbed a proportion of the non-voting stock. The trust held 83.7 per cent of these new voting shares.

At the same time, "Punch" Sulzberger organised a covenant that would be triggered by the dissolution of the Ochs Trust on Iphigene's death. "Punch" Sulzberger, his three sisters and their 13 children each pledged never to sell the Class B voting shares that had been estimated to have a hypothetical value of more than $US1 billion if they ever found their way on to the market. Any family member who wanted to "cash-up" Class B shares had to offer them to the family or the New York Times Company first, and before any of the stock could be sold to any outsider it would have to be converted to non-voting Class A shares. The agreement would stay in force until 21 years after the death of the longest-living descendant of Iphigene Sulzberger who was alive when the covenant was signed (*ibid.*, 585). Tifft and Jones estimate that this secured control of the company in family hands for another century.

The covenant had the effect of combining family interests that otherwise could have evolved into either a series of trusts (at least four trusts representing the families of the four grandchildren provided for in Adolph Ochs' will), or a growing number of individual shareholding family members whose needs and intentions were many and varied. As it stood, however, the family members were apparently unanimous in their desire to protect their combined control of the *New York Times*.

In 1997, the covenant was converted into a new trust (the 1997 Trust), which preserved its provisions. According to a 2013 proxy statement, the 1997 Trust holds 738,810 Class B voting shares (90.3 per cent of the total). Individual trustees also own small additional numbers of voting shares. Through the trust and a number of other instruments, the family owns 6.8 per cent of the non-voting Class A shares. "Non-voting" is a slightly misleading term: in order to get sharemarket listing the family agreed in 1968 to allow Class A shareholders to elect a minority of directors and participate in the appointment of auditors but that is effectively the limit of their voting rights.

The 1997 Trust's stated primary objective is "to maintain the editorial independence and the integrity of the *New York Times* and to continue it as an independent newspaper, entirely fearless, free of ulterior influence and unselfishly devoted to the public welfare".

The covenant and subsequent trust instrument has protected the Ochs Sulzberger family (and the *New York Times*), from the threat of internecine conflict between brothers, sisters, cousins and second cousins. The ready consensus among the 17 signatories to the covenant was fortuitous in the extreme, and stands in complete contrast to the Bingham family that owned the *Louisville Courier-Journal* as well as printing and broadcasting interests. The increasingly public disintegration of that family firm has been described by Tifft and Jones (*ibid.*, 588) as a catalyst for the Ochs Sulzberger clan's decision to opt for unity in 1986. The move came only months before Barry and Mary Bingham announced their intention to sell their business after failing to reconcile differences between their children that had been the cause of growing conflict since the 1970s.

However, while the 1997 Trust provides a large measure of protection against sale of the crucial Class B shares, it does not protect the company from other pressures from shareholders and potential shareholders. A Harvard Business School case study of the New York Times Company by Villalonga and Hartman in 2008 chronicles a bid in 2006 to have the dual-class share system declassified. The promoter of the move declared: "While it may have at one time been designed to protect the editorial independence and the integrity of the news franchise, the dual-class voting structure now fosters a lack of accountability to all of the company's shareholders". The promoter was a Morgan Stanley investment fund that held approximately 8 per cent of the company's Class A non-voting stock. The fund manager,

Hassan Elmasry, urged other Class A share holders to join in withholding their votes on the appointment of directors at the company's shareholder meeting – a symbolic gesture given the family's right to elect a majority of directors. He had preceded the move by producing a report by a financial consultancy that criticised the company's governance structure, and charged that the dual-share structure put the interests of the controlling family above those of other shareholders and made management accountable to the family rather than to public shareholders (2008, 9). There were also claims that the system led to extravagant executive remuneration. When the time came to vote, the total number of abstentions amounted to 28 per cent of the New York Times non-voting stock, which Villalonga and Hartman describe as "a very strong signal of investor discontent" (2008, 1).

In response, the chairman Arthur Ochs Sulzberger Jr. and his cousin, vice-chairman Michael Golden, agreed to forego $US2 million in stock-based pay, but the Ochs Sulzberger family issued an unequivocal refusal to change the dual-share system. Elmasry organised a similar boycott the following year without denting the family's resolve. Defeated, he liquidated the Morgan Stanley fund's holding in the New York Times Company.

If the withdrawal of the Morgan Stanley fund from the New York Times Company share register brought some comfort to the Sulzberger family, it was short-lived. Two hedge funds, Harbinger Capital Partners and Firebrand Partners, began building holdings in the company and by January 2008 their holding approached 5 per cent. They informed the company that they intended to seek four seats on the board, and accumulated further stock until they owned almost 20 per cent of the Class A shares. Faced with a possible proxy battle, Sulzberger did not relinquish any of the existing directorships, but instead, added two more seats to the boardroom table that were offered to the hedge fund group, which reciprocated by declaring that it would not challenge the family's control (McCollam 2008b, 26). The fund holdings were later relinquished. This form of appeasement does not, however, resolve the fundamental problem created by two-tier share systems, which continue to present the danger of a proxy war by major Class A shareholders (or a coalition of shareholders) for a measure of control over the company in which the 1997 Trust elects nine of the 14 directors.

The family's control is also potentially threatened – one might say literally – by default. The company's deteriorating financial position, exacerbated by the economic recession, forced it to borrow a substantial amount of money to meet its short-term commitments. The source of what can only be described as emergency funding was one of the world's richest men, Carlos Slim Helú, who previously had been compared in a *New York Times* editorial opinion to a robber baron, Russian oligarch or Enron executive (Porter 2007). Chapter 2 discussed the problems of rising debt in media companies, and the New York Times Company's willingness to accept a $US250 million loan at 14 per cent interest from Carlos Slim less than 18 months after the editorial opinion was published illustrates the level of pressure that high debt creates. The *New York Times*, which had total debt of $US3.5 billion, was faced with servicing of $US1.1 billion short to medium term debt, and an immediate need to cover a $US400 million credit line that was to expire in May 2009. Slim held 6.9 per cent of the company at the time of the transaction that also issued him with warrants that could, over time, be converted to Class A shares. Accordingly, in its 2013 return to the Securities and Exchange Commission, the company disclosed that Slim had an effective holding of 17 per cent in shares and exercisable warrants.

The arrangement with Slim, whose vast wealth was based on a Mexican telecommunications monopoly, presents two problems for the *New York Times*. The first is financial. A series of covenants were attached to the loan, including restrictions on further borrowing and business activity without Slim's approval. The loan also carried a number of default mechanisms. The covenants meant that Slim could apply considerable pressure, effectively gaining a large measure of control over the company. His business philosophy is based on austerity. He lives modestly, and his companies operate frugally (Wright 2009, 63). His interest in the *New York Times* was said to be simply "a business deal" (Ricchiardi 2009, 53), suggesting that his focus is on its bottom line. No commentator has suggested that his loan to the newspaper company was altruistic.

The second problem presented by his involvement with the *New York Times* was the effect on the newspaper's reputation. Slim is a controversial character – the *Times*' 2007 editorial comment attested to that – whose business operations in Mexico and elsewhere have been subjected to media scrutiny.

Commentators immediately voiced their misgivings over the arrangement with the *New York Times*. The *Seattle Times*, in a widely quoted editorial in January 2009 headed "Newspaper ownership matters in American democracy", stated that the question over Slim's motives would have been better had it not needed to be asked. It went on to describe the New York newspaper as an institution that "should not fall into the hands of a capitalist with loyalties to a foreign state". Such concerns were reinforced in February 2010 by accusations that the newspaper had failed to provide coverage of a major court action involving the JP Morgan Chase bank and a Mexican bank owned by Slim. Criticism did not abate over time. In 2013 Paul Roderick Gregory, an economics professor at the University of Houston and a Hoover Institution research fellow, claimed the *New York Times* "exempts its second largest shareholder (and lender of last resort), Mexico's Carlos Slim, from its motto: printing all the news that's fit to print" (Gregory 2013). Such criticism, and the potentially onerous provisions of the loan, saw the New York Times Company repay it in 2011, two years before it was due. Slim, however, continued to acquire A shares in the company.

Bad times placed strain on the relationship between the Ochs Sulzberger trustees and "ordinary" shareholders but also amplified criticism of Arthur Sulzberger Jr.'s stewardship as chairman and publisher. He bears a doubly weighted cross – heading a company (whose principal assets are newspapers) at a time when news media business models are crumbling, and his selection to head the company had all the hallmarks of primogeniture even if it was not formally acknowledged. The Ochs Sulzberger leadership of the company has some similarities to English history, interspersed with reigning monarchs, regents and would-be usurpers.

"Punch" Sulzberger had no such misgivings and appointed his son, Arthur Ochs Sulzberger Jr., as his successor as publisher of the *New York Times* in 1992 at the age of 40, and as chairman six years later. Between the two appointments, Arthur Ochs Sulzberger Jr. was challenged (unsuccessfully) for the role of chief executive by Lance Primis, a non-family executive who had been appointed president (the business manager) of the company. "Punch" Sulzberger opted for his son.[7] Tifft and Jones state that Primis' mistake was that he did not appreciate that he was president of "an organisation ruled by a monarchy" (1999, 755).

"Monarchy" in this sense clearly includes primogeniture, which, as noted earlier in this chapter, has been identified by researchers as a major source of poor business performance. However, the process does not pre-ordain poor management or stewardship. During "Punch" Sulzberger's tenure, the New York Times Company grew from a $US100 million company in 1963 to a $US1.7 billion company in 1992, and it enhanced its editorial stature by successfully challenging the government over the Pentagon papers and winning a slew of Pulitzer prizes – almost half the Pulitzers won by the *Times* up to 1992 were during "Punch" Sulzberger's term as publisher (*ibid.*, 639) – although the editor for much of the period, A.M. Rosenthal, was controversial. "Punch" Sulzberger also ensured that his son received a "rounded education" in the newspaper business, both inside and outside the New York Times Company. He was, for example, an advertising representative on the 40,000 circulation *Raleigh Times* in North Carolina, an Associated Press correspondent in London and a production executive at the *New York Times*. Former *New York Times* executive editor, Max Frankel, in his autobiography stated that in 1986 "Punch" Sulzberger had asked him to "help me break in my son Arthur as the next publisher" (1999, 415).

Nonetheless, after directing the editorial then overall destiny of the company for two decades, Arthur Sulzberger Jr. continues to carry the burden of questions over the suitability of a chief executive chosen by DNA profile. This is in spite of the fact that many of the criticisms made of him (Auletta 2003, 168–170; McCollam 2008b, 29) could equally be made of many publishers and executive chairmen in the news business. His tenure at the New York Times Company has coincided with arguably the most testing time for that business since its 1896 bankruptcy. Some of his decisions have been questionable – such as paying for a 58 per cent share in an $US850 million 52-storey Manhattan skyscraper that became the company's new headquarters,[8] depleting cash reserves in share buyback schemes and high dividend payments,[9] plus choosing Carlos Slim Helú as a "rescuer" – but much of the company's financial decline and resulting strategies have been shared with others in the industry. He has overseen divestitures, staff cuts (total company headcount down almost 43 per cent between 2008 and 2012) and other budget cuts. Operating costs were cut from $US2.8 billion to $US1.8 billion between 2008 and 2012 in an effort to counter the effects of depressed revenues that also had $US1 billion shaved off over the same period. The most costly exercise for which he will be blamed – the sale of the *Boston Globe* and associated publications for $US70 million in 2013 – was not initially of his making. The purchase of the New England group for a record $US1.1 billion had been one of "Punch" Sulzberger's last acts before handing over the publishing reins to his son. By 2009 the *Globe* was threatened with closure unless significant cost savings were made to overcome what by that stage was a projected $US85 million a year loss.

Shareholders who saw Class A shares drop from a 2002 peak of $US52 to a 2009 low of $US4.13 and only a modest recovery to around $US16.50 by early 2014 would be entitled to ask whether their investment might have fared better had the company's succession policy put ability first and birth a distant second. The answer, however, would not be clear-cut as Arthur Sulzberger Jr. has publishing company contemporaries who have fared worse. Nevertheless, the appointment process for the publisher and chairman roles in the New York Times Company will remain contentious so long as the decisions are made by one member of the Ochs Sulzberger family (with its leaning towards primogeniture) and ratified by his or her relatives.

To date, the Ochs Sulzberger family members have shown remarkable solidarity and a determination to nurture the quality of the *New York Times*, to the point where they have been prepared to accept lower returns than those in peer companies in order to sustain its journalism. With each generation, however, they face the possibility that this cohesion will be tested by the "cousin stage" (Lansberg 1999) that was highlighted earlier in this chapter.

Iphigene Sulzberger was the sole heir when Adolph Ochs died, and at her death her four children inherited her estate. They produced 13 children – the "Fourth Generation" that included Arthur Ochs Sulzberger Jr. – and by 2008 there were 27 members of the so-called "Fifth Generation". Many of the "Fifth Generation" were born before Iphigene died, and the 1997 Trust is set to endure until the last of those dies. McCollam sets out the process by which the family ensures it remains bonded, including induction courses for offspring when they "come of age", and for their spouses when they marry. There are also annual reunions, and an annual meeting with company executives to discuss the business (2008, 29).

Consensus is most easily achieved when small numbers of family members are involved in the decision-making process, but becomes more difficult as the number of stakeholders grows. This situation inevitably will be faced by the extended Ochs Sulzberger family, which will confront the various difficulties associated with consensus determination. "Punch" Sulzberger employed skilful diplomacy in his management of the family and its affairs even in old age. He remained chairman emeritus of the New York Times Company until his death in 2012. His son, however, has a personality that critics say lacks maturity, and at times, resolve (Auletta 2003; McCollam 2008b). A question therefore hangs over whether he can employ the sort of diplomacy and resolve necessary to hold together a family in the face of potential pressure from dissident members, disenfranchised investors and the birds of prey that will gather if the fortunes of the *New York Times* decline and the high-minded resolve of the Sulzberger family suffers dynastic dilution.

An extensive article in *New York* magazine that examined the departure of the company's chief executive, Janet Robinson, in 2011 concluded that with declining company fortunes, there was a fear that "the pressure on the family and the lack of adequate leadership are coming to an inflection point" (Hagan 2012). The article then drew an instructive comparison with what had happened to the Bancroft family when Rupert Murdoch set his sights on the *Wall Street Journal*.

Bancroft family and Dow Jones & Co.

The recent history of the Bancroft family and *Wall Street Journal* publisher Dow Jones is a textbook illustration of the binary effects of structural weaknesses and family disunity. Both elements were exploited by Rupert Murdoch to end a newspaper dynasty and add an expensive jewel to his media treasure chest.

The Bancroft family's association with Dow Jones and the *Wall Street Journal* began when the newspaper's rotund Boston correspondent, Clarence Barron, bought the company in 1902. He went on to expand his publishing business by establishing *Barron's* magazine and increasing the *Journal's* circulation before his death in 1928. Barron had two stepdaughters, Martha and Jane, but on his death Martha did not inherit part of the business. She married a rich shoe manufacturer (Barron believed this secured her financial future) and the Dow Jones shares passed to Jane, whose husband, Hugh Bancroft, became company president. Five years later Hugh Bancroft was dead, a victim of suicidal depression, and his young family was in no position to take over running of the business. The company was left in the hands of the *Journal's* editor, and the Bancroft family thereafter had no active management role (Auletta 2003, 284).

However, it did retain a controlling shareholding that over time became split among three branches of the family. Jane had three children (Jessie Cox, Jane Cook and Hugh Bancroft Jr.) and it is from these siblings that the three branches are descended. Their control was exercised, as in the New York Times Company, by a two-tier voting system. In 2007 Dow Jones had on issue 63.7 million shares in single-vote common stock and 20 million Class B shares that were each entitled to exercise ten votes. The Bancroft family, through a series of interlocking trusts, held 6.4 per cent of the single-vote common stock but 82.4 per cent of the Class B stock. This gave them overall control of 64.2 per cent of the company's shares. If Class B shares were sold, they automatically reverted to common stock with a single vote.

By 2007 there were approximately three dozen family members who were direct beneficiaries. Three family members, plus the administrator of a number of the family's trusts (controlling almost half the Class B shares), sat on the 16-member Dow Jones board of directors.

Dow Jones had something else in common with the New York Times Company: the value of its freely traded single-vote stock had fallen over time – from a peak of $US75 in 2000 to $US33 five years later. Unlike the Sulzberger family, however, the Bancrofts had not consolidated their holdings into a single trust designed to "keep it in the family" when potential buyers inevitably began to gather around a poorly performing company. And unlike the Sulzbergers, the Bancroft family was not united by a sense of stewardship.

The Bancroft family supported the good journalism for which the *Wall Street Journal* was renowned, but did so passively – support meant not interfering. It supported the company's executives, but did not play an active role in management – in contrast to the Sulzberger family. It was nonetheless a major beneficiary and ultimate controller of the company, which one proxy statement had described as "a quasi-public trust".

It had been rare for the family to even discuss the business (Ellison 2010, 18; Nocera 1997), although Jessie Bancroft Cox (the family matriarch who died at the Dow Jones 100th anniversary celebrations in 1982) did block the purchase of a New England newspaper by the company – apparently because it had written something uncomplimentary about one of her horses (*Independent*, 9 June 2007).

However, in 1997 a change occurred within the family that would ultimately lead to the sale of the company to Murdoch's News Corporation. Two Bancroft cousins, Billy Cox III and Elisabeth Goth, had become frustrated at Dow Jones' management, which had faltered badly over a number of business transactions and was delivering reduced profits – a significant proportion of which was being dispersed as dividends to the Bancroft family. Goth had begun what *Fortune* magazine at the time described as "a quest for answers" that "opened the first fissure in what could have been the cosiest partnership between a family and a publicly held company in

America" (Nocera 1997). Other family members and Dow Jones management had been unnerved and angry at what was seen as a disruption of the status quo, despite the fact that Goth had been enquiring into the state of her own substantial bequest (left by her mother, Bettina Bancroft) in a company that *New York* magazine had described as "standing still for the past decade while the rest of the market was in full gallop" (Mitchell 1997). Goth, with the assistance of her cousin, had forced changes that brought new independent directors to the board. More significantly, however, their actions had destroyed the benign nature of the relationship between the Bancroft family and the company. It put the two cousins at odds with older members of the clan.

Their actions also drew into stark relief the difference between non-interference and neglect. The Bancroft family had taken its non-interventionist approach almost to a statutory level. It was, for example, considered unacceptable to voice any criticism of the *Wall Street Journal's* editorial policies (Ellison, 109). The family accepted management decisions without demur, even matters such as the mishandling of the $US1.6 billion purchase of Telerate (a financial data company) that led later to a $US1 billion write-down in its value. Such inaction illustrates that there is a line that family trusts cross at their peril. Stewardship requires an expeditious level of involvement for the good of the business that is not necessarily at odds with the maintenance of editorial independence. By allowing non-intervention to become a form of neglect, the Bancroft family failed the "quasi-public trust" they believed they were serving. And they were protected against external challenge by the protective power of the two-tiered voting system.

Non-interference was the position held by the second and third generations of the family, but it was not universally embraced by the fourth generation. By the time the Dow Jones share price had hit $US33 in 2005, some younger members of the family were not alone in questioning the company's performance. So too did a newly appointed professional trustee (employed by the Bancrofts' long-serving lawyers, Hemenway & Barnes) who advised dissident family members (led by board member Leslie Hill) to challenge management and the board.

The result was an ultimatum to both management and the directors to institute measures that would allow much-needed change in the way the company was operated. It led to the ousting of the chief executive, Peter Kann, a former journalist and Pulitzer Prize winner, who had been a consummate guardian of the "old" Dow Jones ways. It also led to changes to the share structure that prompted further conflict. Company bylaws had stated that if the number of Class B shares held by family members fell below 12 million, they would convert to single-vote common stock and the family would lose control. In a move aimed at providing a source of cash for the Bancrofts, a change to the company articles allowed family members to sell down to 7.5 million Class B shares without triggering the "sudden death" clause. Dissident family members opposed this change and wanted a moratorium on Class B share sales, a cut in Class B dividends (which had been paid at the expense of cash reserves) and the earmarking of half the company's cash flow to repayment of debt (Ellison, 36).

Dow Jones continued to perform poorly, and the immediate prospects for the US economy (and the advertising market) were also poor. The prospect of selling the company had previously been an unspoken subject, but in October 2006 the matter was raised at a family forum to the disbelief of some members. It was raised again, however, at a board meeting in February 2007 so that, when Rupert Murdoch made a bid for the company the following April, family members had begun to take sides on the issue of a sale. Murdoch's offer of $US60 a share was a premium of almost 70 per cent on the current share price. Where the market valuation of Dow Jones had been about $US3 billion, Murdoch was offering more than $US5 billion for the company.

Within the family, the champion for the sale faction was the leader of the 1997 revolt, Elisabeth Goth, while the prime mover in the 2005 assault on the status quo, Leslie Hill, wanted to reject the sale and rebuild the company from within. Ellison notes an interesting difference between the two women. As the sole beneficiary of Bettina Bancroft's interest in the company, Goth stood to receive one-ninth of the family's interest in Dow Jones, while Hill (one of seven children) would receive only one-forty-second of it (2010, 109–110). This illustrates the difficulties that can arise when dynastic dilution creates disproportionate interests among different family members – an effect due to what Wolff describes as "the logic of trusts and the math of reproduction" (2008, 90).

The overlapping trusts also presented problems. Leslie Hill was a beneficiary of the largest trust, the Article III Trust, but the sole trustee was her uncle, Christopher Bancroft, who initially stated he was opposed to accepting the News Corporation offer but later promoted the sale of the family's stake for a higher sum. Administration of a number of the trusts was under the control of four lawyers from Hemenway & Barnes. In the midst of the bid for the company, they were charged with not only providing advice but also trying to reconcile the interests of different family members. And within Hemenway & Barnes, there were generational differences of opinion on the best ways – past, present and future – to serve the interests of the Bancroft family and the *Wall Street Journal*. Three other law firms represented further Bancroft family trusts.

Rupert Murdoch's campaign for control of Dow Jones has been well documented by Ellison, Wolff, Nordberg and Schejter & Davidson (among others), together with numerous newspaper reports including, with commendable corporate transparency, the *Wall Street Journal*. It is a tale of pursuit and persuasion, division and coercion, but ultimately about the power of money. The detail need not be recounted here, beyond noting that after three months of internal discussion the Bancroft family remained divided and the final vote was a split decision. The family controlled 64.2 per cent of the overall votes in the company and the "sell" vote accounted for 37 per cent. The single-vote common stockholders, many of who not unnaturally favoured a sale given the premium being offered by Murdoch, tipped the balance. By the beginning of August 2007, Dow Jones & Co., and with it the *Wall Street Journal*, were part of News Corporation.

Before the sale was concluded, Leslie Hill had resigned as a director in protest. So too, had Dieter von Holtzbrinck, a German publisher who joined the board after an exchange of shares between his family's company and Dow Jones (Nordberg 2007, 718). Holtzbrinck and another non-family director, James Ottaway, had publicly opposed the News Corporation bid, not on financial grounds but over concerns for the *Wall Street Journal's* editorial independence after Rupert Murdoch gained control. Neither man had been swayed by Murdoch's undertakings to the family on editorial independence, which were a much watered-down version of what the family had initially sought, and included a "Special Committee" of "distinguished community or journalistic leaders who are independent" (Schejter & Davidson 2008, 523–526). That agreement appears remarkably similar to the undertakings given before the purchase by Murdoch of *The Times* and the *Sunday Times* and (like Harold Evans) the incumbent editor, Marcus Brauchli, did not long survive the change of ownership. He resigned in April 2008 and three months later became executive editor of the *Washington Post*.

There are a number of significant elements in the sale of the Bancroft family's interests in Dow Jones & Co. that illustrate potential weaknesses in media-owning family trusts. They arise in part because of the makeup of the various branches of the Bancroft family, but all are weaknesses that could be avoided by the use of appropriate mechanisms built into the structure and governance of the family's trusts and by a more constructive articulation of what should be expected of it in the "stewardship" of the company. There were four principal failings:

1. The family was disorganised. It had no established lines of communication beyond an annual family get-together and members were geographically and socially widespread. There was little guidance on how the family members should act in relation to the company. Dow Jones produced a raft of governance documents for directors, management and editorial staff, but the family's conduct was governed by unwritten and largely unspoken "understandings" that were often misinterpreted. Family directors had a reputation for "rubber-stamping" board and management decisions, criticism of the *Wall Street Journal* was frowned upon and there were no memoranda on the maintenance of Clarence Barron's legacy or examples of decisive action (apart from the 1997 revolt) on which they could draw. Discussion over the offer had to be carried out

through hastily convened meetings, conference calls and the use of the legal trustees as educators, intermediaries and canvassers of divided and shifting family feeling. For example, the principal legal trustee, Michael Elefante, was said to be still unsure of the weight of family feeling more than a week after the offer was made by Murdoch (Ellison 2010, 114–115).

2. The family was unprepared for the offer and had not seriously considered the prospect of relinquishing control of Dow Jones. Many family members felt conflicted by (a) the size of the offer, (b) the fact that the prospective buyer was Rupert Murdoch and (c) the knowledge (contained in a letter to family members from the union representing employees) that staff were universally opposed to the sale because they feared that editorial independence would be lost. As a result, there were a variety of positions held by family members and no consensus on what would be best for Dow Jones & Co. and the *Wall Street Journal*. Some opposed any sale, some opposed a sale to News Corporation, while some felt the family should hold out for an even higher price. Many had been accustomed to simply following the advice of their professional advisors, but that counsel was sometimes conflicting. The advisors were struggling with the dilemma of reconciling what was best for shareholders with what was in the wider interests of a publication that had become an American institution. Above all, there was no patriarchal or matriarchal figure to which the entire family could look for sage advice to which they could all subscribe. In other words, there was a lack of leadership.

3. The family's failure over many years to engage in the company's governance meant there was both a lack of knowledge and a certain naivety. An example was a family-prepared statement, proposing a meeting with News Corporation and the consideration of other options, which they assumed would be taken at face value. Non-family directors correctly pointed out that such a statement would be interpreted by the market as an intention to sell and opposed its release, only to find that a copy had already been given to the *Wall Street Journal*. As a result of this statement, directors believed they had a fiduciary duty to proceed to a sale to the highest bidder (Ellison, 124–129). The naivety of family members extended to the search for a mechanism to protect the editorial independence of the *Wall Street Journal* under Murdoch. Ultimately, in spite of what had happened after his acquisition of *The Times* in London, the Bancroft family was willing to allow Rupert Murdoch to construct another Trojan horse. As the negotiations played out, family members were dogged by indecision because collectively they had a fundamental weakness – they did not know the business on which they depended each year for the replenishment of their trusts' coffers.

4. The structure of the trusts and the share structure of Dow Jones were inadequate means by which to ensure continued Bancroft control of the

company. *Fortune* magazine described the Bancroft trusts as a "byzantine web", while the *New York Times* routinely referred to them as "interlocking" (Nocera 1997). Both descriptions point to a level of complexity, which in spite of the stewardship of Hemenway & Barnes over a number of the trusts, meant the Bancroft family's holdings could not be construed as a single voting bloc or even a consistent approach. Unlike the Sulzberger siblings, who had coalesced their holdings into a single trust that was binding on all eligible family members, the Bancrofts had been content not only to allow the initial four trusts to coexist, but for them to be joined by further trusts vested in different family groups for a variety of purposes. There was no systemic way in which the family could speak with a single voice. Further, the Bancrofts did not build a "poison pill" into their trust or share structure to protect the family's assets against future sale through a family rift. The introduction of the two-tiered stock system had been designed to forestall a hostile bid against which the family was united. It was not a defence against a bid in which the principal approach was not a stand in the market, but an attempt to beguile and persuade family members to sell. The Sulzbergers built a mechanism into their trust: the automatic conversion of Class B voting stock into non-voting Class A shares when they were sold that ensured all trustees must be in agreement before the family could sell its control of the New York Times Company. The Bancrofts employed no such mechanism, and as a result the family lost control although half its controlling members were opposed to the sale.

This is not to say that had none of these four factors existed, the Bancroft family would have retained control of Dow Jones and the *Wall Street Journal* in the long term. In a 1997 interview with *New York* magazine, William Cox III said the Bancroft family should not be counted on to continue putting the *Journal's* interests above their own. Did this mean the family might be willing to sell Dow Jones? "Everything has its price", he said (Mitchell 1997, 46). The price, it transpired, was $US60 a share.

If every family has its price, it also has its limits, and those were reached in 2013 in the case of the Graham family when it ended an 80-year association with the *Washington Post*.

The Graham family and the Washington Post Company

The Graham family has some attributes in common with the Sulzberger and Bancroft families. Like the Sulzbergers, the founder of the newspaper company was nominally Jewish. Like that of the Bancrofts, the business was then entrusted to a son-in-law who subsequently committed suicide. And like both families, the Grahams employed trust mechanisms and a two-tiered share system to protect their control. There are, however, several differences that distinguish the Graham family from the other "first families" of American newspaper publishing.

Some of those differences may appear paradoxical. The eldest son had a pre-ordained path to leadership of the company and exercised tight control over voting rights, but the vast majority of directors were independent of the family. The Washington Post Company was renowned as a newspaper publisher, but derived the majority of its revenue from other sources. And it had a large outside shareholder who "bought in" unbeknown to the Grahams but who became the family's acknowledged *éminence grise*.

Much like the way Adolph Ochs purchased the *New-York Times*, the *Washington Post* was bought in a bankruptcy sale in 1933 by Eugene Meyer. In 1948, he decided to pass control of the newspaper to his daughter Katharine and son-in-law Phil Graham. A cash "birthday present" from Meyer enabled Graham to buy shares. Katharine Graham explained in her autobiography that with her concurrence, her husband was given a majority of the shares because her father believed that "no man should be in the position of working for his wife" (2001, 195).[10] At the same time, a self-perpetuating committee modelled on English structures and employed by several newspaper-owning families was set up with "absolute power" to approve or disapprove a buyer, should the Grahams decide in the future to sell the newspaper. The five-member trust was initially comprised of three university leaders, a judge and the head of a large charitable foundation. It did not survive the Graham family's consolidation of ownership over time.

Phil Graham led the Washington Post Company through a process of expansion into other media and consolidation of the Washington market. Acquisitions included radio and television stations, *Newsweek* magazine and the *Washington Times-Herald* that was merged with the *Washington Post*. However, Graham's behaviour became erratic, his relationships with executives deteriorated and his relationship with his wife broke down when he began an affair with a *Newsweek* journalist. Katharine Graham's autobiography details the effects of her husband's mental illness that saw him institutionalised. It was during a respite from institutional care for a bipolar disorder that he took his own life. His death in 1963 complicated matters for Katharine Graham but led, ultimately, to the formation of a series of family trusts. These trusts were the genesis of the Graham family trusts that exist today.

In her first meeting with directors and executives after deciding to assume her late husband's control of the company, Katharine Graham reinforced the dynastic nature of the family's association with the business: "This has been, this is, and this will continue to be a family operation", she said. "There is another generation coming along, and we intend to turn the paper over to them" (Coleridge 1994, 89). She was true to her word. Her son Donald became publisher of the *Washington Post* in 1979 and chief executive in 1991 before becoming chairman two years later on his mother's retirement.

Her granddaughter (and Donald Graham's niece), Katharine Weymouth, became publisher of the *Washington Post* in 2008. However, the Graham family shares a weakness with most other family-controlled public companies. In spite of the long-held assumption that Donald Graham would succeed his mother, there were no formal mechanisms to ensure that a family member would assume the mantle. The company bylaws vested in the directors the power to appoint a chief executive and there was no requirement that preference be given to a family member. In terms of newspaper dynasties, however, the matter would become moot because Mrs Graham's assurance of the *Washington Post* continuing to be a family operation would not survive tectonic shifts in media markets and the Washington Post Company's fortunes.

In 1971 the company went public. Katharine Graham claimed to have had little understanding of the process (*ibid.*, 478), which is almost certainly too self-effacing given her grasp of the business she controlled. A two-tiered share structure was created, with her controlling the majority of the 1 million Class A shares, and her children the remainder. These shares carried 70 per cent of the voting power in the company, in spite of the fact that there were 10 million Class B shares on issue. Class B shareholders were entitled to elect only 30 per cent of the board. Mrs Graham later stated that people bought shares knowing the company was family-controlled, suggesting that she did not envisage assaults similar to those endured (and so far repulsed) by the Sulzberger family at the hand of dissident investors. Mrs Graham (and latterly her son Donald) was astute in her management of investor relations, with significant assistance from her *éminence grise*.

That individual was the chairman of Berkshire Hathaway Inc., Warren Buffett, who bought 10 per cent of the company shortly after it was floated, and stated his intention to buy more. In so doing, he created alarm among the company's advisors, including one who told Mrs Graham bluntly: "He means you no good" (*ibid.*, 555). In fact, Buffett's interest in the company (which in 2013 stood at 23.3 per cent of the Class B shares) was immensely beneficial and, as far as the Graham family was concerned, utterly benign. Renowned as an astute investor, he became a key advisor to Katharine Graham and her son and his presence on the board of the Washington Post Company (where he was described as "lead independent director") was consistently endorsed by shareholders until he decided to stand down in May 2011.

Buffett's relationship with the Washington Post Company was unusual. Although his company was the financial beneficiary of the investment in the company, he entered into an agreement in 1977 under which he gave its voting proxy to the Graham family. Under that agreement (which was amended and extended in 1985, 1996 and 2006) Donald Graham had the right to exercise his voting discretion on 1.7 million Berkshire-owned shares until the agreement expired in 2017. The Graham family had control of

94.5 per cent of the crucial Class A shares, with Donald Graham exercising shared voting rights over the entire family holding, and his sister and two brothers sharing in smaller proportions. Professional trustees also exercised voting rights on behalf of the family. Class A voting rights, together with Class B holdings and the Berkshire Hathaway proxy, meant Donald Graham had undisputed control of the company.

However, to comply with New York Stock Exchange rules the board must meet regularly without its executive members, namely Donald Graham. These sessions were presided over by Warren Buffett until his retirement and the company's proxy statement stated he "collaborates with Mr Graham in reviewing key operational and other matters... and acts as liaison between Mr Graham and the independent directors". Another director, investment counsellor Christopher Davis, assumed the role.

Buffett advised the company on a share buyback programme that enhanced the Graham family's holding (and Berkshire Hathaway's) in the Washington Post Company and endorsed a diversification strategy. It was a strategy that set the Washington Post Company apart from the other American family-owned media businesses examined here. However, the significance of the purchase that created the difference was not initially recognised. In fact, when the acquisition of the Stanley H. Kaplan Company educational services group was suggested in 1984, Katharine Graham said: "I don't give a shit about it, but if you think it will be profitable, let's do it" (Graham, 652). It certainly was profitable and, renamed Kaplan Inc., developed into a revenue and profit generator that eclipsed the *Washington Post* itself. In a statement that would prove prophetic, Donald Graham was moved to say in the 2012 annual report that "the future of The Washington Post Company is the future of Kaplan". The Washington Post Company also benefitted from the purchase of cable television systems that have been consolidated into Cable ONE, which serves approximately 600,000 customers in 19 states with cable television and 644,000 with telephone and high-speed Internet service, and contributed 20 per cent of the group's revenue in 2012.

In 1993, the newspaper and magazine divisions of the company accounted for about 68 per cent of revenue, but by 2002 the proportion had dropped to 51 per cent. A decade later the company had offloaded its magazines, including *Newsweek,* and the newspaper division (comprising the *Washington Post,* the *Slate* digital group, *Foreign Policy* magazine and the company's community newspapers) was contributing only 10 per cent of revenue. Losses in its newspaper division began in 2008 and a deficit of $US192 million the following year led to heavy cost-cutting. Losses were reduced to less than $US10 million in 2010 but rose again to $US53.7 million in 2012.

The *Washington Post* had been forced into rounds of staff reduction since 2003. In 2002 the newspaper had 2610 fulltime employees and 675 editorial staff but a decade later the workforce stood at 1809 and the number of editorial staff had been reduced to 524 across newspaper, magazine and digital operations. *Newsweek*, which lost $US16.1 million in 2008 and $US29.3 million in 2009, was sold for $US1 in August 2010. It ceased print publication in 2012, only to resume a print edition in 2014.

These events may have been the fallout from recession, but they had a negative impact on the company's reputation in some quarters. An article in the *New Republic* in February 2010 painted a picture of staff dissatisfaction, and a newspaper "facing an identity crisis" under publisher Katharine Weymouth and editor Marcus Brauchli (Sherman 2010, 17). It did, however, acknowledge the *Washington Post's* "enduring ability to break important stories – which the paper still does with impressive regularity" (*ibid.*, 21). That article, dismissed in a letter to the magazine by Donald Graham, stands in contrast to a profile in the *Columbia Journalism Review* eight years earlier which offered the following description: "the *Post*, under Don Graham, has maintained a rock-hard stability and commitment to – and investment in – newsroom excellence" (Sherman 2002, 42).

In his annual report commentaries, Donald Graham reinforced an unsentimental approach to the newspaper and the company. He made no attempt to minimise the issues facing the newspaper and magazine industries, and while committing the company to continually seek ways of making its publications profitable, he emphatically rejected the notion that investment in the *Washington Post* (and *Newsweek*) were out of a sense of public service. Investment, he said, was because the company believed the publications could be returned to profitability.

Such comments were made in the knowledge that other operations were producing sufficient profits to allow the company to almost double annual dividends over a decade – from $US5.60 a share in 2002 to $US9.80 in 2012 – and keep investors and family members happy. However, an unforeseen change in the fortunes of Kaplan Inc. tested the family's commitment to the *Washington Post* to the limit.

The educational arm had expanded beyond its original test preparation service when it purchased a chain of vocational schools in Atlanta and for-profit higher education became its mainstay. By 2004 the division was producing more than $US1 billion in annual revenue. However, new regulations governing for-profit colleges introduced by the Obama Administration in 2011 had a serious impact on Kaplan which posted an operating loss of $US105 million in 2012, compared with an operating profit of $US96 million the previous year. The company announced major restructuring to overcome regulatory issues but the combination of Kaplan's downturn and a 44 per cent drop in the newspaper division's revenue over a six-year period created a break point. After the *Washington Post* reported an operating loss of $US53.7 million in 2012 – more than twice the level of loss in 2011 – there were indications of further losses flowing from a 7 per cent drop in the newspaper's circulation in the first half of 2013.

Amid great secrecy, Donald Graham began to seek a buyer for the newspaper division at the end of 2012. It was a signal that the Graham family could no longer sustain the publication and continue to deliver strong dividends to Washington Post Company shareholders. In August 2013 the *Washington Post* and its associated publications were sold for $US250 million to the founder of Amazon, Jeff Bezos. In an interview in the newspaper following announcement of the sale, Katharine Weymouth (who would remain publisher) said that she and Donald Graham had discussed whether the Washington Post Company – a listed company with more than 700 shareholders – was the right place to house the *Washington Post*. "If journalism is the mission," she told the interviewer, "given the pressure to cut costs and make profits, maybe [a publicly traded company] is not the best place for The Post" (Farhi 2013).

Her statement reveals a series of truths. First, even a well-intentioned and engaged family can accept the limits of its tenure as custodian of an iconic newspaper. Second, a family company that opens itself to public shareholding and diversifies its business has a responsibility to shareholders to favour profitable enterprises and divest itself of encumbrances. Finally, the driving need to cut costs and produce profits calls into question the compatibility between the stock exchange and organisations dedicated to public interest journalism.

Yet, even given these truths, the experiences of the Bancroft and Graham families cannot be taken as portents of the death knell for all newspapers controlled by "family firms" – as the Harmsworth family's control of one of Britain's best selling newspapers demonstrates.

The Harmsworth family and the Daily Mail & General Trust

Harold Jonathan Esmond Vere Harmsworth assumed his control of the holding company of London's *Daily Mail* by right. He is an increasingly rare example of British media baronial primogeniture. The fourth Viscount Rothermere's family is the embodiment of the British press baron. The first holder of the title was his great-grandfather, Harold Harmsworth, who formed the company in 1922; followed by his grandfather, Esmond Harmsworth, who did little to enhance its newspapers; succeeded in turn by the third Lord Rothermere, Vere Harmsworth, who resurrected and expanded the media empire until the title passed to Jonathan Harmsworth on his father's death in 1998.

The group's name is misleading. The Daily Mail & General Trust (DMGT) is a public company and is not governed by trust instruments. It is an echo of the original company – Daily Mail Trust Limited, set up in 1922 to consolidate Rothermere's newspaper interests following the death of his brother and business partner, Lord Northcliffe, who had launched the *Daily Mail* in 1896. The company had a capital of £1,600,000 in voting shares, which, according to a contemporary report in Melbourne's *Argus* newspaper, were "subscribed by Lord Rothermere and his friends". Rothermere held a majority. In addition to the share capital, the company offered a similar amount to the public in non-voting debentures. These debentures were covered by a trust deed; hence the naming of the company. The public's involvement on a non-voting basis would continue to the present day, with the debentures later being transformed to non-voting shares. Under the original articles of association, Lord Rothermere was named a director for life and chairman until his death or resignation. The current company articles contain no such provisions, but the voting power of the Harmsworth family can sustain its hold on the chair if it wishes.

The first viscount was an astute businessman with little interest in journalism. Under his brother Lord Northcliffe, journalists had been treated well and business staff relegated to the "back room". Rothermere reversed the status, cutting editorial salaries and elevating managers (Coleridge 1994, 282). Like his brother, however, he had a propensity for interfering in politics and was responsible for an enduring slur on both the *Daily Mail* and the Harmsworth family. It is useful to recount some of that episode to illustrate how family history can deeply affect the family firm.

Rothermere was an early supporter of fascism and Oswald Mosley's British Union of Fascists. He visited Nazi-led Germany, and corresponded with Hitler. This support was reflected in the editorial columns of the *Daily Mail*. The present viscount told me "the family is deeply ashamed of that stance". He is able to rationalise, but not condone, his great-grandfather's ill-judged actions:

> It broke his heart to have two sons die [in the First World War] so he became a pacifist. His marriage broke up and he went to live in Monte Carlo, where he met Princess Stephanie von Hohenlohe who became one of his mistresses. She got him involved in the debate over the Treaty of Trianon that broke up the Austro-Hungarian Empire. He firmly believed that treaty and the Treaty of Versailles would result in another war. So he became very sympathetic to the Hungarian cause and started a campaign that unfortunately sucked him into the fascist cause ... He was also a fervent anti-communist at a time when everyone in Europe was terrified of what would happen if communism prevailed. At that time the fascists were saying they were a popular movement that was not communist and would favour the Establishment. So he fell into that trap along with, I have to say, quite a lot of other people ... He dropped his support for [British fascist leader Oswald] Mosley quite early on and he realised that Hitler was not a pacifist, was not an anti-communist but wanted to dominate Europe and was set on war. At that point [Rothermere] joined forces with Winston Churchill and began pushing very, very hard for re-armament and put his own money into developing the aircraft that

became the Blenheim bomber. He had been absolutely desperate to avoid another war and he had been duped by these people. I don't have conversations about this with many people because I don't want to be an apologist. He was pro-fascist until 1936 or so but he realised he had made a terrible mistake. The sad thing is that when he tried to put something back [into the editorial side of the *Daily Mail*] he was misguided. His brother [Lord Northcliffe] was the sophisticated one and he was just the money man. He was a man with wounded heart who was exploited by Princess Hohenlohe who, it turned out, was a Nazi agent who had been recruited by [German foreign minister] von Ribbentrop and Hitler.[11]

The first viscount's early support for fascism also led to continuing allegations that he was anti-Jewish. The present viscount is adamant that, despite support for fascism, his great-grandfather was not anti-Semitic. Nonetheless, the pre-war editorial policy of the *Daily Mail* that he dictated was unedifying even in a climate of appeasement and the present viscount admits one particularly notorious editorial is still recalled by the left "in order to discredit our editorials and use it as an insult". He told a House of Lords committee in 2008 that the editorial interference by his forebears might have been responsible for the hands-off policy pursued by later generations.[12]

The second viscount (Esmond Harmsworth) continued his father's promotion of business staff at the expense of the company's journalists. He was responsible for the purchase and closure of the *News Chronicle*. His cousin Cecil Harmsworth King provided the Press Association with an excoriating comment, repeated with obvious delight by Greenslade (2004, 325), for his obituary:

> He was a shit. Cold, money-grubbing and completely unsuited to the job he held. When he took over *the Daily Mail* it was the best newspaper in Fleet Street. Look at it now. When he took over the *Evening News* it was the best evening newspaper in the world. Now look at it. Dreadful rags, both of them.

In 1970, when Vere Harmsworth assumed control on behalf of his father, who was beginning to show symptoms of Alzheimer's disease, the company was in danger of going out of business. Its Sunday newspaper had been sold, the evening newspaper was losing money "hand-over-fist", the *Sketch* was losing money and the circulation of *the Daily Mail* was lagging behind its competitor, the *Daily Express*. The third viscount, as he became in 1978, was responsible for a remarkable turnaround (see Taylor 2002).

He had been described during his lifetime as "the last of the proper English press lords... only Vere Rothermere [as he became known] was brought up here, an Englishman, an Old Etonian, a baron with a hereditary peerage, raised to inherit proper English newspapers" (Coleridge 268). He relaunched the moribund *Daily Mail* as a tabloid after merging it with the *Sketch* in 1971,[13] and launched the *Mail on Sunday* in 1982. The *Mail on Sunday* required years of investment before becoming profitable, but is regarded as one of the most successful Sunday launches in recent British newspaper history. He also invested in the company's regional newspaper chain and brought strategic direction to the group.

DMGT had owned an astonishingly eclectic array of businesses, some of which had been acquired over the years from family members. During the 1950s and 1960s, when union power in Fleet Street was at its height, the family's attitude had been to put its money anywhere but in newspapers, and many of these investments eventually found their way into DMGT. By the 1980s, it owned one of the largest independent oil companies in Britain, and was a pioneer of North Sea oil extraction. A forklift firm, one of only two companies in the United Kingdom capable of bending large sheets of glass for shop fronts, 5 per cent of London Taxicabs, and London theatres were among its portfolio of assets.

Associated Newspapers had been only part-owned by DMGT. By borrowing heavily, the company brought Associated Newspapers into the fold as a wholly owned subsidiary and used the sale of the non-publishing assets to pay down debt. The decision to slim down to a publishing group coincided with a move away from Fleet Street, and an end to the power of print unions as computer technology replaced manual typesetting and composition. DMGT, which previously had not even had a bank overdraft, borrowed £500 million to finance the new phase in its development. No sooner had it been completed than Britain plunged into the 1990s recession. A DMGT director of finance, Peter Williams, conceded during an interview with me in 2009 that the company's fortunes were "a bit touch and go" during that period, and he gives much of the credit to Vere Rothermere for the decision to embark on a new strategy that took DGMT into a range of international business-to-business (B2B) commercial information activities (notably Euromoney, which in 2013 had a market capitalisation of £1.5 billion) and avoided reliance on the UK market, on advertising, on newspapers and on regulated businesses.[14]

In 1996 the £75 million operating profit from newspaper activity represented 86 per cent of the total profit for the year. In 2009, with the newspaper market at a recessional nadir, the group's titles again generated £75 million but it represented only 27 per cent of total operating profit – testament to the diversified nature of DMGT, whose adjusted group operating profit in 2013 was £300 million.

Vere Rothermere was a complex character. He was credited with the resurrection of the group, but he did so at arm's length. He was a tax exile who could spend no more than 90 days each year in Britain. He was also a marital exile. His relationship with Patricia, Lady Rothermere, was complicated by a long-term relationship with a Korean consort with whom he cohabited in France and Japan until their marriage after Patricia's death in 1992. Therefore he relied heavily on his lieutenants – *Daily Mail* editor David English and managing director Michael Shields. Distance has been given as a reason for the extraordinary editorial independence enjoyed by English, who was Rothermere's friend and associate for more than 25 years. This does Rothermere a disservice. He and English shared a remarkable empathy and mutual understanding of the newspaper, but the *Daily Mail* was a reflection of English's beliefs and his understanding of its readership. Vere Rothermere did not interfere in what developed into a highly successful formula. When English retired from the editorship to become editor-in-chief and chairman of Associated Newspapers (the DGMT subsidiary that housed its newspaper titles), his successor, Paul Dacre, enjoyed the same editorial independence and Vere Rothermere stated that, although he often disagreed with his editor, "he is entitled to his views in the paper, but if they start to affect the circulation, that will be different" (Davies 2008, 20). The inference is that good business was the sole reason Vere Harmsworth did not breach editorial independence. However, his record includes periods when the newspapers were unprofitable but enjoyed his full support. Max Hastings was editor of the DMGT London evening newspaper the *Evening Standard* at the time of Lord Rothermere's death in 1998, and said of him and his son, the fourth viscount: "I can say that the Lords Rothermere, *père et fils*, are the only newspaper owners I have worked for who have shown themselves sincerely committed to the doctrine of editorial independence" (Hastings 2002, xv).

The present viscount told me his father was a businessman "but he wasn't hugely interested in making money because his passion was journalism and newspapers". He had observed the way that control had shifted from the editorial floor under his father and grandfather so that when he inherited "this dying newspaper empire" he re-established journalistic priorities. Jonathan Rothermere says his father instilled in him the mantra that the business was about investing in journalism:

> To this day we continue to put journalism before management and that is one of the unique parts of our company because it means we basically always understand the value of product rather than strategy or anything else. The most important thing is: You can't have a strategy without a good product. If you look around the world you find that the people who are successful do follow that philosophy. Steve Jobs believed in the product. I'm sure the people at BMW believe in the product. My father was very simple. He wasn't complicated. He didn't want a short-term profit. He didn't want to run the business to pump the share price up. He believed fundamentally in producing a good product and investing in the people who produced that product rather than smoke and mirrors and a cover strategy. Of the general philosophy I learnt as I was growing up, that was what he inculcated [in me]. He was very strong on that.

Vere Rothermere saw himself not as a publisher or journalist, but as a proprietor. In a 1997 interview, he defined the role of newspaper proprietor as a profession that required an understanding of journalists, management and newspaper operations. He said that it was fundamentally a business "and therefore you have to be able to play the same ruthless business games that everyone plays" (Hagerty 1997, 11). Jonathan Rothermere says his father told him that part of the role of chairman was to be a referee between management and editorial "and he said there would never be a day when management don't try to take control of the product". Jonathan Rothermere does not blame management for such a stance "because they feel they could do business better if they had control of the product but ultimately what makes a good manager doesn't mean he's the right person to make a good product because they are two different things".

In the 1997 interview, Vere Rothermere stated that he loathed the thought of retiring and therefore did not think about it. In little more than a year he was dead at the age of 73. Sir David English predeceased him by less than three months. Jonathan Harmsworth became the fourth Viscount Rothermere at the age of 30.

The relative youth of the present viscount on succeeding to the title was due to the fact that Vere Rothermere was 42 when his son was born and had been in real danger of becoming the last Viscount Rothermere. He and his wife, Patricia, had produced two girls: Geraldine (born in 1957) and Camilla (born in 1964). Patricia Harmsworth had been told she could die if she had another child (she had almost died during Camilla's birth). Then his father Esmond decided to marry for the third time in 1966 and his new wife presented the 70-year-old peer with a son. At that point, Vere had no male heir to succeed to the title that, in the tradition of primogeniture, could not pass to his elder daughter. The Letters Patent in 1919 conferred the Rothermere title on Harold Harmsworth and "the heirs male of his body lawfully begotten". Following the birth of a half-brother who was 42 years Vere's junior, the private trusts governing the family's assets were redrafted so that the newspapers eventually would pass to this new male addition. However, in 1967 Patricia presented a son and heir. The trust documents were again redrafted in favour of Vere's son, Harold Jonathan Esmond Vere Harmsworth (Coleridge, 305–306; Greenslade, 224).

Jonathan Harmsworth had been managing director of the *Evening Standard* when his father died. He had not expected to assume the chairmanship of DMGT for some time and nor had the financial markets. In an assessment of the group following Vere Rothermere's death, Greenslade (1998, 40) noted:

The central problem [for the new viscount] will be ensuring that gusts don't dislodge those key elements which have made the company such a formidable performer in the past quarter century, increasing in value from £30 million to £2.5 billion. If that warning sounds far-fetched, given DMGT's track record thus far, it is important to remind one-self of the fragility of media businesses and, even more crucially, of media dynasties. A great deal now rests on the shoulders of 30-year-old Jonathan Harmsworth, the untested, almost unknown, fourth Viscount Rothermere, the new chairman and, given the oddity of the ownership structure, an old-style proprietor.

The ownership structure to which Greenslade refers is seen as a virtue by the family and DMGT executives, but as an unfair anachronism by some investors and analysts. When the new viscount first assumed the title there was no pressure for change, but in the new millennium there has been periodic criticism of DMGT's two-tiered share system. In 2004, investment advocate Pensions Investment Research Consultants (PIRC) gave the following assessment: "It's our view that all equity shareholders bearing the same risks should hold the same voting rights. It should be one share, one vote" (Berens 2004, 7). PIRC and another investment consultancy, Manifest, renewed the criticism in 2010, urging the non-voting shareholders to oppose the annual report in protest against the dual-share structure that allowed Lord Rothermere to control the company. Williams told me, however, that Rothermere and his family would be the largest single shareholder even if forced enfranchisement took place.

Lord Rothermere, through a Bermuda-registered investment trust, Rothermere Continuation Limited, had controlled 59.9 per cent of the ordinary (voting shares) in DMGT. In addition, he and his family own 24 per cent of the non-voting shares. On 1 July 2013 he announced an agreement to acquire the 29.3 per cent controlled by his uncle Esmond Harmsworth (the child of the third viscount's twilight years) as part of a process that will place all the voting shares in the hands of his immediate family (the direct descendants of Vere Rothermere) through the Bermudan trust.[15]

Lord Rothermere has secure control of the group. His sisters, also beneficiaries of the trust, give him full support: "I couldn't hope for more supportive sisters. They are extremely loyal." He and his wife, Claudia, have also secured the peerage. The Hon. Richard Jonathan Harold Vere Harmsworth was born in 1994 and he has three sisters and a brother.

Whether the voting structure that secures the legacy remains in place may depend on the willingness of Vere (he carries his grandfather's name) to perpetuate that legacy and on the group's continued financial success. The latter may determine whether non-voting shareholders will be happy to leave well enough alone. Successful diversification and digital strategies, together with a final dividend that has grown steadily from less than 5 pence a share in 1996 to more than 19 pence in 2013, obviously provide a measure of comfort.

The fourth Viscount Rothermere and the Harmsworth legacy are highly regarded within DMGT management. His relationship with the editor of the

Daily Mail, Paul Dacre, is a continuation of his father's approach. The executive managing editor, Robin Esser, told me Vere Rothermere's relationship with David English had been "very close" and said the proprietor was "happy to be the facilitator of David English's editorial skills", a role that he continued with Dacre.[16] Jonathan Rothermere feels a debt of gratitude to Dacre for helping him through the early years of his chairmanship. In fact, Dacre is one of two men on whom he has placed great reliance. "I don't know where I would have been without Paul," he told me. "I'm really quite dependent on him in many ways and I'm very close to him. We get on very well and I'd like to think that now I've earned Paul's respect so we can have frank and honest discourse about many things. It took a while to get there." The other confidante was Paedric Fallon, a former financial journalist and head of the group's Euromoney subsidiary who died in 2012.

Dacre oversees the editorial policies of the Mail group of newspapers, although he told the Leveson Enquiry "just as I have been given the freedom to edit by our management, I leave the individual editors of the titles – it can't be any other way. You can't edit by remote control." An illustration of the independence of DMGT editors is provided by Esser, who recalls one general election where the *Daily Mail* supported the Conservative Party, the *Mail on Sunday* gave support to Northern Ireland's Social Democratic and Labour Party (SDLP) and the *Evening Standard* endorsed the Labour Party. Britain's national newspapers are known for, and perhaps are expected to exhibit, political bias, and DMGT's nationals are no exception. The *Mail* is regarded as having a highly influential role in British politics, prompting one Labour peer to tell me, somewhat aggrieved, that "policies have been subject to approval by *The Daily Mail* – or the particular views of its editor, Paul Dacre". The comment was made in April 2009 while Labour was still in power. The peer described *Daily Mail* as "the most influential paper by a long way, setting the tone for all media".

The doctrine of editorial independence is not codified, even though it is embedded and observed throughout DMGT. Dacre's authority and that of the other editors is well understood. But so, too, are other aspects of the convention. For example, while national editors are free to determine party endorsement and support, this did not apply to the group's Northcliffe Media regional newspapers that were sold to a consortium in 2012.[17] Editors were expected to be apolitical and local newspapers were not permitted to endorse political parties in local elections. The former managing director of Northcliffe Media, Michael Pelosi, explained to me that most of its regional publications were in single-newspaper markets and endorsing one political party over another would compromise overall community trust. On the one occasion he could recall (when readers had been urged to vote for a particular party) when a heading on the front page had said "Vote Green", the editor was reprimanded and told to limit himself to laying out the environmental issues.[18]

Jonathan Rothermere provides a down-to-earth explanation of his non-interference in editorial issues:

> I may have an opinion, along with everyone else who reads the *Daily Mail*, about what's right and what's wrong but at the end of the day the people who are doing that job are the best at what they do and they are ruthlessly honed to do that job. There is a huge pool of very talented people – the people who get to the top are really at the top of their game. They are elite athletes so the idea that a glorious amateur could come in and start making huge editorial decisions is a dangerous thing.

Esser confirms this policy of non-interference. He told me: "I do not know of a single occasion when the chairman has interfered editorially or even made an urgent request for something to be covered that had not been covered, or whatever. It just does not happen."

The chairman's reputation within DMGT does not rest on being simply an extension of Vere Rothermere's reign. Like a crown prince, he was prepared for the role he assumed in 1998. His education was by British standards unorthodox – first at the spartan Gordonstoun School in Scotland, and then at Duke University in North Carolina. He began his professional training outside the group as a reporter and sub-editor on Glasgow's *Daily Record* – before joining the family firm as deputy managing director of one of DMGT's regional titles in Essex. He then moved on to manage its weekly newspapers in Kent before joining the group's Associated Newspapers (publisher of the *Daily Mail*) in a variety of roles. Much of his reputation rests on his working knowledge of the publishing business. While still in his role at Northcliffe Media, Pelosi described his conversations with Rothermere as "healthy debate and healthy challenges":

> He'll ask some very good questions such as "Look, you have an edition for this newspaper that's way over there and you're only selling 1000 to 1500 copies of that edition. Surely, it would be better to have resources in areas where you have critical mass?" ...He has a thorough knowledge of our publications and when he looks at them he has an eye for publishing.

His knowledge has been put to the test by the recession, during which he has had to oversee a consolidation that rivals his father's re-engineering of the business. DMGT had been trying to sell its regional newspaper group since 2005 but had been unable to find an appropriate buyer. The recession had been hard on Britain's regional newspapers and Northcliffe Media began a series of heavy staff cuts in September 2010. By the end of 2011 staff in the regional group had been cut by 602 (19 per cent of the workforce), with a further 325 (13 per cent) job losses the following year. Cost-cutting resulted in a significant financial improvement before the group was sold in December 2012 to a consortium led by a former newspaper editor and media investor, David Montgomery. The sale ended a 90-year involvement by DMGT in Britain's regional press and was a strong indicator that Rothermere, like his father, puts business before sentiment.

His hardest recession-led decision was the sale (for £6.7 million) of a 75.1 per cent interest in the *Evening Standard* to Russian oligarch Alexander Lebedev. The *Evening Standard* had been the result of his father's prolonged, but ultimately successful rationalisation of the London evening market into which Vere Rothermere had folded the company's loss-making *Evening News* in 1980. The arrangement was initially a 50–50 partnership with Express Newspapers that Vere Rothermere later bought out. Latterly, however, the London paid-for evening newspaper had been losing money in the face of a number of free newspapers, two of which had been launched by DMGT under the present chairman's leadership.[19] A commentary by Dan Sabbagh in *The Times* following the announcement of the sale of the majority stake in the *Evening Standard* stated that Rothermere was "hardly an emotional stranger to the title", as he had been its managing director immediately before his father died but the decision to sell was hardly dismantling the empire: "He is simply recognising reality and moving on."

In a further move that indicated he was no slave to sentiment, Lord Rothermere consolidated the group's radio holdings. Vere Rothermere had initiated a strategy to invest in the radio market in the United Kingdom and offshore. In November 2009, however, the group sold half the shares in its southern hemisphere subsidiary, DMG Radio Australia, to Illyria – the investment vehicle owned by Rupert Murdoch's son, Lachlan. In September 2012 Illyria bought the remaining 50 per cent. In 2014 Boston Consulting Group undertook a review of operations at DMGT's head office and a number of executives left the company.

The flagship title, the *Daily Mail,* and its Sunday companion have been relatively unscathed by recession-led contraction. The newspaper has been able to limit circulation falls to a lower ratio than its competitors and its 21 per cent share of the national market is increasing. The digital version, *Mail Online,* was the most read online newspaper in the world according to Comscore, with more than 50 million unique visitors a month – ahead of the *New York Times* – in October 2012. When Lord Rothermere considered placing a paywall on the site he asked his older children what they thought of the idea. His son Vere told him:

> I wouldn't do that if I were you because all my friends read it – and that's quite an accomplishment – but if you charge for it I don't think any of them would read it. No-one wants to pay for content on the Internet so you would just end up with your traditional demographic and miss out on all the young people.

He "double checked" with his daughters and received the same verdict. *Mail Online* did not have a paywall as it went into 2014.

Recent changes within DMGT are responses to trying times, rather than a desire by Lord Rothermere to stamp his personal mark and move out of the shadow of his forebears. He has not, for example, followed the example of Australian media heir James Packer (who is the same age as Rothermere) in moving away from the family's media businesses. He exhibits many of the traits of a custodian: "I totally agree that we are here to steward the company, make it stronger and more successful and it's the same thing with our titles. That's exactly what we do. We are not here to be the big 'I am'." His tenure as chairman has been marked by caution, rather than the impetuosity of youth that some had expected. The brass-bound desk in his office, originally owned by the founder of the *Daily Mail,* Lord Northcliffe, is symbolic. He regularly invokes his father's legacy and talks openly of the way in which his father instilled in him the values and philosophy that he now follows. He sees it as his responsibility to pass these on – augmented by his own efforts – to his older son and daughters (his younger son was born in 2010):

> I don't talk to them about deals because I'm not really about deals. I'm about the philosophy of what we do and the philosophy of the business. So I think I do discuss that with them. They teach me a lot about technology and I discuss it with them a lot. The whole process of talking to them is talking about the philosophy of products and how they use them. I talk to my son about my philosophy and my attitude and about journalism.

Leadership by an hereditary peer could mark the DMGT as the worst example of family firm primogeniture, one in which the first-born son is not simply favoured by the father, but has his rights enshrined in a state-privileged hereditary status founded on feudalism. However, the success of DMGT under Vere and Jonathan Harmsworth has for the most part, dulled the argument. While the two-tiered share system is the subject of continuing attack, the chairmanship of neither father nor son has been publicly challenged.

The Hon. Richard Jonathan Harold Vere Harmsworth is, as yet, a teenaged unknown quantity. He will succeed to the title but Lord Rothermere places no such certainty on leadership of DMGT:

> Primogeniture can be overplayed. Indeed, I've said to my son Vere that I don't think it's right to put pressure on children, or anyone for that matter, to do something with their life. Everyone should have a right to choose and I'd say the same thing about my daughters. They have a right to choose what they want to do as well. If my son Vere wasn't up to it or didn't want to do the job we would have to think hard over whether there

was another member of my family who was better able to do it. However, I think he really does want to do it.

In fact, the family and the *Daily Mail* are in many ways inseparable. Lord Rothermere speaks of a keen sense of involvement and loyalty to the company by all members of Harmsworth family:

> Everyone sees us as the *Daily Mail*. You've got it plastered across your forehead. That's one thing but we love it, are also deeply grateful for it, and respect it enormously. I wouldn't say we respect everything it says all the time but we respect its independence and we respect its ability to challenge the status quo. We respect its journalistic independence and we respect our philosophy. I think it is definitely something that brings the family together. I don't know what my children would say but I suspect they would say much the same thing.

Would the same degree of certitude exist in a family that has not made the transition from empire builder to next generation? The Murdoch family has yet to confront that question.

The Murdoch family and News Corporation

The Murdoch family and its media interests are in a game that has yet to be played out. While Sir Keith Murdoch left his son the rudiments, it is Rupert Murdoch who has built the media empire with which he is synonymous. The Murdoch family differs from the other families in this chapter, as it is still substantially in its first generation, and one can only speculate on events that might follow the patriarch's death. Therefore, it will not be dealt with in any detail beyond setting out the trust structure that will determine some of its future.

Rupert Murdoch heads two corporations that emerged from News Corporation in the aftermath of the *News of the World* phone hacking scandal and the Leveson Inquiry. He is chairman and chief executive of 21st Century Fox Corporation, which holds the former group's entertainment assets, and executive chairman of New News Corporation, in which newspapers and information services are now held. Before the split in June 2013, News Corporation had assets of $US68 billion and, in common with other family-controlled media groups, a two-tiered share structure: Class A common stock that did not carry voting rights and Class B common voting stock. When Newscorp was split in two, the dual-stock structure was preserved. Stockholders in 21st Century Fox each received one share in New News Corporation for each four shares held. As a result Rupert Murdoch and his family control almost 40 per cent of the voting shares in each group.

The family owns the shares through a series of trusts. The largest is the Murdoch Family Trust, previously known by the obscure title of the A. E. Harris Trust,[20] which is administered by the family's investment vehicle, Cruden Investments. Other trusts used by the family to hold interests in News Corporation include the K. R. Murdoch 2004 Revocable Trust and the GCM Trust that was set up for the benefit of Rupert Murdoch's daughters by his third wife, Wendi Deng Murdoch. Murdoch's three sisters also have interests in the multinational, as did his mother, Dame Elisabeth Murdoch, although she relinquished her stake in a restructuring before her death in 2012 at the age of 103.

Rupert Murdoch's third marriage in 1999 at the age of 68 created new difficulties for a family that was already jockeying for the position of heir-apparent. He had a child, Prudence, by his first marriage and three children (Elisabeth, Lachlan and James) by his second marriage before his third wife gave birth to Grace in 2001 and Chloe in 2003. Under the settlement terms of his divorce from his second wife, Murdoch agreed to never change the trust under which his existing four children would inherit the bulk of their father's interests in the investment vehicle, Cruden Investments (Chenoweth, Wolff).[21] However, with the birth of their stepsisters, the adult Murdoch offspring came under pressure to voluntarily admit the new arrivals to the legacy. Following negotiations, the adult children agreed to provide equal economic participation in the family fortune for their two stepsisters, but they will not be entitled to any future voting rights. In other words, they will be entitled to money but not control. Wolff notes that the adult Murdoch offspring were adamant about the retention of voting rights because their father's third wife, who is their contemporary in years, could potentially exercise more votes than each of them through her daughters' proxies (2008, 354). In November 2013 Murdoch was granted divorce from his third wife, with a private settlement said to be based on a pre-nuptial and two post-nuptial agreements.[22]

The trust arrangement may have secured future control for the older Murdoch offspring but it does not solve the issue of succession to the Murdoch empire. His eldest daughter, Prudence, does not have a direct role in the corporation; his elder son, Lachlan, appeared to be the heir-apparent but abruptly resigned as News Corporation's deputy chief operating officer in 2004 and set up his investment company, Illyria; his youngest son, James, who in 2011 became News Corporation's deputy chief operating officer and was seen as Rupert Murdoch's successor, became enmeshed in the hacking scandal; and his younger adult daughter, Elisabeth, is an independent spirit who had been seen by some as his successor but later criticised the company and brother James over the phone hacking scandal and incurred her father's displeasure. In March 2014 Lachlan was rehabilitated as non-executive co-chairman of both corporations and the apparent successor.

Nothing is pre-ordained although Rupert Murdoch has indicated he would like a family member to succeed him (Auletta 2012). The cleaving of the empire has increased the options: there are now two thrones on which different successors could sit but there are potentially three candidates for those two chairs. And the Murdoch family has yet to face the complications of Lansberg's "cousin stage": by 2013 Rupert Murdoch had 13 grandchildren.

Summary

At this point it is useful to summarise. Each of the major media family trusts examined in this chapter has been subject to the effects of accidents of history and human behaviour. The fortunes of each have been determined by the strengths or weaknesses of key family members and by the robustness or otherwise of the trust structures that attempt to hold together the desires and aspirations of ever-enlarging families.

Family trusts that run news media operations exhibit many of the shortcomings identified in institutional studies of family firms. They do so because they attempt to serve the interests of two groups: the family and the business, when those interests may not always coincide. In the case of news media companies, the problem is compounded by a third imperative – the public interest.

None of the examples canvassed here can be said to be a perfect model for the preservation of good journalism, although they display many of the positive attributes of family firms noted at the beginning of this chapter. In those cases where good journalism *is* being preserved, structural protections go hand-in-hand with the determination of individuals to nurture the "shared dream" of which Lansberg speaks (1999, 75).

Yet even these endeavours may be fragile. When overall company performance in diversified groups is strong (as was the case in the Washington Post Company and is the case in the DMGT), the journalistic values of the core publication appear to be relatively "safe". However, the same cannot be said of secondary publications. The Washington Post divested itself of *Newsweek* and DMGT sold its regional newspaper stable. The New York Times Company does not enjoy the same degree of diversity and is therefore more vulnerable. The company is determined to keep faith with editorial quality on the *New York Times*, but its sale of the *Boston Globe* for less than 7 per cent of the purchase price is evidence of the financial pressure facing the company.

In each case, the desire to maintain editorial quality is tempered by commercial considerations. The family firm has obligations not only to the memory of the preceding generation and the destiny of the next, but also to large numbers of non-family shareholders who have foregone voting power in return for healthy dividends. In preserving their power, each has exposed the company to the weaknesses of the two-tiered share system identified by Villalonga and Amit (2009, 3088–3089). Donald Graham and Lord Rothermere are leaders of diversified businesses. Neither will allow newsprint to fuel a funeral pyre. We might recall that Bhattacharya and Ravikumar believe that the driving force is to bequeath wealth and not necessarily the business being undertaken (2001, 190). Sulzberger, however, may suffer some of the effects of family altruism cited by Schulze et al., who recognise the dangers in putting the family first (2002, 256). Preservation of the Sulzberger family legacy may impair his ability to operate the company in the most commercially competitive manner.

The Bancroft family insulated itself from such considerations, but was a perfect example of the ultimate destruction that can take place in the "cousin phase" of family firm evolution described by Lansberg (*ibid.*, 142). In fact, the family may be seen as the embodiment of many family firm failings even though it played no direct part in the management of Dow Jones & Co. – poor governance, structural weaknesses, the effects of dynastic change and the power of wealth over heritage.

The creator of a media family trust may have the high-minded aim of perpetuating good intentions, and may believe that his or her exceptional abilities have been spliced into the genetic code of succeeding generations. Experience suggests this is by no means certain, and the real weakness of the family trust as a mechanism for preserving significant journalism lies in being unable to choose your offspring. In the following chapter, the legacy of Nelson Poynter and the Poynter Institute is examined. He recognised this fundamental flaw in dynastic succession: "I have not met my great-grandchildren", he was reported as saying, "and I might not like them."

6
The Trinity – Origins and Growth

A handful of newspapers have been invested in a trust or foundation bound to administer them in the public interest. Each has found its way into this unusual form of ownership through unique circumstances that have depended (in one case quite literally) on the way the wind blew.

Each has emerged as a distinctive organisation and collectively they are bound by common purpose rather than by the same legal structure. Nonetheless, the obligations placed on their guardians bear the hallmarks of traditional trusteeship. These guardians are not owners in the ordinary sense, but custodians of enterprises that should endure after them. They have no vested interest beyond ensuring that civil society is the ultimate beneficiary.

This chapter and Chapter 7 examine the three largest trust- or foundation-owned newspapers in the Anglo-American sphere: *The Guardian* in London, the *Irish Times* in Dublin and the *Tampa Bay Times* in Florida. Each of these newspapers enjoys a reputation for high-quality principled journalism, and a commitment to use its columns to provide readers with information that contributes to their ability to function as citizens. Each is bound to pursue a form of liberal journalism established by men and women with a driving determination to serve the public interest. I think of them as a trinity.

There is a strong but necessary emphasis in these chapters on structure and business practice. Organisation and business systems are central to the political economy of the news because they influence and help to shape its form and substance. That is nowhere more so than in the trusts and trust-like bodies that administer these three newspapers. However, commerce has great difficulty in coping with unorthodox structures that do not fit with established concepts of property and markets. The story of these three news-papers is a tale of trying to fit square pegs into round holes, as will shortly become apparent.

I begin by tracing the history of the trinity's transition to their present ownership, because this genesis informs the structure under which each now operates, before examining the subsequent history of each publication to reveal any weakness in its structure. Each newspaper's current governance is as much a reflection of events *after* the change to trusteeship as it is a function of the decision to adopt that form of ownership. Chapter 7 discusses present operations to illustrate the influence that the form of ownership exerts on its journalism. In each case there is a brief look into the future to identify potential challenges that each publication may face.

The three examples face the challenge common to all newspapers, of ensuring that they have a future. They are exposed to the same audience/advertising shift and economic recession as their contemporaries owned by public listed companies. Their responses, however, allow us to examine the effects of different types of ownership on newsgathering, and assess the worth of trustee stewardship as an alternative to ownership of newspapers by publicly listed corporations.

The Guardian represents trust ownership based on the gift of a newspaper by its owners; the *Irish Times* shows that philanthropy is not a prerequisite and a trust can buy a substantial newspaper; and the *Tampa Bay Times* demonstrates that this form of stewardship can exist even where there are legal impediments to formal trust ownership.

Beginnings

The Guardian

Established: 1821
Founder: John Edward Taylor
Trust established: 1936
Benefactor: John Russell Scott
Current owner: Scott Trust Limited
Corporate body: Guardian Media Group
Circulation: 203,069 (December 2013)
Group revenue: £206.8 million (2013)
          [$US316.7 million]*

*Mid-market rate 24.7.2013

The Guardian has been described as the only newspaper with a ghost for a proprietor (Jenkins 1986, 213). That ghost was C. P. Scott, editor from 1872 to 1929 and owner from 1907 until 1914, when he vested most of the shares in his two sons and his son-in-law. He ruled over the *Manchester Guardian* until his death in 1932 and his influence continues to be felt in the newspaper, which changed its name to *The Guardian* in 1959. He was described as one of the great Victorian editors and as an exception among proprietors – willing to sacrifice commercial interests when his conscience demanded (Hampton 2004, 135). It was Scott who was responsible for some of journalism's best-known epithets, the most famous of which was penned in a leading article to mark the *Manchester Guardian's* centennial, 5 May 1921: "Comment is free, but facts are sacred." He established the newspaper as a bastion of liberal journalism, and the principles that he laid down are his ongoing endowment to the newspaper. A single phrase in the articles that govern *The Guardian* ensures that the principles are a doctrinal reality: "on the same lines and in the same spirit as heretofore".

C. P. Scott was the nephew of the founder of the *Manchester Guardian*, John Edward Taylor, and was appointed editor by the founder's son (both were named John Edward Taylor) who had inherited the newspaper. Taylor senior was a Manchester journalist who wrote one of the first newspaper accounts of the 1819 Peterloo Massacre, in which 11 unarmed protestors were killed and 400 wounded at an open-air speech by a radical politician. This spurred his determination to begin his own weekly newspaper. The prospectus stated that the newspaper would contribute to "fixing upon a broader and more impregnable basis the fabric of our liberties". The *Manchester Guardian* became a daily in 1855 after the abolition of stamp duty on newspapers.

Taylor Junior had apparently wished to leave the publication to Scott in his will, but poor execution and the existence of other claimants (whose only interest lay in realising the value of the inheritance) almost took it from Scott's grasp when the proprietor died in 1905 (Taylor 1993, 4). The ensuing struggle to raise sufficient capital to secure full ownership shaped his attitude to future proprietorship. In 1971, his grandson Richard Scott wrote that the experience convinced Scott that the independence of the newspaper would be preserved only if it was owned by members of the family who actually worked on it.[1] In 1914, at the age of 68, he transferred the majority of the shares to his sons, John Russell Scott and Edward Taylor Scott, and his son-in-law C. E. Montague. A formal agreement was made to ensure that shares could not be sold to outsiders and there could be no more than five shareholders. These were not normal shareholders. The company paid no dividend and none was expected. Montague died in 1928 and his holding was divided between the two brothers who were given control of the newspaper – Edward (Ted) Scott as editor and John Scott as manager, under their father's elderly but energetic eye (see Crozier 1934, 327–328). On New Year's Day 1932, C. P. Scott died and his sons were presented with a demand for heavy death duties payable on his holding in the company, which they inherited. Negotiations with the Inland Revenue established that C. P. Scott was a minor shareholder in the business, from which he and his sons had taken only their modest salaries and that death duties were not payable. The ruling was fortuitous, as the company had been enlarged by the acquisition of the *Manchester Evening News* in 1924.

Within four months, Ted Scott was also dead – the victim of a sudden squall that capsized his boat on Lake Windermere. On the car journey to the lake he had discussed the death duties problem with his son, who later recalled: "I distinctly remember his saying that God knows what would happen to the paper if anything happened to him or his brother" (Ayerst 1971, 491). Ironically, the future of the newspaper was being determined (quite literally) by the way the wind blew.

John Scott became sole proprietor of Manchester Guardian and Evening News Limited, following the triggering of an informal agreement between the brothers that on the death of one, the other would acquire his shares. The agreement was in the process of being formalised when Ted Scott died. The death of three family shareholders in four years convinced John Scott that the burden of death duties meant the company could not be kept in family ownership should he too, die prematurely. His solution was an extraordinary one – he decided to give away the newspapers. The advice he was given by his legal advisor, Gavin Simonds, resonates with present-day attitudes to ownership: "You are trying to do something that is very repugnant to the law of England. You are trying to divest yourself of a property right" (Ayerst 1971, 492; Taylor 1993, 4). John Scott's desire to transfer all the shares to a non-commercial entity with no financial interest in the company's profits was challenging both legally and to the Exchequer.

The Scott Trust was not formally established until 1936 and was to run for 20 years. There is no doubt that the threat of overpowering death duties was the prime motivation. John Scott's son Laurence wrote in 1969: "Although people talk of the Scott Trust ensuring the principles and independence of the papers, as indeed it does, John Scott in fact created it with little more in mind than escaping death duties and so avoiding any danger of loss of independence through a forced sale" (*ibid.*, 492). Taylor describes Laurence Scott's view as "revisionism", and believes that John Scott did, in fact, also have higher motives in establishing the trust (*ibid.*, 4–5). This view is reinforced by the fact that John Scott was not prepared simply to take advantage of prevailing market values, and sell the company to facilitate investments that allowed better estate planning. Scott voluntarily divested himself and his heirs of a group then valued at more than £1 million, which included the *Manchester Evening News* for which Lord Beaverbrook and others were reportedly prepared to pay at least that sum had Scott been prepared to sell it. Schlesinger in *The Guardian* in 1986 described the establishment of the Scott Trust as "a remarkable act of public benefaction, and in effect the creation of an institution".

John Scott did, however, arrange the Trust in such a way that the family maintained close connections. In addition to himself as chairman, the other six trustees included his son Laurence and nephew Evelyn Aubrey Montague. The editors of the *Manchester Guardian* (W. P. Crozier, who had succeeded the late Ted Scott) and the *Manchester Evening News* (William Haley) and *The*

Guardian's London editor (James Bone) were also trustees. The sole "independent" was a former Lord Mayor of Manchester, Sir Ernest Simon (who later became the 1st Baron Simon of Wythenshawe) but he was also a director of Manchester Guardian and Evening News Limited. The determination to avoid death duties meant the absence of pecuniary interest was absolute. Trustees did not even receive fees, although a number (including John Scott) were salaried employees of Manchester Guardian and Evening News Limited. John Scott retained the right to appoint and dismiss trustees, who were responsible for appointing company executives. He was, in all but a financial sense, still proprietor. A board of directors oversaw the operations of the company from the beginning and, although the Trust was nominally the shareholder, the board operated with a degree of freedom that was almost comparable to *The Guardian's* editorial independence.

Although the newly minted trust included in its ranks the editors of *The Guardian* and the *Manchester Evening News*, it did not interfere in any way in the editorial direction of the publications. John Scott passed the editorship of the *Manchester Guardian* to Crozier when Ted Scott drowned. Crozier had been on the newspaper's staff for 28 years when he took the editor's chair, and was described as "a 'working journalist' of something bordering on genius" (Hammond et al. 1946, 233). He had organised the newspaper's network of foreign correspondents, and as editor, was responsible for modernising the publication and broadening its appeal. However, during his 12 years at the helm, he was a careful protector (without the need for prompting) of C. P. Scott's vision of the *Manchester Guardian* as an independent organ of opinion and liberal journalism.

The Scott family's gift is unparalleled in British newspaper history. Our next case, the *Irish Times*, found its way into trust ownership not through philanthropy, but as a means of protecting the newspaper from hostile takeover while rewarding its owners for their "generosity".

The *Irish Times*

Established: 1859
Founder: Lawrence Knox
Trust established: 1974
Current owner: Irish Times Trust Ltd
Corporate body: Irish Times Ltd
Circulation: 82,059 (December 2013)
Group revenue: €81.5 million (2012)
                              [$US107.9 million]*

*Mid-market rate 31.12.2012

The *Irish Times* is Ireland's oldest national daily newspaper. Unlike *The Guardian*, it does not owe its ethos or current structure to an enlightened, socially motivated owner/editor. For most of its existence, its owners were businessmen and its editors were employees – although for the most part they enjoyed editorial independence. The founder was a 23-year-old former army officer, Lawrence Knox, who launched the *Irish Times* as a tri-weekly in March 1859. Within 14 weeks its frequency was increased and it became Ireland's first penny daily. Within two years, Knox had increased the number of columns per page to squeeze in more content, and by 1870 had to buy a new press to double the size of the newspaper to eight pages (Oram 1983, 70–71). Knox, in a long editorial announcing the first issue, described the *Irish Times* as a newspaper for "Irishmen loyal to the British connexion", a label that would for a large part of its existence tie it to Protestantism in the eyes of the community (O'Toole 2009, 7). However, under his leadership (although he was never editor), the *Irish Times* established a reputation for moderation and balance.

Knox's premature death at the age of 37 in 1873 led to the purchase of the newspaper (for £35,000) by Sir John Arnott, who was also a supporter of British rule. He announced that he would conduct the opposition to disintegrating forces (i.e. the Nationalists) in a fair and straightforward spirit, without the shadow of offence to any person or party in public life (Oram, 76). In 1898, Arnott died and under the terms of his will, his widow and his son, Sir John Alexander Arnott, held the newspaper in trust for two years while a new entity, Irish Times Ltd, was formed to take over the newspaper and two other publications. Under the new company's articles of association, Arnott was entitled to remain chairman and chief executive until his death or retirement. Three other members of the Anglo-Irish family sat on the board of directors and Arnott and his wife acquired the bulk of the voting shares. Although the structure and voting rights were amended over the years, Arnott retained control (and both positions) until his death in 1940.

The newspaper's offices in Lower Abbey Street, Dublin, placed the *Irish Times* quite literally in the midst of the 1916 Easter Uprising, which it described as "one of the most deliberate and far reaching crimes in Irish history". Its editor, John Healy, was a staunch unionist but the formation of modern Ireland – from the granting of Home Rule in 1914 to the establishment of the Irish Free State in 1921 – occurred on his watch. His pro-British stance throughout was to colour the *Irish Times*' reputation for decades. He died in 1934 and it was for his successor, Robert Smyllie (who later said the *Irish Times* had been "the organ of the British Government"), to refashion the newspaper to better reflect the new nation (O'Brien 2008, 81).

Smyllie had an often brittle relationship with Éamon de Valera and the ruling Fianna Fáil party. He supported the opposition Fine Gael party but his backing ended abruptly when, in government, it withdrew Ireland from the Commonwealth in 1948 and declared a republic. Arnott died during the

Second World War (when Smyllie had some celebrated clashes with the official censors), and his brother Loftus succeeded him as chairman, while his son, Sir Lauriston Arnott, became managing director. A Dublin businessman, Frank Lowe, was co-opted to the board in 1941 and became chairman in 1945 with a brief to modernise the company. Change was necessary. At the end of the 19th century, the newspaper was recording handsome profits in the region of £30,000 (O'Brien, 30) but in the latter part of Smyllie's editorship circulation was falling and profits were low. Lowe introduced a technical modernisation programme but was unable to make inroads in the editorial department. He regarded the management of the department, on which Smyllie had placed his own eccentric stamp, as incomprehensible.

Shortly after Smyllie's death in 1954, when circulation was 35,000 and on some days as low as 25,000 (Brady 2005, 24), Lowe and two other Dublin businessmen (brothers Ralph and Philip Walker) bought out the majority of the Arnott family's holding. He also brought his nephew George Hetherington, whom he had raised, into the partnership. His co-owners joined him on the board, and Sir Lauriston Arnott relinquished the managing director's position. In spite of his failure to fully understand the editorial side of the business, Lowe and his business partners did not interfere with editorial policy.

The three men had invested at a low point in Ireland's economy and the newspaper's revenue and circulation reflected both the parlous state of affairs and the successive appointment as editor of two men who were "next in line" rather than the most able candidates. In 1962, a former British Army major, Thomas Bleakley McDowell, became chief executive of the *Irish Times* after buying an interest in the newspaper, an investment that was described as "hazardous in the extreme" (Brady, 25). Major McDowell (as he was universally known) and Douglas Gageby (who was hired as deputy managing director and who bought a 20 per cent interest in the company) became the agents of change.

McDowell championed Gageby's move from management to the editorship of the newspaper, and he was to serve two terms that totalled 20 years. Under his editorship, the *Irish Times* was transformed from being the newspaper of the Protestant minority – Brady says it was described as the house journal of the "stranded gentry" – to being a truly national newspaper (O'Brien, 165). Circulation had almost doubled to 69,000 by the time Gageby stepped down in 1974 at the end of his first term as editor.

The financial fortunes of the company did not, however, follow the same ever-upward trajectory. In 1968, profits reached £IR76,834 only to drop to £IR29,575 the following year, before bouncing back to £IR68,028 then falling to £IR10,898 in 1971. These fluctuations were in all likelihood a reflection of the fact that the company had no capital reserves and limited liquidity (Brady, 28). By this stage, the last of the Arnott family shareholding had been sold to the five directors, who owned the 70,000 ordinary shares in equal proportions. Under the articles, ordinary shares had to be sold to directors or persons approved by the board. The ordinary shares had five times the voting power of the preferential shares that were traded on the stock exchange. In 1972, the directors decided to inject £IR50,000 of new capital into the company, which was converted to ordinary shares that were distributed equally amongst themselves. This gave the directors unchallengeable voting power over the preference shareholders. In that year, the company returned a record profit of £IR242,134 and in 1973 recorded a phenomenal increase to £IR427,511 (O'Brien, 198–200). The combination of McDowell and Gageby appeared to have reversed the newspaper's fortunes. Both then played a critical role in changing the structure of the company.

The Irish Times Trust was not born out of family tragedy, nor did it display the generosity that saw the Scott family hand over the assets of Manchester Guardian and Evening News Limited without seeking any form of payment. However, like John Scott's action in forming the Scott Trust, the formation of the Irish Times Trust was a defensive action.

In September 1973, the five directors of the Irish Times Company transferred their ordinary shares into a trust held by a firm of Dublin solicitors. Preferential shares continued to be traded on the Dublin Stock Exchange. Eight months later, they announced that the company itself had become a trust in order to prevent a possible takeover of the *Irish Times* by interests "that might not maintain its high editorial standards" (O'Brien, 200). There was, in fact, no pending offer or even expression of interest that might precipitate such a move but three of the five directors (the Walker brothers and George Hetherington) had indicated that they wished to retire and cash up their all-important ordinary shares (*ibid.*, 201–202). This opened the possibility that McDowell and Gageby would be forced to accept new investors with different views on how the company should operate.

McDowell devised a plan that would satisfy the desire by directors to "cash up", prevent a takeover and secure his own control of the business. He sought advice from, among others, the chairman of the Observer Trust, Arnold (later Lord) Goodman.

The solution was complex but involved four key components:

1. He persuaded the Investment Bank of Ireland to invest £IR1,625,000 to purchase the directors' 120,000 ordinary shares.[2]
2. The directors were offered £IR1 for each preference share (which were in two classes that traded at 45p and 54p, respectively). They received £IR13.50 for each of their ordinary shares or a total of £IR325,000 per director. He persuaded the directors to each leave £IR76,000 in the business to purchase the 380,000 preference shares. These were placed in a new entity, Irish Times Holdings, while the operation of the newspaper remained in a wholly owned subsidiary, Irish Times Limited. This was

a necessary distinction to prevent the bank being seen to control the newspaper.

3. The investment by the bank and the directors in Irish Times Holdings was in the form of non-voting redeemable shares and the 100 voting shares would be in the hands of yet another body, the Irish Times Trust Limited – the ultimate controlling entity. The redeemable shares would be progressively bought back from the bank and directors out of profits. In the meantime, the holders were entitled to a 7 per cent dividend (O'Brien, 203–204).

4. McDowell would remain chairman of the operating company and the Irish Times Trust Limited board of governors until he decided to resign or retire (as a condition of the bank's involvement).

In a legal sense, the structure that McDowell created was (as we will see later in this chapter) a precursor to the present status of the Scott Trust. Legally, it was not a trust but a private company limited by guarantee. The element of trusteeship lay in the wording of the memoranda and articles of association in both the Irish Times Trust Limited (for convenience it will be referred to as the Trust) and its operational subsidiary, the Irish Times Limited.

The objects of the Trust began with largely unfulfilled ambitions[3] (to become an educational and social endowment body) before they addressed its relationship with the *Irish Times*. The operating company articles were to be amended to ensure that the object of the Irish Times Limited was "to publish the Irish Times as an independent newspaper primarily concerned with serious issues for the benefit of the community throughout the whole of Ireland free from any form of personal or party political, commercial, religious or other sectional control".

A prohibition on governors being ministers of religion, politicians (and anyone "more than a mere member of a political party or group") or people with media company connections was designed to protect this position. Staff of the *Irish Times* could become governors only with McDowell's permission. The Trust Objects then set out five "principal objectives" that the editorial policy would promote, and three principles that should be followed in the presentation of editorial content. The prescriptive nature of the objectives and principles stood in stark contrast to the Scott Trust's requirement to maintain *The Guardian* "on the same lines and in the same spirit as heretofore".

The *Irish Times* editorial objectives were to be:

• The support of constitutional democracy expressed through governments freely elected.
• The progressive achievement of social justice between people and the discouragement of discrimination of all kinds.

- The promotion of a society where the quality of life is enriched by the standards of its education, its arts, its culture, and its recreational facilities, and where the quality of spirit is instinct with Christian values but free from all religious bias and discrimination.
- The promotion of peace and tolerance and opposition to all forms of violence and hatred so that each man [sic] may live in harmony with his neighbour considerate for his cultural, material and spiritual needs.
- The promotion of understanding of other nations and peoples and a sympathetic concern for their well-being.

The principles governing publication also enshrined core journalistic values. In order to "enable the readers of the Irish Times to reach informed and independent judgements and to contribute more effectively to the life of the community" it required the following:

- News shall be as accurate and as comprehensive as is practicable and be presented fairly.
- Comment and opinion shall be informed and responsible, and shall be identifiable from fact.
- Special consideration shall be given to the reasonable representation of minority interests and divergent views.

Gageby stated later that the editorial policy and journalistic principles were, in fact, what had been practised in the newspaper over the preceding decade (Kearney & Moran 1984, 16). Each governor of the Trust was required to declare annually his or her adherence to the objectives and principles (and confirm he or she had not become a minister of religion or active political party member), but it is noteworthy that neither the memorandum nor the articles included a guarantee of the editor's independence or freedom from interference by the governors. However, the articles of the operating company, the Irish Times Limited, incorporated a section that stated that the directors set editorial policy consistent with the Trust's objectives, but that the editor was solely responsible to the board for the content of the newspaper.

The articles embedded high-minded journalistic principles but they also embedded Major McDowell. Article 52 guaranteed not only his membership of the Trust for as long as he wished it, but also stated that so long as he was there, he would be chairman. And it was to be thus for a very long time indeed.

McDowell's shadow was akin to the influence exerted by the creator of the organisation that assumed ownership of what became *the Tampa Bay Times*, but Nelson Poynter did so from the grave. How he did so is outlined in the following section.

The *Tampa Bay Times*

Established: 1884 (as *West Hillsborough Times*)
Founders: James Montgomery Baggett, Jason L. Edgar & M. Joel
McMullen
Trust-like ownership: 1978
Benefactor: Nelson Poynter
Current owner: Poynter Institute
Corporate body: Times Publishing Company
Circulation: 300,000 (October 2013)
Group revenue: Undisclosed (private company). Holding company income $US151 million (2012).

The *Tampa Bay Times* (it changed its name from the *St Petersburg Times* in 2012) is an American newspaper in every sense, but in one sense it bears a striking resemblance to *The Guardian* in that it, too, is edited by a ghost. The spirit of Nelson Poynter is as pervasive in the modern-day Florida newspaper as C. P. Scott is in the London daily. It was Poynter who transformed the *St Petersburg Times* from an inconsequential local newspaper into an award-winning bastion of liberal journalism that has been described as "perhaps the finest daily newspaper south of the *Washington Post* and east of the *Dallas Morning News*" (Hau 2006). And like the Scott family, Poynter gave his newspaper away.

In 1912, the marginally profitable newspaper was purchased by a partnership that included Poynter's father Paul. He expanded it into a seven-days-a-week newspaper in the boom years of the 1920s, but almost lost it in the Florida land bust. Paul Poynter had also speculated in real estate and incurred heavy debts when the market collapsed. Nelson Poynter joined the company in 1927 – after the newspaper's revenue fell 50 per cent in a month – on the understanding that he would eventually buy out his father's stock (Pierce 1993, 64–65). He became general manager in 1938, and editor in 1939.

In 1945, with the newspaper on a more solid financial footing, his parents signed an option allowing him to buy all of their shares at $US100 each (the market price). His sister Eleanor objected to the arrangement, in what was to become a pattern of sibling rivalry over ownership of the company. In August 1947, agreement was finally reached whereby Nelson Poynter would be allowed to buy all 500 of the ordinary (voting) shares while other members of the family would gain larger numbers of preference (non-voting) shares. Eleanor became the owner of more than $US200,000 in preferred stock, but had no voting power. In a move that would "plague him for the rest of his life and his heirs afterward", Nelson agreed to sell 200 voting shares for $US20,000 to his sister, to help clear the $US50,000 he had borrowed to pay his parents for the voting stock (*ibid.*, 177–178).

Nelson Poynter was deeply concerned about ownership of the paper, particularly in the event of his death. Although only 44 years old in 1947, he sat down and, in an hour, produced what have since become known as the Poynter Principles, a 15-point document that was to be the yardstick against which prospective owners should be judged. It also could stand alongside the recommendations of the Hutchins Commission, which reported in the same year, as a gold standard for responsible newspaper ownership. The principles were to be used in choosing a purchaser for the *St Petersburg Times*, and absolved his executors from a fiduciary obligation to sell to the highest bidder. They were later reduced to ten points by his successor Eugene Patterson, without losing any of their impact, and began with the admonition: "Operating a newspaper must be the honouring of a sacred trust." The principles are set out in Appendix A.

Poynter became an outspoken opponent of chain ownership of newspapers, which he believed could not do justice to local publications, and developed an unbending belief that ownership and control of a newspaper should be in the hands of one person. This belief was to become a central pillar of governance of the organisation after his death, but while he was alive it drove his desire to resolve the unsatisfactory disposition of shares within his family.

He bought his mother's preference shares (in spite of Eleanor's objections), and in December 1955 indicated a desire to exercise an option to buy back the voting shares from his sister. He offered $US100,000 for the shares he had sold for $US20,000 and then raised it to $US200,000. He took the dispute to court after she refused the second offer and repudiated the option agreement, but he dropped the action because his mother regarded litigation between family members as unseemly. Nevertheless, he believed Eleanor had "shown herself to be incompatible with his standards of ownership" (*ibid.*, 204).

Under Poynter's editorship, the *St Petersburg Times* began to establish a reputation for quality liberal journalism. It was one of the first major newspapers in the south to come out against segregation, and in 1954 supported the Supreme Court's landmark Brown decision against school segregation.[4] He supported Democrat presidential candidates to a state that was largely Republican, and often took editorial stands that were unpopular with conservative elements. His liberal stance, and the ownership of the *Congressional Quarterly* that he and his second wife Henrietta had established in Washington in 1945 as an information service on government affairs for regional newspapers, led to accusations that he was a member of a communist front. The FBI maintained a file on him until his death, and there is speculation that the slurs led to his failure to secure television licences in spite of concerted efforts (Pierce, 255–256). His "leftist" reputation would have been enhanced by his decision in 1956 to give a portion of the profits of the newspaper to staff in an enduring profit-sharing scheme.

The *St Petersburg Times* shared in the developing fortunes of Florida and of the city of St Petersburg, which became such a mecca for retirees that it was nicknamed "God's Waiting Room". In the ten years ending in 1971, the circulation of the newspaper increased by 46 per cent, which was more than nine times the national average. In that year, the *St Petersburg Times* also surpassed the circulation of the *Tampa Tribune* across Tampa Bay and became the second largest newspaper in Florida after the *Miami Herald* (it is now the largest daily in the state). In a period when advertising revenue rose by a national average of 20 per cent, the revenue of *The Times* rose 80 per cent (*ibid.*, 264). Editorially, the newspaper achieved growing national recognition and won its first Pulitzer Prize in 1964 for an investigation of the Florida Turnpike Authority that led to the reorganisation of state auditing and bonding practices.

Poynter had begun to groom lieutenants in both editorial and management, and the death of his wife in 1968 may have precipitated his decision the following year to retire as editor and chief executive to become chairman of the board. He appointed Donald Baldwin as editor and president of the *St Petersburg Times* and the Times Publishing Company. It is evident, however, that Poynter continued to assert considerable control over the newspaper and the two men fell out. Baldwin left abruptly in 1971 and Eugene Patterson, who was to articulate Poynter's legacy after his death, assumed the twin roles in 1972.

In the following year, the good times stopped. Florida and the rest of the United States were hit by the oil shock and recession. The *St Petersburg Times* was forced to lay off 150 staff, reduce benefits and publish smaller newspapers (*ibid.*, 298–300). Perhaps as a reaction to the cutbacks, there was a move by a national trade union to unionise the workforce in 1974. A previous attempt in 1945–1946 had been protracted, and exacted a heavy toll on both the staff and Poynter, who previously had good union relations. Although the company successfully resisted attempts to impose court-determined directives, the newspaper lamented the effect on the workforce (*ibid.*, 168–173). The 1974 attempt by the Newspaper Guild (again unsuccessful) was to have a more significant effect on Poynter and the future of the *St Petersburg Times*.

Poynter had been keeping open the possibility that on his death the newspaper would be left to the staff because, as he told his lawyer: "I've never met my great-grandchildren, and I might not like them" (Hooker 1984). By that, he meant that he would not bequeath the *St Petersburg Times* to people he did not know, and therefore could not trust to follow the standards he had set out in 1947. He regarded the Newspaper Guild's campaign as an immature reaction to the recession, and fearful of its future influence on the newspaper, scrapped any notion of bequeathing the company to employees (*ibid.*, 304). He was also determined that the newspaper would not be consumed by one of the chains that by 1974 owned close to 60 per cent of the nation's newspapers. He set about shoring up his legacy.

The Poynter Fund (named in honour of Nelson Poynter's parents) had been set up in 1953 to offer college scholarships. Poynter's original intention was to turn over the company to this foundation, but the plan ran into problems created by the Tax Reform Act of 1969, which set limits on foundation holdings in profit-making enterprises made after the law was promulgated (Simon 1995, 243–254). Educational institutions (which included America's richly endowed colleges) were, however, to be treated as a special case. Poynter's lawyers determined that he could found an educational institution and give the company to it. In 1975, he established the Modern Media Institute (it changed its name to the Poynter Institute in 1984) to provide programmes in journalism education and appointed the former *St Petersburg Times* editor, Donald Baldwin, as its first director. It was governed by a board of trustees (a majority of them employees of the *St Petersburg Times*) and Poynter was its chairman. It was initially financed by the Poynter Fund, which had been bequeathed the company stock held by Poynter's late wife Henrietta. Two years later, Poynter announced that he had willed his controlling interest in the company to the institute.

His will bequeathed 74 per cent of the stock to the Modern Media Institute (MMI), 11 per cent to his third wife (Marion) and 9 per cent to his children. The children later sold their shares to MMI, and Marion Poynter's shares went to the institute as a bequest. The remaining shares were held by Poynter's sister, and included the 200 voting shares he had failed to buy back. Control of the *St Petersburg Times* and the Times Publishing Company would not, however, pass to the institute. The proxy to vote the common stock would pass from Nelson Poynter to the man he had chosen as his successor (Eugene Patterson), and thereafter to whomsoever Patterson chose as *his* successor. Poynter had enshrined the last of the standards he had conceived in 1947: "A publication is so individualistic in nature that complete control should be concentrated in an individual. Voting stock should never be permitted to scatter." It was an unusual arrangement – a not-for-profit non-taxable educational body owned a for-profit organisation (that paid corporate taxes) over which it could not exert any control. Nevertheless, the Inland Revenue Service (IRS) raised no objections.

On 15 June 1978, Nelson Poynter died from a massive cerebral haemorrhage at the age of 74. Like C. P. Scott, he had championed the cause of highly professional, liberal journalism. Unlike the Scott family, he did not feel driven to an act of generosity by the threat of effective foreclosure through inheritance taxes. Like Major McDowell and the other directors of the Irish Times Limited, he was afraid of the consequences of takeover. However, unlike them, he ensured that his trust-like creation did not begin life burdened by debt. In October 1999, *Editor & Publisher* named him one of the 25 most influential American newspaper people of the 20th century.

In 1975, Poynter had drafted instructions for the reporting of his own death. In a memorandum to his successor Eugene Patterson, he said: "Important in the story is to emphasise there'll be no change whatsoever in the Times Publishing Company as a result of my death. I'll haunt you like the devil if the above is not carried out. Just live up to the Standards of Ownership thereafter" (Hooker 1984, 73).

Poynter was to assume a ghostly presence, but his administrators were not haunted by a failure to carry out his wishes. They did so to the letter, but as was the case with all three organisations examined in this chapter, circumstance and personality created a mixture that tested and changed the makeup of the organisation. The next section examines the process of change that led to more robust governance, and prepared each newspaper to face the current media climate, as Chapter 7 will demonstrate. At the risk of belabouring a metaphor: it was the process that put flesh on the bones of a trustee structure.

Trusteeship over time

The Scott Trust and *The Guardian*

There are two histories of the Scott Trust. One is the story of its unusual legal (and for that read taxation) status, while the other is a chronicle of its relationship with the newspaper it is bound to protect. The histories are like sets of railway tracks – they usually run in parallel but at junctions cross over each other in ways that spell danger for unwary train drivers.

The Inland Revenue, already reluctant to accept the Scott family's policy of reinvestment rather than profit-taking, were suspicious of the Trust from the moment it was mooted. Tax officials regarded this reinvestment as undistributed profits and imposed a surtax but the company successfully challenged the impost (Hammond et al., 245). Yet was it merely tax evasion wrapped in the cloak of C.P. Scott's undoubted respectability? Was it the forerunner of a form of estate management that would gain popularity and potentially deny the Exchequer the windfall of death duties? Was it an assault on the very definition of property rights, because in effect, it created something that might (in spite of its apparent contradiction) be described as proprietary non-ownership? In fact, it was designed to be none of these things. It was a solution to what John Scott considered an overriding obligation to continue publication of *The Guardian* "as heretofore", while removing the threat of tax demands that would have forced its closure.

At the time the Trust was being considered, the *Manchester Guardian* was running at a loss but the *Manchester Evening News* was operating at a profit and one subsidised the other. "Profits" were reinvested and, as heretofore, the company paid no dividend. The Inland Revenue found such cross-subsidy difficult to reconcile, and regarded the continued operation of a loss-maker as a whim. It was minded to value the business (for the purpose of duties on the estate of Edward Scott) on the basis of handsome offers for the *Manchester Evening News* from London newspaper magnates. Contemporary newspaper historians admitted that the rejection of such offers and the practice of cross-subsidy were unbusinesslike, and the country's fiscal system was not adapted to accommodate it (Hammond et al., 245). It was only after protracted and skilful negotiation, led by future Lord Chancellor Gavin Simonds, that the trust could be formed. Central to its creation was not only the removal of profit-taking, but also the vesting of operational power in the editors and managing directors of the respective titles.

It was, however, a somewhat uneasy truce with the tax authorities. Under the arrangement, the trust was allowed to accumulate income from Manchester Guardian and Evening News Limited but following a law change, its counsel believed that this accumulation meant the remaining trustees could be liable for estate duties on the death of John Scott. In 1948, the Trust was reconstituted – a new deed in "the spirit of the original agreement" was drawn up to treat accumulated income in a manner that did not risk incurring estate duties.[5] It was to run until the death of the last survivor of a number of C. P. Scott's great-grandsons, which would take the newspaper well into its second century. The new deed also made another change that was one of those railway junctions that spell hazards for the unwary. The chairman would no longer have the power to appoint or dismiss trustees – the principle of collective authority was established but its full significance would not become apparent for some years. John Scott did not challenge the change, and within months of the new deed being signed he was dead.

The introduction of capital gains tax by the Labour government in 1965 created further potential tax problems, because under British law trusts could not exist in perpetuity and the Scott Trust would be liable on winding up or perhaps in a restructuring akin to the 1948 reconstitution. When it returned to power in 1974, the Labour government foreshadowed an even more imminent threat to the future of the Trust. In the following year, it introduced a capital transfer tax that included a provision for taxing trusts that did not distribute their income. According to the then editor of *The Guardian*, Alastair Hetherington, the formula for calculating the payment implied demands – at 7- 10- or 15-year intervals, starting in 1976 – of £2 million or more from the Scott Trust which "would have crippled the *Guardian*, killing it within a few years". Inland Revenue and Treasury officials proved intractable. Hetherington's account of his meeting with one of HM Commissioners of Inland Revenue is redolent of Arthur Clennam's experiences in the Circumlocution Office of Charles Dickens' *Little Dorrit*. The government agreed to a formula to exempt "newspaper trusts where no benefit could accrue to individuals in any way connected with the settlor" only after direct appeals to the Prime Minister, Harold Wilson, and Chancellor of the Exchequer, Denis Healey, and a threat to draw the parliamentary Opposition into the fray (Hetherington 1981, 356–362).

Among the suggestions by tax officials was the restructuring of the Trust, a process that Hetherington describes as "fraught with legal and financial hazards". The Trust had, in fact, examined options for restructuring, one of which was a scheme devised by its lawyers to transform the trust into "a company limited by guarantee". More than 30 years later, when they felt that they needed to confront the inevitable termination of the Scott Trust, the trustees revisited that option.

In 2008, the trust became The Scott Trust Limited, a company limited by shares, in order to forestall future problems with inheritance tax that might arise when the trust inevitably was wound up under English trust law. There is no time limit on the continued existence of a registered company. The trustees transferred to the company's memorandum and articles of association all of the obligations they had assumed under the trust structure. In spite of the change in legal status, it is appropriate to continue reference to "the Trust" rather than "the company" not only to avoid confusion with the operating entities in Guardian Media Group but also because the principle of trusteeship is unchanged. The Scott Trust continues to style itself as such.

The new structure vested shares in each director (trustee) which could only be transferred to other directors, all of whom were required to sign a Deed of Adherence under which they agreed to uphold the objectives that had been based on those that had bound the Trust. By stating that no shareholder could stay on the register for more than ten years without the approval of 75 per cent of the trustees, the articles signalled that most trustees should not serve for more than a decade. Current exceptions are the *Guardian* editor Alan Rusbridger (joined 1997), the chair Dame Liz Forgan (appointed chair in 2003) and a member of the Scott family who has been a trustee since 1988.

The Trust's tax issues have been illustrations of the difficulties, noted earlier, of fitting unorthodox structures within a commercial system that does not envisage or embrace non-pecuniary ownership and the reinvestment of all profits. Equally, they demonstrate that the passage of time has not entirely eroded the view, expressed by the Inland Revenue in the 1930s, that *The Guardian* was a "quixotic luxury".

John Scott had acted like a proprietor. When W.T. Crozier died in 1944, it was Scott who appointed A. P. Wadsworth as the new editor of *The Guardian*. His fellow trustees had merely endorsed the appointment. There is little in Ayerst's "biography" of *The Guardian* to suggest that the first Scott Trust played anything other than a custodial role in the newspaper. Decision-making involving trustees reflected authority drawn from their other positions within the organisation. Under the 1948 deed (again for tax reasons) only one of the five beneficiaries who established the new trust could serve as a trustee *and* as a director of the company. The chosen exception was John Scott's son Laurence, who was managing director.

Laurence Scott exercised considerable influence over the development of the newspaper, but he did so in his executive capacity and not as a trustee. He was, for example, instrumental in the move to front-page news, the dropping of *Manchester* from the masthead and the shift of *The Guardian* to London. He was able to exercise his authority as managing director without recourse to the Scott Trust because it was bound not to interfere in operational matters. A parallel convention prevented him from interfering in editorial policy – his promotion of front-page news had been a delicate *pas de deux* with A. P. Wadsworth, and when the newspaper's well founded opposition to military intervention in Suez in 1956 cost circulation, he simply advised the newly appointed editor, Alastair Hetherington, not to let the financial figures influence his editorial judgement (Taylor, 25).[6]

Laurence Scott was able to dominate the business activities of the company because the Scott Trust was remarkably quiescent even after the 1948 changes. It had been treated, and had therefore acted, "more like the nominated Legco [legislative council] of a nineteenth-century dependency than as a proprietor" (*ibid.*, 90). In other words, it had simply rubber-stamped what was put before it. For instance, it had not been consulted over investment in a weekly newspaper publishing operation that cost the company a large amount of money (and which ultimately failed) but was simply "informed" of the deal and agreed to Laurence Scott's plan. It was briefed on *The Guardian's* editorial policy on the Common Market (that developed into the European Union) but heard the editor's briefing in silence and asked no questions. It served little purpose beyond that of legal custodian of the shares.

The situation may have emboldened Laurence Scott in 1965 when he began the first of three attempts to merge the company with *The Times* in the face of recurring losses by *The Guardian*. Scott held detailed talks with *The Times* (Taylor Chapter 6, Hetherington Chapter 7) and although he informed the Scott Trust chairman (his cousin Richard Scott) of the idea of a merger, did not formally consult the trustees. Alastair Hetherington, who was not then a member of the Scott Trust (unlike his two immediate predecessors), took it upon himself to brief the trust chairman, who was also Washington correspondent of *The Guardian*. However, Laurence Scott broke off the talks and the Scott Trust was not called upon to consider a merger, as was its right under the trust deed.

However, a year later Laurence Scott resurrected merger plans as a counter-proposal to Thomson's acquisition of *The Times* and the *Sunday Times* from the Astor family, and secured a free hand from the Trust to do as he wished after presenting it with a dismal financial report (Taylor, 87). Amid a series of proposals by Laurence Scott, the most serious was a proposed consortium to make a counter-offer for *The Times* that would be more acceptable to the Monopolies Commission than the Thomson offer. If successful, the consortium would then merge *The Guardian* and *The Times*.

Hetherington, who had been in Israel interviewing its foreign minister, returned to Britain to find the Scott Trust in session to consider Laurence Scott's proposal. The *Guardian* editor was firmly opposed to the proposal, although the trustees had been given to understand he supported it. Hetherington effectively secured a postponement of the trust's deliberations, and in the interregnum presented each trustee with a five-foolscap-page memorandum that predicted that *The Guardian* would be completely subsumed in a merged publication and concluded by saying: "To abandon hope of saving the *Guardian* now would be a shameful decision, for which we should not be forgiven" (Hetherington, 165). As Taylor observes, the Trust "was called upon to do something it had never done before: to make a choice" (Taylor, 90).

Trustees were in a position to do so without fearing for their positions. The 1948 deed meant that trustees did not owe their presence to Laurence Scott's largesse because the chairman had lost the right to appoint them. It was a trust that was heavily weighted in favour of *The Guardian*'s traditions.

The trust imposed strict conditions on any consortium, and Richard Scott asserted his position as trust chairman by attending a board meeting for the first time, and informing directors that the editorial staff of *The Guardian* opposed a merged *Times-Guardian*, which they felt would be *The Times* by another name (Hetherington, 166). It was an adroit move that signalled the trust's attitude to the plan, without directly imposing its will on the board. The board withdrew the proposals.

For the first time, the Trust had asserted itself over the company's senior executive, who was the dominant member of the Scott family. At the next board meeting, Hetherington brought an effective end to the Scott family's executive leadership of the company, by moving a no-confidence motion against Laurence Scott, who became a strictly non-executive board chairman.

A number of ill advised financial decisions had been revealed in the course of the crisis, and one outcome was the future (non-voting) attendance of the Trust chairman at all board meetings. Another was the creation of Manchester Guardian and Evening News Ltd as a parent company with separate operating divisions for *The Guardian*, the *Manchester Evening News* and several other operations. This parent company, after a name change to reflect the move to London, became the present Guardian Media Group in 1993. It was during this reorganisation that Peter (later Sir Peter) Gibbings joined as managing director of the *Guardian* subsidiary. He was to become group chief executive, and then chairman, and was responsible for significant diversification in the company's holdings.

Alastair Hetherington believed the trust had been transformed from "feeble protector" to a body that, along with management in the period

1967–1970, not only kept the newspaper alive but returned it to health (Hetherington, 362).

However, Laurence Scott was not quite done. In 1970, amid poor financial results for the Guardian group and rumours that Lord Thomson wished to rid himself of *The Times*, he once again raised the possibility of a merger. This time it was Peter Gibbings who saw off the threat, by setting out the options and concluding: "They are all much inferior to what we are doing at present" (Taylor, 187). Laurence Scott announced his retirement in 1973 and Gibbings became chairman.

Another retirement reinforced the distancing of the Trust from domination by a member of the Scott family. In 1975, Alastair Hetherington announced his retirement as *Guardian* editor in order to take up a position as Controller, BBC Scotland. Laurence Scott had effectively appointed him editor of *The Guardian* (the Trust simply rubber-stamped the appointment), but a new system was devised in 1973 when Hetherington had been offered another external position that he ultimately declined. A form of Electoral College was mooted to consider a replacement, and it was activated when Hetherington finally vacated the editor's chair two years later. The "college" included trustees, directors, executives, staff and union representatives.[7] The ten-member committee recommended Peter Preston as the new editor (from a list of two dozen candidates) and the Trust confirmed his appointment. The process had taken a week, and was conducted behind closed doors with no public declaration of the names of candidates. When the system was used again in 1984 to find a successor to the editor of the *Manchester Evening News*, the guarantee of confidentiality given to each candidate was breached when local union chapel members were asked for their views on one of the hopefuls. The Trust decided to tread cautiously on union representation in future (Taylor, 202).

By the time Preston retired as editor in 1995 to become editor-in-chief of *The Guardian* and the recently purchased *Observer*, Margaret Thatcher and Rupert Murdoch had broken the power of the newspaper unions in Britain, but the choice of Preston's successor was a demonstration of industrial democracy that in all likelihood was duplicated only by the staff-run *Le Monde* in Paris. *The Guardian*'s journalists were given the right to offer to the Trust their own choice of editor. There were four candidates – each of whom produced a manifesto and who staked his claim on hustings (organised by the National Union of Journalists chapel), that allowed staff to quiz them not only on their aspirations for the newspaper, but also their personal politics (Greenslade, 586). Editorial staff voted in a ballot supervised by the Electoral Reform Society and gave Alan Rusbridger 55 per cent of the vote (138 votes out of a possible 251). His appointment was confirmed by the Trust, which had also favoured him as Preston's replacement.

Laurence Scott had played a crucial role in the transformation of *The Guardian* into a London-based national newspaper, and is credited with inspiring a huge circulation increase as a result (Beavan 1986, 172). However, his attempts to diversify the company had also led to some investments that, generously, can only be described as unfortunate (Hetherington, 166–167; Taylor, 89–92). Changes to structure and senior executives following the 1966 crisis led, however, to both growing prosperity and strategic development that saw increasing diversity in the group's activities. In 1968, it took a 20 per cent stake in Anglia Television, and five years later invested in radio. In 1974, with Peter Gibbings now chairing the board of directors, it began a systematic move into regional newspaper markets, first in the Greater Manchester towns of Rochdale and Stockport, but later in Surrey. In 1982, Gibbings negotiated the purchase of a controlling stake in the first of a series of automotive classified advertising publications that became the group's highly profitable Autotrader division. These strategic moves changed the nature of the group, but also began to have an impact on the Scott Trust.

Alastair Hetherington became chairman of the Trust in 1984, and partly as a result of the changes to the company and partly through personal characteristics, began to increase both the profile of the Trust and his own role as chairman. Taylor, in his obituary of Hetherington (1999), says he "brought a new style to that office as a hands-on and interventionist chairman". The new enterprises allowed Hetherington to become involved without impinging upon the sacred ground of *The Guardian*, although Taylor notes that he gave "critical support" to his successor as editor, Peter Preston.

Hetherington's replacement as chairman, Hugo Young, brought a different style to the role but he too, demonstrated that the day had passed when the Scott Trust acted as little more than a rubber stamp on decisions made by a member of the Scott family. A former trustee, Victor Keegan, reflecting on Young's tenure after the latter's untimely death at the age of 64 in 2003, described the trust's role under his chairmanship as "active monitoring". Young presided over a review of the relationship between the Trust and the board of directors, that led to trustees gaining access to more management information and moved the Trust towards more long-term strategic thinking (Keegan 2003).

In 1992, under Young's chairmanship, the Trust for the first time set out its core purpose – essentially an explanation of its understanding of the phrase "as heretofore" – and articulated its broader understanding of how the group would be run:

- To secure the financial and editorial independence of *The Guardian* in perpetuity: as a quality national newspaper without party affiliation; remaining faithful to its liberal tradition; as a profit-seeking enterprise managed in an efficient and cost-effective manner.
- All other activities should be consistent with the central objective. The company that the Trust owns should be managed to ensure profits are

available to further the central objective; not invest in activities which conflict with the values and principles of the Trust.

- The values and principles of the Trust should be upheld throughout the Group. The Trust declares a subsidiary interest in promoting the causes of freedom in the press and liberal journalism, both in Britain and elsewhere.

At the same time it laid out the trustees' formal responsibilities, which were:

- To secure the Trust's own continuity by renewing its membership and by dealing with threats to its existence
- To monitor the organisation, financial management and overall strategy of the Group, holding the Board accountable for its performance
- To appoint and "in extreme circumstances" to dismiss the editors of *The Guardian*, the *Manchester Evening News* (and *The Observer* after its acquisition in 1993)
- To act as a "court of appeal" in the event of any dispute between the editorial and managerial sides of the operation.

This articulation of the Trust's role confirmed its intention to fulfil an active watchdog role over a group that it expected would sustain *The Guardian* above all else.

Young's watch also showed that the Trust was capable of making poor decisions. The purchase of *The Observer* may be seen as a decision fraught with risk (its reputation had been severely damaged by the scandal in which its previous owner "Tiny" Rowland had attempted to use the newspaper to advance his other business interests) – but the handling of the editorship of *The Observer* (and consequent effects on *The Guardian*) was manifestly unfortunate. The Sunday newspaper had had a rapid turnover in editors, and the dismissal of Andrew Jaspan led to public acrimony. The Trust's handling of *The Observer* editorship continued to stutter, and Jaspan's replacement, Will Hutton, held the editorship for little more than two years, a period in which there were numerous staff changes, before he too, was replaced.

The Sunday newspaper had had four editors in five years, and its circulation had dropped towards 400,000. It took concerted effort by the new editor, Roger Alton, and Alan Rusbridger (who also became executive editor of *The Observer*), to restore circulation. *The Observer*'s convulsions were also taking place against the backdrop of *The Guardian*'s controversial exposing of members of Parliament in the "cash for questions" scandal, ensuing libel actions and accusations of conspiracy against *The Guardian* and Rusbridger. The newspaper was vindicated, but not before its critics took the opportunity to question the Trust's stewardship.

The level of public exposure and criticism was unprecedented for trustees who publicly had done little more than acknowledge the Trust's ownership in the Guardian Media Group (GMG) annual report each year. There was no record of the trustees' names in the annual report, and the Trust was criticised for its lack of transparency. The public focus on *The Guardian* and its owner had a beneficial effect: from 2001 it began to include both a statement of its activities (albeit in a circumspect manner) and a list of its members (and their other associations) in the GMG annual report. In the 2001 report, Young stated:

> The Trust does not manage the business. A trustee from an earlier period once said: "It is largely passive, as long as everything is going right". But when the business is as big as this one has become, the sole shareholder has an important strategic responsibility. It is less than a Prime Minister, overseeing every decision, but more than a monarch, confined to listening and warning.

The Trust clearly agreed with the investment initiatives taken by the GMG board, which marked a significant change in strategy. As the new century began, GMG had divested itself of most of its holdings in regional television and began increasing its investment in regional radio stations. It also moved in 2003 to take full control of the high-earning Auto Trader operation. It bought the Greater Manchester television station Channel M, a move that the present chair of the Trust, Dame Liz Forgan, described in 2009 as "a tremendously bold and interesting endeavour". Over time, it proved less than successful, and after failing to find a buyer after selling the *Manchester Evening News*, GMG in 2010 reduced its programme services before closing the operation in 2012.

In 2003 Hugo Young died, but before doing so he chose his own replacement. The present chair, Dame Liz Forgan (who is a former *Guardian* journalist, BBC and Channel 4 executive and a Scott trustee from 1988 to 1993) admitted when I spoke to her that she was appointed by "an undemocratic method".[8] Young was very ill and eventually it was clear he was dying. He telephoned her and asked her to chair the Trust. Forgan hesitated, unsure that she was qualified to take the role, but Young replied: "I don't have to tell you. I know you know." He had assumed, rightly as it transpired, that the Scott principles were deeply ingrained.

In the same year, Rusbridger and the then chief executive of GMG, Caroline McCall, embarked on an audit to ensure that the Guardian Newspapers business "operates in the spirit of the Scott Trust". In an introduction to *Living Our Values: Social, Ethical and Environmental Audit* published in November 2003 they noted that they "perform a fine balancing act between ensuring we are true to our editorial values while also recognizing the absolute need to be commercially competitive".

The report, which was independently audited, was a ground-breaking piece of self-analysis and self-criticism. A decision to publish the findings was made in advance, and the independent auditor, Richard Evans, was given unrestricted access to information and staff to check the conclusions, which he described as "remarkably thorough and honest".

The audit became an annual exercise covering *The Guardian* and *The Observer* (and their websites) and examining environmental as well as ethical "fitness". In 2010, GMG produced a sustainability strategy that extended to other companies in the group and to its joint ventures. While it does not specifically refer to the legacy of C.P. Scott, it states that the strategy is "(D)riven by our unique ownership structure and values – honesty, integrity, courage, fairness and duty to our readers and communities" – the qualities that he promoted.

Rusbridger clearly became a driving force in the final years of the old century and into the new millennium, but he enjoyed strong backing from the Scott Trust in so doing. It supported him during expensive litigation brought by MPs during the illicit payments scandal, approved the innovative development of the newspaper's website and backed his plan to fly in the face of the trend by serious national broadsheet dailies to adopt a smaller format. Rather than move to a tabloid (or "compact") format that can be produced on existing broadsheet presses, Rusbridger and McCall championed a more expensive option – it required an £80 million investment in new printing presses and a format called the Berliner which was popular in Europe.[9] "The business case was so well made and the arguments so overwhelming, the trust was absolutely all on side", said Forgan at the time of the launch of the new format *Guardian* in September 2005. It was judged the world's best-designed newspaper in the Society for News Design's 2005 and 2007 awards. The format change saw the newspaper's circulation rise from 376,816 in 2005 to 394,913 a year later. However, like most of the British nationals, *The Guardian* subsequently went into circulation decline accentuated by the Global Financial Crisis. In June 2013 its audited circulation stood at 187,000.

Beyond Rusbridger's orbit, the Trust was overseeing significant changes in the GMG's businesses. They are worth detailing because they illustrate the benefits of diversified assets and the ability to pay down debt (both of which are issues that have daunted some newspaper groups) and novel capital raising by an organisation that cannot issue shares to the public.

Considerable value had built up in the Trader Media Group (TMG), which by 2006 was worth £1 billion. In 2007 a 49.9 per cent stake was sold to a private equity company, Apax, in the first of two leveraged buy-out joint ventures. There were a number of benefits for GMG and the Trust. It enabled the group to realise some of the value in TMG, and also reduced the debt it carried on its balance sheet. GMG received £700 million in cash from the part-sale, during which TMG assumed additional debt through a finance restructuring exercise. A similar debt restructuring was followed when GMG and Apax jointly purchased the business-to-business operations of Emap, which became the Top Right Group.

GMG's former director of communications, Chris Wade,[10] told me at the time that finance restructuring meant "GMG is not exposed to this debt as it is ring-fenced within these businesses – which makes the situation very different to that in which other media companies have found themselves, that is, with direct exposure to large amounts of debt." A critic of private equity companies, Peter Morris, described the joint ventures with Apax as "risky", although he concedes that the recessionary fall in the value of GMG's portfolio at the time was modest compared to that of many British companies (Morris 2010). In response to Morris' criticism, Wade stated that GMG's strategy over the years had created "a robust financial position for the group, with immediately realisable resources (in cash and via our investment fund) alongside a valuable portfolio of assets". Inarguably, GMG's balance sheet showed an immediate improvement as a result of the joint ventures, and the Trust was provided with a substantial sum for the investment fund that is a vital buffer against the waning financial fortunes of the traditional print newspaper business.

The most recent history of the Trust has been a dramatic demonstration of its single-minded purpose – the preservation of *The Guardian* in perpetuity, and a signal that GMG management and the trustees have been prepared to sacrifice other parts of the group to achieve it. For many years, the *Manchester Evening News* was the guarantor of *The Guardian*'s survival. The loss-making flagship newspaper would have floundered without the profits that accrued each year from the Manchester afternoon newspaper. Over time, other elements of the group (such as Trader Media) eclipsed the profits that were delivered by the *Manchester Evening News* and other titles that had been added to GMG Regional Media. In 2005, the regional newspaper division had delivered a record £32.6 million profit against the national newspaper division's operating loss of £18.6 million. It was, however, a pinnacle from which the only direction was down. GMG Regional Media began posting lower turnover and lower profit each year. In 2009 the regional group's operating profit was a mere £500,000.

The regional newspaper market was on a downturn before the credit-crunch recession took hold (victim largely of the migration of classified advertising to the Internet) but the rapid decline in Britain's economic fortunes accelerated the process. GMG began cost-cutting that prompted an angry reaction from GMG Regional Media journalists. In an open letter, published as a full-page advertisement in *The Guardian* on 31 March 2009, they were highly critical of GMG senior management and of the Scott Trust.

In an editorial published the same day, *The Guardian* stated that its overriding response to the plight of its regional associates was one of sympathy but noted that the 245 jobs being cut were less than the reductions in other regional groups.[11] The editorial noted that the issue was "of far wider significance than one newspaper group and one unhappy group of beleaguered journalists".

Within GMG management, however, there was a general acceptance that cost reductions in the regional papers were both obvious and inevitable. GMG could not afford to subsidise two potentially loss-making divisions. The *Manchester Evening News* had by this stage become a newspaper that was given away free on the city streets of Manchester several days a week. When we spoke in 2009, Forgan summed up the attitude of the Scott Trustees:

> The problem with regional newspapers is that we are not just looking at the effects of recession. We're looking at systemic change. There would have been a much more difficult decision for the Trust [which endorsed the cost-cutting measures] if anybody could be found to say "if you hang on here for a couple of years you can rebuild a regional journalistic enterprise that has the values that the Manchester enterprise currently has and go on delivering profits – not, perhaps, as high as it did traditionally but it can wash its face". That would have been more difficult but nobody is saying that. The model is broken. They [papers like the *Manchester Evening News*] are hugely important. We have done what we can as a trust in talking to government, raising the public debate about what is happening to regional journalism and the importance of it within democratic structures.... There is no viable plan that we can see that can keep the *Manchester Evening News* in any recognizable form – on paper, distributed as it is – going.

GMG and the Scott Trust did not find a way of resuscitating the newspaper that had provided it with annual blood transfusions. In February 2010, GMG Regional Media was sold to the Trinity Mirror Group for £44.8 million – £7.4 million in cash and £37.4 million in consideration of the cancelling of a long-term printing contract with Trinity Mirror. GMG and the Trust released a statement saying the decision to sell was in light of the strategic objective to secure the future of *The Guardian* in perpetuity. An Early Day Motion, signed by 15 Members of Parliament, was tabled on 23 February viewing the sale with regret.

A similar attitude was taken to GMG Radio, which over a period of 13 years grew to be the third largest radio broadcaster in the United Kingdom. It was, nevertheless, a loss-maker and in 2010 recorded a shortfall of £68.6 million – greater than the losses of *The Guardian* and *The Observer* combined. GMG could not contend with two large loss-makers and, in spite of major restructuring in 2011 that reduced the annual loss, decided to sell the 12 radio companies that made up GMG Radio. The initial asking price was £50 million which attracted the interest of Global Radio but a last-minute rival bid saw Global pay £70 million for the assets in 2012. The announcement to staff by GMG chief executive Andrew Miller was a classic refrain:

> The purpose of GMG's portfolio is to support and develop our journalism. This means that we are sometimes faced with the difficult choice between retaining a business that has performed well, as with this case, or deciding that a disposal at an attractive value represents the best way of discharging our responsibilities.

Disposal of significant assets was necessary as GMG and the Trust confronted mounting losses in the two national newspapers. In August 2009, GMG reported annual losses of £89.8 million in Guardian News & Media (the national newspaper division) and as a result the Sunday newspaper's future looked uncertain. *The Observer* does not enjoy the protection afforded to *The Guardian* and, although both endured budget cuts, the 218-year-old Sunday faced the possibility of closure or redevelopment as a mid-week magazine. The National Union of Journalists and the industry publication, the *Press Gazette*, campaigned strongly against closure of the world's oldest Sunday newspaper, and under pressure from both the public and its own journalists, GMG affirmed its commitment to *The Observer* and announced a relaunch (still as a newspaper), that took place the following February. Forgan issued a statement saying the Trust "fully supports the company's thorough and clear-eyed review of its operations". It was the forerunner of a sweeping review that is discussed in Chapter 7.

The Irish Times Trust

The Irish Times Trust was born in buoyant times, and its bankers, its employees and the readers of its newspaper had high expectations. Its "governors", as they were styled, were drawn from academia, the business community and (with some foresight) the trade union movement in both the south and the north. An experiment with the appointment of an *Irish Times* journalist to the Trust was short-lived, and subsequently (unlike the Scott Trust) none of the newspaper's journalists was appointed. Also in contrast to the Scott trust, the editor of the *Irish Times* was not to be a Trust member, but instead, would sit by right on the operating company's board of directors. There was little doubt that Major McDowell was more than first among equals.

Fortunes changed rapidly in the 1970s as the twin effects of the oil shock and the Yom Kippur War sent the Irish economy into recession, and took the newspaper into losses. The company also lost the experienced leadership of Douglas Gageby, who, according to O'Brien (pp. 206–207), resigned as editor amid misgivings among staff about the directors' financial reward and his own apparent embarrassment about the windfall sum he received for his shares in the company. His replacement, Fergus Pyle, was a good journalist, but was unable to maintain the pace of development and innovation that had characterised Gageby's editorship. Newsprint budgets were cut, which resulted in newspapers with fewer pages and a reduced type size to accommodate more content per page (this action, then as now, is fraught with risk as the audience is sensitive to the "readability" of the newspaper), the total staff was cut by approximately 100 and there were three price rises in 18 months. Circulation that had stood at 69,000 when the trust was created in 1974 fell to 61,800 three years later (Brady, 44; Oram, 323). Pyle agreed to stand down, and Gageby, in what was described by staff as "the second coming" (O'Brien, 220), returned as editor in 1977. He said he would take the role for only two years, but stayed for a decade. The company's bankers, who had become extremely worried about the state of their significant investment, wholeheartedly supported his return, according to his obituary in *The Times* (London) in July 2004. Losses incurred in the first years of the Trust had seen the bank loan rise from £1.6 million to £2.5 million (Oram, 325).

Editorially, Gageby was determined that the newspaper would lose its reputation as a Protestant newspaper, and become known as a liberal newspaper serving all of Ireland. A strong supporter of a unified Ireland, he argued for a more secular state. His political views were often at odds with those held by the Trust chair, Major McDowell, who confided to the British Ambassador, Sir Andrew Gilchrist, that he could not persuade Gageby to take a more pro-British line (O'Brien, 188). David McConnell, who retired as chair of the Irish Times Trust in 2010,[12] told me the political climate of the time was "unhappy". He recalls the newspaper in the 1970s as appealing to the Protestant community in Ireland and Ulster, as well as "the intellectual community and people, broadly speaking, who looked outward rather than inward". The dominant Sinn Fein ("ourselves alone") political philosophy of the time was introspective.

McDowell and Gageby, during the latter's first term as editor, had developed a relationship that reflected what Brady described as the "Dawson Formula", under which the editor of *The Times* (London), Geoffrey Dawson, and the proprietor, Lord Northcliffe, had agreed that manager and editor would be separate authorities with their own responsibilities and reporting separately to the board. When the Irish Times Trust was established, the formula was embedded in company articles and it is evident that McDowell, in spite of his pervasive presence in the company, fully honoured it throughout Gageby's second term and that of his successor, Conor Brady (Brady, 204–205).

The company's financial position improved, and after the losses incurred in the first three years of the Trust, it returned a modest profit. In the early 1980s, the Trust ceased to publish accounts, but it is evident that some years were not profitable. Certainly, there was not enough money to allow the Trust to redeem the preference shares held by the bank, until the company received a £IR2.7 million windfall with the 1984 flotation of the Reuters news agency in which it was a part owner. The Trust was presented with a quandary – it wanted to remove the bank from company ownership, but it also needed to replace the *Irish Times'* antiquated printing press. It put £IR1 million towards the £IR3 million purchase of a new press and borrowed a further £IR1 million from the bank and £IR500,000 from the Industrial Credit Corporation. The remainder came from a grant from Ireland's Industrial Development Authority. It then spent the remaining £IR1.7 million from the Reuters float to redeem the preference shares held by the Bank of Ireland. Without the Reuters payout, it is doubtful that the company would have been able to buy back the shares (O'Brien, 227). It could not borrow to fund the repurchase, and until the advent of editorial and advertising improvements made possible by the new press, was not generating sufficient profit to allow it to do so.

Gageby had the critical support of the bank and a level of access to the company budget that Pyle had never enjoyed. He had undisputed control of the editorial department, and with McDowell and the deputy chief executive, formed a triumvirate that ran the company.

By the time Gageby retired in 1986, the *Irish Times* was well on the way to financial health and had earned itself a reputation for the quality of its journalism, which included revelations that two Irish political journalists had their telephones bugged by the Garda Síochána (the Irish Police Service) on orders from the government of Charles Haughey,[13] and for its liberal stance on constitutional prohibitions on abortion and divorce.

The Trust had been stung by its error in appointing Fergus Pyle as editor, and had agreed a process with the NUJ chapel at the *Irish Times* for the appointment of Gageby's successor. Candidates from inside and outside the newspaper were invited to apply for the position, and a short list was drawn up by the board of directors of the Irish Times Limited – which was dominated by McDowell. The short list was then shown to the chapel's representatives who had a right of veto or what Brady calls "a negative sieve" (p. 58). There were only two names on the list, and both were acceptable to the staff. Conor Brady was appointed and would hold the position for 16 years. He was the first Catholic editor of the *Irish Times*.

Under his editorship, the *Irish Times* published a number of stories that continue to resonate through Irish society. It launched an investigation that exposed the Catholic Bishop of Galway, Dr Eamonn Casey, as the father of a child he continued to support, led a campaign against the refusal to allow a 14-year-old victim of sexual abuse to leave Ireland to obtain an abortion and exposed corruption among local councillors. However, the newspaper's attempts to expose corruption in national politics would not reach its peak until after Brady's retirement.

Brady's autobiography provides a valuable insight (Chapter 11: *Working with the Trust*) into the operations of the otherwise "closed" Irish Times Trust and its relationship with the operating company's board. He reveals that his editorial policies (particularly those relating to Northern Ireland) and editorial treatment of issues such as sexual abuse cases and foreign coverage were the subject of vigorous debate among the governors in the portion of proceedings that he would be asked to attend. There were "vigorous arguments", but at the end he was always told to "carry on" as he thought best. He maintains that McDowell was "unfailingly protective" of the editor's independence, refusing to allow discussion of editorial policies at the Irish Times Limited board meetings because he did not believe the editor should be put in a position of defending himself in the presence of subordinates (fellow executive directors). However, he is critical of what he saw as McDowell's increasing domination of the Trust and the company, saying "his Achilles heel was his absolutism" (*ibid.*, 115–117).

Throughout this period, in accordance with McDowell's wishes, the Trust operated entirely out of the public eye. It issued no documentation or statements, and did not even have a mechanism whereby it could meet with staff that were becoming increasingly disturbed by its obscure practices.

A tipping point was reached in 1994, when McDowell appointed his daughter Karen Erwin as deputy managing director.[14] Although she was a distinguished lawyer and able executive, her father's unilateral action was seen as nepotistic (O'Brien, 253). The appointment was opposed by at least one Governor and by Brady. It strained the relationship between McDowell and the managing director, Louis O'Neill. *Irish Times* staff objected to the appointment as "a blatant exercise in nepotism". In the same year, the articles of the operating company were amended to ensure that no board resolution could pass without the approval of the chairman (McDowell) and another trust governor or two governors. (O'Brien, 260).[15]

A system for placing future senior appointments under scrutiny was adopted in 1995, but McDowell was determined that his daughter's appointment would stand. To many it seems that McDowell, having secured his own hold on the paper through the Trust, was creating a dynasty. In 1948, the Scott Trust had moved against familial succession when it rewrote its deed, but there had been no premonition that such a provision would be required in the Irish Times Trust. However, events were set in train that determined it would not be necessary.

In March 1997, amid increasingly vocal criticism, McDowell stepped down as chief executive (although he remained chairman of the operating company) and was succeeded by O'Neill. Two years later, he stood down as chairman of the Irish Times Limited but remained chairman of the Trust. Karen Erwin was given responsibility for corporate governance and all legal matters. In the wake of that move, O'Neill retired as chief executive and precipitated what could have developed into a crisis over the major's daughter.

It did not eventuate. Karen Erwin did not apply for the chief executive's position and avoided both crisis and the need to subject herself to the vetting process instituted in 1995.

A modernisation programme costing £IR100 million (which included the cost of a new press and computer systems) had been started under O'Neill, and was continued by his successor, Nick Chapman. The company had entered into undertakings to "buy out" industrial agreements to facilitate "new technology" (direct editorial computer input and computerised production) as part of the programme. At the time the "Celtic Tiger" was rampant, and a consultant's report predicted that Ireland's burgeoning economy would continue unabated (O'Brien, 258–259). The board and the Trust had no hesitation in financing the modernisation by depleting the cash reserves that had been built up throughout the 1990s. In the economic aftermath of the terrorist attacks of 9/11, in which advertising revenue throughout the Western world plummeted, the Irish Times had no reserves to sustain it. The commissioning of the new press had been delayed, and the severance agreements with production staff had proven costly. Combined with an annual loss of £IR2.35 million in 2001 (after a profit of more than £IR7 million the previous year), the development costs left the company with a deficit of £IR21.7 million (*ibid.*, 264). A total of 250 staff (112 from the editorial department) left the company.

McDowell, who had become an eccentric figure almost Edwardian in appearance, was the focus of blame for the reversal of fortunes, and on 1 December 2001 resigned from the board of the *Irish Times* and from the Irish Times Trust. David McConnell became chairman. It was an appointment that "came out of the blue", and McConnell does not know by what process the decision was made. He does, however, have a more benign view of "the major" than some critics. When I spoke to McConnell in Dublin he said too much blame was placed on McDowell:

> He ended up being the man who fell on his sword. In 2001 the *Irish Times* was going bust. We had 730 employees and we lost a third of them by voluntary severance schemes. [At that point] I am absolutely certain that the *Irish Times* would have been bought by somebody else if it hadn't been protected by the Trust. We had to borrow £IR20 million from the bank to pay for those severance schemes. Can you imagine it? Here is a quality newspaper with a per capita circulation that exceeded the combined broadsheets of the United Kingdom – 120,000 copies.[16] This great newspaper was going bust and, had it been an ordinary institution, the shareholders would have wanted something out of it and there would undoubtedly be people wanting to buy and the board would have sold. However, under the terms of the Trust it could not be done ... Both inside and outside the paper everyone focused on Tom McDowell. The Trust was

blamed and Tom McDowell was personally blamed... Yet, up to this crisis, the *Irish Times* had been phenomenally successful.

McConnell points out that there had been no dissenters among trustees, directors, or executives over the modernisation programme, and no one had been able to anticipate the financial downturn that followed 9/11. He does, however, describe a governance structure that was cumbersome and in need of rejuvenation. When he joined in 2000 he was the only trustee under the age of 60 and some were nearly 90. All members of the Trust were members of the board, and over the years, more and more senior executives became directors. It was, therefore, a very large board but, apart from the governors, there were no outside non-executive directors. "Essentially," McConnell says, "the Trust met the senior management." The Trust retained its voting supremacy, but business was conducted by consensus.

A working party composed entirely of commercial executives (from which Brady was excluded) painted a damning picture of the company's financial position and its governance, and McConnell had to preside over a fundamental reorganisation that he describes as "a terrific challenge". The change that followed in 2002 altered the balance of power.

The Trust's domination of the operating company's board ended, and the Irish Times Limited articles were altered to provide that:

- The number of governors eligible to sit on the board would be reduced to three (a minority)
- Non-executive outside directors could be elected
- The governors' previous 5:1 voting power was withdrawn, and all directors would have a single vote
- The three governor directors would have an effective veto (50 per cent plus one vote) in the following circumstances:

  - The board was contemplating a "significant policy" that was inconsistent with the objectives, principles and standards that had been laid down for the *Irish Times* when the Trust was established; and
  - Two senior legal counsel (one representing the board and one representing the Trust) agreed the matter was a "significant policy". In the event of the lawyers disagreeing, counsel for the Trust would prevail.

There were also significant changes in personnel. The managing director Nick Chapman resigned in November 2001, and settled High Court proceedings he had taken to block the company from removing him. Brady retired as editor a year later.

In many ways, the changes brought the *Irish Times* into line with the disposition of power that had been determined between the Scott Trust and the GMG. And as with the Scott Trust, it had taken a crisis to wrest control from "the founders". Under the new arrangement, each Trust had oversight as owner and custodian, but the operations of the company were left in the hands of professionals and people with corporate board expertise. There were, however, some differences between the Scott Trust and the Irish Times Trust. *The Guardian*'s staff have long been represented on the Scott Trust, but when the staff of the *Irish Times* attempted to gain representation on the Irish Times Trust during the restructuring, McConnell would not agree to have members of the staff sitting over the editor and managing director. The trust did, however, appoint members with links to national union organisations.

McConnell (a slight, bespectacled university professor with an engaging manner and an international reputation as a geneticist) did not try to emulate the major's style, instead applying a more reserved and collegial approach to preserving the newspaper's independence, and ensuring it could endure the financial crisis while "epitomising the values of the newspaper".

Brady describes the changes to the company, which had an inordinately large cost base (due in part to a failure to engage with wage issues) and over-staffing across all departments, as "overdue". Nevertheless, he says the events of 2001–2002 were a shock to a newspaper that had experienced plain sailing for 25 years, and circulation that had been rising for 40 years (Brady, 262–265).

The restructuring, together with a return to economic growth in the republic, led to a return to profit for the group. The downturn had, however, exposed a fundamental weakness in the company's activities. Although it had invested in other businesses (notably a chain of community newspapers, a Metro Dublin freesheet in 2005 and, a year later, the largest real estate website called MyHome.ie[17]), all of the enterprises were susceptible to catching the same cold in an advertising downturn. These investments stood in contrast to those of the GMG, which moved to diversify away from a reliance on UK newspaper advertising, and in time would have a detrimental effect on the company's performance. In turn, this would have an adverse impact on the resources that the *Irish Times* was able to employ.

The Poynter Institute and the *St Petersburg (Tampa Bay) Times*

Nelson Poynter intended the MMI to become the owner of the *St Petersburg Times*, and at his death its nine-member board of trustees was composed largely of present or former executives of the newspaper. Poynter's wife, Marion, was also a member until her retirement in 1991, and the only "outsiders" were academics from Indiana and Yale universities. All trustees were well aware of Poynter's wishes.

Poynter had already secured control of the newspaper in the hands of one person, a move that was not (and has never been) challenged by the institute's trustees after his death. As the nominated successor, Eugene

Patterson became chief executive of the Times Publishing Company as well as editor and president of the *St Petersburg Times*. Under the terms of Poynter's will, the institute became the owner of shares in the Times Publishing Company, but the voting rights on those shares were vested in Patterson and in his successors as company president. Hence, the trustees could advise Patterson but they could not force his hand on the operations of the company or the editorial policies of the newspaper. In any event, as an educational institution it had to maintain its distance in order to sustain its non-taxable status, while benefiting significantly from annual "dividends" from the tax-paying company.

Patterson later acknowledged the responsibility that accompanied the placing of so much power in his hands. In an article in the *St Petersburg Times* in 1998, he recounted a conversation between Poynter and his lawyer on the issue:

> What you lawyers can never understand... is that you can't close every circle. If you're going to accomplish anything in this life, at some point you're going to have to trust somebody. I trust Gene Patterson.

Patterson went on to say that Poynter knew he could not betray that kind of trust, and added that no chief executive of the company would be able to withstand opposition from the newspaper's staff if he attempted to sell Poynter's legacy.

The MMI received annual sums that allowed it to grow exponentially, and to begin to build an investment fund of its own that would augment the amount it received each year from the company's profits. By 1984, when the name was changed to the Poynter Institute, the number of students who attended the institute's courses had risen from 333 to 504, and the board of trustees had been joined by an advisory board which comprised academics and senior journalists from across the United States, that would meet annually to assess and comment on the institute's performance and long-term strategies. It has gone from strength to strength, and is recognised internationally.

Under Patterson's command, the company augmented its Washington-based current affairs magazine by buying a business magazine, *Florida Trend*, which was to become the first of a series of related titles. The *St Petersburg Times* also won a further Pulitzer Prize for a series on the Church of Scientology, an organisation with which the newspaper would have an acrimonious relationship that would persist into the 21st century.

It fell to Patterson and his successor, Andrew Barnes, to deal with a flaw in Poynter's legacy, and the weakness that we have already seen in other family-owned companies – family rivalry that focused on the two hundred voting shares had been left in the hands of Eleanor Poynter, and more significantly, the daughters to whom she bequeathed them. Patterson had made at least one attempt (in 1979) to buy the shares on the terms offered in 1972 but had been rebuffed (Pierce, 370). The offer would have avoided estate duty, but when Eleanor died in 1987 her two daughters were taxed on the legacy. They instructed a New York media broker to sell the shares, which were first offered to the company for $US120 million. Patterson refused to meet the price. He mistakenly believed a further approach would be made, and took no action, which the broker interpreted as lack of interest. The broker found a willing buyer in a man "with one foot in the Texas oil fields and another in cutthroat finance" (*ibid.*, 371).

Robert Muse Bass paid $US28 million for the shares, and entered into a partnership with the daughters that guaranteed them 40 per cent of any gains made on the venture. Bass had a reputation for takeovers and company break-ups, and could not be considered a passive investor. The arrangement was signed in 1988, a month before Patterson retired as chairman and was replaced by Barnes, and started a two-year battle for control of the company. Patterson had nominated Barnes as his successor, after suffering a heart attack in 1984, and appointed him editor and president of the newspaper.

In January 1990, Bass made a bid for all the outstanding stock, through an entity called Poynter-Jamison Ventures Limited Partnership (Jamison was the married name of Nelson Poynter's sister), after failing with a ploy that would have provided him with a much larger share of dividends than Eleanor had received. He offered $US270 million for the stock, $US234 million of which would go to the Poynter Institute. The offer presented Barnes and the trustees with a quandary. On the one hand, such a sum could be invested at a much higher return than the *St Petersburg Times* was generating and suggested that the trustees would best serve their fiduciary duties towards the institute by supporting the sale. On the other hand, selling the company would almost certainly jeopardise the future of the *St Petersburg Times* and the values that had underpinned its publication. Barnes, supported by the trustees, rejected the offer and stated that he was not prepared to "dismantle Nelson Poynter's legacy" (*ibid.*, 373).

Bass had anticipated the rejection, and a week later filed a legal suit based on his initial gambit, which through a restructuring of the share capital would increase his ownership from 5.7 per cent to 40 per cent. The plan involved effective cancellation of preference shares, leaving only the voting shares, of which Bass held 200 (40 per cent). Bass claimed that the primary purpose of the Poynter Institute was not as an educational institution, but to perpetuate absolute control of the Times Publishing Company by management with no oversight. He had, however, singularly underestimated the reaction from the staff, the community and the political establishment. Liberal lawyers offered their services to the newspaper, and the Florida Attorney General, Bob Butterworth, sponsored a bill in the state legislature to protect owners of closely held companies from hostile takeovers. The staff paid for full-page advertisements opposing Bass's move, and a campaign waged through the newspaper's editorial columns gained widespread community support.

In response, Bass's partner, David Bonderman, told the rival *Tampa Tribune* that "the only newspapers that are run by a self-selected group of people that think they have no economic responsibility to anyone are *Pravda* and the *St Petersburg Times*" (Stern 1990, 8–13).

In August 1990, after months of legal arguments, both parties abruptly announced an out-of-court settlement. The *New York Times* reported that the newspaper had agreed to buy the shares held by the "unwelcome investors", but that details of the complex agreement were not disclosed. It quoted analysts as estimating the price paid would be between $US100 million and $US150 million. The agreement allowed for the shares to be acquired in two tranches over three years, with the bulk, according to the *New York Times*, being acquired immediately. The arrangement required the company to incur substantial debt, and to issue a long-term subordinated debenture to the Poynter Institute for preferred shares in order to remove that class from its register. In spite of the cost, Barnes told the *New York Times*: "I just feel wonderful today." He said the debt would not interfere with the newspaper's operations, staff or growth (Jones 1990).

However, the *St Petersburg Times* had yet to finally remove impediments to securing in perpetuity the Poynter legacy.

Poynter's will contained a contingency clause that would be activated if the IRS declined to approve the plan to place ownership in the hands of the Poynter Institute. In this event, the proceeds from the inevitable sale of the Times Publishing Company (aside from the bequests to family members) would pass to Yale University. The IRS approved the Poynter scheme, and Yale received no more than the $US1.5 million Nelson Poynter had given while alive. During the Bass case, it had been estimated that the Times Publishing Company was valued in the region of $US500 million. In January 1991, Yale University asked for the company's financial records because, it stated, it "had an obligation" to determine whether it should challenge the Poynter Institute's tax-exempt status. A successful challenge would yield a handsome windfall for the Ivy League university. Barnes vowed to fight any attempt by Yale to gain ownership, and once again, the *St Petersburg Times* expressed its opposition with indignant invective. On 30 April *the New York Times* carried an Associated Press report containing a statement by Yale's general counsel, Dorothy Robinson: "After careful consideration of this very complex matter, we are persuaded that Nelson Poynter's primary intent in structuring his affairs as he did should not be challenged by the university." Robinson later disclosed that she had been alerted to the possibility of a challenge by Robert Bass's lawyer (Pierce, 377).

The cost of securing ownership and the potential challenge to the Poynter Institute's tax status were instructive, and in the following decades both the institute and the Times Publishing Company would be scrupulous, perhaps to the point of paranoia, in ensuring that such threats would not recur. The manner in which this manifests itself is discussed in Chapter 7.

The newspaper flourished editorially under Patterson and Barnes, securing further national recognition with Pulitzer Prizes in 1980, 1985, 1991, 1995 and 1998. *Time* magazine named the *St Petersburg Times* among the top ten newspapers in the United States in 1984 and repeated the exercise in 1997.

It developed a reputation for its innovative newsroom. In 1977, it took the then-unusual step of appointing a young academic, Roy Peter Clark (currently the Poynter Institute's senior scholar, vice president, and a member of its board of trustees), as the newspaper's writing coach. It was also an innovator in the use of computer-assisted reporting and an early adopter of digital technology (it was a pioneer in electronic archiving). It offered its first Internet service in 1995.

The *St Petersburg Times* also progressively expanded its circulation area, a strategy that Barnes said would have been impossible "if an owner had been demanding immediate profits". However, an attempt to establish a regional edition under a separate masthead, the *Manatee Times*, was abandoned in 1977 after battling unsuccessfully to attract local advertising for four years. In 1999 Barnes also credited the ownership structure with enabling the editorial department to hire sufficient staff and maintain the level of pagination that it needed to discharge its obligations to the community.

The *St Petersburg Times* was to be nurtured under the terms of Poynter's bequest, but the same protection did not extend to the *Evening Independent*, the city's afternoon newspaper that had been bought by Poynter in 1962. Like most evening titles in America, the *Independent* struggled as television began to dominate the market. It survived the transfer of ownership to the institute and the removal by Patterson and Barnes of its long-serving editor, but was closed by Barnes in 1986. The demise of the *Independent* was a signal that the Poynter Institute, like the Scott and Irish Times Trusts, was bound to protect only one title – in this case the *St Petersburg Times*, and business decisions made by the Times Publishing Company during the recent recession have reinforced that reality. Its financial responsibilities have of course, been to both the company and the institute but the separation of entities has always been clear in order to preserve the institute's 501(c)3 tax-exempt status.

Control of the commercial assets owned by the Poynter Institute has been equally clear and stable. Unlike the Scott and Irish Times Trusts, there has been neither dispute over the powers of trustees, nor structural change to overcome unequal distribution or inadequate exercise of power. Poynter's desire to cede control to a single individual has never been challenged, by either the Poynter board of trustees or the directors of the Times Publishing Company. All three successors to Nelson Poynter – Patterson, Barnes and the present incumbent, Paul Tash (who assumed the CEO role in 2004 after four years as Barnes' deputy) – have had undisputed control of the company (on the institute's behalf) and a pivotal role in the affairs of the institute itself, each serving as chairman of the board of trustees. Each has been at pains to publicly assert his anointed role and his right to choose his own successor. Each has reiterated a key phrase in the third of Poynter's Principles: "a newspaper is so individualistic in nature that complete control, and thereby responsibility, should be concentrated in an individual" and periodically reminded readers of the newspaper's ownership and control.[18]

The *St Petersburg Times, Guardian* and *Irish Times* each experienced change for different reasons, and each had different solutions to the problems they confronted. It was an evolutionary process that left each of them better prepared to meet the challenges of an industry in crisis.

7
Modern White Knights

The three newspaper groups studied in the previous chapter now have mature and stable "trustee" governance structures. Each has faced challenges, and made changes to achieve either stability or commercial competitiveness. All have nonetheless remained remarkably true to the vision of the men who saw these three publications as bastions of liberal journalism. By "keeping the faith", *The Guardian*, the *Irish Times* and the *Tampa Bay Times* continue to enjoy journalistic reputations that set them apart from many of the other newspapers in their respective countries.

However, there has been a significant break from the past, inasmuch as trust chairmen no longer exercise autocratic power because the vague notions of governance expressed in founding documents can no longer be exploited. They have been replaced by much more explicit obligations and limitations. This chapter explains how those changes have been put into effect, and how in some cases it has led to a welcome increase in the level of company transparency – an aspect of governance in which the Scott Trust and the Guardian Media Group provide an exemplary lead.

In particular, it shows how the custodians of these newspapers have faced up to the same considerable challenges as their conventionally owned contemporaries – survival against the twin assaults of recession and fundamental media market change. Their responses to these challenges have tested the effectiveness of their current structures to fulfil their obligation to protect the journalism for which their publications stand. Trustees have demonstrated a determination to ensure that editors have a strong voice in how the organisation is run. This stands in contrast to attitudes in many media groups, but as the chapter reveals, there are both differences and similarities in the operation of trustee and profit-driven listed enterprises.

The Scott Trust

The Scott Trust has been operating as a private company for five and a half years at the time of writing, with no discernable change in either the way it perceives its role or in its activities. It remains a trust in every sense except the strict legal definition. It continues to adopt a long-term approach to group strategy, and importantly, has not been panicked by poor trading conditions that have beset the Guardian Media Group (GMG) (and its contemporaries) since the recession began.

The primary purpose in converting the trust to a private company was the elimination of potential inheritance tax liability on the trustees when the Trust reached the end of its "life" in 15–20 years. While the present tax regime does not impose inheritance tax on the Trust, trustees and their legal advisors were mindful of the tenuous nature of tax status, and of the ability of a future Chancellor of the Exchequer to promote a law change that could result in tax bills of millions of pounds. The legal advice given to the Trust was that the most stable, most clearly protected and most robust framework was not a trust deed but registration as a limited company.[1] It also meant that the trustees, who were legally directors of the company, could be indemnified against financial liability. However, a by-product of the change has been the clear articulation of duties and responsibilities that were only implied in the Trust deed, and the enshrining of four provisions in the Articles of Association that cannot be altered (even by a unanimous vote). These provisions are:

- Article 58 (Powers of directors): requires directors (the trustees) to act in a manner that is consistent with securing and preserving the financial position and editorial independence of *The Guardian* in perpetuity, having regard to how that has been pursued "heretofore"; and to promote the causes of freedom of the press and liberal journalism.
- Article 90 (Reserved Board matters): requires the written approval of at least 75 per cent of directors for, among other things, the appointment or removal of the editor-in-chief of *The Guardian*; decisions relating to the disposal of the whole or significant parts of *The Guardian*; altering the memorandum or articles of association; and winding up the company or merging with another firm.
- Article 97 (Dividends and distributions): prevents the payment of any dividends or distributions that provide a financial benefit to shareholders (who must be trustees).
- Article 111 (winding up): requires any surplus remaining after winding up the company to be passed to another company, trust or charity with similar objectives to the Scott Trust; and prevents any distribution of funds to shareholders.

We have seen how past chairmen of the Scott Trust exercised considerable power because governance was understood or even unstated. The current chair, Dame Liz Forgan, told me the new legal entity will prevent anyone from "picking up the Trust and running away with it".

The 11-member Scott Trust board comprises four members who have direct associations with GMG: political economist and *Guardian* columnist Will Hutton, *Observer* Business editor Heather Stewart, editor-in-chief Alan Rusbridger and GMG chief executive Andrew Miller. The GMG company secretary, Philip Tranter, also appears on the board list but is not classed as a board member. As mentioned previously, Trust chair Forgan is a former *Guardian* journalist and another Trust member, Emily Bell of Columbia University's Graduate School of Journalism, was previously the group's director of digital content. The remaining trustees are a former master of Balliol College, economist Andrew Graham; a Law Professor at King's College London, Maleiha Malik; Rothschild executive vice-chairman, Anthony Salz; television documentary maker, Alexander Graham; and a member of the Scott family, Jonathan Scott.

Two Trust board members (the editor-in-chief and the chief executive) also sit on the GMG board of directors. Traditionally, the editor of *The Guardian* did not sit on the group board, but Forgan campaigned for Rusbridger's appointment when she was a non-executive director of GMG. Rusbridger became a director in 1999, and plays an active part in the management of the organisation. Forgan told me:

> The editor of the *Guardian* never used to be on the group board and I fought very hard for that to happen. I don't know whether he curses me for having to go to all the meetings but I still think it was absolutely the right thing to do because, to the extent that there is a kind of tension between the endless appetite and needs of the *Guardian* for resources (and strategic appetite for development) and the ability of the commercial board to service that – in other words, the competition for resources. I thought that so long as the editor did not hear the discussions at the group board about the getting and spending of the total resources of the company, he would always be a sort of remittance child: Outside – given his subvention and told to get on with it, and with no part to play. The board would not understand the editorial ambitions and I just think it's good for journalists to be in the middle of commercial realities to prevent them from being infantile. Otherwise people waste effort fighting for things that can't be delivered.

In the past, the chairman of the group board was a member of the Trust and the chairman of the Trust had tended to be a non-executive director of the company. Forgan and a previous GMG chairman, Paul Myners (who resigned in 2008 to become Financial Services Secretary in the Labour government) altered that arrangement, and the respective chairs now have a standing invitation to attend and speak at any meeting of the other board but do not have voting rights. The purpose of the change was to put some distance between the two boards without diminishing the level of knowledge to which each was privy. However, Forgan acknowledges that should she voice "a principled objection" to a planned course of action by the commercial board, it would be unlikely to proceed, and the GMG chair would in all likelihood forestall a Trust action that was not in the interests of the financial well-being of the group.

The Trust's relationship with the editor of *The Guardian* also has changed. His editorial independence is undiminished, and also unchanged is the Trust's right to appoint (and theoretically dismiss, although Forgan describes this as "a nuclear weapon" or option of last resort) the editors of both *The Guardian* and *The Observer*. However, the Trust has introduced what Forgan describes as "a framework of accountability" to ensure that the editor continues to reflect the values that the Trust is required to uphold. Once a year, the editor reports to the Trust on progress made over the past 12 months. He then presents the plan he proposes to pursue in the following year. Forgan told me she had been worried that there was no formal system of accountability:

> What this [framework] actually does is make a moment where we can look each other in the eye. It makes a safe framework because it is set by the editor and not by the Trust. I think that if the Trust said "These are your objectives for the year" or "This is how we think you've done against them" we would impinge on the independence of the editor. We are getting the editor to set his own objectives and give his own assessment of them. Giving the Trust the ability to discuss them with him is as near as we can get.

The Trust does not issue any appraisals of the editorial performance of *The Guardian*. Forgan does not believe it is the place of the Scott Trust chair to comment on the performance of the editor, and regards a formal public review of the newspaper as "a step too far". She does, however, in the GMG annual report commend examples of outstanding journalism. For instance, in the 2012 report she described *The Guardian's* work on the Wikileaks data and the phone hacking scandal as "a triumphant demonstration of its founding values". However, when Rusbridger presents his annual update before the trustees there is some discussion before they simply say "Thank you". Rusbridger is said to be open in his relationship with other trustees and with Forgan, demonstrating a willingness to discuss editorial matters while not ceding his authority.

Rusbridger does not enjoy budgetary carte blanche. He must argue year by year for the sum he believes necessary for the national newspaper division to discharge its editorial functions The editorial budget he presents must be approved by the Guardian Media Group board as part of the overall budget package put forward by the Guardian News & Media executive committee (the national newspaper division has an executive committee that includes Rusbridger and ten other executives).[2] Each year he produces business plans, and admits that projects have been rejected when acceptable business cases have not been made. However, he is able to make decisions on non-commercial grounds because his newspaper has been exhorted by GMG to be "profit-seeking, not profit-making". In other words, it must operate efficiently, but does not face the same dire consequences as listed company publications that operate at a loss.

The relationship with *The Observer* is more at arm's length. The editor, John Mulholland, does not sit on the Trust or either of the commercial boards, and Forgan concedes that within the organisation the status of *The Observer* "was always a bit ambiguous" and so too were the Trust's obligations towards it. Did it have the Trust's protection or didn't it? This has been clarified by a statement from the trustees that the Sunday does not enjoy the formal protection that the Trust is required to provide to *The Guardian*. However, Forgan says that although there is no formal obligation, the trustees are "absolutely mindful of the fact that they have something precious and important in their charge". It is a responsibility that she believes weighs heavier on a trust than it would on a public listed company, and this sense almost certainly swayed the Trust (and the commercial boards) towards redevelopment of the Sunday newspaper rather than accepting the alternatives of closure or digital transmutation.

There was also a lack of clarity in the relationship between *The Guardian* and *The Observer*, which the Trust has resolved by creating the position of editor-in-chief over both publications. Rusbridger, who represents their interests in the various forums, currently holds the position. However, the relationship between the two newspapers is best described as evolutionary. While *The Observer* is not a Sunday edition of *The Guardian*, there has been some integration of resources. Forgan acknowledges that "with every day that passes it is harder and harder to draw a line between the corporate entities that are the *Guardian*, the *Observer*, and the website".

Integration affords a measure of protection for the Sunday newspaper in a commercial sense, but it does not alter *The Observer's* formal status with the Trust. If push came to shove, the interests of *The Guardian* would be paramount, and *The Observer* could be disentangled from its stable mate. This is a position supported by both Rusbridger and the Trust. Forgan puts it succinctly:

> The core purpose of The Scott Trust is to secure the financial and editorial independence of the *Guardian* in perpetuity. Although we regard *The Observer* as very precious, if the media landscape were to deteriorate to the point that publishing both titles was no longer viable, then our priority would be the *Guardian*.

The Trust's legal (and emotional) attachment remains with *The Guardian*, in whatever medium it is produced. While Forgan is sincere in articulating the Trust's championing of good journalism wherever it is found, the recession highlighted an unsentimental belief that the Trust will do whatever is necessary to protect *The Guardian* in whatever form (print or digital) it takes. The group's non-journalistic assets are treated as essentially commercial investments to which the Trust does not owe the same level of responsibility "in perpetuity", and the *Manchester Evening News* was sold when the company and the Trust determined that it was heading towards the point where it would constitute another (unsustainable) loss-maker in the group. However, Forgan concedes that the Trust held off making "really regrettable but unavoidable" decisions about GMG Regional Media, and with hindsight, it would have been wiser to acknowledge that the regional newspaper business model was broken by 2007.

The Trust in the 21st century has attempted to correct the anonymity and apparent inactivity that characterised much of its past. It has a strong presence on the Guardian Media Group website and in the GMG annual report, and is explained in GMG staff induction programmes. It is also more assertive in ensuring it is kept abreast of group operations. However, the Trust is far from being an interventionist owner and remains a reserve authority in most respects. Forgan says her most important message to potential trustees is: "You hardly do anything. When the sky falls in you are very important, but otherwise you don't have to do anything, and you certainly don't have anything to do with the content of the paper."

While the trustees have no say in the content of *The Guardian* or its sister publications, they are bound to uphold editorial independence. The editor-in-chief is described by Forgan as "a very powerful person", adding that C. P. Scott was an editor, and the Scott Trust was established to protect that power. Scott himself recognised that newspapers were both a business and more than a business, and laid down that "an editor and business manager should march hand in hand, the first, be it well understood, just an inch or two in advance" (Taylor 1993, 38).

Alan Rusbridger's power within Guardian News & Media is considerable, and his authority on editorial matters is, theoretically, absolute. However, he exercises it in a peculiarly *Guardian* way which is different to that normally associated with large newspapers. "My perception of [conventionally structured newspapers] is that they tend to be edited in quite a pyramidical structure," he told me.

> The *Guardian* is edited under a very flat structure, and the most symbolic way of describing that is that in most [other] places the editorial conference is chaired by an editor with a small group of senior colleagues. In the *Guardian*, certainly as long as I have been here (he joined the newspaper in 1979), the day begins with an open conference at which

anybody can come along and challenge or critique the paper. We some-times get 60–70 people at morning conference. People speak up if they feel we have overstepped on ethical or journalistic or policy issues and that is a fairly significant constraint on my power.

He seeks views at such open conferences on major editorial policy deci-sions. Before every General Election, there is a discussion amongst the staff over which party *The Guardian* should support. A similar discussion took place over whether Britain should adopt the euro. Rusbridger does not feel bound by the outcome of these deliberations, but although he does not think "consensus" describes the process, he is conscious of the need to take his colleagues' collective views into account. "If I had set this newspaper in favour of war with Iraq, I don't think the staff would have allowed that. Every morning people would have come in and challenged me."

Two years after he assumed the editorship, *The Guardian* became the first British national newspaper to appoint an internal ombudsman (known as the readers' editor) "to collect, consider, investigate, respond to, and where appropriate come to a conclusion about readers' comments, concerns, and complaints in a prompt and timely manner, from a position of indepen-dence within the paper". The full-time readers' editor fields more than 25,000 emails, calls and letters a year and is responsible for corrections and clarifications in the newspaper and on its websites. He has complete edi-torial autonomy (although readers may appeal his decisions to an outside independent ombudsman) and can be dismissed only by the Scott Trust, which is also responsible for the appointment. A similar position, estab-lished by Roger Alton when he was editor, exists on *The Observer*. The 12-paragraph terms of reference for the readers' editor are published on *The Guardian*'s website, along with the newspaper's editorial code that was updated in 2011 in part to strengthen privacy provisions in light of the News Corp phone hacking scandal that *The Guardian* had played a leading role in exposing.

The first readers' editor, Ian Mayes, admitted that some initially regarded the role as "eccentric", a form of flagellation or exhibitionism, but he described the principle as a simple one: "News organisations that, almost by definition, constantly call others to account should be more readily account-able and open themselves, and should be seen to be so" (Mayes 2004). Rusbridger, in a further display of "outreach", wrote to 50 people in high pro-file public service and private sector executive roles, asking them to evaluate the coverage of their work by both *The Guardian* and its competitors. The responses were published over two weeks in *The Guardian*'s media sections on 10 and 17 January 2005. The preface – the late Anthony Sampson's last essay – stated: "There can be no doubt about the genuine anguish of many distinguished people who feel aggrieved or simply resigned to the misrepre-sentations of the press." Rusbridger noted two months later that there had been almost no reaction among other media to the survey. *The Guardian* has a well-deserved reputation for keeping its contemporaries under scrutiny and there was no better illustration than the painstaking work of a team led by Nick Davies that exposed the activities that saw to the closure of the *News of the World*, the arrest of News Corporation editors and reporters and the establishment of the Leveson Inquiry in the wake of the phone hacking scandal.

The GMG group itself has comprehensive public interest disclosure and anti-corruption policies and operates an internal "whistle-blower" policy that includes provision of a confidential hotline for staff. Its anti-bribery and corruption committee reports regularly to the GMG board.[3]

Rusbridger practices a rare (perhaps unique) form of check and balance that owes much of its existence to the newspaper's ownership by the Scott Trust and its objectives. He explained his attitude during testimony to the House of Lords enquiry into ownership of the news in 2007, during which he acknowledged both the power of his position and the need for an internal process to assay his decisions. He went on to explain to the committee that *The Guardian's* staff produced better journalism because of the presence of the readers' editor:

> they think twice before they write any sentence now because everything they write will be contestable [by readers] and, if they get it wrong, it will be corrected the next day and they don't like that. Having this independent mechanism within the paper absolutely affects the standard of journalism which I think is getting better.

He noted that none of the other nationals (with the exception of *The Guardian's* companion Sunday title), had opted to follow his newspaper's example. That has since changed in the scramble by media to be seen as responsible self-regulators in the wake of the Leveson Report and *The Sun* appointed its first ombudsman in 2012.

Rusbridger was also the moving force behind the development of *The Guardian's* presence on the Internet, and the increasing integration between online and print areas of the newsroom. His ambition for a fully integrated editorial department with staff able to move freely between digital and paper environments was enhanced by the £8 million move in 2008 from cramped and threadbare quarters in Farringdon Road, to a new headquarters in King's Cross. The move was criticised in some quarters as an expensive luxury but it consolidated far-flung sections of the editorial department. The website *theguardian.com* has grown in popularity since its launch (as Guardian Unlimited) in 1999. Within two years it had 4.5 million unique users a month and was website of the year in the UK Press Awards. By May 2013 there had been almost a 10-fold increase to 40.9 million monthly unique users and *The Guardian* had decided to firmly nail its colours to the digital mast. In 2011 it announced a "digital first" strategy – to counter a continuing decline in print revenue. It said at the time that it wanted to increase digital revenue from £38 million that year to more than £90 million by 2016. Announcing the five-year plan, Rusbridger said newspapers had to adopt an "open" digital philosophy that embraced contributions beyond the ranks of its own journalists and said there needed to be "a greater focus of attention, imagination and resource on the various forms that [the] digital future is likely to take".

The plan included expansion in the US market with the launch in May 2012 of *Guardian US*, a New York-based digital service that has a staff of 35. The following year a similar move was made into Australia with a 21-strong team of journalists serving the *Guardian Australia* digital platform. By the time the Australian service launched in May 2013 *The Guardian* was the third most read English language newspaper website in the world after the *Daily Mail* and the *New York Times*. By March 2013 digital revenue had reached almost £56 million, a 30 per cent annual gain that exceeded losses in print revenue. For the year ended March 2014 it reported digital revenue of £70 million, an increase of 25 per cent on the previous year. This was a key equation: if digital revenue gains could more than replace print revenue losses *The Guardian* could avoid the dire scenario predicted by chief executive Andrew Miller in 2011: that the company could run out of money in three to five years.

The newspaper division of the group had operating losses of £41.6 million in 2011, £44.2 million in 2012 and £30.9 million in 2013 as its titles were exposed to the cold realities they shared with most of their contemporaries – declining print advertising and circulation revenue. Irrespective of their high journalistic ideals, *The Guardian* and *The Observer* have been required to cut costs. Guardian News & Media was no stranger to redundancies with voluntary severances in 2002 and widespread staff cuts announced in 2009 that led to more than 100 journalists taking redundancy. The "Digital First" strategy saw continuing negotiations with employees and the National Union of Journalists to further reduce staff numbers. Sixty journalists took voluntary redundancy in 2013 but there have been no forced redundancies – in marked contrast to the trend in newspapers elsewhere. The overall workforce in the Guardian Media Group fell from 4314 in 2008 to 1717 in 2013, due largely to business divestiture.

The voluntary nature of GNM's redundancy initiatives blunted some of the potential criticism of the cuts, and Rusbridger has been careful to insulate certain parts of the editorial operation. In the lead-up to the introduction of the 2009 cuts he said: "I'm completely clear that I'm not going to cut news, I'm not going to cut foreign news, and I'm not going to cut comment." He is determined to protect *The Guardian*'s network of foreign bureaux and international coverage and argues that such a strategy, while journalistically beneficial, may also be commercially sound as other organisations cut foreign correspondents and open the field for syndication services. The launch and growth of the US and Australian operations significantly strengthened coverage in those areas. GMG confirmed to me in 2013 that the news and foreign budgets had been protected and *The Guardian* had maintained its complement of reporters, foreign writers and stringers. The *Guardian*, in contrast to many of its contemporaries, decreased rather than increased its reliance on freelancers. These cuts were largely due to reductions in pagination but, again in contrast to many other newspapers, it did not reduce its freelance rates of pay.

Rising annual losses by the newspapers were manageable when GMG's overall profits returned year-on-year growth for the group. However, the recession resulted in operating losses by the group in 2009 and 2010. While GMG's overall financial health was not in question (its combined cash balance and investment fund remained reasonably robust), shortfall led not only to staff reductions but also to operating budget cuts, as well as moves to outsource production of some non-core elements of the newspaper and to reduce rates for freelancers and casual employees. A decade of the national newspaper division's annual losses is set out in Table 7.1.

The national newspaper division registered significant savings of £26.8 million through cuts and restructuring in 2010 and followed this with a programme aimed at cutting a further £25 million over five years. In 2012/2013 printing costs were cut by £9 million, due in part to a redesign that reduced pagination, and a reduction of almost £3 million in the editorial budget – largely voluntary editorial staff redundancies.[4]

Cost-cutting and the quest for digital revenue are common strategies in the newspaper business. The core purpose of the vast majority of companies is to return dividends to investors and it is here that GMG differs from most

Table 7.1   Guardian News & Media annual loss

Year ended March	Turnover (million)	Loss before exceptionals and amortisation
2004	£227.5	£6.2 million
2005	£233.8 (+3%)	£18.6 million
2006	£237.4 (+1.5%)	£19.3 million
2007	£245.7 (+3.5%)	£15.9 million
2008	£261.9 (+6.6%)	£24.9 million
2009	£253.6 (−3.3%)	£33.7 million
2010	£221.0 (−12.8%)	£30.9 million
2011	£198.2 (−10.3%)	£31.1 million
2012	£196.2 (−1%)	£44.2 million
2013	£196.3 (+0.05%)	£30.9 million

Source: Guardian Media Group Annual Reports.

of its contemporaries. The chief executive of the Guardian Media Group, Andrew Miller, began his 2012 annual review by saying:

> Our core purpose is to deliver the financial security that allows The Scott Trust Limited to achieve its central objective: the editorial independence of the *Guardian* in perpetuity. The group's strategy is to use its portfolio of assets (see Table 7.2) to support the *Guardian* while we go through the tumultuous period that the media industry is experiencing.

The way in which those assets are employed has been a constant challenge for GMG and the Scott Trust in the new millennium. In 1977, the Manchester Guardian and Evening News company had a turnover of £25 million. Twenty years later, the group's turnover was £348 million from the four divisions that represented national and regional newspapers, trade publications and broadcasting. By 2007, the group turnover had peaked at £593.9 million, and ushered in the era of joint-venture operations that realised value in the enterprises and allowed the down-paying of debt.

A former GMG director of strategy, Steve Folwell, outlined to me four levels of investment that continue to be the group's investment strategy.[5] The first is the core elements of *Guardian/Observer*/theguardian.com and "brand extensions from the *Guardian*" which would include the US and Australian digital editions. The second is the investment fund (derived largely from unlocking some of the value of the businesses through divestiture or partial sale to joint ventures) that is diversified away from news media "and

Table 7.2 Guardian Media Group structure 2013

Entity	Operations	Contribution 2013
Guardian News & Media	*Guardian Observer* theguardian.com	Operating loss £30.9 million
GMG property services	Software companies and business-to-business websites	Profit £1.9 million
Joint ventures	Digital and print classified publications (Trader Media Group*)	Profit £73 million (GMG share)
	Business-to-business media products (Top Right Group)	
Investment fund Other entities	Externally managed fund Includes contract production	£253.7 million invested Undisclosed

*Trader Media Group sold in 2014 but its 2013 contribution was significant.

the things that the *Guardian* depends upon". The third is in what Folwell described as "safe-haven assets" that ought to deliver consistent returns over time. These investments are in media but are deliberately chosen because they do not have a high dependency on advertising – if *The Guardian*'s advertising volumes drop, these companies will not be subject to the same downturn. Until their sale to Trinity Mirror in a declining market, the regional newspapers formed part of the safe-haven portfolio, and had in the past produced what he called "fantastic returns". In this category sat the Trader Media Group and Top Right Group (formerly known as Emap). The fourth is in "riskier ventures" that have future potential and attributes that match the Scott ethos of community service. This included Manchester's Channel M until its closure in 2010 and, with the benefit of hindsight, would also probably describe GMG's investment in radio in its latter stages. Specialist external fund managers operate the investments in a diversified range of assets that reduce the group's reliance on the UK market. It represents a significant financial shock absorber for the group in general, and *The Guardian* in particular.

The investment fund is a result of realising the value that had built up in the Trader division of the group. Part of the sum raised from the sale of 49.9 per cent of the division funded the joint-venture acquisition of Emap (Top Right Group), but the remainder was used to boost the group's investment fund and cash reserves from a modest £35.3 million in 2007 to £260.8 million in 2010. Losses saw some drawdown in the fund but in 2013 it stood at £253.7 million, boosted by a contribution from the sale of radio companies. In March 2014 the fund received an even more significant boost from the sale of the remaining 50.1 per cent of the Trader group for £619 million and the trust announced *The Guardian*'s future was "secure for generations to come".

The single-minded purpose of the group in protecting the Scott legacy has created issues outside the Guardian News & Media division. When market downturns led to staff reductions (in regional newspapers and radio for example) there was a natural tendency for a redundant worker to see his or her sacrifice as a consequence of "protecting *The Guardian*" The attitude was manifested in the March 2009 full-page advertisement placed by *Manchester Evening News* staff, who alleged they were forced to endure cuts "to service the on-going expansion of the *Guardian* – which is losing many millions but still paying executive bonuses". The symbiosis that needs to exist between the national newspaper and other operations in the group is one that must be carefully managed, and *The Guardian* must be seen to be pulling its weight (and sharing the pain), to prevent seeds of resentment germinating in other parts of GMG. In recent years, *Guardian* staff would say, that has been the case.

The *Guardian* and *The Observer* are publications in transition. Despite swift denials in October 2012 that it was considering an end to its print editions,

The Guardian is moving inexorably towards a digital future. It is also moving even further from its Manchester beginnings to become an overtly international news organisation with distinct London, New York and Sydney editions. It does so, however, without losing sight of the Scott legacy and tradition.

The challenge has been to find ways in which sufficient revenue can be raised to sustain the sort of journalism that C. P. Scott would have desired. "Monetising" the web is as elusive for GMG as it is for other newspaper publishers although the increases in digital revenue have been encouraging. The greatest hope, however, may lie in the size and income of the investment fund. In December 2012, when GMG was first engaged in talks over the sale of its remaining interest in the Trader Group, the city editor of the *Financial Times*, Jonathan Guthrie, in his Lombard column advised GMG to sell its interest to create "a nest egg an ostrich would envy". Those talks ended in failure to agree a price but the eventual sale of the interest resulted in an overall £1.4 billion return on what had initially been a very modest investment in Autotrader. The group is now able to make further significant diversified investments that are impervious to the issues facing the news media industry.

GMG can look to an exemplar in the trust family, the Wellcome Trust, for investment examples. The Wellcome Trust, to which we will return in the concluding chapter, was founded in 1936 as custodian of the pharmaceutical company that bore its name. In its first 20 years, in which the company's performance was lacklustre, it distributed only a total of £1.2 million to researchers. In 2014 – and no longer owner of a pharmaceutical firm – it has a widely diversified investment portfolio worth £16.4 billion and makes grants amounting to more than £720 million in a year. An investment fund even a fraction of that size, but diversified outside the media to withstand the winds of change, could well allow the Scott Trust to meet its obligation to "preserve the financial position and editorial position of the Guardian in perpetuity".

The Irish Times Trust

The separation of the Irish Times Trust from the operation of the entities that it owns is even more pronounced than the buffer between the Scott Trust and the Guardian Media Group. The crisis of 2001 and resultant changes to its articles have reduced the Irish Times Trust to two formal roles: as the holder of the company's shares that appoints the board, and as a court of appeal to which deeply divided groups of directors may resort after jumping a legal hurdle. The first role is unchallenged, and the second has been avoided.

No longer subservient to a dominating managing director, the current company board membership is based on business and administrative experience. The Trust is represented on the company board by three of its members with strong administrative or legal backgrounds including the Trust chair, Tom Arnold. There are four independent non-executive directors including the board chairman, Dan Flinter. Flinter is a former executive director of the Industrial Development Authority and sits on the board of Dairygold, Ireland's largest farmer-owned business. The other independent directors also have strong business backgrounds. The remaining members of the board are the managing director, Liam Kavanagh, the editor, Kevin O'Sullivan and his deputy, Denis Staunton. Kavanagh and O'Sullivan report independently to the board.

The Trust itself, in addition to Arnold who is the former chief executive of a worldwide humanitarian agency, is comprised of finance and policy advisors, academics, a lawyer, a former trade union leader and a former arts administrator. One trustee is from Northern Ireland.

If any criticism could be levelled at the make-up of the board and the Trust, it would be that for all the social and commercial attributes, there is a significant gap – a conspicuous absence of independent news media expertise that could offer advice or guidance based on experience. Apart from the three executive directors, the only independent news media experience lies with trustee Rosemary Kelly, who does not sit on the company board. She is a former head of public affairs and company secretary for BBC Northern Ireland who has also worked for UK broadcasting regulator Ofcom. When senior executives seek to justify decisions or policies to their fellow board members, they do so to an essentially lay membership. The Irish Times Limited is not, of course, alone among media companies in failing to co-opt independent industry expertise on to its board, but the 2001 restructuring was a missed opportunity to balance industry knowledge and commercial prowess by veering entirely towards the latter. The desire to increase the independent commercial input on the board is understandable given the financial crisis in which the company found itself in 2001, but the absence of significant journalistic or media experience on the Trust (in contrast to the Scott Trust and Poynter Institute) exposes a potential weakness.

The Trust meets regularly following monthly board meetings, and is briefed on board matters by its nominees under a policy that trustees should be kept fully informed on business activities. The chairs of the Trust and the board meet frequently between board meetings (on which both sit) in what former chair David McConnell described to me as "a continuous working relationship that I don't think is onerous and which absolutely is not meant to be directive but supportive". The editor and managing director also formally report twice yearly to the Trust, and brief trustees "by way of information" on any major issues that arise in the interim.

The board meets its statutory obligations in the public reporting of its annual accounts, but has not been moved to emulate the fulsome annual reports and social audits published by the Guardian Media Group. The Trust continues to maintain a dignified silence. Media historian Mark O'Brien, author of a history of *the Irish* Times, remains highly critical of the Trust's lack of public exposure[6]:

> The Trust is a secretive body in many ways... If you stopped the ordinary Joe or Jane Citizen on the street and asked them who's on the Irish Times Trust or what they do I don't think even the regular readers of the newspaper would appreciate that it's run by a trust, what it means to be run by a trust, and what that means for the journalism of the newspaper. If only the Trust came out into the limelight – not in a dictatorial way – and said "we have oversight, we're not interfering but we will give an assessment every year of what we think of the journalism".

O'Brien's desire for an annual assessment by the Trust is unlikely to be realised. Even the Scott Trust stops short of making such a judgement on the editorial performance of *The Guardian*. The Irish Times Trust will not venture into an area where it may be accused of attempting to exert control over the editorial content of the *Irish Times* – which McConnell described as "forbidden territory". While the board is responsible for editorial policy and the appointment of the editor, McConnell could not recall any instance in recent memory when either the trustees or directors had called the editor to account for editorial content.

Nor does McConnell believe it is the role of the Trust to set future business strategy, a task that he believes is best left to company executives. "The Trust is not set up to second guess management," he told me. "It's not a body of experts on newspapers." Rather, the Trust is a body whose role is essentially as the custodian of reserve powers. If for example, an editor was consistently failing to observe the editorial requirements set out in the company's articles, the Trust would be forced to act, and short of some other solution, remove the editor. Similarly, with responsibility for the appointment of directors, the Trust would be capable of changing the make-up of the board if it felt members were failing to meet the company's objectives.

McConnell was, however, strongly of the view that such powers should never be held over management or directors. He believed they should never have to be used, or even threatened to be used and saw a free flow of information between the three elements of the governance structure as the key to a good working relationship. In his view, the governance structure has a cohesion that has avoided tension or conflict: "In a funny sort of way, I'd like to think that if, as a group (the senior management, directors, and trustees), were in a room discussing something – we might do that to discuss something but we haven't – you might find it difficult to determine who was from what."

The contemporary Irish Times Trust may appear to be a shadow of its former incarnation, but, when the assertive Major McDowell was in power, the Trust represented little more than a rubber stamp to ratify his wishes. Its present form is a more legitimate use of the trust structure. It may be seen to have handed executive power to the commercial board but the realities of modern news media business require no less.

When he was appointed editor in 2011 Kevin O'Sullivan moved to improve the profile of the Trust which, he accepted, had little public recognition. Information on the trustees and their role was placed on the newspaper's website where O'Sullivan wrote: "The Irish Times Trust and its Articles of Association give the newspaper and its website a special position among media organisations by protecting its editorial content from commercial and other sectional interests."

The explicit nature of the editorial objectives set out in the company articles requires the editor and his staff to provide forms and levels of editorial content to which other Irish publications are not bound. The objectives also act as a guarantee against attempts to curtail such coverage. They represent the most detailed formal mandatory prescription for the editorial policy in any of the newspapers examined in this study, and exceed even those of the *Toronto Star* that were laid down in the Atkinson Principles. O'Sullivan believes they give the editorial staff a touchstone:

> Every day there are stories in the *Irish Times* that you would not get anywhere else. Our more extensive reportage on a particular issue that you won't find in other Irish newspapers ... is influenced by the trust and the articles. All of the articles still apply and are even more important now. In my view the issue of independence is really critical because we are in a scenario where there are fewer newspapers in the Irish market. There is a growing dominance of one particular employer in a multi-media sense [Denis O'Brien, who is the largest shareholder in independent News & Media and owner of extensive broadcasting interests] and that domination in my view doesn't give you the best mix of a diverse media. In that mix the *Irish Times'* independence is critical.[7]

The objectives are deeply inculcated in the editorial department and strongly reflected in the content of the newspaper, which O'Sullivan has described as "the most important national forum for thinkers and doers in Irish society":

> We offer a platform for critical, constructive and divergent comment in the different spheres including business, politics and public affairs, culture, the environment, health and education. We have moved in recent years from being a newspaper of record to a newspaper of reference.

Political coverage is a strong example of the way in which the objectives manifest themselves in the *Irish Times,* which maintains a staff of four political correspondents plus a "colour" writer on politics. It is one of a small number of newspapers in the English-speaking world (and unique in Ireland) that continues to carry pages dedicated to parliamentary chamber coverage. O'Sullivan believes that, in the wake of the economic crisis and banking bailout, political coverage is vital. He signalled from the beginning of his editorship that it was an area that would not be compromised by cutbacks. "If anything," he says, "we have increased our firepower in this area."

> There are huge questions about transparency in government, account-ability and the future of Irish democracy that have arisen from all this turmoil and I would like to think the *Irish Times* is at the forefront in covering this, evaluating it and suggesting ways forward.

The *Irish Times* has a proud record of uncovering political misdeeds, some-times at significant risk. In 2006, for example, the newspaper revealed payments made by businessmen to the former Taoiseach (prime minister), Bertie Ahern, when he was minister of finance. Ahern later resigned. O'Sullivan's predecessor as editor, Geraldine Kennedy, controversially destroyed evidence (that could lead to identification of the informant) rather than risk seizure. A four-year court battle followed, resulting in a decision that enshrined in Irish law the right of journalists to protect sources. O'Brien has described the drawn out saga as an example of the *Irish Times* fulfilling its main function of "exposing the underbelly of Irish political life to public scrutiny" (2008, 271).

O'Sullivan's approach differs significantly, however, from that of his predecessor. Kennedy practiced a traditional form of editorship based on a clearly defined hierarchy. "One of the very strange things about this place – and maybe newspapers generally – is how autocratic the structure is," she told me in 2009. "They're not democracies, and even though a lot of my reporters may be very left-wing and may disagree with me, they do respect that the editor has the final word." O'Sullivan, on the other hand, told me in 2013 that his management style is very different and he has instituted a flatter structure based on collective decision-making:

> I think you have to bring people on and involve them in the decision-making. Whether it's an ethical decision or a basic news priority, I would advocate that we have to talk more about details, weigh up issues. With time pressures there's a requirement for quicker decisions but in certain instances I would say to people "Look, it's a very controversial story so let's step back for a second and look. Are we doing it correctly? Are there issues in terms of fairness and balance? Do we need to go back on any-thing?" That's a new approach I have put in place. It comes from a basic belief that collective decision-making gives you a better decision.

It is easy to see parallels with Rusbridger's approach at *The Guardian*.

The *Irish Times* editors' comments, taken together with those of Rusbridger and the staff of the *Tampa Bay Times* later in this chapter, demonstrate a further key finding in relation to trustee-run newspapers. Although there are prescriptions for the journalistic values to be followed, the governance structures allow considerable freedom to accommodate both the personality of the editor and the culture of the newsroom.

O'Sullivan's relationship with the commercial side of the business is also clearly defined. He decides each day on the number of pages in the newspaper – in contrast to many publications where the pagination is dictated by commercial departments – and will "open up" the *Irish Times* when circumstances (such as the death of a giant of Irish literature, poet and Nobel laureate Seamus Heaney in 2013) require it. He says it would be "impossible for us" if cost alone was the ultimate dictator although he must be conscious of it. He describes his relationship with the managing director Liam Kavanagh as "close, while still respecting our different requirements and independence":

> The whole market is in such turmoil you cannot not have that degree of cooperation. The complexity is such that the scale of decision-making requires that degree of cooperation. That doesn't mean I have suddenly become commercial or am dictated to by a particular advertiser or whatever but we do need to cooperate – everyone in the room recognises that now.

In theory the board sets the editorial policy, but it is apparent that directors and trustees have been willing to leave such matters to the editor. O'Sullivan told me he does discuss stories with directors and trustees, particularly on controversial subjects "because I feel it's important to explain the context of how we make certain decisions". He says there is a strong appetite for discussion on such stories but a clear understanding that he will not take direction. Here is another parallel with Rusbridger, who listens but at the end of the day makes his own decisions.

In the event of a serious challenge to editorial independence by the board or management, the editor could seek the support of the Trust. However, there is no provision under the company articles for a direct formal appeal by the editor to trustees. To do so formally, the editor would have to approach the matter as a director (O'Sullivan sits on the board) and invoke the "significant policy" clause under which the Trust's representatives on the board could have an effective right of veto. There have been no signs, however, that such a threat to his authority is likely.

However, neither the Trust nor the board have been able to shield the editorial department from the impact of the crisis in the Irish economy that began to unfold late in 2007. Kennedy and O'Sullivan had to contend with both staff cuts and reduced budgets. Sixty staff from the newspaper were made redundant in 2008 under what was termed a "voluntary parting scheme", and in 2009 pay cuts of 5–10 per cent for staff were introduced, with reductions of 15–20 per cent for senior executives.[8] In 2011 an additional 16 editorial positions were lost as part of a cost-reducing exercise designed to cut up to 30 from the overall staff. O'Sullivan took up his appointment during that exercise. The overall workforce involved in printing, publishing and distribution dropped from 571 in 2007 to 447 in 2012.

Like all editorial departments, the *Irish Times* has high fixed costs, related largely to staffing. Budget cuts have reduced the amount of discretionary spending available to O'Sullivan. "It's a considerable challenge in terms of reporter/correspondent firepower," he told me:

> We are considerably diminished in comparison with 7 or 8 years ago (during Ireland's economic boom)...I think we've been very prudent. In many ways we've tried to protect our content generators, to use that awful term. They're our most important things in terms of our interface with readers and we would be worried about anything that undermines that. So we need to fight to retain that key edge in terms of content and to a large extend we have done that. We still have our network of foreign correspondents and, if anything, we've enhanced it.

The network of foreign correspondents is unusually large for a newspaper with a circulation under 85,000. It maintains correspondents in London, Belfast, Washington, Paris, Brussels and Berlin, and freelance writers on retainer in Rome, China and South America. In addition the newspaper has a roving foreign correspondent, Mary Fitzgerald, who has covered war zones such as Libya and Syria and the conflict in Egypt. It also has permanent stringers (freelancers) in the Middle East, South America and Sydney. The newspaper's foreign coverage is influential. Conor O'Clery, who established the newspaper's Beijing bureau in 1996, credits the *Irish Times'* coverage (of China's economic potential) with bringing about a change in Irish foreign policy (O'Clery 2009).

The *Irish Times* was an early entrant into the Internet, beginning in 1994 with simple text-based online pages. In 2008, the online news staff that worked for the company's website Ireland.com were integrated into the *Irish Times* newsroom, and the site was rebranded as irishtimes.com. In October 2010, while attracting 2.3 million unique visitors a month, it was judged the country's best website. The online presence has experienced significant growth. The number of page impressions a month rose from 13 million in 2005 to 23 million in 2009 and 43.6 million in 2013. The Internet statistics are in contrast to the circulation of the newspaper itself, which was relatively static from 2004 to 2007, when it stood at 119,000. Circulation went into decline during the recession and in 2013 the newspaper was selling little more than 84,000 copies a day. Given the relative stability of circulation of the *Irish Times* before 2007, it is reasonable to assume that the recent decline is recession-based although the consequences are serious.

The Irish Times company, with a turnover in 2012 of €81.4 million, is small by comparison with both the Guardian Media Group and Poynter's Times Publishing Company. Its commercial activity in the new millennium is a story of growth bookended by losses. The company recovered quickly from the crisis that led to losses of £IR2.35 million (€2.98 million) in 2001 and £IR2.8 million (€3.55 million) in 2002, and posted a profit in 2003.[9] This signalled a run of steadily rising turnover and operating profit that was brought to an abrupt end in 2008 as Ireland descended into financial crisis and a prolonged period of austerity. A decade of the company's changing fortunes is set out in Table 7.3.

Ireland's Gross Domestic Product grew by an average of 5.7 per cent between 2000 and 2007. Between 2008 and 2011 it declined by 5.4 per cent before returning to low growth. The recession highlighted structural vulnerabilities in the reliance on advertising-based revenue across the various businesses in the Irish Times group. Its newspaper advertising revenue declined by 23 per cent in 2008 and 42.5 per cent in 2009 before moderating to a downturn of 7.8 per cent in 2010, 4.1 per cent in 2011 and 6.1 per cent in 2012.

The Guardian Media Group embarked on a strategy to reduce its reliance on the UK advertising market. The Irish Times Limited investment strategy has been tied to both the Irish market and to businesses that are closely allied to the company's core media competencies and markets.

In 2004, there was a robust debate over the future of the company, with one group of directors wishing to see a diversification programme to

Table 7.3 Irish Times Limited profit and loss 2003–2012 (€ millions)

Year	Turnover	Operating profit*	After-tax profit
2003	95.18	6.97	8.39
2004	104.35	15.27	14.98
2005	113.25	18.08	12.98
2006	129.42	22.66	37.29
2007	137.19	21.92	18.76
2008	124.26	6.41	(37.85)
2009	92.12	(4.62)	(27.88)
2010	85.98	(0.63)	1.06**
2011	86.76	2.45	(1.89)
2012	81.45	1.65	(0.78)

*Before exceptionals; **Reflects pension credit.
Source: Irish Times Limited Directors' Report & Annual Accounts.

safeguard future earnings and another group warning that diversification could compromise the primary task of the company which was to publish the *Irish Times* (O'Brien, 271). The outcome was a series of acquisitions and start-ups that appear to be an attempt to meet both objectives, but which could not provide a buffer against a severe downturn in the Irish economy. In addition to the *Irish Times*, the company owns or has shareholding in the following:

- Itronics – electronic publishing and training services (100 per cent)
- MyHome – real estate website (100 per cent)
- Gazette Group Newspapers – community newspapers (63.8 per cent)
- Gloss Publications – magazine publishing (50 per cent)
- Sortridge – advertising sales representation (50 per cent)
- Fortunegreen – free metro newspaper joint venture (33.3 per cent)
- Digital Media Brokers – digital sales representation (50 per cent)
- Entertainment Media Networks – online entertainment (31.7 per cent).

Itronics was established in the 1990s to manage the company's Internet developments. The subsidiary has generally been loss-making or only marginally profitable. Myhome.ie, a leading online property portal which operates through a group subsidiary called DigitalworX, was bought by the Irish Times in 2006 at the height of the property boom for €50 million (financed from the sale of the D'Olier Street headquarters at a time of record property prices). Then the Irish property sector collapsed, with residential prices being halved. As a long-term strategy that shores up the company against migration of classified advertising to the Internet, the purchase was sound. However, the Irish Times was forced to write down the value of goodwill in the subsidiary in 2008 and 2009. By 2013, there were signs that the Irish property market was beginning to stabilise.

Shortly before the financial crisis of 2007 the company took a 47 per cent holding in the Gazette Group, which publishes eight free community newspapers in the outer suburbs of Dublin, and later raised this to a majority stake and took management control. The group accumulated losses and in June 2013 sought protection from creditors before being placed under examinership. This is a rescue process by which companies that are insolvent are helped to recover during a 100-day "breathing space" in which they can be restructured. After a capital injection the group reported to the court in September 2013 that it had returned to profit. However, the Irish Times' half share in the women's magazine *The Gloss* has also failed to produce dividends. After sustaining losses, and the rebuffing of a purchase offer,[10] it ceased to be a stand-alone magazine in 2009, when it began to be inserted into the *Irish Times* on the first Thursday of every month.

The Fortunegreen joint venture with Associated Newspapers introduced the *Metro Ireland* free newspaper to Dublin in 2005. In 2010 it merged with the rival *Herald AM* after the free newspapers lost an estimated combined sum of €11 million. By the end of 2011 – and no longer locked in a newspaper war – the *Metro Herald* was breaking even. In 2013 it had a daily distribution of 65,000 copies and 50,000 subscribers on a companion website.

Participation in these ventures should be put in context. Liam Kavanagh told me that, with the benefit of hindsight, media deals at the time now look very expensive. However, the Irish Times was not alone, nor did it venture in at "the deep end".

> We participated in many [negotiations] but succeeded with really only one of substance, which was MyHome. Others we looked at, but didn't get and were very fortunate to have missed out. Examples were the Leinster Leader regional newspaper group bought by Johnston Press for €139m and Emap's Irish radio assets bought by Denis O'Brien [largest shareholder in Independent News & Media which is publisher of the rival *Irish Independent*] for over €200m. At the other end of the scale, and just at the end of 2007 as the crash was clearly on its way, INM bought the *Sligo Champion*, a small regional paper for about €20m. The multiples in all of the above were well into the late teens. To some extent these prices pushed us towards start-up/younger businesses. If the price to buy was so high why not build brands that were complementary to our own or where we could bring some support?

Kavanagh led a renewed drive into digital initiatives in the Irish Times group. It was among the first newspapers in the world to start a website (1994) which was redeveloped and now has about 630,000 unique users per month. It is in comScore's *Top 20 Sites in Ireland* – one of only five Irish-owned and -operated websites to make the list. The site did not have a paywall at the time of writing – in keeping with *The Guardian* and the *Tampa Bay Times*. An online electronic version of the print newspaper and a related tablet app have paid subscriptions and the newspaper's electronic archive attracts charges.[11] Like all newspaper publishers the Irish Times group struggles to derive sufficient revenue from digital to replace print losses. In 2012 it began a series of incubator programmes for digital start-ups, including experiments to define the next generation of digital advertising. Kavanagh said at the end of the first programme:

> We have been a very heavily print dominated and very traditional news organisation. This project required us to come out of our comfort zone. I was conscious that the organisation could have rejected the digital disruptors when they arrived, which would have posed serious difficulties. If we did not embrace this challenge then it would have said serious things about whether the organisation could change.

The Irish Times Limited had the great misfortune to begin its expansion programme shortly before the Irish economy went into freefall, and much of the criticism of its investments has been with the benefit of hindsight.[12] Some aspects of its strategic approach have helped the business. It is debt averse (it has no net debt) and its acquisitions and the construction of a modern printing plant at CityWest (together with a €20 million expansion in 2004 that increased its value to €70 million) were funded from revenue and cash reserves. The plant is part of the company's diversification strategy and about half the capacity of the printing plant is used for contract printing – including the Cork-based *Irish Examiner* and its related titles – that is a useful source of revenue. This has prevented the company from being faced with the debt servicing burdens that have beset groups (such as the rival Independent News & Media) that borrowed heavily to expand.

Liam Kavanagh continues to face major challenges as commercial helmsman of the Irish Times including coping with investment decisions that were not of his making. A stuttering restart to the Irish economy does, however, offer the prospect of a sustainable return to operating profits. Where the strategy employed in more buoyant times by Kavanagh's predecessor Maeve Donovan leaned towards expansion beyond the *Irish Times* itself, he has been keen to invest in digital platforms that enhance the *Irish Times* brand. It is clear that, whatever the direction, chief executives have been the driving strategic force, backed by their board of directors. The Trust, on the other hand, has been treated as a reserve power. It could intervene if the actions of managing director or board place the future of the *Irish Times* in jeopardy. Since the onset of the global financial crisis there have been some close calls but the governors have not been panicked into intervention.

Tampa Bay Times

The role of trustees in the running of the *Tampa Bay Times* differs fundamentally from that of its two counterparts. Indeed, apart from holding the shares in the holding company in a manner that prevents their sale, the trustees of the Poynter Institute effectively have no other part to play in the commercial enterprise. The functioning of the Times Publishing Company and its titles is an enduring recognition of Nelson Poynter's third principle that states, in part, that "a newspaper is so individualistic in nature, that complete control, and thereby responsibility, should be concentrated in an individual". Control of the company is firmly in the hands of Paul Tash, who is chairman and chief executive, and until he relinquished the title in May 2010 to concentrate on business operations was editor of the newspaper. It is a position that, as one observer put it, gives Tash "the kind of operational clout that Donald Graham or Arthur Sulzberger might envy".[13]

Tash's hold extends to chairmanship of the Poynter Institute's board of trustees, but that board is no longer dominated by company executives. Apart from Tash, only the president of the group's Florida magazine company sits on the 11-person board, which also includes the institute's president, Dr Karen Dunlap. No company executives sit on the institute's national 18-member advisory board drawn from prominent academic and media institutions.

The board of the holding company, Times Holding Company, consists only of Tash and three company executives, and Tash exercises all voting rights to the shares in the company held by the institute. With the exception of two Poynter representatives,[14] the board of directors of the Times Publishing Company – the principal operating entity, which publishes the *Tampa Bay Times* – is composed of company executives and bears a closer resemblance to a group executive management team than a conventional board. There are also three subsidiary boards, each chaired by Tash who, nonetheless, emphasises where his ultimate responsibility lies: "Although my day job is at the *Times*," he says, "my responsibilities originate from Poynter."

The vast majority of the company's operations are in publishing. In 2009, the company sold the Washington-based publishing interests that had been nurtured by Nelson Poynter and his first wife. *Congressional Quarterly* and its weekly record of congressional activity, *CQ Weekly*, were sold to the Economist Group, reportedly for more than $US100 million, and *Governing* (established after Poynter's death) was sold to the California-based media company, e.Republic. As a result, the activities of the company are not only largely restricted to publishing but also firmly based in Florida (see Table 7.4).

There is a focus on marketing within the group, which delineates its structure by brands rather than divisions. The traditional circulation department found in most newspapers was reorganised in 2006 to become an audience development department, with a strong sales and market development emphasis. Brand managers were appointed for each publication, with control over budgets to increase audiences.

There is a strong sense that there is room for initiative but it is equally clear that major decisions must have the approval of Paul Tash and that

Table 7.4   Times Publishing Company operations

Tampa Bay Times	Seven-day morning newspaper (circulation 340,260 March 2013)
*tbt (*Tampa Bay Times)	Free weekday daily newspaper (distribution 431,500 copies/week)
tb-two	Free print and online newspaper distributed to students
Florida Trend	Monthly business magazine (Average circulation 51,400)
Tampa Bay Newspapers	Five weekly and three monthly newspapers (combined circulation 160,000)
Senior Living Guide	Services directory for senior citizens
Tampa Bay Expos	Events marketing

much of the development of the group is driven by him. This suggests that Tash has extraordinary power, and in a strictly structural sense that is the case. However, it is power exercised through a process of agreement and delegation. Executive control of the Poynter Institute is in the hands of Karen Dunlap, but while the breadth of commercial activities requires Tash to delegate responsibilities, Tash is in firm control of the business. As he put it when I interviewed him: "She has her day job, and I have mine."[15] Tash's relinquishing of the role of editor and the structure of subsidiary enterprises are examples of his willingness to delegate responsibility within the company's publications. The delegation extends to a high degree of autonomy within the editorial board of the *Tampa Bay Times*, which in 2013 received the Pulitzer Prize for editorial writing.

Dunlap told me the institute's relationship with the company is clear: "we own it, but we don't manage it", and that there is a clear distinction between her role as operational chief executive of the institute, and Tash's "fiduciary responsibility of bringing together the trustees to help in the strategies and the big operations" which she then carries out. While acknowledging potential conflict of interest through also sitting on the Times Publishing Company board, Dunlap states that in reality, no conflict has arisen because of the climate of trust that exists between Tash and herself, and the fact that "it is in the best interests of the institute to have a strong newspaper".[16] It appears to be a relationship that owes more to personal rapport than institutional framework. Such a climate of trust is also present in *The Guardian* and the *Irish Times*. Dunlap told me:

> We talk regularly – it's showing mutual respect and trust – and have a monthly lunch. We'll bring up problems and he lets me know sometimes about things he thinks would be a good idea and I kid him sometimes about his patience and willingness to accept that we don't do it that way ... By the time he goes forward to the board (of trustees) I'm in agreement with what he is doing. We discuss things formally and informally. If we were having a finance committee meeting and there were some things that he had to do formally there, it would be very unusual for anything to come from that meeting that he and I had not agreed on in advance. The board is generally agreeable to those decisions but it's the normal trustee process: If the finance committee approves something it takes it to the board and the board has an opportunity to discuss, to object ... I don't detect any lack of free expression but we don't have significant disagreements in the board. I credit the chairman for that. He does a good job.

This separation of roles is important because the Poynter Institute is ever mindful of the need to maintain an arm's-length relationship with both the Times Publishing Company (a tax-paying entity) and the *Tampa Bay Times* in order to secure its 501(c)3 tax-exempt non-profit status. In order to maintain that status, the institute is also required to refrain from any form of political advocacy. It is important therefore that it be seen to be distanced from the newspaper's endorsement of political candidates and its stance on political issues. The association is handled with the finesse of diplomatic relations, and manifests itself in ways that may at first sight appear excessive, but which illustrate the determination to protect not only the institute's non-profit tax status but also its standing as an educational entity – which is vital to the preservation of the Poynter Institute's ability to hold all of the Times Holding Company shares. For example, there are established policies that require the *Tampa Bay Times* to pay the going rate for any use of Poynter facilities or staff, and to avoid employing journalists immediately after they complete institute courses. The company can second personnel to the institute – the dean of faculty, Stephen Buckley (previously managing editor of the newspaper), was originally seconded but is now on the permanent staff of the institute – but the process cannot operate in reverse. It is a peculiarity of Poynter's tax status, but the effect is similar to the separation between "owner" and newspaper achieved through very different means at *The Guardian* and the *Irish Times*. A similar tax status prevents some of the American start-up operations discussed in Chapter 8 from offering commercial services.

The unusual nature of the Poynter Institute's ownership of a major Florida commercial enterprise has led to periodic calls for greater disclosure of financial information. The legal disclosure requirements on the institute do not extend to detailed information on the activities of the Times Publishing Company, which as a private company is not obliged to report publicly on its financial activities each year. This aspect of the company's policy, which in terms of corporate transparency stands at the opposite end of the spectrum to the Guardian Media Group, renders it vulnerable to criticism.[17] Disclosure should be the default position for a news media company whose daily stock-in-trade is to press others to reveal facts and figures. The Guardian Media Group, no doubt influenced by Rusbridger's attitude to open access, is a model in this regard. Could the Times Publishing Company's lack of transparency be due to placing so many responsibilities, in accordance with Nelson Poynter's wishes, in the hands of one person? Would there be greater internal pressure to open the company books if power was more distributed?

Until recently, the Poynter Institute's sustained source of income was dividends from the publishing group although it had received grants from philanthropic organisations such as the Knight Foundation amounting to $US1–2 million a year. The institute's annual tax return up to the global financial crisis gave a glimpse of the Times Publishing Company's growth and pointed to the consistency of the company's contribution to the institute (see Table 7.5). Although the investment income also reflected the proceeds from investment funds worth approximately $US20 million, the

Table 7.5   Sustaining the Poynter Institute

Year	Times Holding Company total income ($US)	Poynter investment income ($US)*
2002	262,763,621	6,464,408
2003	280,205,139	6,339,122
2004	296,000,000	6,360,074
2005	317,278,240	6,492,238
2006	335,000,000	6,766,929
2007	308,000,000	3,695,344
2008	n/a	8,675,388
2009	274,700,000	(5,072,158)
2010	159,000,000	4,502,597
2011	151,000,000	989,828
2012	151,440,000	891,678

*Includes SP Times and income from investment portfolio.

bulk was derived from the subsidiaries of the Times Holding Company. After investment income was almost halved in 2007, the contribution was above average in the following year to largely restore the balance. The company's ability to continue to balance the institute's books through annual dividends has now, however, largely evaporated. Dunlap admitted in 2012 that it was "no longer viable" to rely on the Times Holding Company to fund Poynter's activities and that a foundation had been established to solicit philanthropic funding (Mullins 2012). The company has, however, provided more than $US150 million to the institute since Nelson Poynter's death in 1978 and Paul Tash believes it will continue to provide funding in the future. In 2013 he told me: "In the last few years of economic crisis, very few news companies – including this one – have generated operating results sufficient to pay dividends. We expect gradual improvement in that position with economic recovery and gains in our market share."[18]

There is a strong attachment within both organisations to Nelson Poynter's views on independent ownership. Several years before Dunlap made her admission about the newspaper's inability to meet the future funding needs of the institute, Tash told me that the Poynter Institute "has a sense of pride in owning an accomplished journalism organisation and that it would be directly counter to its own mission (to uplift journalism around the world) by demanding profits that forced it into being a plundering owner of the newspaper". In an interview with the *New York Times* he said: "We don't put out a newspaper to make money, we make money so we can put out a great newspaper" (Krauss 2007). After the sale of the *Boston Globe* and the *Washington Post,* Tash was asked whether the *Tampa Bay Times* could be put up for sale. He responded emphatically that it would not be sold and that its relationship with the Poynter Institute was a solid one that worked well (Brown 2013). In fact, for the institute to sell the Times Publishing Company would fly in the face of the Poynter bequest. Nelson Poynter was committed to journalism education but the establishment of the organisation that bears his name was as much a legal device to secure the future of the *Tampa Bay Times* as it was an expression of his educational aims. Just as the Scott Trust is committed to stewardship of *The Guardian*, the Poynter Institute could be legally bound to maintain its ownership of the *Tampa Bay Times*.

Paul Tash's attitude to the newspaper's future is clear and Nelson Poynter's foresight in vesting remarkable power in the hands of one person suggests the *Tampa Bay Times* will not follow its Washington and Boston counterparts into new hands. And, while he cannot bind his successor to any course of action, Tash is in a position to ensure that his successor has the same inextricable links and commitment to the newspaper and to Poynter's legacy.

There is a safe-deposit box in St Petersburg that contains the name of his successor. Tash chose the name, in fulfilment of Nelson Poynter's wish that each leader appoint his own successor and as insurance against an untimely demise, committed it to the vault on 14 May 2004 when he assumed command of the Times Holding Company and all of its offshoots. Only he knows whether the same name remains in the box a decade later. He has the sole right to choose his successor without consultation, and is under no obligation to remain with his initial choice. Nor is he obliged to signal the identity of the new chief executive before announcing his retirement (compulsory at 65) some time before 2020, although it is almost certain that he will do so. He has not publicly nominated a successor and says the elevation of Neil Brown to the editorship of the *Tampa Bay Times* "is in recognition of his outstanding work running our news report". It would be premature, therefore, to assume Brown will be given the top role.

Andrew Barnes had been chosen by Gene Patterson in 1984 and assumed the role of chairman and chief executive in 1988. Paul Tash served an apprenticeship under Barnes that made it increasingly clear over time that he had been chosen as Barnes' successor. He was appointed executive editor in 1992 and Barnes told the *American Journalism Review* in 2004 that he had had Tash in mind when he invited a dozen candidates for the executive editor's job to answer the question: "What do you see as the main challenges and opportunities facing the company and what would you do if you were in charge?" In an article in the *Tampa Bay Times* in 1999 he publicly acknowledged Tash as his choice for the position of chairman and chief executive.

A member of the *Tampa Bay Times* staff told me during anonymous interviews at the newspaper that before Tash was revealed by Barnes as his likely successor there were several other people who had been mentioned as candidates: "They scared the hell out of me, and when Tash was appointed, all I could say was 'thank God'."

The Editor of Editorials at the *Tampa Bay Times*, Tim Nickens, believes that Tash exemplifies a culture that is instilled partly through the Poynter Institute's ownership of the newspaper and its values, and partly through a steady and logical progression of successors "who have come from the inside, from within the system, and who have been groomed on a long glide path". Nickens adds that while the institution is bigger than one person, the chief executive puts his imprint on it: "It's a matter of emphasis and direction and reacting to the changing environment – within an unchanging foundation of the values and the sort of journalism that we do." For his part, Tash acknowledges the power of his position, and when I asked what checks and balances are imposed upon him, replied that he subscribes to the view, expressed by Barnes, that he "answers to an idea":

> I subscribe to that idea. I might express it a little differently but I answer to conscience, I answer to the terrific legacy of Nelson Poynter. I don't mean that in the sense that everything must be maintained as it was on the day he died but it is a tremendous thing that the man did – giving away his life's work in order to preserve it. I take that generous, hugely generous, decision that he made as a tremendous obligation. I will be the last chairman (God willing and unless something weird happens) who has a memory of him as a living human being. So you ask how do you inspire that sense of purpose and duty and possibility in those who come later and don't remember this man.

Tash, like those before him, demonstrates an almost religious attachment to the memory of Poynter and what he would expect. It is a belief system that permeates the *Tampa Bay Times* and the Poynter Institute, just as there are physical reminders such as photographs, framed copies of the Poynter Principles and (at the Poynter Institute) Poynter's Royal typewriter. There is also a sense of continuity in the manner in which the chief executive manages the company due, in all likelihood, to what Tash calls the "inculcation" of values – embodied in Poynter's "sacred trust" – that takes place during the apprenticeship period. Tash is an example of appointment-from-within. In an article marking the newspaper's 125th anniversary, he noted that "we don't have rotating editors and executives, moving through town on their way up the corporate ladder" (Tash 2009). There is no requirement that the successor must be an insider – Eugene Patterson was "brought in" by Nelson Poynter, but the value placed on the organisation's culture suggests he or she will emerge from the ranks.

The management style also owes much to Poynter's determination to give control without ownership. No chief executive of the Times Publishing Company has been able to profit financially beyond his salary and modest bonuses, and has therefore not been tempted into decisions based on personal gain. Tash's remuneration is modest by American executive scales.

In 2011, his salary and bonus amounted to $US512,000 – roughly midway between that of Irish Times managing director, Liam Kavanagh ($US350,000) and that of Guardian Media Group CEO, Andrew Miller ($US885,000) in the same year.[19] Staff members attest to his approachability and collaborative style. This collegial style permeates to lower levels of the company although the desire to reach consensus at those levels may occasionally delay the decision-making process.

Like Rusbridger, Tash has been an innovative contributor to the company's development. In September 2004, four months after he assumed command, the Times Publishing Company launched *tbt** (*Tampa Bay Times**) as a free weekly tabloid that targeted readers in the 25–35 age group. Two years later *tbt** became a weekday daily with an initial print run of 42,500 that has since more than doubled.[20] In 2013 the company also began a joint venture to distribute a local edition of the military newspaper *Stars & Stripes* to personnel serving at MacDill Air Force Base, which houses 14,500 military and civilian personnel and their dependents.

Tash was also a strong supporter of a ground-breaking editorial service that began in the *Tampa Bay Times* and online in 2008. Politifact was devised by the newspaper's Washington bureau editor to track promises the *Tampa Bay Times* identified as having been made by incoming president Barack Obama and to check (through a multiple-step verification process) the validity of statements by members of Congress, the White House, lobbyists and interest groups. The service, which won a Pulitzer Prize in 2009, was then also "regionalised" to scrutinise political statements in Florida through a partnership with the *Miami Herald*. It directly holds those in the political arena to account for the veracity of their statements, and has since been extended to a range of newspapers in other states. In 2013 it established its first international franchise when Politifact Australia was launched.

Under Tash's leadership, the newsroom was restructured to reflect the increasing opportunities that the Internet and interactive journalism provide in editorial operations. The *Tampa Bay Times* newsroom includes a NOW desk, that covers and updates breaking news stories on tampabay.com, tbt.com and politifact.com. The newspaper's staff have also won awards for the use of computer-assisted reporting.

However, it is in the area of investigative reporting that Tash displays his commitment to Poynter's journalistic legacy, and for which his newspaper has gained a national reputation. It is best exemplified by the *Tampa Bay Times'* reporting on the Church of Scientology. Coverage of the organisation dates back to its arrival in Florida, and earned the newspaper a Pulitzer Prize in 1980. During Tash's editorship there were special investigations in 2004 and 2006, and in 2009 when the *Tampa Bay Times* embarked on a major investigative series that drew on the experiences of former members of the congregation. Investigations into the Church of Scientology's activities continue under Brown's editorship and are led by two reporters, Joe Childs and Thomas C. Tobin who in January 2013 revealed a prolonged investigation of Scientology by the Federal Bureau of Investigation. In retaliation, the Church of Scientology has initiated concerted publicity campaigns against the newspaper and threatened lawsuits. Tash told me he believes publication of material criticising such a formidable organisation was also materially assisted by the fact that he is not subject to corporate or share market pressure. It is a sentiment that can be equally applied to *The Guardian* and the *Irish Times*:

> That work is directly tied to ownership that is private and independent because if we had been part of a chain – and particularly if we had been part of a chain that was publicly held – finding no satisfaction here in trying to derail that work, the officials of the church who are so vehemently opposed to that sort of coverage would have reverted to the corporate offices, would have threatened (as they often do), very expensive and consuming litigation. They would have gone to the home office because they didn't get any satisfaction here and the bosses at the home office would have said: "Let's slow it down, let's have a look at the review" and, failing that, they would have tried to exert pressure through the public markets and for a publicly held company that sort of exposure would be very annoying if not worrisome. This [the Church of Scientology] is an organization that backed down the Inland Revenue Service. So writing about them, covering them... this is not easily done. I think it's a clear example of the kind of work that is better able to be done because of our ownership structure.

Editorial staff to whom I spoke described Tash's decision-making role as "huge". One staff member contrasts the decision-making process at the *Tampa Bay Times* with his experience in a newspaper owned by a publicly traded company:

> That paper did some extraordinarily good investigative work, but the final word on things came from another division on a different floor and, after the sale of the newspaper, from another state. It's helpful here when you are seeking an answer that you can go up [to Tash's office] and get the answer.

Staff believe that while Tash might take the business into consideration, his editorial decisions were made "in terms of the journalism". It is an attitude that was present in his predecessors, and is also evident in the behaviour of O'Sullivan, Rusbridger and *their* predecessors – suggesting again, that it is a function of the type of organisation within which they operate.[21]

Each of Nelson Poynter's successors has faced a defining challenge. For Patterson, it was the translation of Poynter's dying wishes and the closure of the money-losing *Evening Independent*. For Barnes, it was securing the ownership of the Times Holding Company shares and resisting the Bass takeover bid. Tash's defining challenge has been in ensuring the survival of both the *Tampa Bay Times* and the Poynter Institute during a recession that, in the 2010 trough, made Tampa Bay one of the economically weakest metropolitan areas in the United States.[22]

The advertising revenue of the *Tampa Bay Times* in 2009 was roughly half that of 2006. Driven by the Florida real estate crash that saw state-wide house prices fall by more than a third in that period (and continue below the national average into 2013), the revenue decline extended to retail, automotive sales and employment advertising. The company recorded a $US3.3 million loss in 2008, and has been forced to cut millions of dollars from its operating costs. It had made previous economies – eliminating quarterly cost-of-living salary adjustments for full-time staff in 2001 and reducing the width of the newspaper (with commensurate newsprint savings) in 2006 – but the pressures facing the company after the credit crunch of 2007 had not been seen in decades.

The American newspaper industry in the same period experienced widespread and deep staffing cuts. The Times Publishing Company was not immune, and in 2008 offered an early retirement scheme that was accepted by 200 employees. In the same year it introduced a pay freeze that was extended in February 2009 when it also suspended its contributions to employees' pension plans. Seven months later, Tash announced the 5 per cent across-the-board pay cut and the phasing out of health care coverage for retirees on the company's health plan. By March 2010, the overall staff had been reduced by one-third (about 350 people) over a three-year period. In addition, the number of pages in each day's editions was reduced, some regional editions had been discontinued and some stand-alone sections such as business coverage were incorporated into the body of the newspaper. To overcome the problems of reduced space, the *Tampa Bay Times'* news stories were shortened and greater use made of the tampabay.com website to carry material that could not be accommodated on paper. In total, the company reduced its operating costs by more than $US70 million but it was not enough. The effects of recession continued to be felt and in 2011 the company instituted another temporary 5 per cent pay cut (which took $US1 million out of the wage bill) and the laying off of 6 per cent of the workforce. Announcing the five-month pay cut, Tash told staff: "I am fed up with this recession, like each of you, and I'm tired of having to bring tough news about its effect on the company and all of us." He added that he was not discouraged because of the gains being made to increase the newspaper's reach.

The recession had a great impact on American newspapers because of their higher reliance on advertising revenue than their British counterparts (Lanchester 2010, 5), and cuts have been made across the country. This raises

207 Modern White Knights

two questions: is the *Tampa Bay Times* management no different from that in newspapers that are under much-criticised chain-ownership or in publicly held companies, and have cutbacks had similar effects to those on newspapers under those forms of ownership? By their nature and severity, cutbacks could be expected to have a seriously negative impact on staff morale, and in many American newspapers that has been the case. It appears, however, that for a number of reasons the *Tampa Bay Times* is different.

From comments gathered during interviews with staff at the newspaper, it appears there is general acceptance that the company delayed cost-cutting measures longer than most of its contemporaries (there is some concern among staff that it may have waited *too* long and deepened its losses). Nickens, looking back on the 2009–2010 cutbacks, told me he did not detect bitterness during the process but rather, an acceptance that the newspaper was "not where it needed to be", and that cost reductions were necessary: "I saw some cases where the person who had been told we no longer had a job for them was comforting the editor who had told them the job was no longer there." Even after the 2011 layoffs there was a continuing belief in the company's commitment to quality journalism and the newspaper's position as a primary news source.[23]

There may be an element of "there-but-for-the-grace-of-God-go-I" in the prevailing support by staff for the *Tampa Bay Times*. They had been watching their closest competitor across Tampa Bay, the *Tampa Tribune*, which had been subject to budget cuts since 2007. In 2011 its workforce was reduced by 20 per cent in a single culling and the following year the newspaper was sold to a California private equity company for $US9.5 million – less than the value of the land and buildings that housed the newspaper's Tampa headquarters. Tash has taken advantage of the *Tribune's* weakened state to expand his newspaper's circulation area and, consequently, to rename the *St Petersburg Times* to better reflect its new catchment area.

There is a sense that the Times Publishing Company has tried to protect its editorial functions, although there have been noticeable reductions in the "machinery" of the newsroom – reporters' "beats" have been reduced, as has some local coverage.

Tash has been at pains to balance short-term financial needs against long-term effects. At the height of the recession he told me: "We didn't cut deeper because we were afraid that doing so would cause long-term damage to the relationship with readers and advertisers and that by doing such damage we would be diminishing the long-term value of the franchise when things started to improve." He added that he was certain that if the Times Publishing Company had been publicly listed there would have been deeper cuts. Again we see parallels with *The Guardian* and the *Irish Times*.

Since making those comments Tash has lost much of his ability to minimise budget restraints. The Times Publishing Company has been forced into survival mode because The Tampa-St Petersburg area had, by mid-2013, seen only 5.5 per cent economic growth over the four years since the region bottomed out at the end of 2009. In the good times the company had benefitted from the fact that it was not required to meet a set profit target, which in publicly held companies had often been driven by market expectation to levels in excess of 20 per cent (in many markets, not only the United States). The Times Publishing Company had a 10 per cent margin guideline, but did not use that as a measure by which to set its cost base. One staff member commended the company for foregoing high profit margins, recounting the case of another corporation that continued to deliver 15 per cent profit margins, not from revenue growth but from continually cutting costs. Tash told me, rather ruefully, in 2013:

> Before the recession hit in full force, our guidelines on profit margin set a range from a floor of 10 percent to a ceiling of 20 percent. From today's perspective, the concern that we might generate too much profit seems historically quaint.

Until the recession, the company and investment in mutual funds had been expected to generate around $US6 million a year in dividends to the Poynter Institute, with some profit retained for company development. Like the Guardian Media Group and the Irish Times, it was not burdened by the high levels of debt that many of its acquisitive contemporaries have had difficulty in servicing. It is difficult to gauge accurately the current state of the Times Publishing Company's balance sheet as it does not publish its accounts but it is clear from the Poynter Institute's annual tax returns that all has not been well. The value of the institute's net assets fell by more than $US22 million in the decade to 2012, the year in which its income from investments and securities (the sum that includes income from the Times Holding Company) was only 12.2 per cent of the 2002 total of $US6.5 million. Both the institute and the holding company have sold property assets to make up shortfalls and Dunlap's concession that the newspaper was no longer a "viable" source of financial support did not appear to describe a short-term issue.

The institute's solution has been to seek alternative finance through a new funding-raising foundation. By inference, the *Tampa Bay Times* will concentrate on self-sustainability with the hope of a return to providing dividends to Poynter. Would the outlook have been different if the *Tampa Bay Times* was no more than one of the assets of a publicly listed company? Media General divested itself of all of its newspaper assets in 2012 and prominent mastheads – the *Washington Post, Boston Globe, Orange County Register* and *Philadelphia Enquirer* among them – changed hands. Tash's statement that the *Tampa Bay Times* was not for sale could not, under such an ownership scenario, be taken at face value.

The *Tampa Bay Times* has largely avoided curtailing the activities that have earned it a national reputation. It has retained the long-form civic journalism that was once (but is no longer) a hallmark of many US newspapers. It has continued to mount lengthy and expensive investigations and special reports. The Pew Centre's 2013 State of the News Media Report identified the paper as one of four "top metros" that "produce a strong daily report and find the resources for high-impact special projects". Since 2007 the newspaper has had eight finalists and three winners in the Pulitzer Prize awards (it has won a total of nine Pulitzers). In 2012 Neil Brown, after appointing an investigations editor, announced more resources were being put into investigative journalism.

The newspaper was candid with its readers about the effects of the recession. Brown acknowledged cuts and fewer pages on weekdays, but believes the economies were made in areas that were no longer of interest to the broad readership. Investigative reporting and narrative story-telling, he told readers, had been preserved (Brown 2009). The newspaper compensated for lost coverage by substituting web-based material for regional newspaper sections and its website is now highly localised. It began an experiment it called Pro-Am, in which students from three colleges and residents wrote short stories on local events. Contributors were vetted and either accepted, rejected or sent to the Poynter Institute for training (for which the *Tampa Bay Times* pays). The newspaper also avoided a cost-cutting measure that has seen coverage of state government dramatically curtailed by the closure of bureaux in state capitals. Rather than follow suit, the *Tampa Bay Times* (which had cut its Tallahassee bureau staff from four to three) combined its resources with the *Miami Herald* (which had two reporters in the state capital) in 2009. Under the arrangement the newspapers split costs, the bureau chiefs of the two newspapers rotate leadership duties and reporters' beats have been reorganised to avoid duplication.

Nevertheless, no organisation can endure the privations of recession without an effect on staff morale and reader loyalty. However, the *Tampa Bay Times* went into the bad times with a deep reservoir of goodwill and commitment by staff to the newspaper. In 2001, the *Columbia Journalism Review* published a four-page report on the newspaper in which reporters credited it with more freedom to innovate, more support, more guidance, fewer administrative mandates and fewer power struggles than they had encountered in other (group-owned) newspapers at which they had worked (Baker 2001). Almost a decade later, Nickens maintained that "overall that's still very much true". In addition, the staff are inculcated with the values that trace back to Nelson Poynter, in the same way that there is an ethos left on *The Guardian* by C. P. Scott. Another executive stated that "the tenets and commitment have not changed: the 10 principles are pinned up around the place". Staff are also well aware that the *Tampa Bay Times* is *not* a non-profit enterprise even though its owner has that status. They accept that it is (and must be) run on a commercial basis. This has led to a pragmatism that is summed up by one staff member: "The recession has taken its toll. The cuts have led to real inroads in local coverage and it remains to be seen if that will be reinstated in better times. But I'll take this boat anytime. It's prepared to accept smaller profits to preserve its journalism."

Tash has not been tempted to follow the strategy of the Guardian Media group in diversifying away from his region's advertising-based markets.

Am I confident that I could pick the [right] business? I don't know. If it was another Kaplan [the educational business that became a major profit centre for the Washington Post Company] great, but if you bought the wrong thing you could end up dragging the company down.

The company's attention, he says, is consumed by the publishing business – the newspapers and the magazines – and "getting through this storm and positioning the company more strongly". And Paul Tash must also be mindful of Nelson Poynter's attitude, enunciated in his 1947 "standards of ownership", towards the creation of a large media group: "A 'chain' owner cannot do justice to local publications or radio stations. His devotion and loyalty to any one area is bound to be diluted or divided if he has other ownerships and interests."

Summary

Throughout this chapter, parallels have been drawn between the newspapers that form what I term the Trust trinity. While none has been immune from the effects of changes to news media markets, each has exhibited a determination to preserve the core journalism to which the creators of their unique forms of ownership committed them.

The three have varying degrees of resilience that I identify as the degree to which they have diversified with subsidiaries that are not subject to the same changes in market conditions as their parents. The uncertainty of news media markets mean that such commercial buffers are prudent components of future strategy for publications that must continue to make decisions that give full weight to the importance of the civic journalism they are committed to uphold.

The chapter showed that such an editorial commitment is common to all three newspapers, and is embedded in ways that are not found in most publicly listed newspaper companies. Not only are there codified obligations that pass from editor to editor, and trustee to trustee, but each has an enduring culture founded on the principles of liberal journalism practised by men who loomed large in their past.

However, the parallels are accompanied by differences. Each newspaper is in a different form of ownership, although all have trusteeship in common. Each has a different relationship with its trustees, although all trustees have reserve powers. Each has a different attitude to disclosure of its financial details, although all place profit second to the needs of their flagship newspapers. The editor-in-chief of each newspaper has a different level of control in the organisation, although all are the undisputed custodians of editorial policy.

In the final analysis, the value of trust-like ownership of these three newspapers comes down to a single question: would *The Guardian,*the *Irish Times* and the *Tampa Bay Times* enjoy the same reputations as civic-minded, values-driven newspapers if they were owned by profit-driven, publicly listed groups? They would in all likelihood be subjected to the same indiscriminate "economies" that have debilitated many of their contemporaries in recent years.

8
The Electronic Age

The press is the medium with the longest history of trust ownership but it does not have a monopoly on this form of news media governance. In the electronic age broadcasters and news services have used trustees as a guarantor of editorial independence and as a bulwark against state interference. Now they are emerging as guardians for the growing ranks of not-for-profit and low-profit start-ups that aim to secure the future for serious journalism in the digital age.

They may not bear the formal trustee title but irrespective of the name by which they are identified – they include governors, board members, directors, advisory councillors and governance officers – they are people who are charged with upholding public service principles and the independence and integrity of the journalism that their organisations produce. Those organisations may be legally constituted as trusts or they may not. As this chapter will demonstrate, it is possible to pursue all of the ideals of guardianship while, for whatever reason, operating under another legal structure.

The chapter begins by examining public service broadcasting, a system that usually takes the form of one or other of two exemplars: Britain's BBC and the United States' Public Broadcasting Service (PBS). The former is wholly state-funded and the latter largely depends on philanthropy. There are aspects of the structure of both forms of PSB that determine their trust-like behaviour and which provide some insights into governance that might be employed (or avoided) by news media trusts that could emerge in the future. The same can be said of some news agencies that are similarly interrogated before the chapter moves to an outline of organisations that have been established to compensate for the deficit in investigative and civic journalism caused by cost-cutting in traditional newsrooms. Finally, the chapter outlines the emergence of hybrid structures based on the low-profit limited liability company (L^3C) in the United States, its United Kingdom equivalent the Community Interest Company (CIC) and India's social business model – all of which recognise the public service contributions of social agencies that embrace the efficiencies of for-profit business. It may offer a means of preserving significant journalism while recognising the realities of altered media economics. In so doing it may create a new class of trustee structure.

Public service broadcasters

Public service broadcasters share a number of common characteristics that help them to achieve their principal goal of engaging viewers and listeners (and digital media users) in a dialogue about public life (Freedman 2008, 147). First and foremost is a dedication to the public interest and a sense that their services are a public good that contribute to the democratisation of public life (Scannell 1989, 136). They have a commitment to what Scannell describes as properly public, social values, and these are reflected in a concomitant commitment to high programme standards (*ibid.*, 164). Their charters include cultural and educational imperatives, and wide accessibility as part of their role to reflect the national character in all its diversity. Each plays a vital journalistic role, sometimes providing the only non-partisan reportage in a media environment increasingly populated by outlets determined to promote a particular point of view. This journalistic contribution extends to a commitment to the reporting of political assemblies (be they congressional or parliamentary) that is matched by few commercial media organisations. Their governance structures are designed to protect, preserve and enhance these attributes while maintaining a necessary distance from political influence.

It is common for PSBs to be constituted under empowering legislation. For example, Australia's ABC and SBS, which had been constituted under the Broadcasting and Television Act, are now covered by their own legislation – the Australian Broadcasting Corporation Act 1983 and the Special Broadcasting Service Act 1991. CBC-Radio Canada is governed by provisions of the Canadian Broadcasting Act 1991, and the New Zealand public service broadcasters by the Radio New Zealand Act 1995, the Television New Zealand Act 2003 and the Maori Television Service Act 2003. In India, public service broadcasting was under direct government control until the enactment of the Prasar Bharati Act in 1997, which granted autonomy to All India Radio and the Doordarshan television network through a corporation required to maintain editorial impartiality and protected by the Indian Supreme Court from unjustified government interference. In post-apartheid South Africa a new Broadcasting Act in 1999 reconstituted the South African Broadcasting Corporation (SABC had been originally established in 1936) under a new charter subject to oversight by an Independent Broadcasting Authority. In the United States, where public service broadcasting is based largely on regional and local cooperatives that depend on donations and philanthropy for their survival, a Corporation for Public Broadcasting (CPB) was initially established under the Public Broadcasting Act in 1967, and from it grew the PBS and National Public Radio (NPR). In each case, a feature of the legislation is the provision of clauses that distance the relevant organisations from direct government control and provide journalistic and programming independence.

In Europe, where public service broadcasting is idiosyncratic (Tunstall 2008, 250), arguably the most complex legislative arrangement for public service broadcasting exists in Germany. The German Constitution mandated the creation of public service broadcasting and also its decentralisation to prevent a resurgence of the wartime national broadcasting system that had been a powerful Nazi propaganda tool. Each Land (state) was required to establish a corporation to provide public service broadcasting under legislation that required a number of common principles, but which also reflected regional needs. Following German reunification and some consolidation, there are now nine such corporations running regional television and radio stations, plus digital services. They also formed a collective (ARD) under an inter-regional treaty to operate a national television network.

The exception to legislative mandate is the BBC, which has operated under a succession of Royal Charters since 1926. These instruments have created what Born describes as a "contradictory" relationship between the corporation and Parliament. Although the British government has oversight of the BBC's performance as each charter comes up for its (usually ten-year) renewal, and sets the public licence fee on which the BBC depends, it cannot claim the BBC as a direct instrument of state. The charter establishes the BBC as an independent corporation. Attempts to "rectify" this situation by making the BBC subject to empowering legislation (and hence directly answerable to Parliament) failed when a new Royal Charter was granted in 2006, in spite of strong representations opposing the structure by the House of Lords Select Committee on the BBC's Charter Review. The review changed the structure of the BBC and created the BBC Trust which, in spite of its name, is not a legal trust entity.

Protection from government interference is more apparent than real in most of the jurisdictions with which we are concerned. In particular, the ability of governments to control PSB finances has been a powerful lever that has affected levels of production and the commitment to certain broadcast services. Governments have a long-standing record of ambivalent attitudes towards their public service broadcasters, and even the BBC is not immune (Freedman et al. 2007; Humphreys 1999).

In many jurisdictions, governments have reserved the right to determine both the governance structure and membership of PSB boards. The majority of PSBs operate a two-tiered system of governance (a board and an executive committee) that separates the appointed board from the day-to-day operations of the broadcaster. In part, this represents the same separation of board and management found in commercial enterprises, but it has the added purpose of distancing political appointees from operational decision-making. Some legislation also requires the appointment of advisory boards to monitor programme content. Appendix B shows the similarity between the legislatively (or Royal Charter) driven structural elements of governance in different jurisdictions. German PSBs are each governed by different state (Land) legislation and have been omitted.

PSBs are also subject to the oversight of external regulatory bodies that police public and commercial broadcasters. In Britain, the BBC is required to conform to Office of Communications (Ofcom) codes under its agreement with the Government, while in Australia the ABC and SBS defer to the Australian Communications and Media Authority (ACMA) in appeals over complaints. New Zealand broadcasters[1] SABC and Prasar Bharati are each subject to complaints procedures adjudicated by independent broadcasting authorities set up for that purpose. In North America, CBC/Radio Canada is subject to programme and policy oversight by the Canadian Radio-television and Telecommunications Commission (CRTC), while in the United States the Federal Communications Commission has oversight within the confines of the First Amendment. In each case, commissioners or authority members are government appointees. Coupled with dependence on state funding, this means PSBs may be subject to three tiers of political patronage.

In structural terms, the governance of most PSBs is unremarkable. The boards of all of the PSBs in Appendix B, with the exception of the BBC, operate in much the same manner as any board of directors. For example, a former managing director of SBS, Shaun Brown, told me that organisation operates a "conventional governance relationship" in which the board scrupulously follows the dictate that it is there to set strategy and hold the managing director accountable while the chief executive's responsibilities are to deliver on those strategies and to meet SBS's charter obligations.[2] Like his counterparts, Brown had wide management powers including the right to hire and dismiss staff. PSBs do diverge from conventional corporate governance, however, by being subject to public service requirements either by statute or internal charter. These measures represent valuable templates for the documenting of public interest obligations to which trustees and executives in news media organisations might be held and, as an example, an extract from the charter of the SABC is included as Appendix C.

The BBC Trust is different because it is a solution to a problem highlighted in 2006 in the course of the review that usually precedes the renewal of the corporation's Royal Charter. The Hutton Report into the corporation's handling of the so-called "dirty dossier" on Iraqi weapons of mass destruction and the subsequent death of Dr David Kelly had raised concerns about the robustness of BBC governance.

At the time, the BBC was controlled by a Board of Governors whose relationship with the operational affairs of the broadcaster had been the subject of ongoing criticism. On the one hand there were charges of interference, while on the other, there were claims that the Governors and the executive were too close for the former to discharge a role as representative of the public interest (or licence-payer). Born's analysis of the running of the corporation, in the years immediately preceding the restructuring that saw the creation of the BBC Trust, concluded that "extensive reforms" were necessary to overcome "the vexed issues of governance and self-regulation, which lay at the heart of the BBC's escalating political difficulties in recent years" (2005, 505). While Born saw those reforms being achieved from within, a March 2005 Green Paper on the review envisaged a radical restructuring.

The Green Paper stated that the then-current BBC Board of Governors had to carry out two potentially conflicting roles: running the BBC, and assessing how well it was performing, and judged that "this model is increasingly out of step with best corporate governance" (2005, 6). The 2006 Royal Charter required the BBC to establish two bodies to overcome the conflict: the BBC Trust would set the overall strategic priorities for the corporation and provide oversight, and an Executive Board of the BBC would be responsible for delivery of BBC services. It bears some similarity to European corporate supervisory boards. In Germany for example, it is common for companies to have a two-tiered board structure in which a supervisory board is responsible for the appointment and supervision of an executive or management board. Such a two-tiered system is required by the European Union for registration as a European Company or SE (Societas Europaea).

When the new structure came into effect in January 2007, the separation was symbolised by the installation of the Trust and its support body, the Trust Unit, in offices far removed from Broadcasting House. The Trust Unit employs about 70 people, the majority of whom are London-based. The unit advises trustees on their duties, manages the Trust's supervisory and regulatory functions and provides independent assessments of proposals from the BBC's Executive Board.

The Trust negotiated a framework agreement with the Government, required under the Royal Charter, which elaborates some of the obligations that the Charter imposes and sets out the process by which the corporation will be funded. It imposes on the Trust an obligation to keep BBC spending under continual review. The Trust is also responsible for negotiating with the Culture Secretary the level of licence fee payment that is the BBC's principal source of income. The Royal Charter itself set six public purposes for the BBC to fulfil, and the Trust has in turn produced a series of "purpose remits" that document priorities that trustees set the Executive board in each of the areas which include "sustaining citizenship and civil society", "promoting education and learning" and "stimulating creativity and cultural excellence".

The framework agreement also required the Trust to establish a complaints procedure, through which viewers can seek redress over programme content. The BBC has a three-tiered complaint system under which the Trust acts as an appeal authority on matters of impartiality and inaccuracy, and some commercial matters. Aside from those three areas of concern that are regarded as the province of the BBC alone, complainants can take their concerns to the outside complaints authority, Ofcom.

The trust's oversight of the BBC is carried out through seven committees: audience and performance, finance and compliance, editorial standards, strategic approvals, remuneration and appointments, audience councils and general appeals. Each committee is composed of between three and six trustees. Oversight is a combination of process (the Executive Board is required to report regularly and to submit significant proposals for approval) and proactive governance when major issues arise – an eventuality to which we will return. The committees carry out periodic reviews within their respective briefs. The editorial standards committee, for example, has reviewed the impartiality of coverage of the Arab Spring and of refugee issues.

A month before standing down in April 2011 the Trust's first permanent chairman, Sir Michael Lyons, stated that the Trust was "not a traditional regulator, in fact not really a regulator at all, but with significant powers and resources to challenge BBC management and to shape the BBC on behalf of the public who own it".[3] He went on to say that even now, within the corporation, there are some who do not fully understand the Trust's "parental powers and responsibilities". To remove any misconceptions he then outlined the purposes – "the reality, not the fiction" – of the Trust:

- Fundamentally it is a supervisory board with some regulatory functions. Most notably the oversight of accuracy and impartiality, just like the Governors before us.
- It is markedly more separate from the Executive than was the case with the Governors and has its own professional support staff.
- It approves strategy and headline budgets; the Executive manages the day-to-day functions of the BBC and the Director-General is both chief executive and Editor-in-Chief, with the Trust there to protect the independence of that latter role.
- The Trust has one significantly different power compared with the Governors – it has the authority to approve new BBC services, a power that used to lie with the Secretary of State.

  - The charter defines these roles and focuses the Trust on the fundamental duty of representing the public interest in its governance of the BBC.
  - This translates, first of all, into guarding the independence of the BBC, for on that independence hangs the high level of public trust that the BBC enjoys.
  - But it also translates into a consistent challenge from the Trust to the Executive to do better in terms of value for money, impartiality, distinctiveness and better serving the BBC's many different audiences across the U.K.

In other words, the Trust had set itself apart from the operations of the BBC. As the representative of the public, it could function as auditor and defender without becoming a cheerleader for the corporation. This distance is what particularly distinguishes the Trust from the Governors that it replaced. However, recent events precipitated by investigation into allegations of sexual offences by the late entertainer Jimmy Savile and others employed by the BBC, together with the fallout from a *Newsnight* current affairs programme that made similar allegations against "a leading Conservative politician from the Thatcher years" (see the section on stand-alone non-profit journalism later in this chapter), have raised questions over whether the distance is too great for effective control. Leaving aside the behaviour of those under police investigation, the various enquiries into the BBC's handling of related issues revealed systemic problems in the day-to-day operations of the corporation – including the scale of severance payments to senior staff leaving the organisation – of which the Trust was unaware. The chairman, Lord Patten, gave evidence to the Pollard Review of a *Newsnight* investigation into the Savile affair after examining documents on that matter and said he had found that parts of the corporation "existed in parallel universes". He said he had found some aspects of the corporation's structure and function were "chaotic". A fellow trustee, Anthony Fry, in July 2013 told a separate enquiry by the House of Commons Public Accounts Committee into BBC severance payments that some BBC staff were "out to lunch" over salary expectations. Lord Hall, appointed director-general in April 2013 after two predecessors had fallen on their swords in quick succession, told the same enquiry that since taking up his position he had found the BBC organisation to be "over-complex, over-layered".

This suggests that the Trust was unaware of fractured reporting lines, cultural shortcomings and managerial decisions involving considerable sums of money in spite of the oversight by Trust committees, the production of numerous policy documents and guidelines, regular meetings with the director-general of the BBC, and a succession of reviews on matters as diverse as participation in broadband television services and content bias. It further suggests that the structural change that led to the creation of the BBC Trust should also have included a mandate for it to oversee internal reorganisation to address the deficiencies identified by Born.

In a parliamentary debate on the BBC Trust in 2013[4] a Conservative MP, Rob Wilson, castigated the corporate level of the BBC, saying he had "rarely encountered such poor management at any level in any organisation", and describing a "woeful lack of active leadership by the BBC Trust". The response by Edward Vaizey, Parliamentary Under-Secretary of State for Culture, Communications and Creative Industries, highlights the systemic problem:

> In terms of the BBC Trust's role as the guardian of the licence fee revenue, its strategic functions include setting the strategic direction of the

BBC and assessing the performance of BBC services. BBC Trust oversight of the BBC, however, does not extend to interference in editorial decision-making and involvement in operational management. It is the regulator of the BBC, but it does not run the BBC on a day-to-day basis.

In an enterprise as large and complex as the BBC, do trustees need to have an ability to oversee not only what is done but also *how* it is done? The chairman of the House of Lords Select Committee on Communications, Lord Fowler (a former minister in the Thatcher government), has been critical of the BBC's governance structure since it was first mooted. He told me[5] that the structure was "a complete nonsense" that prevented the normal corporate processes under which a chief executive and directors interacted with each other around a board table. Instead the executive (led by the director-general of the BBC) was separated from the board of directors (the BBC Trust) not only organisationally but also physically. The creation of an Executive Board with non-executive members had allowed the director-general to function as an executive chairman, a position that was out of step with present-day views of corporate governance.

Lord Fowler was committed to the replacement of the Royal Charter (which he describes as a "period piece that was a reaction to the Hutton Report") with legislation that would bring the corporation under parliamentary oversight in terms of how it was organised, and holding it accountable for the spending of the public's money. He also believed that the regulatory functions of the BBC Trust should be passed to Ofcom: "It regulates the rest of the television and radio industry so why not the BBC?" In short, he saw no real place for the Trust in an environment where the BBC would have conventional corporate governance and be subject to external regulatory oversight. It would, in effect, be run along similar lines to ITV (without the advertising revenue).

The Trust must tread two parallel fine lines: it has twin roles as regulator and authoriser, plus it must (under the terms of the Royal Charter) preserve its separation from the day-to-day operations of the BBC. The concept of independence has taken on almost religious significance within the corporation and has allowed directors-general to turn that separation to advantage and to create what one journalist described – and Rob Wilson was only too happy to repeat in the 2013 Westminster debate – as "a totalitarian state". This sense of internal sovereignty has led to a certain delicacy in the handling of major projects for which the executive requires Trust approval, and has led to a degree of reserve in relationships between the two bodies. As a result the Trust's ability to oversee *how* things are done has been less than optimal. Acrimonious exchanges between the Trust and a former director-general, Mark Thompson, during the 2013 parliamentary enquiry suggest the gap was wide indeed and raise questions over the part played by the personalities of individuals.

This contrasts with the more familial relationship the Scott Trust has with the Guardian Media Group and the Irish Times Trust has with its enterprise. In both cases the culture is one where the trust is seen as the friend and protector of the publication. In the case of the BBC the corporation has seen the BBC Trust as an obligation under the Royal Charter. Its role as an adjudicator of complaints – a task that does not fall to any of the newspaper-owning trusts – puts further distance between the BBC Trust and the executive. There is, however, a reluctance to pass the regulatory responsibilities entirely to Ofcom, thus increasing the power of an already potent authority. From a public interest standpoint, there could also be political fallout (an avoidable risk in the Conservative-Liberal coalition) from passing all oversight of the BBC to an organisation (Ofcom) established to privilege the role of consumers over that of citizens (Freedman 2008, 118).

When I put questions about the BBC Trust to its chairman, Lord Patten, he felt constrained by an internal review process that had yet to conclude. However, he made the following points:

> The BBC is a unique organisation, within public service broadcasting and within the media more widely. The governance system that has been established by the BBC's Royal Charter attempts to provide an appropriate oversight structure for a large public service broadcaster that operates within a competitive commercial landscape, both in the United Kingdom and globally. The Trust's responsibilities are therefore not only to determine the strategic direction of the Corporation in the interests of licence fee payers and audiences, but also to ensure that its decisions are made in the knowledge of the BBC's impact in the wider market. The need for adequate oversight in the spending of large amounts of public money, and the responsibilities of the Trust to weigh issues of public value against possible market impact, sit alongside our responsibilities to protect the editorial and operational independence of the BBC. It is my view – and the view of those who established this structure, well before my arrival at the BBC – that these functions are best discharged separately from the executives who have been appointed to manage the day-to-day operations of the Corporation. It is for this reason that the Trust exists, separate from the management and the industry regulator, and explicitly holding the BBC to a high standard.[6]

I asked him whether there was a danger in judging the BBC governance structures on the basis of a single incident like the Savile scandal or the severance payment issue and he responded:

> I do think that there is danger in reaching conclusions on any system of governance in such circumstances, and fundamentally that the current model – while not perfect – provides a workable means of overseeing and

regulating the BBC in the public interest. Nonetheless, I feel that we must have a system that works under the strains and pressures that the BBC inevitably faces. Those who pay the licence fee have a right to expect this from us.

So the structure remains controversial – a halfway house between internal and external regulation – but for the purposes of this study the BBC Trust is a useful example of highly codified separation of functions between trustees and the executive. The Royal Charter[7] sets out in detail the functions of both bodies and the manner in which they should interact. Section 24 contains 17 provisions detailing the Trust's functions, while Section 38 details nine functions that are reserved to the executive. The Charter also binds the BBC to provisions in the Framework Agreement that give additional functional detail, setting out the Public Value Test that the Trust is required to apply to all new services proposed by the executive. The Agreement also sets out procedures under which the Trust develops protocols and codes of practice to be followed by operational units of the BBC, and gives the Trust specific powers to direct the Executive Board on the allocation of "an appropriate amount" of programme schedule time for news and current affairs. Explicit in the Royal Charter and implicit in the Framework Agreement is the need for the Trust and the Executive Board to play different roles within the BBC and "never act together as a single corporate body".

Explicit in both documents is the guaranteed independence of the BBC from government. However, the corporation has found throughout its long history that it is not immune from political pressure and recent controversy is likely to increase that pressure. Nonetheless, it is not alone, as most PSBs will attest.

The principal means by which governments assert influence over public service broadcasters who theoretically shelter under an "independent" umbrella, are appointment processes and appropriation of funds. Indirect influence is applied through regulatory bodies that are also subject to influence through government appointment processes. There are inherent limits in PSB autonomy, because the public service operation is "a creature of legislation and politicians, and can only go so far astray" (Herman & McChesney 1997, 5). Interference in bodies such as the BBC, ABC, SBS, CBC/Radio Canada, TVNZ and Radio New Zealand needs to be kept in perspective – it is far less intrusive than in state-owned broadcasters in less democratic regimes and must be judged alongside the services that the PSBs *are* able to deliver. Nevertheless it illustrates the need to be aware of the limitations of apparent safeguards.

Dependence on funding that is controlled by outside agencies is a fundamental weakness. The systems that fund the BBC, the United States' CPB[8] and the New Zealand Broadcasting Commission (NZ on Air) are attempts to place funding at one remove from direct government appropriation but in fact, in each case the government of the day exercises control over any movement in the level of funding. In the case of the BBC, the licence fee negotiating process has been called "profoundly political" (Freedman, 162). The coalition government in the United Kingdom imposed a six-year freeze on the level of the fee in 2010, the National-led government in New Zealand froze Radio New Zealand funding "for the foreseeable future" in March 2010 and the Obama Administration's 2012 Budget proposes cuts to public broadcast funding. CBC/Radio Canada's hybrid funding system (a combination of federal funds, subscription fees and advertising revenue) depends on an annual appropriation from the Canadian Government for more than 70 per cent of its income, which has been subject to cuts. In Australia, a triennial funding system operates for both the ABC and SBS. The former has been relatively successful in securing funding increases, while the latter's calls for additional money to fund digital services were largely ignored by the Liberal government. In 2012 a Labor-led Government provided a funding boost of $158.1 million over four years.

Hence, politicians may not exert control over content such as news and current affairs, but they have a significant influence over how much content is produced and how it is done. It is the same type of control that management and major shareholders exert over the news budgets of newspapers – as editor then editor-in-chief of the *New Zealand Herald* over almost a decade, I worked with an editorial budget that was ultimately decided by the chief executive. It is a situation in which finance controllers do not infringe the letter of editorial freedom (they do not attempt to determine the nature of content) but their effect on editorial output can be profound in terms of quantity and quality.

Radio New Zealand is a good example of such effects. Peter Cavanagh, who retired as chief executive and editor-in-chief in 2013, did not believe that government used financial approvals as a coercive means of dictating content. However, he had no doubt about the effects of inadequate funding. In 2007, the then government commissioned a review of Radio New Zealand funding to be carried out by the accountancy and auditing group KPMG, which had conducted a similar review of the ABC for the Australian government. The study found that Radio New Zealand baseline funding was 20 per cent below what was considered necessary to sustain services. This baseline would have added $NZ8–9 million to the existing budget of $NZ32 million. The following year, the PSB was granted an additional $NZ2.6 million but subsequent appropriations were frozen at $NZ34.3 million for the foreseeable future without any compensating reduction in Radio New Zealand's Charter obligations. Cavanagh told me[9]:

> It may be possible for us to perform at an adequate level in the future but not at the same level we are [achieving] at the moment. The Charter is a qualitative not quantitative document and quality is a subjective thing.

I think we'll probably need a few years in the future before we can look back at this time to see whether we were producing at the same qualitative rate that we are currently... Now the most optimistic person in the world could not possibly say that we can maintain our performance at the same rate of qualitative output in all of our Charter areas over that time without any increase in funding. It just won't happen so there will undoubtedly be reduced qualitative outputs. One of our challenges over the next couple of years will be to work out how to maintain the highest quality that we are able to maintain for the funding and resources that we have and to provide the best service we can within our means.

Radio New Zealand's dilemma is apparent elsewhere. In each jurisdiction, PSB directors/trustees have limited ability to influence the political decision-making process on funding, while remaining vulnerable to criticism for failing to protect the interests of their organisations. In 2012 the president of CBC/Radio Canada, Hubert Lacroix, announced service cuts in the face of a $C115 million reduction over three years in government funding. In South Africa the SABC was forced to go cap-in-hand to the government in 2010 to resolve a financial crisis that had put it R1 billion in debt. The resulting R1.4 billion National Treasury guarantee drew the corporation even closer to a government to which it had already been accused of being subservient.

The South African experience is an example of the need for public interest-driven news organisations to employ structural mechanisms that limit, as far as possible, the ability of external agents to exert undue influence. None has been wholly successful to date. In 2006 the International Federation of Journalists accused the SABC of self-censorship by "politically influenced managers" after a documentary on South Africa's president Thabo Mbeki was withdrawn from broadcast. The corporation has been periodically accused of manipulating news coverage to favour the ruling African National Congress party. Successive British governments (before, during and after the Hutton report) were accused of intrusive interventions in the affairs of the BBC (Born 2005, 500). The Conservative-led government's choice as head of the BBC Trust of a former chairman of the Conservative Party (Lord Patten) to replace the Labour government's choice of a former Birmingham City Council Labour councillor and advisor to Gordon Brown (Sir Michael Lyons) preserves a perception of continued political patronage and promotes controversy. The incoming BBC Trust chairman was the first, however, to appear before a House of Commons select committee in a pre-selection hearing (although a veto of his appointment was unlikely) and, as chairman, Lord Patten has not displayed closeness to the Conservative-led government, nor has he been immune from criticism. In 2005, a review by the United States CPB's Inspector-General Office lent weight to claims during the George W. Bush Administration of conservative political bias by the presidentially appointed board and led to the resignation of its chairman. The Inspector

General (charged with independent audits and reviews within the corporation) found that the CPB chairman had applied a "political test" in the appointment of a chief executive and that the organisation allowed the chairman and CPB executives to operate without "appropriate checks and balances". DeBrett's review of Television New Zealand (2010, 161–182 concludes "a history as political football has left public service broadcasting in New Zealand without the cushioning of traditions or collective public memory to inspire public support". An Australian Senate inquiry found: "The overwhelming view of submissions received by the inquiry was that the ABC has become politicised, has lost its independence, and accordingly, has lost the confidence of the public" (Australian Senate 2001).

Over time, a significant element of such allegations has been the appointment process. As set out in Appendix B, the vast majority of the PSB boards are appointed by the executive wing of government, and political links are to be found in many of them. A proposal by the Australian Labor Party (which would have been implemented had it won the 2004 election) was to replace appointments by Cabinet with a civil service selection panel, operating under the British Nolan rules, which would interview candidates for advertised vacancies (Inglis 2006, 558–559). The 2001 Senate inquiry had recommended a selection panel made up of both houses of Parliament. Neither proposal was adopted, but they represent an unfulfilled desire to distance selection processes from those who would seek to derive benefits from the appointments.

In political terms, these benefits range from acquiescence over controversial government policies to the application of internal pressure aimed at modifying news coverage that is critical of the government. Empowering acts and charters set a framework of independence, but require resolve on the part of directors/trustees (and executives) to resist informal pressures. Political appointment is not, of course, a sentence of subservience, and there are numerous examples of such appointees standing against the will of government when they believed proposed actions were not in the interests of a PSB or of the public. For example, a former chairman of the ABC, Maurice Newman, was described as "notoriously his own man" despite the fact he was the Prime Minister's friend (Simons 2007, 172). Nonetheless, in an industry in which the public interest is to the forefront, transparency and distance are elements that should be given expression in an appointment structure. None of the PSBs under study here has gone more than partway towards this goal although India's Prasar Bharati has come closest with a once-removed appointment process by a committee comprising the chairman of the Council of States (the Upper House of Parliament), the chairman of the Press Council of India and a presidential nominee. Its recommendations are, however, still subject to presidential approval.

Politicians unhappy at the news coverage they receive from PSBs are wont to claim the broadcasters are failing to "meet their charter obligations regarding fairness and accuracy". As Cavanagh noted, qualitative provisions are inherently subjective. However, it is evident from comments made by all of the PSBs under study that charter provisions are taken seriously and their annual reports list outputs that contribute to meeting these obligations. They give substance and media context to the phrase "public service".

News agencies

The national news agencies of Britain, North America, Australasia and India see themselves as bastions of unbiased, accurate reportage. Their owners have, in the main, practised trust-like stewardship.

In 1941, Reuters News Agency was in disarray and came close to collapse at the very time that its international news coverage of the war effort was most needed. It was rescued when the Press Association (PA; owned by Britain's provincial newspapers) joined forces with the country's national newspaper owners and later, the news agencies of Australia, New Zealand and India. The result was an organisation that set journalistic benchmarks and which operated, under the terms of their formal agreement, "in the nature of a trust" (Read 1992, 244).

In the 70 years since the Reuter Agreement was signed much has changed. Reuters is no longer a cooperative, but is in the hands of a Canadian corporation (largely owned by the descendants of Lord Thomson of Fleet) that is centred on business information. The Press Trust of India withdrew from the partnership after only four years, the New Zealand Press Association (NZPA) no longer exists and Australian Associated Press (AAP) has been forced to augment its news services in a bid to meet the challenges of a declining market in traditional media. The surviving agencies have endeavoured, however, to maintain the guarantees of journalistic independence and quality that are exemplified by the 1941 document. Yet none is a legal trust. With the exception of Thomson Reuters and Canada's domestic agency, Canadian Press, which was restructured in 2010 as a for-profit corporation in a financial rescue deal, each is a form of cooperative in which the owners forego dividends in order to sustain the agency's newsgathering capacity.

The development of successful national news agencies in the English-speaking world has been based on the cooperative model with ownership vested in member news organisations. The need for these organisations to adopt a form of self-interested neutrality in order to share information led to boards of directors acting as custodians of a service provider rather than as drivers of profit and corporate efficiency. Some wrote the concept of service above profit into Articles of Association, while others publicly bound the board to codes of practice adopted by their news service. Some were content to defer to strong (sometimes legendary) managers who ensured that their agencies embodied the concepts of service and trust. Hand-in-hand with instruments to safeguard editorial independence and journalistic values went anti-competitive provisions that enhanced the economic value of membership and locked out other potential subscribers. Anti-competitive strategies reached a climax in the *United States v Associated Press* in 1945 when the US Supreme Court ruled such "closed shops" violated the Sherman Antitrust Act.

Here is not the place, however, to canvass the history of wire services. Rather, it is useful to highlight four aspects of news agency governance that contribute potential ingredients to trust structures of the future.

The first relates to Reuters, and the trust deed signed on 28 October 1941. The deed, endorsed by the wartime British government, stated that the parties "will regard their respective holdings of shares in Reuters as in the nature of a trust rather than as an investment" and committed them to ensure:

(a) That Reuters shall at no time pass into the hands of any one interest group or faction.
(b) That its integrity, independence and freedom from bias shall at all times be fully preserved.
(c) That its business shall be so administered that it shall supply an unbiased and reliable news service to British, Dominion, Colonial, Foreign and other overseas newspapers and agencies with which it has or may hereafter have contracts.
(d) That it shall pay due regard to the many interests which it serves in addition to those of the Press.
(e) That no effort shall be spared to expand, develop and adapt the business of Reuters in order to maintain in every event its position as the leading world news agency.

The two shareholders each appointed four trustees and the independent chair was nominated by the Lord Chief Justice. When the AAP and the NZPA became shareholders in 1946 and the Press Trust of India in 1948,[10] each was allowed to appoint a director and a trustee. The role of the trust was to "act in a consultative capacity with the board", and it had the power to reject nominations to the board and to dismiss directors (Read 1992, 244–245). The PEP Report on trusts acknowledged the Reuters agreement, but made no comment on its effectiveness. However as later events were to prove, the deed was no more than a shareholders' agreement that could be altered (*ibid.*, 234). Its provisions also could be sidestepped, as in the acceptance of money from the Foreign Office that was characterised as a commercial contract but which was in fact a subsidy that flew in the face of "integrity, independence, and freedom from bias" (*ibid.*, 326–332).

The flotation of Reuters as a public company in 1984 (on the back of its lucrative move into financial data services) led to restructuring that altered the trust deed and the trustees played an active role in protecting what had become known as the Reuters Trust Principles. The result was the creation of a Founders Share Company that held one special share with overriding voting rights in certain circumstances. Under the new structure, the trustees could invoke the Founder's Share to prevent a single group acquiring control, and could prevent any move to vary the Founder's Share's protective power (*ibid.*, 364). Additional trustees with no connection with Reuters or the newspaper industry were appointed.

The trust was reckoned to have been strengthened by the flotation and restructuring. When associated transactions had the effect of increasing Rupert Murdoch's holding of Reuters "A" shares to 23 per cent (*ibid.*, 403–404), the possibility of trustee intervention was sufficient to force divestiture. However, this apparent strength did not prevent the merger of Reuters and the Thomson Corporation (an effective takeover by the latter) in 2008 when the article that had kept Murdoch at bay was ignored. It was clear evidence that the deed protected only those things that directors wished to protect at any given time.

Nonetheless, when Reuters merged with Thomson, the mechanism that had protected the editorial integrity of the agency was maintained and the Founder Share and Founder Share Company provisions were written into the new articles of association (Article 1.5).

The second example is the Press Trust of India, whose company articles serve as a model that places the principles of good journalism at the core of the business. Its Memorandum of Association incorporates a barely modified version of the Reuters trust deed provisions set out above. In addition to those principles of independence, the company's main object – undertaking the work of a news agency – requires it to transmit news "which shall at all times be free of bias". The articles also require the company "to oppose and resist, either directly or indirectly, any legislation which may seem disadvantageous to the company".

The third noteworthy example is the way in which the Press Association in Britain has applied the trustee principle. The PA Group's memorandum of association sets out the objects of the company, that include (Section 3a) the collection and dissemination of news and information "on as reliable and impartial a basis as reasonably possible". It then goes on to list a wide range of other functions that contribute to the group's broadening commercial interests. Section 3a is a somewhat equivocal rendition of the journalists' mantra of independence and impartiality, and in 2007, driven by the increasingly commercial focus of the group in the face of rapidly declining fortunes in its traditional newspaper market, the board decided that it needed another mechanism to demonstrate the independence of its traditional editorial services. It established a consultative committee, known as the Press Association Trust, to oversee editorial activities and altered its articles of association (Article 97a) to require the three-person Trust to provide an annual audit of editorial performance.

The Trust is composed of a former newspaper editor-in-chief, a former BBC Controller of Editorial Policy and an emeritus professor of journalism. Its audits have included an assessment of allegations, based on research by Cardiff University, of PA reliance on press releases (Davies 2008); the effects of the financial crisis on PA's editorial staffing; and a review of reporters' activities during the phone-hacking scandal. However, the Trust is a recent development, and has yet to find itself in a situation where it must challenge either the board or management of the agency. It remains to be seen whether it represents an effective check on boardroom and management power and a guardian of the public interest, but it should nonetheless be seen as a useful *potential* safeguard.

The final example is a means by which the self-interest of stakeholders can be kept in check, and is found in the operations of the AAP and Canadian Press.

Australia's newspaper conglomerates (News Corporation and Fairfax Media) have a competitive and antipathetic relationship that, as they are the two principal shareholders of the AAP, could spill over to the agency's operation with disastrous effects. However, my review of the news agencies of Australia and New Zealand (Ellis 2010, 106–121) found such difficulties have been anticipated in the company memorandum and in a management agreement. The former includes in the company objectives "To preserve the integrity, independence, and freedom from bias of the company's services by, amongst other things, maintaining a balance of control between members" that prevents one group outvoting the other (a situation that could have arisen when Fairfax Media merged with another shareholder, Rural Press in 2007 but led instead to a redistribution of votes) and which has promoted a degree of consensus that has had the boardroom nicknamed "Switzerland".

However, while the shareholders could be kept in balance, there was also a need to ensure that their own interests did not interfere with the agency's operational autonomy. A former chief executive of AAP, Clive Marshall (now chief executive of the Press Association in the United Kingdom), negotiated a formal management agreement with the board that established an arms-length relationship between directors and management and gives AAP a free hand to develop and sell services. The agreement extends to editorial independence and the editor-in-chief of AAP, Tony Gillies, told me that neither shareholders nor the editors of their newspapers apply pressure to the agency over news coverage.[11]

The combination of company articles and shareholder-management agreement is a belt-and-braces approach that has worked well at AAP, and illustrates the advantages of not relying on a single element of formal governance to provide appropriate environments and safeguards. It stands in contrast to its near neighbour, the New Zealand Press Association (NZPA), which shut down in 2011 after 131 years of service. This followed the withdrawal, amid growing rivalry, of Fairfax Media, that was one of the two

Australian-owned newspaper groups that were the principal owners of NZPA. Its parent company is also a major shareholder in AAP where inter-group antipathy had been held at bay. Fairfax and its New Zealand competitor, APN News & Media, then set up rival internal news services that had significant gaps in domestic geographic coverage.

A similar fate could have befallen Canadian Press in 2010 when it was faced with a $C34.4 million pension fund shortfall that threatened its survival. Three of Canada's largest newspaper publishers, Torstar, Globe & Mail and Square Victoria (the parent company of Montreal's *Le Presse*), combined to acquire the cooperative news agency established in 1917. The trio formed a for-profit entity, Canadian Press Enterprises (CPE), and restructured the agency's finances and operations. The publisher of the *Globe & Mail* and the publisher of the *Toronto Star* are co-chairs of the company and each of the three shareholders has two seats on the board. The chief executive was recruited from a group that had left the old Canadian Press cooperative in 2007. Co-chair Phillip Crawley of the *Globe & Mail* describes the governance as "three-way ownership".

The president of CPE, Malcolm Kirk, agrees that the organisation is seen as acting in the best interests of the news agency rather than of individual shareholders. He told me in 2013 that, although he is unaware of any formal agreement like that negotiated by Clive Marshall while at AAP, his organisation enjoyed complete editorial independence:

> There is an acknowledgement that we want CPE to be a for-profit enterprise but, as it stands, I can tell you we don't have *any* interference at all or intervention at board level. We are expected to secure the very best pricing we can for our products and services but I think there is a pervasive sense of fairness.[12]

The old Canadian Press agency was governed by a statute that prohibited it from distributing profits. The reconstituted agency is not a cooperative and has no such provision. Kirk describes financial self-sustainability as a "bare minimum" and believes that would be the view of shareholders. He has more ambitious financial goals and expected the break-even point to be reached in 2014, aided by a diversification strategy that includes new digital services as well as the Pagemaster outsourcing service – licensed from AAP, where it is a significant contributor of revenue – that now sub-edits and paginates much of the *Toronto Star*, the *Globe & Mail* and a number of other publications. Central to the financial strategy, however, is the maintenance of core news agency services that, Kirk says, retain the editorial values and standards of the old Canadian Press.

Governance structures that protect the ability of news agencies to function as non-partisan, accurate gatherers and distributors of news and information in the public interest may take on added significance in a future where traditional newspaper and broadcasting newsrooms are under increasing cost pressures.

The editor of the *Guardian*, Alan Rusbridger, told a Media Standards Trust seminar in 2009 that the decline of local news reporting warranted a government subsidy to the Press Association to undertake local public service journalism, which he described as a "kind of utility" which was as important as gas and water (Holmwood 2009). The PA at the time was attempting to start a pilot scheme to redress its own decline in local council and court coverage. Rusbridger's comments were in response to an alarming decline in local news coverage in Britain, but it is a phenomenon also seen elsewhere.

There is a heavy reliance on news agency material in mainstream newsrooms, which is growing as the number of journalists in those newsrooms and their satellite bureaus declines (Davies 2008, 74–108). News agencies therefore see opportunities to become the principal provider of bread-and-butter content on a more economic basis than individual publications and broadcasters can achieve. Already, international news agencies have come under more pressure to provide foreign coverage in newspapers and broadcast outlets that previously fielded their own overseas correspondents (Moore 2010, 43). Malcolm Kirk also believes CPE is in "a very advantageous position":

> We see a media landscape where journalistic resources are declining so in very many respects we become much more useful to many customers who simply do not have the resources they once had.

News agencies represent important components in the growth and maintenance of national character and social awareness (Day 1990, 238). Should their influence increase further, the governance structures under which they operate will assume even more importance – nowhere more so than in cases where commercial interests take over from the traditional cooperative. The majority of the mechanisms discussed above should be seen principally as reserve powers. The primary responsibility for adhering to editorial values and standards in the provision of public interest journalism lies at an operational level and within the editorial department. Nevertheless, the provision of even reserve powers is an important element of trustee governance.

Stand-alone non-profit journalism

While news agencies may play a special part in future news media, a range of other entities also has grown up to fill the vacuum left by the degradation of traditional news services (Compaine & Cunningham 2009; Deuze 2007; Picard & van Weezel 2008). They range from incorporated not-for-profit organisations and cooperatives, through university adjuncts, to loose forms of social media. Their purpose is to fill specific needs within the journalistic spectrum, and they have flowered particularly in the United States. These organisations are worthy of their own research project and this section will limit itself to examining governance aspects of the more institutionalised enterprises. Structurally, these are conventional but they provide a number of insights. They show, for example, that stand-alone non-profit organisations set up solely to carry out a journalistic function *can* attract tax-free status and philanthropy that is currently unavailable to existing newspapers with a circulation/advertising revenue base. However, recent experience demonstrates the need to build safeguards into philanthropic funding models and to seek a diversified range of donors. An examination of these start-ups also shows that the vision and drive displayed by their founders largely determine the culture and editorial ethos that develops within them. What has yet to manifest itself, however, is a formal framework that ensures a founder's legacy will endure after he or she has gone.

Stand-alone organisations without formal links to newspapers or broadcasters are not new. The oldest still in existence in the United States is the Center for Investigative Reporting that was established in California in 1977. It has since been joined by a raft of similar organisations in other states, the most prominent of which are the Center for Public Integrity (1989) and ProPublica (2008). Each of these three organisations has been registered as a non-taxable, non-profit 501(c)3 corporation eligible to receive grants and donations. The incorporation documents in each case are designed to conform to the requirements of the federal Internal Revenue Code for non-profit organisations, and do not include provisions to safeguard editorial integrity, although they all state that their purpose is to produce and distribute investigative journalism in the public interest. Their status (designed to facilitate tax-deductible donations as well as exemption from paying taxes), precludes them from selling the results of their editorial endeavours or from selling advertising space. Strict provisions are applied by the Inland Revenue Service (IRS) to ensure that eligibility is maintained. The model, therefore, is more appropriate for an emerging class of editorial organisation than one that is likely to be adopted by existing newspapers or commercial broadcasters. It is the reason why the *Tampa Bay Times* is a taxable business while its owner, the Poynter Institute, is a non-taxable 501(c)3 educational organisation unable to siphon any philanthropic funding into the business.

Typically, these American non-profits have conventional boards of directors that include founders, academics, prominent journalists and philanthropists. For example, the executive chair of the Center for Investigative Reporting board, Phil Bronstein, is a former editor of the *San Francisco Chronicle* and several directors represent charitable foundations; the Center for Public Integrity has a large 19-person board that includes Arianna Huffington (founder of the *Huffington Post*), Craig Newmark (founder of craigslist) and *60 Minutes* correspondent Steve Kroft; while ProPublica's board includes its founder Paul Steiger and cornerstone donor Herbert Sandler. Each organisation also maintains at least one advisory board that includes an honours list of academics, journalists, lawyers and community representatives including the *New York Times'* executive editor Jill Abramson (dismissed May 2014), CNN correspondent Christiane Amanpour, academics Ben Bagdikian and Geneva Overholser and former chairman of the Federal Reserve Paul Volcker. Each operates under an internal code of conduct that is tailored to the complexities of investigative journalism.

The newsrooms of not-for-profit news organisations vary in size and structure. Hyper-local newsroom Alhambra Source in southern California, for example, has a staff of 1.5 people while the three organisations mentioned above have newsrooms that resemble mid-sized mainstream media. The Center for Investigative Reporting (CIR) has 49 newsroom staff while the Center for Public Integrity has a full-time newsroom staff of 32 and ProPublica has a staff of 37 full-time journalists. Each organisation is led by a veteran journalist – the CIR by Robert Rosenthal (former managing editor of the *San Francisco Chronicle*), the Center for Public Integrity by Bill Buzenberg (former vice president for news of NPR) and ProPublica by Steve Engelberg (former editor-in-chief of *The Oregonian* and investigative editor of the *New York Times*).

The methods of distributing their investigative endeavours vary from organisation to organisation. Some, like the Center for Public Integrity, operate a creative commons approach under which their stories are available to all media outlets for publication. Others, like ProPublica, typically negotiate exclusive arrangements for first publication of major investigations with partner publications that range from the *New York Times* to the *Denver Post* and *Albany Times Union*. Material is placed in a creative commons environment after exclusive first publication, and ProPublica proactively "pushes" stories to individual newspapers. Its president, Richard Tofel, told me the choice of placement is determined by where the story will have the greatest impact and that exclusivity invariably means better display of a story. A ProPublica staff member was awarded a Pulitzer Prize in 2010 for an investigation, published by the *New York Times*, into the care of casualties at New Orleans' Memorial Medical Center in the aftermath of Hurricane Katrina; two staff won a Pulitzer for national reporting (on the behaviour of bankers during the financial crisis) the following year; and a co-production about a 1980s massacre in Guatemala, aired on public radio's highly popular *This American Life*, won a Peabody broadcasting award in 2013.[13]

Substantial funds are needed to sustain the quality and range of investigative projects undertaken each year and the major American organisations benefit from that country's tradition of philanthropy. Annual tax returns show that ProPublica received grants and donations worth $US36.6 million between its inception in 2007 and 2011, the Center for Public Integrity received $US30.8 million over the same period and the CIR received $US25.4 million between 2008 and 2012.[14] Despite these significant sums, philanthropic support requires considerable fund-raising effort on the part of these organisations. An Aspen Institute forum on future models for journalism in 2009 noted that there was reluctance on the part of charitable foundations to "fund media".

A core issue has been the ability to tap into a stream of grants and donations that allow similar-sized budgets to flow from year to year. Equally important, however, is the need to secure a range of donors to prevent over-dependence on one source. This prospect faced ProPublica, which was established on the basis of a multiple-year grant from its principal supporter, the Sandler Foundation.

Herbert and Marion Sandler were instrumental in the establishment of ProPublica, and in 2007 made what Tofel describes as "a minimum three-year rolling commitment" under which their foundation indicates at the end of each year whether it will roll over the funding. As a result the organisation was able to place a three-year horizon on its financial planning but the foundation did not see itself as the sole funder of the enterprise and Sandler became, according to Tofel, a "principal fund-raiser" on ProPublica's behalf. The Knight Foundation, which is a strong supporter of journalism projects, made a grant under which three-quarters is devoted to a fund-raising development strategy. In its 2009 tax return, ProPublica disclosed that the Sandler Foundation contributed 70 per cent of the $US6.4 million received in grants and donations. Six of ProPublica's donors were committed to funding for two or more years. When I visited ProPublica's offices in the financial district of New York, both Steiger and Tofel emphasised that diversifying the donor base was a high priority.[15] By January 2013 ProPublica had more than 2300 donors and its founding funders were contributing only 39 per cent of the total raised.

Diversified funding is simply a sensible strategy. ProPublica had an indication of potential problems when its foundation donor came under public criticism. The Sandlers were the owners of a respected financial institution, Golden West Financial Corporation, the sale of which in 2006 provided a $US2.4 billion fortune that they then applied to philanthropic projects like ProPublica. However, during the credit crisis the Sandlers were subjected to high profile media criticism from the *New York Times* (among others), and were included in a *Time* magazine list of "people to blame for the financial crisis". A five-page investigation by the *Columbia Journalism Review* (March/April 2010, 40–44) largely exonerated the Sandlers, and between January and June 2009 the *New York Times* issued three corrections to its 25 December 2008 front-page criticism of them.

Steiger admits the episode caused concern among the staff "but it was not worrisome for me because, as someone who covered this stuff as reporter and mostly as editor, I understood the difference between what Golden West was doing and what the engines of disaster were doing". Steiger told the staff that ProPublica was monitoring the issue, and if he and the managing editor saw something that they believed merited investigation, ProPublica would do so. He also invited staff to suggest any aspects of the controversy that they thought the organisation should pursue. In the final analysis, ProPublica's reputation was not tarnished (nor in the long run was the Sandlers'), but the episode highlighted the need for organisations such as ProPublica to scrutinise their funding sources, not be overly reliant on a single source whose removal could cause severe financial problems and place a clear distance between donor and editorial output. In 2010 a similar start-up, The Fiscal Times, provided a story to the *Washington Post* on federal spending, but did not disclose that its own financial backer, Peter G. Peterson, had a strong interest in the subject and connections to some of the experts quoted (Pérez-Peña, *New York Times*, 18 January 2010). The *Washington Post* later acknowledged it should have made the disclosure. Browne advises organisations to be wary of philanthropic funding because of "potentially competing and hidden agendas" (2010, 901). ProPublica has in place board resolutions to prevent such associations. Steiger told me:

> [At the formative stage] the Sandlers and I were discussing how it [ProPublica] would operate. I said I thought the best way would be for them to have no knowledge of what we were working on and there should be no intervention in what we were working on from them or any other board member or donor. They agreed with that with no argument whatsoever and it was their idea to make it part of the minutes at the first two board meetings. [It is a board resolution that] I think would be immutable.

Many news media companies observe similar conventions, but Tofel was unaware of any other organisation that had codified editorial independence to this degree through board resolution.

It is obvious that an investigative organisation like ProPublica must be seen to be reputable. The consequences should that reputation become tarnished could threaten its viability. A British counterpart was taken to the brink by such an episode. The Bureau of Investigative Journalism, which operates out of City University in London, was the organisation that seconded an investigative journalist who worked on the BBC *Newsnight* story that wrongly linked former Conservative Party treasurer Lord McAlpine to a child sex abuse scandal. As a result the BBC suspended all co-productions with the Bureau and its founding editor, Iain Overton, resigned in spite of claiming that the Bureau had no editorial input into the programme. Three Conservative MPs moved an Early Day Motion in the House of Commons calling on the bureau's backers to "cut all ties and refuse to donate any more money to TBIJ". However, a later Motion by a Labour MP praised the work of the bureau under Overton's editorship.

The Bureau of Investigative Journalism is funded through a trust established by the initial backers of the project, computer entrepreneur David Potter and his journalist wife Elaine. A separate trust, the Centre for Investigative Journalism, is a charity established by the Potters to fund journalism education. There does not appear to be any direct relationship with TBIJ beyond several shared trustees including the Potters. The bureau's trustees also include a former chairman of the *Financial Times*, Sir David Bell, and prominent media lawyer Geoffrey Robertson QC. The trustees and the bureau's editorial advisory board (which includes the head of journalism at City University Professor George Brock) conducted an enquiry into the BBC affair. They subsequently issued a statement that, although the bureau had played no direct role in the *Newsnight* programme and could not be held responsible for its content, the Trustees consider that a serious mistake was made in agreeing to the secondment of a member of its staff to the BBC, "without retaining the necessary degree of editorial control, and are taking action to ensure this does not happen again". They added: "It is clear that there was a failure within the Bureau of editorial and managerial controls and the surveillance thereof by the trustees. For this the trustees accept responsibility and add their regrets for these failings." The episode could have caused closure but the bureau battled on to restore its reputation and in June 2013 three of its staff were awarded the Martha Gellhorn Prize for an ongoing investigation into the United States' covert drone war in Pakistan, Somalia and Yemen. The project had been initiated under Overton's editorship. In evidence to the Leveson enquiry he summed up the ethos that permeated his newsroom:

> Everyone involved in the Bureau shares a common belief that democracy itself is imperilled by the absence of honest information and a robust watchdog to hold governments and the powerful to account.

Culture, as we have already seen, is an important element of any newsroom. The culture of these start-ups owes much to the vision of their founders who seek to inculcate it as rapidly as possible into a body of journalists (experienced and inexperienced) who come from a variety of backgrounds to work in an organisation with no pre-existing heritage. The background of the founder therefore strongly informs the ethos that develops. In the case of the CIR, two of its founders, Lowell Bergman and David Weir, were former staff writers on *Rolling Stone* magazine. Charles Lewis was a producer on CBS's *60 Minutes* before establishing the Center for Public Integrity, and both Steiger and Tofel had distinguished careers on the *Wall Street Journal*. In each case, their former employment influenced the values that they brought to their new undertakings. Tofel (a former lawyer), for example, rewrote the Code of Ethics at the *Wall Street Journal* before writing ProPublica's code as its founding general manager. He admits to "plagiarising myself" although

ProPublica's code also drew on those of other news organisations. Steiger explains the cultural development process:

> First of all, the Sandlers and the board are committed to the principles here and I have been lucky enough to assemble a team led by Dick Tofel and Steve Engelberg and they totally embrace the principles and helped refine and shape them. Then we have a very strong collection of senior reporters and senior editors that all share that vision. And we're all busy, not only doing stories and pumping out a website, but also creating a culture so the kids who are the web posters are embracing and refining that culture themselves. So there is an engine in development here that I think is building a lot of momentum and [which] can continue.

In a farewell email when he left in 2004, Charles Lewis encapsulated the ethos that had grown during his 15 years leading the Center for Public Integrity. In it he said:

> The Center must always maintain courageous, fearless "edginess" and a willingness to expose abuses of power, from Presidents to multibillion dollar corporations. But edgy and compelling must also always accompany fair and accurate at the Center for Public Integrity, and nothing beneath this standard should ever be published. There is no such thing as too careful when it comes to information gathering...The stakes are very, very high just as the opportunities to create high impact national and international journalism are extraordinary. Don't ever let the bastards get you down or intimidate you. But also, don't ever, in any way, enable them to diminish your credibility as a truth-teller.
>
> (Lewis 2007, 18)

He told me the email was "the closest thing I ever did in my time at the centre to setting forth what I think is the way it should be done", but added: "No-one at the centre has a copy. It's not up on the wall."[16] With hindsight, Lewis believed he should have done more to codify the values and ethos of the centre, but admitted that it was now too late to commit to paper the values that he inculcated during his period of leadership. It was one of several regrets he had about governance of the operation:

> The frustrating thing about discussing founders is that founders don't go to Founders' School and they don't read books on founding. It's all based on instinct and adrenalin [and] your wits. And even after you've done it and succeeded there is not enough of a sense [of the need] to preserve what you've created. I hate to admit that and I'm deeply proud of what I did at the centre...I knew how temporal life is. I knew how temporal it is with people and I knew about my time with those 15 years

[at the centre] after I created it. I did understand that whoever came after me... would have different sensibilities. I was reluctant, a little shy and, with humility, wasn't sure it was my place to codify my vision... Was my humility misplaced? Yes it was.

Lewis also believes that insufficient attention was paid to succession planning. His attempts to groom successors within the centre failed, and after extending his departure date by a year, he was unwilling to further extend his tenure. The events that followed his decision highlight the need for three things:

- A board must recognise the stresses on a chief executive when he or she is facing burn-out.
- It must instigate a succession process early enough to avoid deadline-driven decisions.
- A board must have sufficient independent representation to function as a governance body rather than a support mechanism for the founder who almost invariably chooses the inaugural directors.

None of this was present when the replacement of Lewis was considered. His successor remained in the post for only 16 months. Lewis explains the consequences in a report on non-profit journalism:

> The mark of a true institution is one that has been able to survive one or more leadership transitions. I came to the sober realization a few years ago, after passing a milestone birthday, that at some point the founder has to leave the building, for the long-term wellbeing of the enterprise. The past two transition years have been very difficult to watch. Most of the Center's carefully assembled, very talented, senior staff had quit by the fall of 2005; the successor executive director's 16-month tenure ended abruptly in June 2006, followed by an acting executive director for another six months. During this time, with a few notable exceptions, the reports, while undeniably important and fulfilling a public need, were generally unremarkable, generating neither substantial news media coverage nor web interest. Worse, some stories even required embarrassing public corrections. Fundraising revenue to the Center for 2005 and 2006 was only about half what it had been in 2004, and in early 2007, the number of full-time staff was reduced by one-third
>
> (Lewis 2007, 21–22)

The centre recovered after the arrival of its present executive director and the appointment of a number of new directors that changed a founder's board into a governance board (*ibid.*, 23). However, Lewis is somewhat rueful that the necessary processes were not put in place *during* his 15-year tenure.

It seems in the nature of organisations such as the CIR, the Center for Public Integrity and ProPublica that their concentration is on the present and on survival rather than on the preservation of the short heritage that they have been able to build. While still editor-in-chief and president, Paul Steiger was more sanguine about his successor at ProPublica:

> The board will decide on my successor. We don't have a name in the safe [a reference to my asking whether ProPublica followed the same convention as the *Tampa Bay Times*], but we are a very flat structure and the board knows the people here and the board has a sense of who is outside. I think if I got hit by the proverbial train the board would deal with it.

In the event, his two deputies succeeded to each of his posts on his retirement at the end of 2012, aged 70, to assume the role of executive chairman.

As Downie and Schudson demonstrated in their 2009 study *The Reconstruction of American Journalism*, the field of non-profit journalism is full of experimentation, risk and hope. Like the endeavours themselves, the governance of these entities is a work in progress. So, too, is the determination of where they might fit into conventional thinking. Just as the Scott Trust's ownership of the *Guardian* was regarded by tax authorities as an assault on the concept of property rights, present-day incarnations for the preservation of public interest journalism inhabit something of a twilight zone.

The most established, such as the American examples canvassed above, have the benefit of substantial and sustained philanthropy. Others, however, lead a tenuous existence that may be hostage to the uncertainty of crowd-sourced funding and the goodwill of volunteer journalists. It is the nature of experimentation that many fall by the wayside. However, for those with well-founded structures and the ability to produce the journalism to which they aspire, there is a need for a niche in established systems that recognise social purposes.

Some find sanctuary in tertiary institutions. For example, the Investigative Reporting Workshop established by Lewis after he left the Center for Public Integrity is a non-profit professional newsroom that is part of the School of Communications at American University in Washington where he is a professor of journalism. All editorial staff are faculty members. In the southern hemisphere, the Australian Centre for Independent Journalism is part of the University of Technology, Sydney (UTS), and receives the majority of its funding through public short courses it runs at UTS. Its director, Tom Morton, is a member of the Faculty of Arts and Social Sciences and is seconded part-time to the centre. In 2013 it collaborated with *The Guardian*, Global Post and a reader-funded investigative website, New Matilda, to log reports of abuse in Australia's asylum-seeker detention centres. In Britain, the Bureau of Investigative Journalism is based at City University in London but its association is more distanced than the other examples. The Bureau receives subsidised office space and facilities from the university and has a relationship with its Department of Journalism where senior members of the staff are guest lecturers.

The bureau provides a useful example of the difficulties faced by such ventures in gaining recognition for its social function. It is funded through a separate charitable trust because it has been unable to secure charitable status for itself. It has made two unsuccessful applications to the Charities Commission on the basis that "it has a clear charitable purpose in promoting citizenship and democracy". Overton admitted that a major funding application by the bureau had been rejected because it did not have charity status. The commission determined that investigative journalism was not a charitable activity in itself and could gain charitable status only if it advanced a charitable aim such as education. The confusingly titled Centre for Investigative Journalism also established by David and Elaine Potter is solely devoted to education and enjoys charity status. That status could have been compromised if the bureau had been folded into its structure. The bureau's funding body (the Trust of the Bureau of Investigative Journalism) has as its first stated object "the advancement of education", presumably in the hope that it would assist in attaining charity status. In spite of a 2012 recommendation by the House of Lords select committee on communications that investigative journalism should be considered a charitable activity, the culture secretary Jeremy Hunt stated that "government is not currently inclined to legislate" to recognise investigative journalism as a charitable activity.

The new economics of journalism may require a change of policy to give charitable status to entities like the bureau in order that donors can claim the tax benefits of their philanthropy and any other income made tax-free. Alternatively, they could be recognised as organisations entitled to be registered as companies serving a social purpose. On both sides of the Atlantic a form of company has emerged that receives such recognition in exchange for a commitment to reinvest the majority of any profit back into the business.

The trusts and institutions that own *The Guardian*, the *Irish Times* and the *Tampa Bay Times* lie between the non-profit organisation and the familiar profit-centred public company. Their profits go towards sustaining their endeavours (and in the case of the Florida newspaper, maintaining an educational institution) rather than returning dividends to shareholders but their operating arms pay taxes like any other corporate.

Social purpose company structures have emerged in the United States, where they are known as Low-profit Limited Liability Companies (L^3Cs) and in Britain, where they are known as Community Interest Companies (CIC). India, too, recognises a social business model. In many ways, L^3Cs and CICs are the antithesis of the high-profit, bottom-line-driven commercial media groups that are the norm. They sit in the gap between non-profit and commercial enterprises, and receive tax concessions for putting social purposes ahead of profit. L³Cs and CICs are being suggested as an alternative for news media, but would require legislative change to make "the news" a social purpose. It could be the basis for news media trusts that cannot achieve charity status because they sell their content.

The structure serves two worthwhile purposes. First, it provides a governance structure that is an appropriate recipient of tax concessions that contribute to viability, and secondly, it could overcome potential legal issues associated with establishing media organisations as charitable bodies. Disseminating the news in the ways with which we are familiar is not yet a charitable purpose, and those run by profit-driven corporations doubtless never will be. However, should an epiphany (unlikely as it may sound) lead to decisions to cast some publications as serving principally social purposes, the L³C or CIC may provide an appropriate structure within which they can operate.

The first legal recognition of the L³C structure took place in 2008 when Vermont amended its company laws. By 2013, the L³C was recognised in nine states and 711 L³Cs had been registered although none was devoted to public interest journalism. Nevertheless, the L³C is subject to continuing interpretation and legal development and, along with its British equivalent, is being seen as a possible pathway down which sections of the financially battered news media may pass. It may be a means by which the news media organisations of the future could attract capital in an environment where newspapers and television stations are no longer seen as attractive investments, and news websites have a lower earning capacity than their traditional counterparts once enjoyed.

There are, however, hurdles aplenty. The most significant of those barriers is the difficulty in persuading legislators and tax officials that a newspaper (or any of the other traditional forms of news media) can be included within the rubric of social purposes. Schmalbeck (2010, 251–271) mounts an argument that they *should* be included, but freely concedes there are many features of contemporary newspapers that would be hard-pressed to defend their existence in terms of "achieving a lessening of the burdens of Government", "advancement of education and science" and "promotion of social welfare". He finds little in the current L³C laws to accommodate newspapers – most politicians would subscribe to the view that newspapers *increased* their burden. However, it is a situation that could be remedied through a unilateral ruling by the IRS or by Congress to alter the qualification for L³C status. There are good grounds, Schmalbeck says, for seeing that done:

> So we are left saying, I think, simply that publication of a newspaper *should* qualify as a valid charitable objective. This is an activity that involves tremendous positive externalities that cannot be easily captured by the publisher, but which are essential to the political, economic, and social health of the community served by the particular newspaper. This

is so clear to many individuals that they would be willing altruistically to support the publication of the newspaper with disinterested contributions. And newspaper publishing is perhaps the single best example of an activity that is in the public interest, but which should nevertheless not be conducted by the government, since criticism of government performance is one of its greatest services, and accomplishment of that goal would be compromised by government ownership and operation.

(ibid., 270–271)

The model has yet to migrate, but it does offer potential that is not limited to North America. As Schmalbeck notes, because the core problem of newspapers is a financial one, the solutions presumably come in the form of new financial structures (*ibid.*, 251). The L³C offers the potential of a viable financial structure that because of its inherent social purpose is an ideal vehicle for a self-sustaining (as opposed to profit-centred) news media trust.

Lessons

It is clear that news media trusts do not have a monopoly on governance in the public interest. There are other structures that have the potential to shore up the gathering and distribution of democratically significant and socially sustaining journalism. However, the purpose in detailing the governance of these other entities has been to show that there are lessons in them for the types of trust that are our primary focus.

Public service broadcasters, for example, will be instructive should state subsidies form part of the private sector media landscape, as Rusbridger suggests might happen in the case of PA coverage of local/regional matters. PSBs show how external bodies can have an overriding influence, either formal or informal, through control of finance. Should some form of state funding eventuate, PSBs could show that an impenetrable barrier must be put between politics and those who allocate the funds to say, trust-run newspapers or news websites. PSBs also offer lessons for such trusts about mechanisms that help to sustain the journalistic pursuit of the public interest.

News agencies show how trust-like agreements and documented executive powers can enshrine journalistic values and separate the interests of the shareholders and the agency. They also illustrate the inability of a trust-like agreement to prevent the inevitable consequences of rising monetary value, and the irresistible urge to realise that value even when the result is the destruction of a cooperative and ownership being placed in the hands of a foreign corporation (as was the case with Reuters in the initial flotation and then the final sale to Thomson).

The growth of investigative journalism units to fill a gap in the editorial landscape has provided proof that, in the United States at least, philanthropy can go hand-in-hand with a public-spirited desire by the founders of such organisations to hold power to account through good journalism. These are young organisations whose ethos and embryonic heritage owes much to the character and vision of those founders. In the digital age they represent the most likely area of development for trustee ownership. It requires a tectonic shift in thinking before commercial shareholders willingly place an existing mainstream media outlet in the hands of altruistic trustees. It is far easier to start an enterprise with trusteeship in mind. The lesson here, however, is that the demands of the present can draw attention away from the medium and long-term future that should be secured – as much as is possible – by foundational decisions. As Charles Lewis noted: "The mark of a true institution is one that has been able to survive one or more leadership transitions."

There is much to commend Schmalbeck's belief that the solution to financial crisis in the news business lies in emerging structures, altered to accommodate public interest journalism. The nature of the news business has been irrevocably altered by developments in digital technology aided and abetted by business strategies that have, with the benefit of hindsight, been found to be foolhardy. So the future of democratically significant journalism should not be fettered by the past. The concluding chapter will argue, however, that to secure its future will require identification of several dependent paths and acceptance of the inevitability that whatever emerges must be a product of bricolage – the weaving of old institutions into new ones.

9
Conclusions – Possibilities and Realities

Journalism cannot be divorced from the business and ownership structures within which it is housed, just as the media are an inseparable part of a broader socio-political environment. Yet little attention is paid to ensuring that those structures are capable of nurturing the journalism necessary to sustain that environment. This book set out to determine whether trusts and trust-like stewardship are capable of providing a sustaining framework within an industry that is struggling to find alternatives to a flawed business model. The normative qualities of most kinds of trustee stewardship are inherently positive, so this exercise has been an appraisal, based on a number of cases, of the practical application of that form of governance in an industry with fluctuating fortunes and strong personalities.

There will be solutions to the current disturbing state of mainstream media. Some of those solutions will be revolutionary, others evolutionary. There are enormous opportunities for low-cost entry to the open-ended world of digital broadband, while – if they wish – large conglomerates have the resources to sustain and enhance their mainstream news media outlets with quality, professional journalism rather than entertainment-driven content. Some new ventures will be short-lived because they have been ill-conceived, and there will be further faltering and failure of established organisations – the demise of the New Zealand Press Association after 131 years as the country's national news agency and the near-death experience of Canadian Press are cases in point. Voids may be created by failures (that others can then seek to fill) but faltering outlets may be saved by changes that are not limited to their newsrooms and the content they produce. Private sector news media organisations that make a significant contribution to the public interest may be sustained by including ownership structure in the mix of novel restorative changes.

The study has shown that in each case, the use of trusts and trust-like structures in the news media has been a reaction to unique circumstances. Unique circumstances mean each of the trustee news media studied here has been different, although each shares elements with its counterparts. Each has also been modified over time in order to meet changed circumstances or the challenges of conflicting aspirations. This chapter draws together observations made throughout the book, and concludes that a trust does offer structural protection and journalistic focus, but trustee governance requires careful crafting, is difficult to attain and will owe its success or failure to not only the skill and insight of trust founders in establishing appropriate institutional structures and guarantees but also the personalities of key players.

At the beginning of the book I stated that it would strive to produce a game plan for the future sustenance of democratically significant journalism. Now it is time to reveal the game itself. Think of the news business as a game of chess but no ordinary board game. Instead, envisage a three-dimensional game of chess akin to that described by Isaac Asimov in the short story *A Perfect Fit*: "a makeshift setup of eight chessboards balanced on pegs, one above the other". Unlike conventional chess, it plays in three dimensions and, in our case, the aim is not to capture the king but to occupy particular territory. Each board in the stack represents a particular form of influence on the news game – financials, market, technology, regulation, governance, leadership, culture and engagement – and each space has a value. An organisation's place on a particular board will be determined by its performance on scales along each horizontal axis, acknowledging that some measurements will be inherently subjective. Each board interacts with those above or below it, either influencing or being influenced by them. For example, a high level of civic engagement serving a diverse range of communities is likely to have a strong culture based on social benefits. Conversely, a weak internal culture that places little store by social benefits will betray both ineffective leadership and poor civic engagement. Figure 9.1 is a diagram of the 3-D chess game.

A media outlet is most likely to produce democratically significant journalism if its trustees aim to occupy particular optimum quadrants that contribute to such an outcome. News media with different aspirations – entertainment-driven tabloids, for example – would say that some of their optimum quadrants lay elsewhere on the boards. Just as the market orientation of a publication can affect its performance within the matrix so, too, can the preferred strategies employed by the organisation. Hence, a publication's position will be influenced by the overarching decisions made by its chessmaster.

Further factors complicate the picture: the interactive influences symbolised by each board are neither equal nor uniform. The effect of financial performance permeates through other layers of the matrix in ways that factors such as regulation and engagement do not. The market is more of an influence in a field of several media players than in a monopoly. Technology uptake must be seen in light of the technological environment within which the news organisation is situated. Regulation may exert a stronger influence

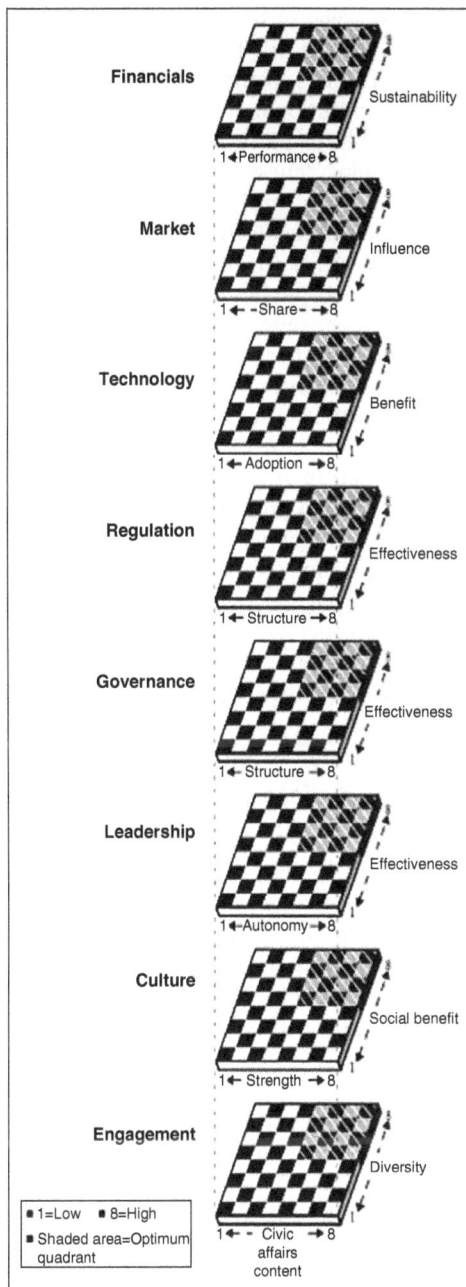

Figure 9.1   Three-dimensional media performance matrix
Graphic: Richard Dale.

in times of political stress – war or terrorism, for example – than in periods of peace and prosperity. And so on. The interactions are, indeed, complex and this complexity contributes to the industry's uniqueness and has had significant effects on its institutional development.

A publication that is able to place itself in the top right quadrants of the culture and engagement "chessboards", at the same time as satisfying the requirements to occupy similar positions on the other boards, will be well placed to meet the obligations that are set for it by a democratically engaged society. This study suggests trustees determined to maintain an organisation committed to public interest journalism are likely to play the game to end on the upper right quadrant on each board. The position is optimised by governance and regulation that facilitate sustainable civic journalism and that means an internal structure predicated on stewardship and on external regulation that recognises a growing need for arm's length support.

Before proceeding to what might be called the end-game, it is useful to consider some elements encountered thus far, beginning with a definition of the type of news game we may wish to play – the production of democratically significant journalism. This we defined as the type of reportage, commentary and analysis that helps citizens make informed judgements about politicians and bureaucrats (together with others in positions of power), and hold them to account. It provides catalysts and platforms for debate, and in its broader coverage, contributes to the social and cultural well-being of society.

Chapter 1 examined the ways in which we can identify socially responsible news media at a time when journalists may feel they have been transported into a violent Xbox game rather than placed within the stylised symbolism of a chessboard. In spite of the challenging nature of the times, we found that journalism is underpinned by universal enduring qualities that are manifested in both the institutional nature of newsrooms and the norms that guide its practitioners. This chapter also introduced the term "bricolage" which, in an institutional sense, means the recombination and reshuffling of pre-existing available components or other institutional components to form a new entity. Bear the word in mind as we enter the end-game because, if we may borrow from Thelen's approach to media analysis that we encountered in the first chapter, we should "strive for creative combinations that recognise and attempt to harness the strengths of each approach."

In the period since the Second World War, various approaches have been used by news media in their quest for changing goals amid changing fortunes. Chapter 2 traced the rise and decline of newspapers as a business and presented evidence of the factors that have contributed to the weakening (and in some cases failure) of the business model under which newspapers have operated: investor pressure that led to the use of cost-control in editorial departments as a profit smoothing mechanism; an institutionalised view that acquisition equalled growth; and the financing of these acquisitions by large-scale borrowing serviceable only when there were healthy cash flows. The financial crisis in which newspapers found themselves was produced by a misguided view that the companies had to expand or die, by incaution bred by market expectations and personal incentives and by unquestioning collective industry belief in the "legitimacy" of their strategies. The victim in this crisis was the professional, print-standard journalism that became squeezed between budget cuts and the Internet that some saw as its replacement. However, while citizen journalism and blog-based commentary made valuable contributions, they were not substitutes for the influential journalism that emanated from professional newsrooms serving mass audiences and employing people trained to observe the normative values of journalism. A key factor was the unparalleled access by mainstream journalists to the holders of power because of their organisations' audience reach.

Throughout its recent history the news media were subjected to official scrutiny, never more so than in the wake of News Corporation's phone hacking and the Jimmy Savile sex scandal. Media accountability for perceived failings was the catch-cry of public enquiries held over many years in Britain, North America, South Africa and Australasia but they achieved little in terms of fixing structural weaknesses in the news media. Chapter 3 revealed a history of either failure to confront issues of ownership and structure or effective nullification by powerful interests determined to maintain the status quo.

History is a vital component of this book, and detailed examination of different types of newspaper trusts and trust-like stewardship in Chapter 4 revealed lessons that can (and have) informed the development of more robust and purposeful institutions. These lessons can be drawn from altruistic trusts charged with serving the public interest or from those that have existed to protect family fortunes or power. The following are instructive:

- The British PEP report on trusts placed great importance on the form of a trust, the selection of its first trustees, and the process for their replacement. Yet it was under no illusion that a trust necessarily created editorial independence, or was capable of turning a poor newspaper into a very good one.
- The most common use in North America was endowment trusts established to protect family assets for the benefit of family members, but there were exceptions. Trusts were used to allow staff members a share of ownership (for example, at the *Kansas City Star*), to allow religious institutions to own publications (notably the *Christian Science Monitor*) or to bequeath newspapers (such as *The Day*) for charitable purposes. Trust status was also used in an attempt to secure ownership of newspapers

virtually in perpetuity, but as the case of the Frank E. Gannett Foundation showed, legislation and market forces could conspire against such desires. Legislation could thwart the wishes of benefactors to establish trusts, but the example of the *Toronto Star* showed that determined executors could enshrine the benefactor's values in a company's articles and ethos.

- A trust could be hostage to its founder while he or she was alive and such influence could persist from the grave. Trustees could be usurped or marginalised when other owners were involved in an organisation and such owners could jeopardise editorial independence. A complex relationship existed between trustees and editors that required careful and explicit codification and exercise of each party's powers.

The family endowment trusts encountered in the history of newspaper trust development bore many of the characteristics of the family firm: loyalty, sole leadership, integrated decision-making, "Shared Dreams", family-centric altruism, primogeniture, sibling rivalry, an expanding beneficiary base and inefficient management. Chapter 5 examined the Ochs Sulzberger, Graham, Bancroft and Harmsworth families that over successive generations controlled newspapers with international reputations. It found, however that the "family firm" in the modern media world had become one in which the family was the privileged holder of a class of shares that secured control of a company which had opened its doors to public shareholders and their capital.

The Ochs Sulzberger family's control of the *New York Times* provided several lessons: carefully constructed trust instruments and covenants can minimise the likelihood of internecine conflict; inculcating each generation with appropriate family values can sustain an ethos that will put journalism before profit; primogeniture opens the company to criticism (whether justified or not); dual voting systems can be maintained by resolute family unity but require adroit management of shareholder relations; and such control can be compromised by circumstance (such as the financial rescue package provide by Carlos Slim).

The principal lesson from the Graham family was that although it had been subjected to heavy budget cuts, the survival of the *Washington Post* was helped by a diversification strategy (also adopted by the Guardian Media Group) that added a division outside the news media that was not subject to that industry's financial fluctuations. Donald Graham's pragmatic leadership and eventual sale of the newspaper also told us that trusts do not, of themselves, generate a sentimental attitude towards the business.

The Bancroft family provided two important lessons: the first was that lack of involvement in a company's affairs could be as damaging as overt interference in its operational management. The Bancroft family's "hands-off" attitude left the company with no clear sense of strategic direction. The second lesson was that in the absence of restrictive clauses to prevent sale of a controlling interest, factions could be exploited, particularly when coupled with the maxim "everyone has their price".

The Harmsworth family are British media aristocracy and as such, presented a striking case study in institutionalised primogeniture and the lottery that it represented for the protection and promotion of the editorial fortunes of the *Daily Mail* and its sister publications. Fortuitously, both the third and fourth Viscounts Rothermere proved to be able leaders who displayed strong support for their editors-in-chief and the concept of editorial independence along with a degree of business acumen. The family, like its counterparts across the Atlantic, benefitted from a two-tiered share structure that had been criticised by other shareholders seeking a greater say in the Daily Mail & General Trust (DMGT). However, for decades DMGT resisted the temptation to raise capital through rights issues and limited the number of shares. Through two family trusts, Viscount Rothermere also exercised full control over the family's voting shares. It was a further lesson in the maintenance of company stability.

Each of these family trusts contributed to the ethos that guided highly influential and prestigious newspapers but the principal purpose was to protect family interests. In every case, the continued existence of a commitment to journalism was due to the men and women who led the dynasty and their close associates. It is a theme that runs throughout this book: structure cannot be divorced from the strength of those who lead it.

Three newspapers in trust or trust-like ownership have been at the core of this book, and inspired my interest in trustee stewardship of news publications. *The Guardian*, the *Irish Times* and the *Tampa Bay Times* are newspapers whose journalism is outstanding, and whose political influence is greater than their circulation numbers would suggest. Chapters 6 and 7 explored why that should be so.

A survey of the origins of each publication and the circumstances that led to a dramatic change in the nature of its ownership provided little common ground. As noted at the beginning of this chapter, the move to trustee stewardship involved novel reactions to unique circumstances. However, all three newspapers had already established reputations as liberal publications that had taken principled stands on significant issues. In other words, there was an established tradition of liberal journalism. Two of the three had owner/editors (C. P. Scott and Nelson Poynter) with a well developed sense of the requirements of good journalism and the role of the newspaper in the community and in democratic society.

None of the newspapers at the time of the ownership change would have been considered a strong financial performer, but all could have been takeover targets. Trust (or in the case of the *Tampa Bay Times*, educational institute) ownership was a means by which that undesirable possibility was kept at bay.

It was at this point that similarities between the organisations ended, but they were to prove fundamental to the future ethos of each newspaper. As the unique circumstances played out, each enterprise found its own trustee structure, but all built into their articles an obligation to pursue high journalistic ideals solely in the public interest – even the tantalisingly simple phrase "as heretofore" that had been C. P. Scott's last wish for the running of *The Guardian* was the embodiment of such ideals. And each expressed the desire to continue to do so in perpetuity.

Chapter 6 examined the development of each of the three trusts (for the sake of convenience let us regard the Poynter Institute in the same way as its two counterparts) and found that in all cases there were significant structural and governance changes over time. Some alterations were legal adjustments to account for law changes and taxation interpretations, but others were to overcome weaknesses exposed by events.

The first three decades of the Scott Trust's existence were dominated by members of the family whose generosity led to its formation. However, the relationship exposed two weaknesses in the arrangement: a readiness by descendants of a benefactor to display proprietorial tendencies, and a power imbalance created by allowing such a descendant to be both trustee and managing director in an environment where the powers of a trust are effectively unstated.

The final decade of the 20th century saw what might be regarded as a maturing of the Scott Trust in providing active governance of the Guardian Media Group (GMG) through a well-constructed articulation of its responsibilities and those of the executive. Structural maturity is not, however, a complete defence against risk-taking and the purchase of *The Observer* (followed by the appointment to a succession of editors) illustrated that trustees and executives acting together could expose an organisation to risk. Public exposure of the consequences of such actions, however, led to one wholly beneficial outcome: the Scott Trust and GMG became, in the first decade of the 21st century, a model of transparency and public accountability. The one constant throughout the history of the Scott Trust was its commitment to preserve and promote the liberal journalism of the *Guardian.*

The Irish Times Trust's history is shorter than that of the Scott Trust, but there was a remarkable similarity between the two in terms of the exercise of power. The *Irish Times* had not been a family newspaper, but one of the architects of the trust in which it was vested acted with the same proprietary style as members of the Scott family. The position of Major Tom McDowell was protected by the trust deed, and as trust chairman and chief executive he acted like an owner (but an attempt at nepotism was a step too far). It was an example of concentrated power that ran counter to the broader interests of a trust board and turned trustees into little more than window-dressing.

However, McDowell did not interfere editorially. He and his fellow trustees and directors clearly felt bound by prescriptive editorial objectives and principles that provided both focus and commitment. The enshrining of an editorial ethos in the company articles undoubtedly contributed to the *Irish Times* emerging as a liberal newspaper serving all Ireland. Its status allowed it to attract journalists who gave it added weight as a politically important journal. As a result the editorial principles have assumed an immutable place in the company's Articles of Association but the adoption of new articles in 2002 show that such documents are not necessarily set in stone. The changes fundamentally altered the balance of power between trustees and management. We saw here the enactment of an important principle: trusts should oversee and managers should manage. It is debatable whether *too much* power was vested in the Irish Times Ltd's executive board, but this argument is tempered by the fact that the trustees' power of veto was well entrenched.

Concentration of power was at the centre of Nelson Poynter's plans for the *Tampa Bay Times*. He believed that to be successful, the newspaper must be under the firm hand of one person who chose his or her successor. The system established on his death has provided strong leadership for the newspaper, but it stands or falls on the quality of the person chosen for the role, and therefore, must be seen as a potential institutional weakness. Although the Scott Trust's experience with the *Observer* editorship showed trustees to be as capable as individuals of making mistakes, collective leadership generally has more checks and balances.

There are further lessons to be taken from the development of the Poynter Institute and its ownership of the *Tampa Bay Times*. The first relates to the danger of a structure in which significant shares are not held by the trustees (in that case shares were held by Poynter's sister and her family). Resolution of that problem proved expensive for the institute. The second is the delicate relationship between an educational body (or perhaps a charity) and its commercial enterprise. A tax-free status is essential for the former, and a robust separation between the entities is necessary to preserve it.

Mature governance structures emerged from the development of the three "trusts", and a significant legal change took place when the Scott Trust was transformed into a private company. It offered better protection from tax liability, but interestingly, was accomplished with no discernable change to the way in which trustees governed. The important point that this raises is that organisations can operate with all the provisions and principles of trustee stewardship without the formal shell of legal trust status. Indeed, given tax authorities' apparent difficulty in categorising trusts that operate commercial enterprises, the new structure of the Scott Trust may be a model for others to follow.

The policy of transparency pursued by the Scott Trust and the Guardian Media Group is also worthy of emulation, not only by future enterprises but also by their counterparts who meet only minimum legal requirements. The Poynter-owned Times Holdings Company, in particular, does not practice the level of financial disclosure they exhort other bodies to follow. This highlights the need for trust ownership to practise higher standards of accountability as a concomitant element of the special relationship with the public. That said, the cornerstone mastheads of the three organisations continue to stand for liberal journalism pursued in the public interest, and Chapter 7 examined how a sense of stewardship determined the way in which they faced the considerable challenges that had been canvassed in Chapter 2.

The different business structures of each organisation described in Chapter 7 have influenced their ability to withstand the rigours of recession and the downturn in audiences for traditional media. However, two common elements stand out in their responses: a commitment to the maintenance of core journalistic resources that many other editors have been unable to secure; and a determination to protect the principal newspaper – the founder's central bequest – even at the expense of other publications and assets in the group.

The editor is central to the performance of most newspapers (a few figureheads are still to be found) but Chapter 7 illustrated the signal importance of the editor-in-chief in trust-run publications. The senior editors – Rusbridger, O'Sullivan (Kennedy before him) and Tash (until he relinquished the role to concentrate on management of the group) – were each shown to have institutionalised power in both the business and editorial sense. Each was a director of the respective operational board, and two were members of the "trust" board as well. The chapter demonstrated that, in addition to this institutionalised power, each possessed a dominant personality (albeit expressed in different ways) that was impressed on the respective publications. Each was shown to be a champion of the type of journalism that holds political power to account. Once again, it was an illustration of the fact that personalities cannot be divorced from the equation in assessing the institutional effectiveness of trust ownership.

Nonetheless, one should not lose sight of the fact that the appointment of an editor is ultimately the responsibility of the trustees, and even the Poynter Institute would be forced to intercede if the "name in the vault" nominated by the incumbent was manifestly inappropriate. It is equally significant that the editor-in-chief in each case has established a good professional relationship with the chair of the trust, or in the case of the *Tampa Bay Times*, the president of the Poynter Institute.

Chapter 7 explored the business approaches of the three organisations in response to current financial problems, and found that diversified interests had acted as buffers, particularly for the *Guardian* and the *Tampa Bay Times*. The flexibility to divest loss-making or non-core activities was equally helpful, but low debt was undoubtedly a pivotal factor in the short-term future of all three organisations. The implicit degree of caution that is embodied in trustee stewardship acts as a moderating influence on balance sheets, and it is significant that none of the trust-owned groups have the debt millstones that have plagued their corporate counterparts.

The overarching business lesson drawn from that chapter is that trustees must recognise that the modern media world is complex and survival requires the expert skills of professionals. This suggests the desirability of a two-tiered system of governance in which trustees safeguard core purposes and values including editorial independence while directors oversee business strategy and management.

Such a two-tiered system was present in the BBC Trust model set out in Chapter 8, which examined the governance of public service broadcasting and the new start-ups that have emerged to fill gaps in the journalistic landscape. That chapter found that charters that set out the values and obligations were taken seriously by public service broadcasters and gave them a clear sense of direction. These are instruments that could be readily employed in organisations other than state-owned enterprises, supplementing trust deeds and articles of association in a way that allowed fixed-term reviews and (when necessary) more routine change than formal alteration to articles. However, the chapter also illustrated how even the most diligent drafting of empowering documents did not fully immunise a public service broadcaster against either outside influence and interference (particularly when there were external elements of financial control) or internal dysfunction.

Philanthropically supported organisations, set up primarily to undertake investigative journalism, are trusts in all but name. They operate similar governance structures to the newspaper trusts discussed in the previous two chapters, albeit without commercial enterprise. However, they exhibit two traits that the newspaper trusts have left behind: a pervasive founder influence (a function no doubt of their relatively recent formation) and a less codified approach to governance (perhaps as a result of the way in which 501(c)3 status dictates incorporation documentation).

That notwithstanding, these bodies represent a viable form of trust-like governance for journalistic undertakings. Large-scale philanthropy (an established part of American society but less ubiquitous elsewhere) has made it possible for these organisations to be established as charitable institutions. That application is limited and limiting, because it precludes commercial revenue generation. The L^3C structure discussed in Chapter 8 is a means by which trustee governance might be maintained, while allowing an enterprise to generate enough commercial revenue to sustain itself.

As the book explored trust ownership and governance throughout the 20th century and into the present millennium, it encountered numerous elements that contribute to (or detract from) the use of this form of ownership and oversight by organisations engaged in journalistic endeavours. Positive and negative attributes emerged over successive chapters. Trusteeship could promote and protect such journalism, but there were potential shortcomings in this form of governance. When it was poorly constructed, or placed in the hands of people who were able to usurp its collective role by exercising dominant personal power, it became a weak vessel.

Most trusts and trust-like entities were sentenced to pass through periods of adversity or uncertainty, and not all emerged to become stable and sustainable enterprises. Each, however, contributed something to our understanding of the dynamics of trusteeship in the news media. We can learn even more, however, by briefly looking outside the news media to what can be regarded as an exemplar: the Wellcome Trust, which is the United Kingdom's largest non-governmental source of biomedical research funding with assets worth £16.4 billion and charitable activities that in 2013 amounted to £726 million. Ironically it is an example to follow not only for its positive attributes but also for the lessons learned as it progressed fitfully towards its present model status. It demonstrated the need, for example, to underpin the trust with an appropriate legal instrument. For many years it was hostage to a benefactor's last will and testament, under which it was established, and that increasingly proved inadequate and which required numerous declaratory court applications. The early operation of the trust, which had inherited the Wellcome pharmaceutical company, showed the absence of robust and clearly delineated procedures could draw trustees and managers into disagreement and potential conflict. It also highlighted the limitations of an investment strategy based solely on the traditional core business, which in the case of the Wellcome Trust limited its income for many years. However, most importantly, the current governance structure and strategy of the Wellcome Trust is a model that others might follow.

In 1998, the trust began negotiating with the Charities Commission for a new trust constitution that modernised the wishes of the benefactor, provided a modern working structure and consolidated the numerous court rulings that littered its past. The new constitution and articles, granted in 2001, are a model of clarity. However, the real benefit of the trust's 2001 constitution and associated documents lies not in their commendable clarity, but in the flexibility that they embody. The breadth and depth of powers and functions set out in the documents allow the trustee considerable freedom of action within clearly set responsibilities. The three schedules to the constitution set out powers to be exercised in furtherance of the trust's aims, plus administrative and investment powers. They anticipate situations that may sit outside the present framework, and provide both the capacity to amend the constitution and the safeguard of an approval process through the Charities Commission that is likely to obviate the need for resort to the High Court. The documents recognise the complexity of the environment in which the trust operates, and the fact that the organisation is entrusted with husbanding very large sums of money through diversified investment.[1]

In parallel with the empowering 2001 documents, the Wellcome Trust operates model systems of internal organisation and governance. Overall responsibility lies with a ten-person board of governors, which in 2013 comprised six professors in the life sciences (five British, one American), two banking and investment directors, one healthcare company director and a retired senior civil servant.

Below the governors is a trust director/chief executive and nine-member executive board that manage the day-to-day activities across six divisions led by a directorate.

The board of governors sets the overall investment policy and the spending limit on grants. The investment committee, comprising two governors, four external (expert) members and up to four staff members, oversee investment strategies and the detail of investment policy. Decisions on actual investments are made by a professional investment team (within the Investment Division) which is insulated from the possible influence of the day-to-day financial needs of the trust, which are handled by a finance department in another division. The trust's £16.4 billion endowment is in a widely diversified investment portfolio that is no longer weighted towards the pharmaceutical industry.

There is a clear separation of the investment and granting activities of the trust, at operational as well as governance levels. The tight focus on respective roles below board level avoids what Wellcome's former company secretary, John Stewart, sees as "the real danger of mixed motives" in which marginal investments could be made because they may also have a charitable outcome. Mixed motives lead, he says, to bad investments and bad charitable outcomes:

> We have been very careful to separate the two things out. It's actually quite dangerous to mix them. What I used to say when we debated this internally was that, when someone was coming to us on an investment basis we should look at it as a good investment and, if it was a good investment, we should put money into it for investment purposes and not pretend that we also wanted to get a charitable benefit. The flip side is also true. If it's a good charitable use of money we should do it for charitable purposes and not look at the financial return.[2]

A strategic grants committee comprising the board of governors, the trust's chief executive, and two divisional directors make up the principal body overseeing the grants process but grant applications themselves are considered by a large number of advisory committees – currently 30 – comprising external experts from different fields but no members of the trust's staff. Biomedical research carries strict requirements in ethics and probity, that are reflected in the committees' consideration of grant applications and rigour applied to the process, which also involves a peer review of grant applications by members of an international body of expert referees numbering several thousand.

That trust operates under flexible instruments that offer sufficient freedom of action while protecting assets and objectives. Its internal governance and operational structures ensure the separation of business and non-commercial activities in a way that would be usefully employed in news media operations (with journalism designated a non-commercial activity). It also underlines the benefits of risk management through diverse investment strategies that act as financial shock absorbers, already demonstrated by the Guardian Media Group and the Daily Mail & General Trust.

The size and purpose of the Wellcome Trust are far removed from those of most newspaper publishing, but there are valuable lessons that can be applied. The following are some of the attributes drawn from the Wellcome Trust experience that are instructive when considering the structure of news media trusts which aim to deliver quality journalism:

- Clear trust deed objectives
- Flexible trust instruments that offer sufficient freedom of action while protecting assets and objectives
- An appropriate balance between trustee powers and liabilities
- Trust assets sufficiently diversified to protect their overall financial position
- Comprehensive investment risk management
- Lack of nostalgia (the Wellcome Trust has no special attachment to pharmaceutical companies as investments). Not to be confused with a sense of history, which the Wellcome Trust has in abundance
- Comprehensive internal governance and operational structures to ensure the separation of business and non-commercial functions
- Separated management functions
- Financial transparency to ensure that trust objectives are optimally pursued

Taken together, the Wellcome Trust and the newspaper trusts (or trust-like bodies) examined in the book provide a long list of moves that can be employed (and avoided) in our end-game – the future model for public interest journalism. They are summarised in the table on page 259.

Bricolage and the end-game

More than 50 years ago the PEP report on newspaper trusts ended with the observation that it would "be necessary to watch the performance of trusteeship over many more years before its success of failure can be measured". Those many years have passed and my conclusion is that this form of stewardship can meet that laudable aim but that it does not guarantee it.

It is equally clear that no single media entity under trustee stewardship provides a perfect model for others to emulate. Even the Wellcome Trust, which may now provide us with an exemplar, endured 65 years of legal uncertainty and periodic conflict that cannot be detailed here (see Lilja 1997; Williams 2010). And its scale and purpose require us to take from it principles rather than detail. We are left therefore with the task of planning our end-game from fragments of past play.

We have seen that there are no guarantees that a trust established to protect the interests of family members will protect the journalism in any publication in which the family has an interest because the focus of these trusts is family, and any other benefits are incidental. Yet they may embody a "shared dream" that we can usefully employ. Similarly, trusts established to ensure continuity of ownership and prevent the breaking up of media groups have a primary responsibility that offers no quality guarantees or protection of editorial resources. Yet there are merits in the way they protect publications in perpetuity. The trinity of publications that this book has keynoted have attributes that preserve and promote core editorial values and journalistic excellence. Yet each has struggled financially. The start-ups that promise to fill the gaps created by mainstream media cutbacks have laudable aims and a growing number of successes. Yet they depend on the generosity of philanthropists and the cooperation of mainstream media to achieve those aims.

In the short term the most likely new application of trustee stewardship is with emergent digital ventures that will, in effect, start with a clean stack of chessboards. So our end-game will set up the chess pieces for a new enterprise and, like good players, we will draw on past gambits for opening moves. In order to do so, however, we must risk mixing our metaphors and return to the subject of bricolage.

The derivation of the word is *bricoler*, French for to do odd jobs or repair. The meaning it has taken on in English is vaguely derogatory: something created from what is immediately to hand and put together as an assemblage of haphazard or incongruous elements. Institutional theorists have given it a distinct contextual meaning that recognises, as sociologist David Stark noted in an influential paper, "the new does not come from the new – or from nothing – but from the reshaping of existing resources" (Stark 1992, 301). Stark was examining social change in Eastern Europe after the fall of communism and there are some parallels with changes – present and future – in the news media landscape. He noted, for example, that "if we assume that it is in the 'ruins' that institutional materials will be found for reconstructing the economy, we should expect that structural innovations in the economy are more likely to entail complex reconfigurations of [existing] institutional elements than their immediate replacement" (*ibid.*, 302). Post-communist democracy in Eastern Europe had the same ultimate goals as the Marxism it replaced – the maintenance of society and management of its economy – but the elements were arranged differently to achieve those goals by other means. So, too, are the ultimate goals of serious journalism unchanged but the elements may need to be reordered to achieve those goals by other means.

However, Stark also wrote a book examining divergent interpretations of worth in times of rapid change and a chapter on new digital start-ups suggests the change may be so pronounced that our bricolage approach will need to leave significant flexibility in the game plan (Stark 2009, 81–117). That, of course, is no different to the way in which a successful chess player's strategy takes account of an opponent's moves but it suggests the reordering of elements must be creative as well as utilitarian. Stark and a colleague conducted a two-year ethnographic study within a start-up company and found that, although the form of the firm and the shape of its projects borrowed from past models, the dynamics were different. Multiple levels of contestation, from relative values to inter-disciplinary implementation, created a dissonant environment in which creative friction required complex coordination and discursive pragmatism to bring projects to fruition. It was not a hierarchy (the pyramidical structure we find in most newspapers) but what Stark termed a "heterarchy" (the simultaneous existence of different orders of worth – that "make assets of ambiguity").

Such notions could pose problems for a book based on hierarchical institutions but, I contend, a trust structure can bring order without destroying the creative quality of digital chaos. A trust should sit outside the operational activities of a news organisation. In so doing it allows for an operational structure that can accommodate Stark's "heterarchy" if the enterprise believes this will put it at the cutting edge of digital developments in news media. So long as the structure contains sufficient lines of communication to keep trustees informed (and to allow them to intercede if its imperatives are being subverted or ignored), the operational dynamics can be varied according to need.

Irrespective of whether public service journalism is produced by "old" or "new" technology and within a hierarchy or heterarchy, it will be subject to the influences acknowledged by our stack of eight chess boards so, first, we might put into our game plan those elements that need to survive in both the analogue and digital environments if we are to preserve the positive qualities of public service journalism. We should take as a given a commitment to the ethics and principles that (as Figure 1.2: *Common principles in Anglo-American journalism* shows) have developed a universality in newsrooms in the English-speaking world. The essence of these principles must be enshrined in any trust deed or similar instrument in order that they permeate the entire organisation, although the detail may also be set out in codes of practice and guidelines (so ably demonstrated by *The Guardian*). Beyond that we can create a list of positive attributes drawn from Table 9.1

Table 9.1 Lessons from history

Chapter 4: Historic trusts (20th century development)	Chapter 5: Family Trusts (Family-run newspapers)	Chapters 6–7: The Trinity (*Guardian, Irish Times, TB Times*)	Chapter 8: PSB & start-ups (TV/radio, agency, investigators)	Chapter 9: Exemplar trust (Wellcome Trust)
• Memoranda and codicils morally bind trustees. • Founders can "direct from the grave". • Proprietors can usurp advisory trusts. • Relationship between trustees, "proprietors" and editors is finely balanced. • Flexibility is the key to both the governance and operation of a long-running trust.	• Interaction of family unit, individual family members and the business itself. • Need for formal governance often ignored. • Exhibit shortcomings of many family firms. • Strong individuals can nurture family's "shared dream". • Primogeniture can weaken leadership. • Generational family expansion is potential source of friction.	• Circumstances dictate nature of ownership. • Tax law is a deciding factor. • Family/former owners may exercise hold on leadership. • Clear demarcation required between trustee and executive roles. • Business and editorial transparency is not always forthcoming. • Dominant editors play key roles. • Public service can be enshrined in trust deed or company articles. • Editorial departments cannot be isolated from financial realities. • Trust-owned newspapers preserve core editorial functions. • Need diversified business strategies.	• Politicised appointment processes. • Political intervention possible in spite of protective legislation. • Two-tiered governance system advisable. • Charters mandate services and performance requirements. • Formal management agreement may serve purpose similar to charter. • Survival of editorial values depends on the goodwill of controlling interests. • Status of start-ups strongly influenced by tax laws. • Over time, independent trustees should replace founder appointees. • Guiding principles should be codified. • Robust, transparent funding processes are essential. • Formal processes required to ensure succession and renewal.	• Appropriate legal structure. • Balance between trustee powers and liabilities. • Clear trust objectives. • Flexibility. • Pragmatic business approach. • Diversified trust assets. • Comprehensive risk management. • Comprehensive internal governance. • Separated management functions. • Financial transparency. • Constructive trustee/executives relationship.

that should be formally embodied in any new enterprise to serve this type of journalism.

- A legal structure appropriate to the enterprise
- An appropriate funding model (commercial, state, L³C/CIC, philanthropic or hybrid)
- A clearly articulated "shared dream" that embodies principles of public service and the tenets of good journalism, together with a commitment to sustaining core editorial functions
- Flexibility to accommodate changes over time
- A two-tiered governance structure with clear demarcation between oversight and executive roles but constructive lines of communication between tiers
- Transparency – both financial and internal governance
- Robust appointment processes at governance and operational levels
- Processes for succession and renewal

A well developed and appropriate trust deed or company articles and a robust business plan are prerequisites for entry to the game but they do not guarantee success or even a long game. We have seen the importance that attaches to the founders and leaders in all of the enterprises examined here and the calibre of such people in an organisation faced with the challenging task of producing and sustaining civic journalism cannot be underestimated. Our governance chessboard is foundational but our leadership board may be a game changer as so many of the boards on our 3-D game – regulation, perhaps, excepted – will be profoundly influenced by these people. On one hand they will have an overriding effect an enterprise's performance on the engagement and culture planes while on the other their leadership will be critical in financial performance and market success (however that might be defined). And their ability to harness and exploit technology will be vital as journalism is increasingly practised at the digital frontier.

The right structure and the right people are vital but even given those components a civic journalism enterprise is not guaranteed success. It can be helped by the right regulatory environment – one that, for example, grants charitable status to this area of news media to attract philanthropy (be it from foundations or crowdsourcing) or accepts it as a candidate for Low-profit Limited Liability Company (L³C) and Community Interest Company(CIC) status. And, of course, it can be helped by generous benefactors. However, the real test will lie in its ability to survive for a significant period of time. In the short term that will require a high degree of realism in setting expectations of the enterprise. The desire to establish a large, full-functioning newsroom is enticing but a start-up may have few – if any – full-time editorial staff until it has established itself in the marketplace.

It may wish to produce a daily outpouring of public interest content when its resources and finance are sufficient to sustain only periodic projects. In the medium term it must strive to be financially self-sustaining either by commercial activity or through donors with long-term commitment. In the long term it must be flexible in its structure and aim for diversified sources of revenue that allow it to weather periodic storms that batter the new media sector. There are no certainties of success, only game plans that improve the odds.

Thus far we have considered start-up enterprises as the most likely candidates for trust-like stewardship but could an existing major newspaper or news organisation move into a form of trust ownership? In other words, is there another "Scott family" or group of "Irish Times shareholders" or a "Nelson Poynter" willing to gift a "*Guardian*" to a trust? In the course of this research, I interviewed numerous people in the United Kingdom, Ireland, North America, South Africa, India and Australasia. The views of some have been presented here, but all contributed to my understanding of the realities of the news media landscape. The overwhelming consensus is that there will not be another Scott Trust.

There are a number of reasons for this view, not least of which is the very small number of major newspapers left in private ownership. As far as investors are concerned, listed media companies exist only to increase the value of tradable securities and to produce dividends. Such investors do not practice collective philanthropy. The fiduciary duty that directors owe to their investors requires them to attempt to realise value in the sale of even an ailing newspaper, which in today's market may mean the buyer assuming a level of debt. It is unlikely that a trust would be willing and able to assume such a burden. Directors see even closure of a title as a better alternative when a company can write off its losses. Put plainly, the economics of major media companies, afflicted by the strategies set out in Chapter 2, represent an impediment that would daunt the most public-spirited potential trustee.

A more likely prospect lies in the regional or local market where in Britain and America at least, large-scale closures have already occurred. Here the scale may be such that groups of individuals could either take over a title or, more likely, start a new digital news enterprise. However, the form of ownership would require careful thought. Not-for-profit status may be difficult to reconcile with a business model that still requires the sale of advertising, and a cover price to cover staffing and operating costs. With the right regulatory recognition a variation of the L^3C structure may enable a regional or local newspaper trust to operate in a self-sustaining manner while attracting tax concessions that improve its viability. Such enterprises could operate as local cooperatives but they may not be as robust or enduring as a trust as each member would retain an ownership share and would be at liberty to act out of self-interest. An intriguing alternative suggested to me was the purchase of a newspaper by an altruistic local resident, who could place the oversight of the publication in the hands of a local board of trustees – as an alternative to hands-on local ownership and direction by what were described as "not media barons but media squires". Hands-on local ownership is not inherently undesirable but it relies entirely on the intentions – good or otherwise – of the owner and of his or her successors.

However, legal structure should not be seen as an insurmountable impediment. As this research has demonstrated, workarounds can and do exist. The focus should be on the type of governance that would be employed. Trustee stewardship, manifested in a number of the ways described in preceding chapters, represents a means by which agreed journalistic objectives and values can be entrenched.

The consensus appears to be that trusteeship is a viable option at these levels but not at national level. However, that consensus is based on the belief that a national newspaper is too large a financial commitment (in the form of invested capital or accumulated debt) to be gifted by present owners or afforded by those who would seek to emulate the Irish Times Trust. It is a pragmatic view with which it is difficult to argue, although the value of newspaper assets has dropped alarmingly and could yet bring them within reach. Further, it ignores the possibility (unlikely though it may be in an era of government fiscal austerity) of state assistance for the creation of a new public service news organisation based on the written word.

Over time, the news has become a less attractive investment. Declining revenue, combined with decreased direct competition through newspaper mergers and closures, has seen fewer resources deployed in newsrooms in the struggle to maintain profitability. Perversely, although the number of media outlets and users has grown exponentially in the digital age, the breadth and depth of news coverage by mainstream media has diminished. Society may have no alternative but to seek creative ownership solutions if it wishes to retain a mass-audience alternative to the quality journalism produced by state-owned public service broadcasting. The need for multiple sources of such journalism is self-evident, not least because the notion of a state-owned monopoly on newsgathering carries with it significant difficulties. However, the time may have come when we must regard public interest journalism as the basis of only a self-sustaining operation and not one that delivers profits to its backers.

The United States Bill of Rights invested the press with an untouchable quality. Commercial enterprise throughout the 20th century reinforced the proposition that as conscientious custodians of the public interest, the news media could be left to be masters of their own destiny. In the 21st century, there is a strong case for institutional change if commercial enterprise cannot guarantee the supply of democratically significant journalism and a commitment to the public interest that transcends other interests (and there is ample evidence that in many quarters it is failing to do so). This book has found that those newspapers with trust ownership or trust-like governance possess a uniquely enshrined, sustainable commitment to journalism, and a determination that their newsrooms will not become what the Canadian Davey Commission on the Press described as "bone yards of broken dreams". In 1989 Leo Bogart stated that "the worst appears to be over" for US newspapers facing declining revenue and readership (1989, 49). It was the year in which Tim Berners-Lee proposed the World Wide Web, and Rupert Murdoch launched Sky Television in Britain. Obviously, there are risks in prediction and what follows may owe more to hope than certitude. It is safe to say, however, that digital technology *will* deliver an information-rich future. The contributions of citizens (informed and otherwise) will sit alongside the work of professionals. There is potential for more news, more analysis and more high quality journalism. There is scope for the newspaper to move to a multimedia iPad/tablet platform that retains in-depth reportage and analysis without the burden of printing and distribution costs. At the other end of the spectrum, there is potential for this type of journalism to be further fragmented and eroded.

My prediction is that in time, this journalism will recover when citizens realise the democratic deficit that results from its loss. New structures will evolve where the old forms of ownership and governance are found to be inadequate or inappropriate. Trusteeship will be seen as a natural expression of the public interest, in a segment of the news media that will regard income as the key to editorial sustainability rather than shareholder satisfaction. It will be regarded not as quixotic but as a white knight.

Appendix A: The Poynter principles

In 1947, Nelson Poynter set down 15 guiding principles for the *St Petersburg Times*. In 1979, his successor, Eugene Patterson, consolidated them into ten principles that now guide the *Tampa Bay Times*.

1. Operating a news publication must be the honoring of a sacred trust. We cannot compromise with the integrity of the news. Neither can we forget that our privilege of freedom under the First Amendment burdens us with a companion responsibility to exercise it fairly, carefully and in the public interest.
2. We will be sensitive to the unusual obligations that any worthy publication bears to the community in which it operates, aggressively volunteering service to the public with enthusiasm and never waiting to be prodded into it with reluctance. Because a chain owner's devotion to any one area is bound to be diluted or divided, we owe a commitment to our community to retain local, independent ownership of this newspaper.
3. To maintain our independence, we must resist debt, build reserves, sustain financial strength, forbid voting stock to scatter, and determine that a newspaper is so individualistic in nature that complete control, and thereby responsibility, should be concentrated in an individual.
4. Because a news organization encumbered with outside interests cannot best serve its public purposes, our editorial policy and news coverage will not be tinctured by ownership in enterprises not related to our primary mission of informing the public.
5. The manager of any department of our particular enterprises should have a well-rounded appreciation of and respect for the contributions that are made by staffers in all departments.
6. Second to staff, modern equipment should be regarded as vital to the service of our readers and advertisers, and essential to the achievement of our goal of highest excellence. Dividend policy will take into account these capital needs.
7. We seek to assemble a staff on which every member is above average, and so we must be willing to compensate staffers above average, and then expect the staff to demand of itself performance above the average.
8. Our profits are to be shared with the staff on a formula that recognizes contribution to the enterprise.
9. Pensions are to be paid that promise dignified retirement to members of the staff who devote their lives to the institution.
10. Our publications' policy is very simple: Merely to tell the truth.

Appendix B: Government-mandated governance in PSBs

	Board of directors	Chairman	Managing director	Advisory boards	Charter	Interference protection
BBC (UK)	Govt appointed trustees (12) Trust appointed executive board	Govt appointed	Trust appointed Director General may chair Executive Board	Trust appointed regional audience councils (4) chaired by trustee	Objects, purpose and mission embodied in Royal Charter	Independence from interference in content and management
CBC/ Radio Canada	Govt appointed directors (12)	Govt appointed	Govt appointed	Board committees for English and French broadcasts	No charter Legislative and regulatory requirements	Journalistic, creative and programming independence
ABC (**Aust.**)	Govt appointed directors (Max. 7 plus CEO)	Govt appointed	Board appointed	Board appointed advisory council plus staff committee	Charter of functions and obligations	Subject to direction only in notified matters of national interest
SBS (**Aust.**)	Govt appointed (Max. 8 plus CEO)	Govt appointed	Board appointed	Board appointed Community Advisory Committee	Charter of functions and obligations	Subject to direction only in notified matters of pub- lic/national interest

(Continued)

	Board of directors	Chairman	Managing director	Advisory boards	Charter	Interference protection
Radio New Zealand	Govt appointed Board of Governors (Max. 9)	Govt appointed	Board nominated Govt appointed	None specified	Charter of functions and obligations subject to review by Parliament	Independence from interference in content and management
SABC* (South Africa)	12 non-executive board members appointed by president	Appointed by president	Board appointed	None specified External advisory group for Minister	Charter in Broadcasting Act	Independence from interference in content and management
Prasar Bharati (India)	15 member mixed board: 7 president appointed on advice	Appointed by president on advice	Internal recruitment board	None specified	Act includes functions and obligations Subject to review by Parliament	Constitutional protections but subject to notified Government direction in national interest
CPB** (USA)	President appointed ratified by Senate (max. 9)	Elected annually by board	Corporation president appointed by board	Required to report on minority interests	Policy on PSBs in Public Broadcasting Act	Prohibited

*SABC has two separate services (public service and commercial) overseen by a 15-person board. The 12 non-executive directors are appointed on advice from the National Assembly. **The Corporation for Public Broadcasting (CPB) is the steward of U.S. federal government investment in public service broadcasting.

Appendix C: Charter of South African Broadcasting Corporation SABC (Extract)

Objectives of Corporation

The objectives of the Corporation are

(a) to make its services available throughout the Republic;

(b) to provide sound and television broadcasting services, whether by analogue or digital means, and to provide sound and television programmes of information, education and entertainment funded by advertisements, subscription, sponsorship, licence fees or any other means of finance;

(c) to acquire from time to time a licence or licences for such period and subject to such regulations, provisions and licence conditions as may be prescribed by the Authority;

(d) to provide, in its public broadcasting services, radio and television programming that informs, educates and entertains;

(e) to be responsive to audience needs and account on how to meet those needs;

(f) to provide other services, whether or not broadcasting or programme supply services, such services being ancillary services;

(g) to provide television and radio programmes and any other material to be transmitted or distributed by the common carrier for free to air reception by the public subject to section 33 of this Act;

(h) to provide to other bodies by such means and methods as may be convenient, services, programmes and materials to be transmitted or distributed by such bodies and to receive from such other bodies services, programmes and materials to be transmitted by stations of the Corporation for reception as above;

(i) to commission, compile, prepare, edit, make, print, publish, issue, circulate and distribute, with or without charge, such books, magazines, periodicals, journals, printed matter, records, cassettes, compact disks, video tapes, audio-visual and interactive material, whether analogue or digital and whether on media now known or hereafter invented, as may be conducive to any of the objects of the Corporation;

(j) to establish and maintain libraries and archives containing materials relevant to the objects of the Corporation and to make available to the public such libraries and archives with or without charge;

(k) to organise, present, produce, provide or subsidise concerts, shows, variety performances, revues, musical and other productions and performances and other entertainment whether live or recorded in connection with the broadcasting and programme supply services of the Corporation or for any purpose incidental thereto;

(l) to collect news and information in any part of the world and in any manner that may be thought fit and to establish and subscribe to news agencies;

(m) to carry out research and development work in relation to any technology relevant to the objects of the Corporation and to acquire by operation of law, registration, purchase, assignment, licence or otherwise copyright and designs, trade marks, trade names and any other intellectual, industrial and commercial property rights;

(n) to nurture South African talent and train people in production skills and carry out research and development for the benefit of audiences;

(o) to develop, produce, manufacture, purchase, acquire, use, display, sell, rent or dispose of sound recordings and films and materials and apparatus for use in connection with such sound recordings and films;

(p) to develop and extend the services of the Corporation beyond the borders of South Africa.

Organisation

(1) The Corporation consists of two separate operational entities, namely

(a) a public service; and
(b) a commercial service.

(2) The public and commercial services of the Corporation must be separately administered.

Public service

(1) The public service provided by the Corporation must

(a) make services available to South Africans in all the official languages;
(b) reflect both the unity and diverse cultural and multilingual nature of South Africa and all of its cultures and regions to audiences;
(c) strive to be of high quality in all of the languages served;
(d) provide significant news and public affairs programming which meets the highest standards of journalism, as well as fair and unbiased coverage, impartiality, balance and independence from government, commercial and other interests;
(e) include significant amounts of educational programming, both curriculum based and informal educative topics from a wide range of social, political and economic issues, including, but not limited to, human rights, health, early childhood development, agriculture, culture, justice and commerce and contributing to a shared South African consciousness and identity;
(f) enrich the cultural heritage of South Africa by providing support for traditional and contemporary artistic expression;
(g) strive to offer a broad range of services targeting, particularly, children, women, the youth and the disabled;
(h) include programmes made by the Corporation as well as those commissioned from the independent production sector; and
(i) include national sports programming as well as developmental and minority sports.

(2) The public service provided by the Corporation may draw revenues from advertising and sponsorships, grants and donations, as well as licence fees levied in respect of the licensing of persons in relation to television sets, and may receive grants from the State.

Commercial services

The commercial services provided by the Corporation must

(a) be subject to the same policy and regulatory structures as outlined in this Act for commercial broadcasting services;
(b) comply with the values of the public broadcasting service in the provision of programmes and service;
(c) commission a significant amount of their programming from the independent sector;
(d) subsidise the public services to the extent recommended by the Board and approved by the Minister; and
(e) be operated in an efficient manner so as to maximise the revenues provided to its shareholder.

Notes

2 Journalism's Crisis

1. US analyst John Morton interviewed by Dean Roper for WAN-IFRA www.ifra.net
2. WAN-IFRA public statement 3 June 2013.
3. After the introduction of computerised editorial input and pagination had radically reduced the number of pre-press printing staff.
4. Pew Research Center, *Understanding the Participatory News Consumer: How Internet and Cell Phone Users Have Turned News into a Social Experience*, 1 March 2010.
5. South Africa and India are not numbered among this group as their political and economic development created unique circumstances for the development of their news media.
6. "Back from the brink", *The Economist*, London, 7 December 1991, Vol. 321, No. 7736, 77 (2 pages).
7. Television's evening news audience also declined – from 52.1 million in 1980 to 28.8 million in 2004 (*State of the Media 2005* report by the Project for Excellence in Journalism).
8. The number of hours spent watching terrestrial television also declined – from 108.5 hours in 1994 to 90.8 hours in 2006 (*Ownership of the News*, House of Lords Select Committee on Communications 2008, Vol. 1, 24).
9. No nationwide Australian circulation figures are available for 2001–2002. For this exercise, the midway point between 2000 and 2003 figures (2,750,000) has been applied in both years. There are inconsistencies between sets of World Association of Newspapers data on Australian circulation between 1999 and 2003 and the apparent circulation decline 2000–2005 of 17 per cent may be overstated. Australia represents approximately 3.5 per cent of the combined average daily circulation of the six countries.
10. Clay Shirky, Address to Shorenstein Center, Harvard University, 22 September 2009. Transcript downloaded from http://www.niemanlab.org/2009/09/clay-shirky-let-a-thousand-flowers-bloom-to-replace-newspapers-dont-build-a-paywall-around-a-public-good.
11. Methodologies for determining readership differ between the countries under examination. Analysis has been limited to assessing trends within individual countries between 2005 and 2008, the latest year for which figures were available in all cases.
12. *Source*: *World Advertising Trends 2006*, World Advertising Research Centre, Henley-on-Thames.
13. News Corporation's debt rose from $US11 billion in 2000 to $US14.3 billion in 2009. The diversified conglomerate's assets of more that $US62 billion, a cash balance of $US6.5 billion (at the end of 2009) and decreasing reliance on advertising revenue allowed the group to maintain stable credit ratings.
14. Annual revenues were combined and synergies allowed the consolidation of services, with resulting reductions in costs
15. In some cases, executives in acting CEO roles also received entitlements.

16. Jensen and Meckling (1976) and An et al. (2006) found that equity holding by managers tended to lower debt-to-equity ratios. Acquisition raised the asset base of these companies at the same time as it increased the debt servicing burden.
17. UK House of Commons Culture, Media and Sport Committee, *Future for Local and Regional Media* April 2010, 12.
18. *Life in the Clickstream: The Future of Journalism,* Sydney 2008, Media Entertainment and Arts Alliance.
19. Dublin-based Independent News & Media was paid £1 for *The Independent* and the *Independent on Sunday* but agreed to pay Lebedev £9.25m over ten months to take on the paper's liabilities and obligations.
20. The *Monitor's* Editor, John Yemma, told *Poynter Online* on 23 October 2009 that 93 per cent of the printed daily's 43,000 subscribers agreed to switch to the new weekly print magazine and its circulation had increased to 67,000 fully paid subscribers plus 18,000 trial subscribers in seven months. Page views on its daily website had increased 20 per cent in the same period.
21. Even the model of public service broadcasting, the BBC, was not immune to the effects that the medium had on the news. It was as aware of visual impact as its commercial counterparts (Born 2005).
22. US total includes broadcast television and cable TV.
23. *Sources*: AA/WARC and US Television Bureau of Advertising.
24. *Shaping the Future of the Newspaper*, Vol. 1, No. 5 May 2002, attempted to measure everything from editorial resources and reader research to editorial performance and journalistic content. The purpose was to create a newspaper editorial department performance evaluation system that had strong corporate overtones.
25. A 2008 Digital Future study by the Annenberg School of Communication at University of Southern California found that 21 per cent had cancelled newspaper or magazine subscriptions because content was available online and 27 per cent stated they would not miss the print edition of their newspaper if it was no longer available.
26. Aspen Institute 2007, *Next Generation Media: The Global Shift* (Richard P. Adler, *rapporteur*).
27. Browsers such as Microsoft *Explorer* and Mozilla *Firefox* and search engines such as *Google* and *Yahoo*.
28. Dan Gillmor of the *San Jose Mercury News* in a foreword to *We Media* (Bowman & Willis 2003).
29. Les Hinton, "They're stealing our lifeblood", *British Journalism Review*, Vol. 20, No. 3 September 2009, 13–18.
30. Marshall's coverage of the firing of eight US attorneys under political circumstances contributed to the resignation of US Attorney-General Alberto Gonzales. In September 2009 *The Atlantic* listed him among America's 50 most influential commentators. Staff numbers cited are as at May 2012.
31. Jay Rosen: http://journalism.nyu.edu/pubzone/weblogs/pressthink
32. *New York Times* Sunday Book Review 11 July 2004.

3   Media under Scrutiny

1. "The contemporary British Press – 1. The trend of ownership", *The Economist*, 3 November 1928, 786–787.
2. Fyfe 1936, 144.

3. Steed 1938, 20–23.
4. PEP was an independent non-party organisation of about 100 members drawn from industry, central and local government, the media, the medical profession and universities. *The Report on the British Press: A Survey of Its Current Operations and Problems with Special Reference to National Newspapers and Their Part in Public Affairs* was the result of a three-year study by its Press Group. In a preface Steed acknowledged its influence on his own book.
5. Quoted in Hocking's monograph in the US Hutchins Commission Report on Freedom of the Press, entitled *Freedom of the Press: A framework of principles*, 1947:197.
6. In 1941 the FCC began a three-year investigation of newspaper ownership of radio stations. Its record of proceedings ran to 3500 pages and 400 exhibits but no new rules were promulgated (*Michigan Law Review*, Vol. 75, No. 8. (Aug., 1977), 1723).
7. US newspaper companies invested in radio in the 1920s and 1930s. Broadcasting in the United Kingdom remained state-owned throughout the war.
8. An interesting aspect was the footnoted comments by other commission members that created a subtext that gave some insight into the attitudes and tensions within the enquiry. For example, Hocking stated that ownership of newspapers "conferred no privilege of deafness" toward radical opinions. Fellow commission member Archibald MacLeish penned a footnote stating that "on the contrary", minority ownership of a general right "may impose a duty" to publish the widest possible range of opinions (Hocking 1947, 99).
9. See McChesney and Scott (2004).
10. In 1967 Raymond Williams produced a similar study in the United Kingdom and also characterised four systems – authoritarian, paternal, commercial and democratic – all of which he said were "all to some extent active, in practice or in local experiment, in contemporary Britain". The main struggle over the past generation had been between the paternal and commercial systems and it appeared the commercial had been "steadily winning".
11. The Economist Intelligence Unit produced a three volume study, *The National Newspaper Industry: A Survey*, in 1966, while in 1967 and again in 1970 the National Board for Prices and Incomes investigated the costs and revenue of national daily newspapers.
12. Purchase of Oldhams Press by Daily Mirror Newspapers (1962 Royal Commission Report, 10).
13. Cited in US Congressional Committee Report 97-V, November 1981.
14. Chadwick (1989), 247 (Table 5).
15. Richard Ackland, "Inquiry into Media Ways Sure to Test Fink tank", *The Age*, Melbourne, 16 September 2011.
16. Shaw recounts numerous exchanges between the newspaper industry and the commission chairman, Judge Helm van Zyl, that indicate the commission's desire to influence the establishment of a "voluntary" disciplinary body (1999, 169–179). In a chronology of media history in South Africa submitted to the Truth & Reconciliation Commission, the Freedom of Expression Institute stated that the commission's final report was in nine volumes and ran to 4250 pages including its annexures. It weighed 60 pounds (27 kilograms) and had cost R355,000. It did call for a statutory Press Council to reprimand, fine and impose "self control and discipline", as well as to maintain a register of journalists with special registration for overseas transmission rights. However, the industry's efforts to

forestall state control led to the compromise that saw the establishment of an industry-appointed Board of Reference empowered to reprimand.

17. India was subject to emergency regulation 1975–1977 and, while freedom of expression is guaranteed by the Indian Constitution, a framework of laws – some dating to colonial times – that cover criminal and civil libel, contempt, official secrecy, national security and incitement have constrained the news media.

18. In June 2013 Kevin Rudd retook the prime ministership from Julia Gillard, who had previously deposed him. Conroy was a Gillard supporter.

19. Established by mainstream broadcasters to oversee their online content, which was not subject to oversight by the Broadcasting Tribunal.

20. *Media Transformation, Ownership and Diversity*, a discussion paper presented to the ANC National General Council in September 2010.

4 Genesis of Media Trusts

1. Contained in a motion placed before the House of Commons on 29 October 1946 by two MPs (both journalists) calling for the Royal Commission. Quoted in Royal Commission Report (p. 3).

2. In 1978 PEP merged with the Centre for the Study of Social Policy and was renamed the Policy Studies Institute, which became part of the University of Westminster in 2009. PEP produced an extensive *Report on the British Press* in 1938 and a further report on press ownership in 1955.

3. The editor of *The Observer* from 1908 to 1942 was J. L. Garvin, who enjoyed a good relationship with the owner, Viscount Astor, until a disagreement over wartime editorial policy saw him ousted over what Astor claimed was a breach of contract. In 1948 David Astor (son of the trust founder) became editor, replacing Ivor Brown, who had taken the chair while David Astor did military service. For a positive view of David Astor's editorship see Roy Greenslade, *Press Gang*, 2004, London Pan Macmillan (p. 24). Greenslade notes that Astor always ensured that appointees to the trust chairmanship were people who held views similar to his own.

4. Charles Hyde was the grandson of the founder of the *Birmingham* Post, John Frederick Feeney, and inherited the company from his uncle. He is credited with playing a major role in the modernisation of the Press Association in Britain in the 1920s (Moncrieff 2001, 77; Scott 1968, 160). His contempt for the mass-circulation London papers was a reflection of his traditionalist beliefs and dignified approach to journalism. In 1921 he was created Baron Hyde of Birmingham. He died without an heir in 1942 and the baronetcy became extinct.

5. Deeds of trust used by British news agencies to secure their news service functions. Important principles and safeguards were incorporated in the Reuters Trust Principles that are discussed in Chapter 8. Also examined in that chapter is the recent formation of a trust by the (British) Press Association, to ensure that its editorial objectives continued to be met as it diversified its range of activities.

6. The trustees did retain an ownership interest that continues to be reflected in the shareholding.

7. Layton agreed to an amendment to Article 105 that recognised the editor's responsibility to maintain the general character and tradition of *The Economist* and that "with a view to doing so" the editor would meet with the board of directors "from time to time" (Edwards, 739n).

8. The committee of notables that was supposed to afford *The Times* a measure of trustee protection indirectly had its origins in the insanity of a major shareholder, Lord Northcliffe, and the calamity over ownership that surrounded his madness and subsequent death (Times History 678–721, 740–766).

9. Legislation had been passed the previous year requiring sale or merger of newspapers to be referred to the Monopolies & Mergers Commission under certain circumstances. The 1977 Royal Commission on the Press noted that seven cases had been referred to the commission since the enactment of the law and all were approved (Royal Commission Report 1, 10). Jenkins (1986, 54) described the Monopolies Commission enquiry into *The Times* purchase as "an extraordinary parade of Fleet Street self-importance" and "an Establishment initiation rite" [for Thomson]. Thomson's offer to add four independent directors to the Times Holdings Company board (which he did) was characterised by the Monopolies Commission as "window-dressing" because they lacked any real power (Evans 1983, 128).

10. The more populist William Randolph Hearst may have been expected to join the attack, but instead issued instructions that Mrs Eddy and the Church of Christ, Scientist were not to be criticised. Hearst's infant son was reportedly cured of a wasting illness by a Christian Science practitioner (Peel, 495n). Paradoxically, the *Monitor* has been the recipient of seven Pulitzer Prizes.

11. The early *Christian Science Monitor* was innovative. In 1912 it set up a complete newspaper plant at the Republican national convention in Chicago and issued special editions from the venue, while in 1928 it became one of the newspapers that invested in Press Wireless Inc. to provide radio communication for news distribution (Lee, 285, 558).

12. During the First World War, the US Post Office used the Espionage Act as a pretext to suppress issues of socialist and left-wing publications that were critical of the war, by ruling that they were no longer eligible for the cheaper second-class mail rates that newspapers received (Starr 2004, 277).

13. United States Court of Appeals No. 475, Docket 84–6222, June 1985.

14. *American Journalism Review,* April–May 2012.

15. Voting shares held by the foundation were converted to 15.9 million shares of Gannett stock, making it the largest shareholder. Preferred shares converted at a rate of one preferred share to 40 shares of common stock, providing a "bonanza" for shareholders (Neuharth 1989, 182).

16. Available at www.parl.gc.ca/39/1/parlbus/commbus/senate/com-e/trans-e/rep-e/repfinjun06vol1-e.htm.

17. Critics claim the English-language press, in fact, treated their non-White staff as second-class citizens and that their opposition to apartheid was essentially self-serving because the racist policies had negative economic effects (Horwitz 2001, 39–40).

18. Independent News & Media in 2013 sold its South African business for R2billion ($219.6 million) to a consortium of local investors led by Iqbal Survé.

19. *Grassroots* described itself as a newsletter. Newspaper licensing in apartheid-era South Africa required the deposit of a R40,000 bond – which the community groups could not afford to pay. *Grassroots* avoided registration by publishing every five weeks, avoiding one of the definitions of a newspaper that stated in must be published at least monthly.

20. The author, as editor and editor-in-chief of the *New Zealand Herald*, was not subject to direct editorial interference, but managerial control of budgets greatly influenced the *level* of coverage each year.

5 Keeping It in the Family

1. Pulitzer Inc. (which owned 14 daily newspapers, including the *St. Louis Post-Dispatch*, and more than 100 non-daily publications) was sold to Lee Enterprises in 2005 for $US1.46 billion.
2. Rupert Murdoch's father, Sir Keith Murdoch, has been called the "founder of a media empire" (Younger 2003) but his legacy was, in fact, modest – two Adelaide newspapers after Sir Keith's widow sold his Queensland interests.
3. The Harvard survey, conducted in association with the Centre for Management and Economic Research at École Polytechnique, involved a comparison with non-family firms and found a number (such as Nestlé) that were managed like family firms.
4. Passing on the Crown – Family Business; Family Businesses. *The Economist*, 6 November 2004.
5. Bloom and Van Reenan ascribe the higher incidence of primogeniture in Britain and France to their Norman origins under which the rights of the first-born were enshrined in law. Such rights were abolished in the United States following the War of Independence. German inheritance has generally been based on the Teutonic principle of equal division between all sons (2007, 1382).
6. Adolph Ochs' estate planning had, however, been negligent because he would not transfer any shareholding during his lifetime and the resulting death duties left the family facing a bill of almost $US6 million. Tifft and Jones (*ibid.*, 169–170) describe the "ingenious" plan that Arthur Sulzberger devised to pay the death duties without the family relinquishing voting power or resorting to bank loans that could compromise the independence of the *New York Times*. The New York Times Company offered to buy non-voting preferred stock from the trust and Ochs relatives (who had received the stock as gifts in the 1920) – providing the finance to pay the estate duties – and retired it.
7. The New York Times Company board ratified such appointments but the choice was the prerogative of "Punch" Sulzberger (and his father before him). His son was not appointed CEO but the position was downgraded and the eventual appointee reported to Arthur Ochs Sulzberger Jr. rather than to the board of directors.
8. In March 2009 Bloomberg reported that the company had been forced into a partial sale and leaseback agreement to raise $US225 million. It has an option to take back ownership in 2019 for $US250 million.
9. On 13 April 2004, the company's board of directors authorised the repurchase of up to $400 million worth of Class A shares. In 2007 the dividend was increased by 31 per cent but dividend payments to both Class A and Class B shareholders were suspended from the fourth quarter 2008 and remained through 2012 (New York Times Company Annual Report 2012).
10. A total of 3325 Class A shares were transferred to Graham and 1325 to Katharine which, with their existing holding, gave them a combined total of 5000 shares. Other shares classified as Class B were transferred to a charitable foundation and repurchased by the Grahams in 1957, giving them total ownership of the company. Katharine's siblings were given sums of money by their father, rather than an interest in the newspaper.
11. Lord Rothermere, interviewed by telephone 18 September 2013.
12. House of Lords Select Committee on Communications, 1st Report of Session 2007–2008 "The Ownership of the News" Volume II: Evidence, p. 542 (HL Paper 122-II).

13. Jonathan Rothermere told me his father had wanted to redevelop the *Sketch* along lines that Rupert Murdoch would later successfully employ with the *Sun* but the second viscount had forced him to choose one newspaper and close the other. He chose the *Daily Mail*.
14. Peter Williams was interviewed in London, 1 April 2009. He retired in March 2011.
15. The non-voting shares are freely traded on the London Stock Exchange but the tiered share structure led to their removal from the FTSE index of public companies in 2012. The voting shares are listed on the exchange but are very rarely traded.
16. *Daily Mail* executive managing editor, Robin Esser, interviewed by author in London, 1 April 2009.
17. Northcliffe Media, which published 77 titles, was sold in December 2012 to the Local World consortium. DMGT received cash proceeds of £52.5 million and shares representing a 38.7 per cent stake in Local World. The consortium also bought the regional publisher Illiffe News and Media.
18. Michael Pelosi was managing director of Northcliffe Media when interviewed by the author in London on 3 April 2009. He retired in March 2011.
19. In 1999 Lord Rothermere introduced the successful *Metro* free morning newspaper concept on London transport and followed it in 2006 with the evening, *London Lite*, which was embroiled in a free sheet war with News Corporation's *London Paper*. The free sheets had a negative impact on the *Evening Standard*. After the sale, both *London Lite* and the *London Paper* closed. Lebedev relaunched the *Standard* as a free newspaper and set it on the road to profitability. DMGT's 2012 annual report stated *Metro* "continued to perform strongly".
20. According to Chenoweth (2001, 114) the name is derived from another Australian businessman, A. E. (Ted) Harris, who suggested they swap names in their trusts in the interests of anonymity. Ted Harris is now deputy chairman of APN News & Media, whose interests include New Zealand's largest daily newspaper, the *New Zealand Herald*.
21. Murdoch's mother, Dame Elisabeth, held 10 per cent of Cruden that were to transfer to Rupert Murdoch on her death in 2012 (Chenoweth, 315).
22. *The Guardian* 20 November 2013. http://www.theguardian.com/media/2013/nov/20/rupert-murdoch-wendi-deng-divorce

6   The Trinity – Origins and Growth

1. Scott, Richard, "On the same lines and in the same spirit", *Guardian*, 5 May 1971, p. 14.
2. In 2005 Brady estimates that in current dollars (allowing for inflation) the loan would have been worth €30 million.
3. A Dublin magazine, *The Phoenix*, regularly criticised the Trust for failing to meet its charitable objectives, which were to have been discharged through the Irish Times Foundation (Brady, 118).
4. Poynter Timeline 1903–2005 compiled by the library director of the Poynter Institute, David Shedden. A number of date references in this chapter are derived from the timeline.
5. For a brief moment, the newspapers reverted to ownership by Scott family members. When the 1936 trust was wound up, the assets of the company were divided

among five Scott beneficiaries who immediately settled the shares on a new Scott Trust.

6. It was a short-term problem: circulation in June 1956 was 163,000, dipping to 155,000 in August but rising to 180,000 in November (Greenslade 2004, 137).

7. Hetherington (352–356) records the various proposals for union representation. The Trust had a well-established policy that it would not concede to the union the right to mandate any of its members for executive positions. However, it took "a friendly view" to the initial proposal for union representation on the Trust and engaged in protracted talks. By the time Hetherington retired "(T)he exploration, unfortunately, became stuck in soft sand." There has been a long-standing tradition that at least one *Guardian* staff member should sit on the trust although he or she should not be seen as a *representative* of the staff because of potential conflict of interest.

8. Interviewed in London 2 April 2009.

9. The Berliner format is 470 mm × 315 mm while a tabloid format is 430 mm × 280 mm. The broadsheet format previously used by *The Guardian* was 749 mm × 597 mm. *The Observer* adopted the new format in 2006.

10. Chris Wade left GMG in 2012 to join Sir Martin Sorrell's WPP Communications and was replaced as head of communications by Oliver Rawlins.

11. More than 1000 each by Johnston Press and Northcliffe Media and 800 by Trinity Mirror.

12. McConnell, Professor of Genetics at Trinity College Dublin, was interviewed in Dublin on 26 March 2009. The current chairman is Tom Arnold, chair of the Constitutional Convention set up in 2012 to consider proposed amendments to the Irish Constitution.

13. The bugging was to determine the sources of stories about challenges to Haughey's leadership and one of the journalists, Geraldine Kennedy of the *Sunday Tribune*, would later become editor of the *Irish Times*.

14. In the same year the articles of the operating company were amended to ensure that no board resolution could pass without the approval of the chairman (McDowell) and another Trust Governor or two Governors. In 1997, Governors on the board of directors were given five votes for each executive director's vote (O'Brien, 260).

15. In 1997, Governors on the board of directors were given five votes for each executive director's vote (O'Brien, 260).

16. Ireland's population at the time was 3.84 million. The three quality dailies in the UK had a combined circulation of 2.1 million for a population of 58.8 million.

17. The purchase of MyHome.ie involved an upfront payment of €40 million and a further €10 million once performance targets were met. The site had over 300,000 users a month.

18. Patterson, Eugene, "Nelson Poynter still lives through the newspaper he gave away", *St Petersburg Times*, 15 June 1998; Barnes, Andrew, "Who owns the St. Petersburg Times? Why it matters to readers", *St Petersburg Times*, 26 December 1999; and Tash, Paul, "Who owns the *Times*, and why it matters", *St Petersburg Times*, 7 August 2005).

7   Modern White Knights

1. The company was initially registered on 24 September 2008 as Scott Place 1001 Limited, but changed by special board resolution a week later to the Scott Trust

Limited, a move the chair Dame Liz Forgan describes as "a great joy". She was interviewed in London 2 April 2009.

2. The group's chief executive, Andrew Miller, flattened the management structure by removing the position of managing director of Guardian News & Media (the incumbent left the company) and taking on the role of executive chairman of the news subsidiary to ensure a common approach between GNM and GMG.

3. The GMG Anti-Bribery and Corruption Committee is made up of directors and senior managers from Editorial, Legal, Finance, Commercial, HR, Risk and Communications.

4. Rusbridger's remuneration in 2009/2010 (£411,000) was £33,000 less than in the previous year. The reduction was to his base salary and he receives no annual bonuses. In 2012/2013 he again opted for a 10 per cent reduction in his base salary (from £439,000 to £395,000) and a 50 per cent cut in the company's contribution to his pension.

5. Interview London 2 April 2009. Folwell resigned in December 2012.

6. O'Brien was interviewed in Dublin 27 March 2009.

7. O'Sullivan was interviewed by telephone 24 September 2013.

8. A voluntary redundancy scheme aimed at reducing the staff by 40 workers had also been offered in 2005.

9. Euro conversion, for the purpose of comparison, is at the rate (0.787564) prevailing when the new currency was introduced in 2002. Restructuring costs took the total 2001 loss to £IR21.7 million (€27.55 million).

10. "Owners vow to stick with troubled magazine", *Irish Independent*, 26 April 2009.

11. The ePaper, as it is known, has a small circulation of 2278 with a further 2350 copies on eReaders.

12. The lacklustre performance of the subsidiaries and joint ventures prompted the *Irish Times* chapel of the NUJ to pass a motion in June 2009 saying that "on-going investment in loss-making projects poses a serious threat to employment" at the newspaper. The NUJ Irish Secretary, Seamus Dooley, in a letter to both the board and the Trust, said:

> The reason for this motion is widespread concern for the future and it should be seen in a positive light, coming from workers who, like their colleagues in sister unions, have been prepared to take more than their fair share of pain. We want to see employment protected across the board but the first priority must be to ensure the survival of the *Irish Times*.
>
> (*Irish Journalist* Summer 2009, 2).

In 2005 staff had complained about executive salary levels.

13. McCollam, Douglas, "Somewhere East of Eden: Why the St Pete Times Model Can't Save Newspapers", *Columbia Journalism Review*, March/April 2008, pp. 50–51.

14. One Poynter representative on the Times Publishing Company board is the president, Dr Karen Dunlap. The other is the dean of faculty, Stephen Buckley, who joined the board in 2006 when he was managing editor of the newspaper.

15. Tash was interviewed in St Petersburg FL, 13 April 2010.

16. Dunlap was interviewed in St Petersburg FL, 15 April 2010.

17. The only area in which the company makes full disclosure of financial information is the Tampa Bay Times Fund, a non-profit offshoot that makes grants to non-profit organisations and offers scholarships to college students. Tash is president of the fund (established by Nelson Poynter in 1953), whose investments

stood at $US11.2million in 2012 and from which grants totalling more than $23 million have been made since its inception.

18. Email from Paul Tash, 21 September 2013.

19. Remuneration for GMG chief executive Andrew Miller totalled £573,000 in 2011 (the latest year for which comparable figures were available) while that of the managing director of the Irish Times Company, Liam Kavanagh, totalled €270,000. Both figures were converted to $US at the rate prevailing on 31 December 2011.

20. *tbt* is an example of the difference that private and independent ownership can make by allowing a longer-term view of strategy. Its continual growth drew the attention of newspaper companies throughout the United States, and Tash began receiving calls from executives wishing to emulate its success. A year after it was launched, he received a call from the chief executive of a large, well-known public company: "He asked 'Is it making money?' I said 'Not yet, I think it will be another year but it's headed in the right direction'. There was a long pause at the other end of the telephone and he said 'That's going to be tough for us to do then'." A year later it was profitable.

21. Paul Tash interview St Petersburg FL 13 April 2010.

22. The Brookings Institution's *Metro Monitor* report in March 2010 ranked Tampa in the 19 weakest-performing of 100 metropolitan areas, with 12.4 per cent unemployment. From that trough it emerged in June 2013 to rank in the overall top 25 metropolitan areas.

23. A laid-off journalist, Ester Venouziou, in a blog headed "My thoughts about the St Pete Times layoffs" posted on her website LocalShops1.com on 22 October 2011, took issue with the way the cuts had been announced and an absence of managerial reductions but also said: "I still believe the *Times* is devoted to quality journalism, and that it will continue to be one of the area's top sources for news, in spite of dwindling resources and a skeleton staff."

8 The Electronic Age

1. Television New Zealand is state-owned but operates two fully commercial networks. It is no longer subject to a public service charter.

2. Brown was managing director of SBS from 2006 to 2011. He was interviewed in Sydney 2 June 2009.

3. Speech at the London School of Economics 9 March 2011.

4. Westminster Hall debate 24 April 2013. Mr Rob Wilson, Conservative MP for Reading East, moved a debate on the role of the BBC Trust in oversight of the BBC. The Parliamentary Under-Secretary of State for Culture, Media and Sport, Mr Edward Vaizey, responded on behalf of the Government.

5. Interviewed in London 23 March 2009.

6. Email from Lord Patten on 10 October 2013 in response to correspondence.

7. The Royal Charter and service agreements can be found at http://www.bbc.co.uk/bbctrust/governance/regulatory_framework/charter_agreement.html.

8. Federal funding accounts for only 15–20 per cent of the aggregated revenues of public broadcasting stations in the United States.

9. Cavanagh interviewed in Wellington 15 June 2010.

10. The Press Trust of India withdrew from the partnership in 1952 over coverage of news in the Indian zone. A tense relationship existed between India and Pakistan, which had fought a brief war in 1947–1948 over territory in Kashmir.

11. Gillies was interviewed in Sydney 5 June 2009.
12. Malcolm Kirk was interviewed by telephone from Toronto 11 October 2013.
13. ProPublica's second Pulitzer Prize in 2011 was for a series on the financial crisis. It ran on the organisation's own website and was the first Pulitzer awarded for a contribution that did not appear in print.
14. The CIR merged with another Californian not-for-profit news organisation, Bay Citizen, in April 2012 and its income, principally from grants and contributions, in that year was $US11.1 million ($US5.4 million in 2011).
15. Steiger and Tofel were interview in New York on 20 April 2010.
16. Lewis was interviewed in Washington D.C. on 19 April 2010.

9 Conclusions – Possibilities and Realities

1. The Wellcome Trust Constitution, Memorandum of Association and Articles of Associations can be found at http://www.wellcome.ac.uk/About-us/Organisation/Governance/Constitution/
2. Interview with John Stewart, London 23 March 2009. Stewart retired as company secretary in January 2012.

Bibliography

Adler, Richard P. 2007. *Next-Generation Media: The Global Shift.* Aspen, Colorado: Aspen Institute Forum on Communications and Society.

Alexander, Alison, James Owers, Rod Carveth, C. Ann Hollifield, and Albert N. Greco, eds. 2004. *Media Economics: Theory and Practice.* Mahwah, NJ: Lawrence Erlbaum.

Allen, David S. 2001. The First Amendment and the doctrine of corporate personhood: Collapsing the press-corporation distinction. *Journalism* 2 (3):255–278.

Altheide, David L. 1984. Media hegemony: A failure of perspective. *The Public Opinion Quarterly* 48 (2):476–490.

Altschull, J. Herbert. 1984. *Agents of Power: The Role of the News Media in Human Affairs.* New York: Longman.

Alysen, Barbara. 2005 The changing newsroom: Shifts in journalism work practices and the implications for journalism educators. *Australian Studies in Journalism* 14:61–78.

Amar, Vikram David. 1999. From Watergate to Ken Starr: Potter Stewart's "Or of the Press" a quarter century later. *Hastings Law Journal* 50 (April 1999):711–715.

Andrews, Paul. 2003. Is blogging journalism? *Nieman Reports* 57 (3):63–64.

Anon. 1952. Local monopoly in the Daily newspaper industry. *The Yale Law Journal* 61 (6):948–1009.

An, Soontae, Hyun Sueng Jim and Todd Simon. 2006. Ownership structures of publicly traded newspaper companies and their financial performance. *Journal of Media Economics.* 19 (2):119–136.

Arrese, Angel. 2005. Corporate governance and news governance in economic and financial media. In *Corporate Governance of Media Companies,* edited by R. G. Picard. Jönköing, Sweden: Jönköing International Business School.

Asimov, Isaac. 1983. A perfect fit. In *The Winds of Change and Other Stories.* New York: Doubleday.

Aspen. 2009. *Of the Press: Models for Transforming American Journalism.* Washington DC: Aspen Institute.

Auletta, Ken. 2003. *Backstory: Inside the Business of News.* New York: Penguin.

———. 2007. Can the *Los Angeles Times* survive its owners? In *-30- The Collapse of the Great American Newspaper,* edited by C. M. Madigan. Chicago: Ivan R. Dee.

———. 2012. The heiress. *New Yorker* 88 (39):10 December 2012.

Australia, Senate Environment Communications Information Technology and the Arts References Committee Commonwealth Parliament of 2001. *Above Board? Methods of Appointment to the ABC Board.* Canberra: Commonwealth Parliament of Australia.

Australian Institute of Political Science (41st: 1975: Canberra ACT) and Gersh Major. 1976. *Mass Media in Australia: Proceedings of the 41st Summer School, Australian Institute of Political Science.* Sydney: Hodder and Stoughton.

Ayerst, David. 1971. *Guardian: Biography of a Newspaper.* London: Collins.

Bagdikian, Ben. 1973. Shaping media content: Professional personnel and organizational structure. *The Public Opinion Quarterly* 37 (4):569–579.

———. 2000. *The Media Monopoly,* 6th ed. Boston, MA: Beacon Press.

———. 2004. *The New Media Monopoly.* Boston: Beacon.

——. 2005. Grand theft: The conglomeratization of media and the degradation of culture. *(25 Years of Monitoring the Multinationals)* 26 (1–2):35(2).

Baker, C. Edwin. 1989. *Human Liberty and Freedom of Speech*. New York: Oxford University Press.

——. 1994. *Advertising and a Democratic Press*. Princeton, NJ: Princeton University Press.

——. 1998. The media that citizens need. *University of Pennsylvania Law Review* 147 (2): 317–408.

——. 2002. *Media, Markets, and Democracy, Communication, Society, and Politics*. Cambridge; New York: Cambridge University Press.

——. 2007. *Media Concentration and Democracy: Why Ownership Matters, Communication, Society, and Politics*. Cambridge; New York: Cambridge University Press.

Baker, Russ. 2001. A happy newsroom, for Pete's sake: Why people like working for the St Petersburg Times. *Columbia Journalism Review* September/October 2001: 54–57.

Baldwin, Elizabeth. 1977. The mass media and the corporate elite: A re-analysis of the overlap between the media and economic elites. *Canadian Journal of Sociology/Cahiers canadiens de sociologie* 2 (1):1–27.

Bardoel, Jo and Leen d'Haenens. 2004. Media meet the citizen. Beyond market mechanisms and government regulations. *European Journal of Communication* 19 (2):165–194.

Barley, Stephen R. and Pamela S. Tolbert. 1997. Institutionalization and structuration: Studying the links between action and institution. *Organization Studies* 18: 93–94.

Barnes, Andrew. 1999. Who owns the St. Petersburg times? Why it matters to readers. *St Petersburg Times* 26 December 1999.

Barnett, Stephen. 2004. Media ownership policies: Pressures for change and implications. *Pacific Journalism Review* 10 (2): 8.

Barnett, Steven. 2008. On the road to self-destruction. *British Journalism Review* 19 (2): 5–13.

Barron, Jerome A. 1967. Access to the press – A new first amendment right. *Harvard Law Review* 80 (8):1641–1678.

Barry, Paul. 2007. *The Rise and Rise of Kerry Packer Uncut*. Sydney: Bantam.

Beavan, John. 1986. The miracle of the guardian. *The Political Quarterly* 57 (2):172–181.

Becker, George J. 1959. Upton Sinclair: Quixote in a Flivver. *College English* 21 (3):133–140.

Belloc, Hilaire. 1918. *The Free Press*. London: George Allen & Unwin.

Bennett, W. Lance. 2003. The burglar alarm that just keeps ringing: A response to Zaller. *Political Communication* 20:131–138.

Bennett, W. Lance and Steven Livingston. 2003. A semi-independent press: Government control and journalistic autonomy in the political construction of news. *Political Communication* 20 (4):359–362.

Bentley, Clyde H. 2008. Citizen journalism: Back to the future? In *Carnegie-Knight Conference on the Future of Journalism*. Discussion paper prepared for the *Carnegie-Knight Conference on the Future of Journalism*, Cambridge, MA. 20–21 June 2008. Cambridge, MA.

Berens, Camilla. 2004. Viscount discounts FTSE code. *Financial Management* 1 March 2004.

Bhattacharya, Utpal and B. Ravikumar. 2001. Capital markets and the evolution of family businesses. *Journal of Business* 74 (2):187–219.

Blasi, Vincent. 2002. Free speech and good character: From Milton to Brandeis to the present. In *Eternally Vigilant: Free Speech in the Modern Era*, edited by L. C. Bollinger and G. R. Stone. Chicago: University of Chicago Press.

Blood, Rebecca. 2003. Weblogs and Journalism: Do they connect? *Nieman Reports* 57 (3):61–63.

Bloom, Nicholas and John Van Reenan. 2007. Measuring and explaining management practices across firms and countries. *Quarterly Journal of Economics* 122 (4): 1351–1408.

Blumler, Jay and Michael Gurevitch. 1995. *The Crisis of Political Communication*. New York: Routledge.

Boczkowski, Pablo J. 2005. *Digitizing the News*. Cambridge, MA: The MIT Press.

Bogart, Leo. 1989. Newspapers in transition. In *American Media: The Wilson Quarterly Reader*, edited by D. G. Philip Cook and L. Lichty. Washington, DC: Wilson Centre Press.

———. 1996. What does it all mean? *Media Studies Journal* 10 (2–3):15(13).

Bollinger, Lee C. 1991. *Images of a Free Press*. Chicago: University of Chicago Press.

Bollinger, Lee C. and Geoffrey R. Stone. 2002. *Eternally Vigilant: Free Speech in the Modern Era*. Chicago: University of Chicago Press.

Born, Georgina. 2005. *Uncertain Vision: Birt, Dyke and the Reinvention of the BBC*. London: Vintage.

Bowman, Shayne and Chris Willis. 2003. We Media: How audiences are shaping the future of news and information, edited by J. D. Lasica. The media Center at the American Press Institute. http://www.hypergene.net/wemedia/download/we_media.pdf

Boyce, George. 1978. The fourth estate: The reappraisal of a concept. In *Newspaper History: From the Seventeenth Century to the Present Day*, edited by G. Boyce, J. Curran and P. Wingate. London: Constable.

Boyce, George, James Curran, and Pauline Wingate, eds. 1978. *Newspaper History: From the Seventeenth Century to the Present Day*. London: Constable.

Boyd-Barrett, Oliver, ed. 2010. *News Agencies in the Turbulent Era of the Internet*. Barcelona: Government of Catalonia.

Boyd-Barrett, Oliver and Chris Newbold, 1995. Approaches to media a reader. In *Foundations in Media*, edited by O. Boyd-Barrett. London: Arnold.

Boyd-Barrett, Oliver and Terhi Rantanen, eds. 1998. *The Globalisation of News*. London: Sage.

Boyd-Barrett, Oliver, Colin Seymour-Ure, and Jeremy Tunstall. 1977. *Royal Commission on the Press: Studies on the Press (Working Paper Number 3)*. London: HMSO.

Boyd-Barrett, Oliver and Daya Kishan Thussu. 1992. *Contra-Flow in Global News: International and Regional News Exchange Mechanisms*. London: John Libbey & Co.

Brady, Conor. 2005. *Up with the Times*. Dublin: Gill & Macmillan.

Brenner, Marie. 1988. *House of Dreams: The Bingham Family of Louisville*. New York: Random House.

Brighton, Paul and Dennis Foy. 2007. *News Values*. London: Sage.

Brown, Jo-Lynn. 2013. Times says it's not for sale as other properties change hands. *Tampa Bay Business Journal* 6 August 2013.

Brown, Neil. 2009. At the St Pete Times, Pulitzers and beyond. *St Petersburg Times* 3 May 2009.

Browne, Harry. 2010. Foundation-funded journalism. *Journalism Studies* 11 (6): 889–903.

Bruns, Axel. 2005. *Gatewatching: Collaborative Online News Production*. New York: Peter Lang Publishing.

——. 2008. *Blogs, Wikipedia, Second Life, and Beyond: From Production to Produsage*. Edited by S. Jones, Digital Formations. New York: Peter Lang.

Canada, Royal Commission (Kent Commission). 1981. *Royal Commission on Newspapers*. Ottawa: Canadian Government Publishing Centre.

Canadian Parliament. 1970. *Special Senate Committee on Mass Media (the three volume Davey Report)*. Ottawa: Government of Canada.

Carter, Roy E. Jr. 1958. Newspaper "Gatekeepers" and the sources of news. *The Public Opinion Quarterly* 22 (2):133–144.

Chadwick, Paul. 1989. *Media Mates: Carving up Australia's Media*. Melbourne: Sun Books (Macmillan).

Chami, Ralph. 2001. *What Is Different about Family Businesses?* edited by the International Monetary Fund. Washington, DC: IMF Institute.

Chenoweth, Neil. 2001. *Virtual Murdoch: Reality Wars on the Information Highway*. London: Secker & Warburg.

Chester, Jeff and Gary O. Larson. 2005. Sharing the wealth: An online commons for the nonprofit sector. In *The Future of Media: Resistance and Reform in the 21st century*, edited by R. W. McChesney, R. Newman and B. Scott. New York: Seven Stories Press.

Chomsky, Daniel. 1999. The mechanisms of management control at the *New York Times*. *Media, Culture and Society* 21 (September 1999):579–599.

Chrisman, James J., Lloyd P. Steier, and Jess H. Chua. 2008. Toward a theoretical basis for understanding the dynamics of strategic performance in family firms. *Entrepreneurship Theory and Practice* 32 (6):935–947.

Cohen, Elliot D. 2005. *News Incorporated: Corporate Media Ownership and its Threat to Democracy*. Amherst, NY: Prometheus Books.

Cohen, Noam. 2008. Blogger, Sans Pajamas, Rakes Muck and a Prize. *New York Times* 25 February 2008.

Coleridge, Nicholas. 1994. *Paper Tigers*. London: Mandarin.

Commission on Freedom of the Press. 1947. *A Free and Responsible Press: A General Report on Mass Communication: Newspapers, Radio, Motion Pictures, Magazines, and Books*. Chicago, IL: University of Chicago Press.

Committee on Energy and Commerce. 1981. Telecommunications in transition: The status of competition in the telecommunications industry. United States House of Representatives.

Compaine, Benjamin. 2002. Global media. *Foreign Policy* (133):20–28.

Compaine, Benjamin and Brendan Cunningham. 2009. Nonprofit models, media ownership and diversity, and advertising prices. *Journal of Media Economics* 22 (3):115–118.

Compaine, Benjamin M. and Douglas Gomery. 2000. *Who Owns the Media? Competition and Concentration in the Mass Media Industry*, 3rd ed. Mahwah, NJ: Lawrence Erlbaum Associates.

Comrie, Margie and Judy McGregor. 1992. *Whose News?* Palmerston North, NZ: Dunmore Press.

Connolly, William E. 1974/1983. *The Terms of Political Discourse*. Princeton, NJ: Princeton University Press.

Cook, Timothy E. 2005a. *Freeing the Presses: The First Amendment in Action, Politics@media*. Baton Rouge, LA: Louisiana State University Press.

——. 2005b (1998). *Governing with the News: The News Media as a Political Institution*. 2nd ed. Chicago: University of Chicago Press.

——. 2006. The news media as a political institution. *Political Communication* 23 (2): 158–171.

Cottle, Simon, ed. 2003. *Media Organisation and Production: Media in Focus*. London: Sage.

Couldry, Nick and James Curran. 2003. *Contesting Media Power: Alternative Media in a Networked World, Critical Media Studies*. Lanham, MD; Oxford: Rowman & Littlefield.

CQ Press. 2004. *Issues for Debate in American Public Policy: Selections from The CQ Researcher*, 5th ed. Washington, DC: CQ Press, Division of Congressional Quarterly Inc.

Craik, Jennifer, Julie James Bailey, and Albert Moran. 1995. *Public Voices, Private Interests: Australia's Media Policy, Australian Cultural Studies*. St. Leonards, NSW: Allen & Unwin.

Crawford, Nelson Antrim. 1969[1924]. *The Ethics of Journalism*. New York: Knopf, Johnson Reprint Corp.

Crofts, William. 1989. *Coercion or Persuasion: Propaganda in Britain after 1945*. London: Routledge.

Croteau, David and William Hoynes. 2000. *Media/Society: Industries, Images, and Audiences*, 2nd ed. Thousand Oaks, CA: Pine Forge Press.

———. 2001. *The Business of Media: Corporate Media and the Public Interest*. Thousand Oaks, CA: Pine Forge Press.

Crozier, W. P. 1934. "C.P.S." in the office. In *C. P. Scott of the Manchester Guardian*, edited by J. L. Hammond. London: G.Bell & Sons.

Cunningham, Stuart and Graeme Turner. 2002. *The Media & Communications in Australia*. Crows Nest, NSW: Allen & Unwin.

Curran, James. 2000. *Media Organisations in Society*. London: Arnold.

———. 2002. *Media and Power*. London: Routledge.

———. 2005. What democracy requires of the media. In *The Press*, edited by G. Overholser and K. Jamieson. New York: Oxford University Press.

———. 2007. Reinterpreting the democratic roles of the media. *Brazilian Journalism Research* 3 (1):31–54.

Curran, James and Michael Gurevitch. 2005. *Mass Media and Society*, 4th ed. London: Hodder Arnold.

Curran, James, Michael Gurevitch, and Janet Woollacott. 1977. *Mass Communication and Society*. London: Edward Arnold in association with the Open University Press.

Curran, James, Shanto Iyengar, Anker Brink Lund, and Inka Salovaara-Moring. 2009. Media system, public knowledge and democracy: A comparative study. *European Journal of Communication* 24 (1):5–26.

Curran, James and David Morley. 2006. *Media and Cultural Theory*. Edited by James Curran and David Morley. London; New York: Routledge.

Curran, James and Myung-Jin Park, eds. 2000 *De-westernizing Media Studies*. London: Routledge.

Curran, James and Jean Seaton. 1997. *Power without Responsibility: The Press and Broadcasting in Britain*, 5th ed. London: Routledge.

———. 2003. *Power without Responsibility: The Press, Broadcasting, and New Media in Britain*, 6th ed. London: Routledge.

Dahl, Robert. 2000. *On Democracy*. New Haven: Yale University Press.

Dahlgren, Peter. 1995. *Television and the Public Sphere: Citizenship, Democracy and the Media, The Media, Culture and Society Series*. London: Sage.

Daily, Catherine M. and Marc J. Dollinger. 1992. An empirical examination of ownership structure in family and professionally managed firms. *Family Business Review* V (3):117–136.

Dalhberg, Lincoln. 2007. The Internet, deliberative democracy, and power: Radicalizing the public sphere. *International Journal of Media and Cultural Politics* 3 (1): 47–64.

Davis, Aeron. 2003. Whither mass media and power? Evidence for a critical elite theory alternative. *Media, Culture & Society* 25:669–690.

Davies, Nick. 2008. *Flat Earth News*. London: Chato & Windus.

Davis, Peter. 1983. Realizing the potential of the family business. *Organizational Dynamics* 12 (1):47–56.

Day, Patrick. 1990. *The Making of the New Zealand Press: A Study of the Organizational and Political Concerns of New Zealand Newspaper Controllers 1840–1880*. Wellington, NZ: Victoria University Press.

Deans, Jason. 2011. Lord Patten confirmed as "preferred candidate" for BBC Trust chairman. *The Guardian* 25 February 2011.

DeBrett, Mary. 2010. *Reinventing Public Service Television for the Digital Age*. Bristol: Intellect.

Delli Carpini, Michael X. 2000. Review of Michael Schudson, The good citizen: A history of American civic life. *Public Opinion Quarterly* 64 (Winter 2000): 546–549.

DeMott, Deborah A. 2008. Guests at the table?: Independent directors in family-influenced public companies. *Journal of Corporate Law* 33 (4):819–863.

Dennis, Everette E. 1989. *Reshaping the Media: Mass Communication in an Information Age*. Newbury Park, CA: Sage.

———. 1992. *Of Media and People*. Newbury Park, CA: Sage.

Deuze, Mark. 2007. *Media Work*. Cambridge: Polity Press.

Dewey, John. 2004. Our Un-Free Press (1935). In *Our Unfree Press*, edited by B. S. Robert McChesney. New York: The New Press.

Donaldson, Matthew, Chloe Heffernan, Andrew Lambeth, Debbie Matthews, Kim Mazur, John Miller, Geraldene Peters, Tomachi, Aotearoa Independent Media Centre., Planet TV., and Auckland Doco Collective. 2004. *Whose News?* Auckland: Auckland Doco Collective, videorecording.

Dordick, Herbert S. 1997. Invisible crisis: What conglomerate control of media means for America and the world. *Media Mergers* 47 (3):158(3).

Dorgan, Stephen J., John J. Dowdy, and Thomas M. Rippin. 2006. Who should – and shouldn't – run the family business. *McKinsey Quarterly* 2006 (3):13–15.

Downie, Leonard and Robert G. Kaiser. 2002. *The News about the News: American Journalism in Peril*, 1st ed. New York: A.A. Knopf.

Downie, Leonard and Michael Schudson. 2009. The reconstruction of American Journalism. *Columbia Journalism Review* (November–December 2009):28–51.

Doyle, Gillian. 2002a. *Media Ownership: The Economics and Politics of Convergence and Concentration in the UK and European Media*. London: Sage.

———. 2002b. *Understanding Media Economics*. London: Sage.

Doyle, Gillian and ebrary Inc. 2002. *Media Ownership: The Economics and Politics of Convergence and Concentration in the UK and European Media*. London; Thousand Oaks, CA: Sage. http://site.ebrary.com/lib/auckland/Doc?id=10076779

Drezner, Daniel W. and Henry Farrell. 2008. Blogs, politics and power: A special issue of Public Choice. *Public Choice* (134):1–13.

Drinnan, John. 2011. News, interrupted. *New Zealand Herald* 18 February 2011.

Duckworth, Michael, Leanne Lodder, Michael O'D Moore, Sara Overton, and James Rubin. 1990. The bottom line from the top down. *Columbia Journalism Review* (July–August 1990):30(3).

Dunlap, Karen. 2004. A study of nonprofit ownership of news media. In *Breaux Symposium: News in the Public Interest: A Free and Subsidized Press.* Louisiana State University, Baton Rouge: Reilly Centre for Media & Public Affairs, Manship School of Mass Communication, Louisiana State University.

Dyer, W. Gibb, Jr. and David A. Whetten. 2006. Family firms and social responsibility: Preliminary evidence from the S&P 500. *Entrepreneurship Theory and Practice* 30 (6):785–802.

Eddleston, Kimberly A. 2008. Commentary: The prequel to family firm culture and stewardship: The leadership perspective of the founder. *Entrepreneurship Theory and Practice* 32 (6):1055–1061.

Edwards, Ruth Dudley. 1993. *The Pursuit of Reason: The Economist 1843–1993.* London: Hamish Hamilton.

———. 2003. *Newspapermen: Hugh Cudlipp, Cecil Harmsworth King and the Glory Days of Fleet Street.* London: Secker & Warburg.

Ellis, Gavin. 2010. Australia and New Zealand: Two agencies on parallel tracks that sometimes diverge. In *News Agencies in the Turbulent Era of the Internet,* edited by O. Boyd-Barrett. Barcelona: Government of Catalonia.

Ellison, Sarah. 2010. *War at the Wall Street Journal.* Australian ed. Melbourne: Text Publishing Company. Original edition, United States: Houghton Mifflin Harcourt.

———. 2012. Ghosts in the newsroom. *Vanity Fair* (620), April 2012.

Entman, Robert M. 1989. How the media affect what people think: An information processing approach. *The Journal of Politics* 51 (2):347–370.

Epstein, Marcus, Walter Block, and Thomas E. Woods Jr. 2007. Chesterton and Belloc: A critique. *The Independent Review* 11 (4):579–594.

Evans, Harold. 1983. *Good Times, Bad Times.* London: Weidenfeld & Nicolson.

———. 2009. *My Paper Chase.* London: Little, Brown.

Fallows, James. 1997. *Breaking the News: How the Media Undermine American Democracy.* New York: Vintage.

Farhi, Paul. 1999. How bad is big? *American Journalism Review* 21 (10):28.

———. 2013. Washington Post to be sold to Jeff Bezos. *Washington Post* 6 August 2013.

Fee, C. Edward and Charles J. Hadlock. 2000. Management turnover and product market competition: Empirical evidence from the U.S. newspaper industry. *The Journal of Business* 73 (2):205–243.

Finlayson, James Gordon. 2005. *Habermas: A Very Short Introduction.* Oxford: Oxford University Press.

Fish, Stanley. 1994. *There's No Such Thing as Free Speech: And It's a Good Thing, Too.* New York: Oxford University Press.

Flew, Terry, Jason Sternberg, Cratis Hippocrates, and Australian Key Centre for Cultural and Media Policy. 1999. *Media Wars: The Pen May Indeed Be Mightier than the Sword.* Nathan, QLD: Australian Key Centre for Cultural and Media Policy.

Freedman, Des. 2008. *The Politics of Media Policy.* Cambridge: Polity.

Friedman, James. 1983. *Oligopoly Theory.* Cambridge: Cambridge University Press.

Friedman, Ted. 1998. From heroic objectivity to the news stream: The Newseum's strategies for relegitimising journalism in the information age. *Critical Studies in Mass Communication* 15 (3):325–335.

Friend, Cecilia and Jane B. Singer. 2007. *Online Journalism Ethics: Traditions and Transitions.* Armock, New York: M.E. Sharpe.

Fyfe, Hamilton. 1938. *Press Parade: Behind the Scenes of the Newspaper Racket and the Millionaires' Attempt at Dictatorship.* London: Watts & Co.

Galik, Mihaly. 1996. Foreign capital is welcome here. *Media Studies Journal* 10 (2–3):139(8).

Galpin, Timothy J. and R. Greg Bell. 2010. Social entrepreneurship and the L3C structure: Bridging the gap between non-profit and for-profit ventures. *Journal of Business and Entrepreneurship* 22 (2):29–39.

Galtung, Johan and Mari H. Ruge. 1965. The structure of Foreign News. *Journal of Peace Research* (2):64–91.

Gans, Herbert J. 2003. *Democracy and the News*. New York; Oxford: Oxford University Press.

———. 2004 (1979). *Deciding What's News: A Study of CBS Evening News, NBC Nightly News, Newsweek, and Time*. Evanston, Ill: Northwestern University Press. Original edition, 1979 Random House.

Garnham, Nicholas. 2000. *Emancipation, the Media and Modernity: Arguments about the Media and Social Theory*. Oxford: Oxford University Press.

Garnham, Nicholas and Fred Inglis. 1990. *Capitalism and Communication: Global Culture and the Economics of Information*. London; Newbury Park: Sage.

Geering, John. 2001. *Social Science Methodology: A Criterial Framework*. Cambridge: Cambridge University Press.

Gershon, Richard A. 2006. Issues in transnational media management. In *Handbook of Media Management and Economics*, edited by A. Albarran, M. Wirth and S. Chan-Olmsted. Mahwah, NJ: Lawrence Erlbaum & Associates

Gilens, Martin and Craig Hertzman. 2000. Corporate ownership and news bias: Newspaper coverage of the 1996 Telecommunications Act. *The Journal of Politics* 62 (2):369–386.

Gissler, Sig. 1997. What happens when Gannett takes over: Culture clash and some disturbing changes at two formerly family-owned newspapers (Des Moines Register and the Louisville Courier-Journal). *Columbia Journalism Review* 36 (4): 42–48.

Gitlin, Todd. 1996. Not so fast. *Media Studies Journal* 10 (2–3):1–6.

———. 2003. *Media Unlimited: How the Torrent of Images and Sounds Overwhelms Our Lives*. 1st Owl Books ed. New York: H. Holt.

Globe & Mail. 1999. "Torstar's Family Values". 2 January 1999. Section B.

Golding, Peter and Philip Elliott. 1979. *Making the News*. London: Longman.

Graber, Doris. 2003a. The media and democracy: Beyond myths and stereotypes. *Annual Review of Political Science* 6:139–160.

———. 2003b. The rocky road to new paradigms: Modernising news and citizenship standards. *Political Communication* 20:145–148.

Graham, Katharine. 2001. *Personal History*. London: Phoenix Press. Original edition, 1997. New York: A.A. Knopf.

Greenslade, Roy. 1998. Challenge for the mail heir. *Management Today* (October 1998):40–45.

———. 2004. *Press Gang: How Newspapers Make Profit from Propaganda*. London: Pan Macmillan.

Gregory, Paul Roderick. 2013. *Why doesn't the New York Times Expose Carlos Slim?* http://www.realclearmarkets.com/articles/2013/03/12/for_155m_did_carlos_slim_buy_silence_from_the_times_100195.html

Griffen-Foley, Bridget. 2000. *The House of Packer: The Making of a Media Empire*. St Leonards, NSW: Allen & Unwin.

Gunther, Richard and Anthony Mughan, eds. 2000. *Democracy and the Media: A Comparative Perspective*. Cambridge: Cambridge University Press.

Gurevitch, Michael. 1982. *Culture, Society, and the Media*. London; New York: Methuen.

Gurevitch, Michael and Jay G. Blumler. 1990. Political communication systems and democratic values. In *Democracy and the Mass Media*, edited by J. Lichtenberg. Cambridge: Cambridge University Press.

Gurevitch, Michael and James Curran. 1996. *Mass Media and Society*, 2nd ed. London; New York: Arnold; Distributed in the USA by St Martin's Press.

Habbershon, Timothy G., Mary Williams, and Ian C. MacMillan. 2003. A unified systems perspective of family firm performance. *Journal of Business Venturing* 18:451–465.

Habermas, Jürgen. 1996. *Between Facts and Norms: Contributions to a Discourse Theory of Law and Democracy*. Cambridge: Polity Press.

Hagan, Joe. 2012. A New York Times Whodunit. *New York* 4 June 2012.

Hagerty, Bill. 1997. Life, politics, sex – and owning newspapers. *British Journalism Review* 8 (4):6–12.

Haley, Michael and Lara McMurtry. 2006. *Equity & Trusts*, 1st ed. London: Sweet & Maxwell.

Halliday, Adele, Dougal Blackburn, World Vision Canada, Canadian International Development Agency, and World Vision of New Zealand. 2006. *Media Literacy for Global Citizenship: An Educational Resource for Years 7 to 10 that Supports English, Media Studies and Social Studies Curricula*. Auckland, NZ: World Vision New Zealand.

Hallin, Daniel C. 1992. The passing of the "high modernism" of American journalism. *Journal of Communication* 42 (3 Summer).

Hallin, Daniel C. and Paolo Mancini. 2004. Comparing media systems: Three models of media and politics. In *Communication, Society and Politics*, edited by W. L. Bennett and R. M. Entman, 1st ed. Cambridge: Cambridge University Press.

Halloran, James. 1974. *Mass Media and Society: The Challenge of Research. An Inaugural Lecture*. Leicester: Leicester University Press.

Hamilton, Denis. 1989. *Editor-in-Chief: The Fleet Street Memoirs of Sir Denis Hamilton*. London: Hamish Hamilton.

Hamilton, James. 2004. *All the News that's Fit to Sell: How the Market Transforms Information into News*. Princeton, NJ: Princeton University Press.

Hammond, J. L., C. E. Montague, and H. D. Scott Nichols. 1946. *C.P. Scott 1846–1932: The Making of the Manchester Guardian*. London: Frederick Muller.

Hampton, Mark. 2004. *Visions of the Press in Britain, 1850–1950*. Champaign, IL: University of Illinois Press.

Hargrave, Andrea Millwood, Geoff Lealand, Paul Norris, and Andrew Stirling. 2006. *Issues Facing Broadcast Content Regulation*. Wellington: New Zealand Broadcasting Standards Authority.

Harris, Michael. 1978. The structure, ownership and control of the press 1620–1780. In *Newspaper History: From the Seventeenth Century to the Present Day*, edited by G. Boyce, J. Curran, and P. Wingate. London: Constable.

Harrison, John, Geoff Woolcock, and Sue Scull. 2004. Social capital and "the media": Dimensions of the debate. *Australian Studies in Journalism* 13:8–33.

Hasings, Max. 2002. *Editor: An Inside Story of Newspapers*. London: Macmillan.

Hass, Nancy. 2009. True to type. *Vogue* July 92–131.

Hassan, Robert and Julian Thomas. 2006. *The New Media Theory Reader*. Maidenhead: Open University Press.

Hau, Louis. 2006. Why newsrooms pray to St Petersburg. *Forbes.com* 4 December 2006.

Hefner, Christie. 1996. Thinking outside the box. *Media Studies Journal* 10 (2–3):65(3).

Held, David. 1980. *Introduction to Critical Theory: Horkheimer to Habermas.* Berkeley, CA: University of California Press.

———. 1996. *Models of Democracy,* 2nd ed. Stanford, CA: Stanford University Press.

Hennessy, Peter. 1993. *Never again: Britain 1945–1951.* New York: Pantheon.

Herman, Edward S. and Robert Waterman McChesney. 1997. *The Global Media: The New Missionaries of Corporate Capitalism.* London; Washington, DC: Cassell.

Herring, Susan C., Lois Ann Scheidt, Sabrina Bonus, and Elijah Wright. 2004. Bridging the Gap: A genre analysis of weblogs. In *International Conference on Systems Science.* Hawaii: IEEE.

Hetherington, Alastair. 1981. *Guardian Years.* London: Chatto & Windus.

Hinton, Les. 2009. They're stealing our lifeblood. *British Journalism Review* 20 (3): 13–18.

Hitchens, Lesley. 2006. *Broadcasting Pluralism and Diversity: A Comparative Study of Policy and Regulation.* Oxford; Portland, Oregon: Hart Publishing.

Holmwood, Leigh. 2009. Decline of local news may allow corruption in public institutions to grow, Guardian editor warns. *The Guardian* 22 July 2009.

Hooker, Robert. 1984. The Times and its times: A history. *St Petersburg Times* 25 July 1984.

Horrocks, Roger and Nick Perry, eds. 2004. *Television in New Zealand: Programming the nation,* 1st ed. Melbourne: Oxford University Press.

Horwitz, Robert B. 2001. *Communication and Democratic Reform in South Africa.* Cambridge: Cambridge University Press.

Hoskins, Colin, Stuart McFadyen, and Adam Finn. 2004. *Media Economics: Applying Economics to New and Traditional Media.* Thousand Oaks, CA: Sage.

House of Lords. 2008. *The Ownership of the News,* Communications Select Committee. London: The Stationery Office.

Hulbert, Mark. 2007. How many quarters in a row can earnings really grow? *New York Times* 23 September 2007.

Hume, Ellen. 1996. The new paradigm for news. *Annals of the American Academy of Political and Social Science* 546:141–153.

Humphreys, Peter. 1999. Germany's "dual" broadcasting system: Recipe for pluralism in the age of multi-channel broadcasting. *New German Critique* 78:23–52.

Hunter, Dan. 2003. Cyberspace as place and the tragedy of the digital anticommons. *California Law Review* 19 (2):439–519.

Hutchins, Robert (Chair). 1947. *A Free and Responsible Press. A General Report on Mass Communication: Newspapers, Radio, Motion Pictures, Magazines and Books.* Chicago: University of Chicago Press.

Inglis, K. S. 2006. *Whose ABC? The Australian Broadcasting Corporation 1983–2006,* 2 vols. Melbourne: Black Inc.

Innes, Duncan. 1984. *Anglo American and the Rise of Modern South Africa.* London: Heinemann.

Islam, Roumeen. 2002. *The Right to Tell: The Role of Mass Media in Economic Development, WBI Development Studies.* Washington, DC: World Bank.

Ives, E. W. 1967. The genesis of the state of uses. *English Historical Review* 82 (325): 673–697.

Jackson, Joseph. 1999. *Newspaper Ownership in Canada: An Overview of the Davey Committee and Kent Commission Studies,* edited by Political and Social Affairs Division. Canada: Government of Canada.

Jaspan, Andrew. 1996. The trust that went bust. *New Statesman* 9(411):16–19.

Jenkins, Henry. 2006. *Convergence Culture: Where Old and New Media Collide*. New York: New York University Press.

Jenkins, Simon. 1986. *The Market for Glory: Fleet Street Ownership in the Twentieth Century*. London: Faber and Faber.

Jensen, Klaus Bruhn, ed. 2002. *A Handbook of Media and Communication Research: Qualitative and Quantitative Methodologies*, 1st ed. London: Routledge.

Jensen, Michael C. and William H. Meckling. 1976. Theory of the firm: Managerial behavior, agency costs and ownership structure. *Journal of Financial Economics* 3 (1976):305–360.

Johnson, Paul. 1998. Who will run the Scott Trust when the sackings have to stop? *The Spectator* 8 August 1998:22.

Johnson, Shaun. 1991. Resistance in Print 1: *Grassroots* and alternative publishing, 1980–1984. In *Studies on the South African Media: The Alternative Press in South Africa*, edited by Keyan Tomaselli and P. Eric Louw. Bellville SA: Anthropolis.

Jones, Alex S. 1990. St Petersburg Times Agrees to Buy Out Bass Investors. *New York Times* 18 August 1990.

———. 2009. *Losing the News: The Future of the News that Feeds Democracy*. New York: Oxford University Press.

Josephi, Beate. 2005. Journalism in the global age: Between normative and empirical. *International Communication Gazette* 67 (6):575–590.

Kachaner, Nicolas, George Stalk and Alain Bloch. 2012. What you can learn from family business. *Harvard Business Review* November 2012: 102–106.

Kaplan, Richard L. 2002. *Politics and the American Press: The Rise of Objectivity, 1865–1920*. Cambridge: Cambridge University Press.

———. 2006. The news about new institutionalism: Journalism's ethic of objectivity and its political origins. *Political Communication* 23 (2):173–185.

Karp, Jonathan. 1996. Conglomerates – a good thing for books. *Media Studies Journal* 10 (2–3):123(3).

Kearney, Richard and Dermot Moran. 1984. Public responsibility and the press: 1 Richard Kearney and Dermot Moran talk to Douglas Gageby. *The Crane Bag* 8 (2):13–23.

Keegan, Victor. 2003. In Scott we trust. *Guardian* 29 September 2003.

Kent, Tom. 1981. *Royal Commission on Newspapers*, edited by Government of Canada. Ministry of Supply and Services Ottawa.

Kesterton, W. H. 1984. *A History of Journalism in Canada, Carleton Library Series*. Ottawa: Carleton University Press.

Knight Commission. 2009. *Informing Communities: Sustaining Democracy in the Digital Age*. Washington, DC: Aspen Institute (Knight Commission on the Information Needs of Communities in a Democracy).

Koss, Stephen. 1984. *The Rise and Fall of the Political Press in Britain Volume 2: The Twentieth Century*. London: Hamish Hamilton.

Kossoff, Mirinda J., ed. 2005. *History of the Burroughs Wellcome Fund 1955–2005*. Raleigh, NC: Historic Preservation Foundation of North Carolina.

Kovach, Bill and Tom Rosenstiel. 2001. *The Elements of Journalism: What Newspeople Should Know and the Public Should Expect*, 1st ed. New York: Three Rivers Press.

Krauss, Clifford. 2007. Balancing bottom lines and headlines. *New York Times* 30 September 2007.

Lanchester, John. 2010. Let us pay. *London Review of Books* 16 December 2010:5–8.

Lane, Robert E. 1996. "Losing Touch" in a democracy: Demands versus needs. In *Elitism, Populism & European Politics*, edited by H. J. Oxford: Clarendon Press.

Lansberg, Ivan. 1999. *Succeeding Generations: Realizing the Dream of Families in Business.* Boston: Harvard Business School Press.

Lanzara, Giovan Francesco. 1998. Self-destructive processes in institution building. *European Journal of Political Research* 33:1–39.

Lasswell, Harold D. 1927. *Propaganda Techniques in the World War.* New York: Knopf.

Lazarsfeld, Paul. 1942. The daily newspaper and its competitors. *The Annals of the American Academy* 219 (January 1942):32–43.

Lazarsfeld, Paul and Robert Merton. 2009 [1948]. Mass communication, popular taste and organized social action. In *Key Readings in Media Today: Mass Communication in Contexts,* edited by Brooke Erin Duffy and Joseph Turow. New York: Routledge.

Lecours, Andre. 2005a. New institutionalism: Issues and questions. In *New Institutionalism: Theory and Analysis,* edited by A. Lecours. Toronto: University of Toronto Press.

——, ed. 2005b. New institutionalism: Theory and analysis. In *Studies in Comparative Political Economy and Public Policy,* edited by M. Howlett, D. Laycock and S. McBride. Toronto: University of Toronto Press.

Lee, Alfred McClung. 1939. Trends affecting the daily newspapers. *Public Opinion Quarterly* 3 (3):497–502.

——. 1947. *The Daily Newspaper in America: The Evolution of a Social Instrument.* New York: Macmillan.

Lessig, Lawrence. 2004. *Free Culture: How Big Media Uses Technology and the Law to Lock Down Culture and Control Creativity.* New York: Penguin.

Leveson, L. J. 2012. *An Inquiry into the Culture, Practices and Ethics of the Press.* London: The Stationery Office.

Lewis, Charles. 2007. The growing importance of nonprofit journalism. In *Working Paper Series.* Boston: Harvard University, John F. Kennedy School of Government.

Liebes, Tamar. 2005. Viewing and reviewing the audience: Fashions in communication research. In *Mass Media and Society,* edited by J. Curran and M. Gurevitch. London: Hodder Arnold.

Liebling, A. J. 1964. *The Press.* New York: Ballantine Books.

Lilja, J. R. 1997. *International Equity Markets – The Art of the Deal.* London: Euromoney Books (Wellcome Trust reprint).

Lindblom, Charles. 2001. *The Market System: What it is, How it Works, and What to Make of it.* New Haven: Yale University Press.

Lippmann, Walter. 1922. *Public Opinion.* New York: Harcourt, Brace & Co.

Livingstone, Sonia. 2005. On the relation between Audiences and Publics. *LSE Research Online.* http://eprints.lse.ac/archive/00000437

Lorimer, Rowland and Jean McNulty. 1987. *Mass Communication in Canada.* Toronto: McClelland and Stewart.

MacDonald, Gerard Alastair. 1973. The News Media Ownership Act of 1965: A case study in the relationship of press and polity. Thesis (MA, Political studies), University of Auckland.

Macdonald, Gilbert. 1980. *In Pursuit of Excellence: One Hundred Years Wellcome 1880–1980.* London: Wellcome Foundation Limited.

Madigan, Charles M., ed. 2007. *-30- The Collapse of the Great American Newspaper.* Chicago: Ivan R. Dee.

Maguire, Miles. 2003. Wall Street Made Me Do It: A preliminary analysis of the major institutional investors in U.S. newspaper companies. *Journal of Media Economics* 16 (4):253–264.

Mansell, Robin, Rohan Samarajiva, and Amy Mahan. 2002. *Networking Knowledge for Information Societies: Institutions & Intervention.* Netherlands: Delft University Press.

Mantzavinos, C., Douglass North, and Syed Shariq. 2004. Learning, institutions, and economic performance. *Perspectives on Politics* 2 (1 (March 2004)):75–84.

March, James G. and Johan P. Olsen. 1984. The new institutionalism: Organizational factors in political life. *American Political Science Review* 78 (3): 734–749.

———. 1989. *Rediscovering Institutions: The Organizational Basis of Politics.* New York: The Free Press.

Margolis, Mac. 1996. In the company of giants. *Media Studies Journal* 10 (2–3):147(11).

Mayer, Henry. 1964. *The Press in Australia.* Melbourne: Lansdowne Press.

Mayer, Martin. 1993. *Making News.* Boston, MA: Harvard Business School Press.

Mayes, Ian. 2004. Trust me – I'm an ombudsman. *British Journalism Review* 15 (2): 65–70.

McChesney, Robert W. 1996. *Corporate Media and the Threat to Democracy.* New York: Seven Stories Press.

———. 1999. *Rich Media, Poor Democracy: Communications Politics in Dubious Times.* Urbana: University of Illinois Press.

———. 2004. Welcome to Havana, Mr Corleone: Issues of media ownership and control. *Pacific Journalism Review* 10 (2):20–31.

———. 2007. *Communication Revolution: Critical Junctures and the Future of Media.* New York: The New Press.

McChesney, Robert Waterman, Russell Newman, and Ben Scott. 2005. *The Future of Media: Resistance and Reform in the 21st Century,* 1st ed. New York: Seven Stories Press.

McChesney, Robert Waterman and John Nichols. 2002. *Our Media, Not Theirs: The Democratic Struggle against Corporate Media,* Rev. ed. New York; London: Seven Stories; Turnaround.

McChesney, Robert W. and Ben Scott, eds. 2004. *Our Unfree Press: 100 Years of Radical Media Criticism,* 1st ed. New York: The New Press.

McChesney, Robert Waterman, Ellen Meiksins Wood, and John Bellamy Foster. 1998. *Capitalism and the Information Age: The Political Economy of the Global Communication Revolution.* New York: Monthly Review Press.

McCollam, D. 2008a. Somewhere East of Eden: Why the St. Pete Times model can't save newspapers. *Columbia Journalism Review* (March–April 2008).

———. 2008b. Sulzberger at the Barricades: Arthur Sulzberger Jr is racing to transform the embattled *New York Times* for the digital age. Is he up to the job? *Columbia Journalism Review* XLVII (2):24–31.

McGregor, Judy 1991. *News Values and the Reporting of Maori News.* Palmerston North, NZ: Department of Human Resource Management, Faculty of Business Studies, Massey University.

———. 1996. *Dangerous Democracy?: News Media Politics in New Zealand.* Palmerston North, NZ: Dunmore Press.

———. 2002. Restating news values: contemporary criteria for selecting the news. In *Communication: Reconstructed for the 21st Century: Refereed Proceedings of the Australia and New Zealand Communication Association International Conference, Queensland July 2002.* Edited by Mary Power. Coolangatta: Massey University.

McGregor, Judy and Margie Comrie. 2002. *What's News?: Reclaiming Journalism in New Zealand.* Palmerston North, NZ: Dunmore Press.

McGregor, O. R. 1977. *Royal Commission on the Press,* Parliament: Her Majesty's Stationery Office.

McManus, John H. 1994. *Market-Driven Journalism: Let the Citizen Beware.* Thousand Oaks, CA: Sage.

McNair, Brian. 2003. From control to chaos: Towards a new sociology of journalism. *Media, Culture & Society* 25:547–555.

Melvern, Linda. 1986. *The End of the Street.* London: Methuen London.

Merrill, John C. 1977/1995. *Existential Journalism.* Ames: Iowa State University Press.

Meyer, Philip. 1995. Learning to love lower profits. *American Journalism Review* 17 (10):40–44.

——. 2004. *The Vanishing Newspaper: Saving Journalism in the Information Age.* Columbia, MO: University of Missouri Press.

Michalski, Jerry. 1996. Are your intentions honorable? *Media Studies Journal* 10 (2–3):127(4).

Milner, Henry. 2002. *Civic Literacy: How Informed Citizens Make Democracy Work.* Hanover, NH: University Press of New England.

Mitchell, Chris. 1997. Beating the Dow. *New York* 30 (7):44–46.

Mnookin, Seth. 2004. *Hard News: The Scandals at the New York Times and Their Meaning for American Media.* New York: Random House.

Mogridge, Fiona Margaret. 1998. *The Globalisation of Broadcasting: A Study of the Future of Local Television Content in New Zealand.* Auckland: University of Auckland.

Moncrieff, Chris. 2001. *Living on a Deadline: A History of the Press Association.* London: Virgin Books.

Moore, Aaron J. 2002. Ownership: A chill in Canada. *Columbia Journalism Review* 2002 (March/April):11(1).

Moore, Martin. 2010. *Shrinking World: The Decline of International Reporting in the British Press.* London: Media Standards Trust.

Morris, Peter. 2010. Who guards the Guardian? *Prospect* September 2010.

Morrow, Raymond Allan and David D. Brown. 1994. *Critical Theory and Methodology.* Thousand Oaks, CA: Sage.

Mosco, Vincent and Janet Wasko, eds. 1984. *The Critical Communications Review: Changing Patterns of Communications Control,* 2 vols. Norwood, NJ: Ablex Publishing.

——. 1988. *The Political Economy of Information.* Madison, WI: University of Wisconsin Press.

Mott, Frank Luther. 1962. *American Journalism: A History 1690–1960.* New York: Macmillan.

Mukerji, Chandra and Michael Schudson. 1991. *Rethinking Popular Culture: Contemporary Perspectives in Cultural Studies.* Berkeley: University of California Press.

Mullins, Richard. 2012. Newspaper no longer a "viable" source for support, media institute says. *Tampa Tribune* 2 June 2012.

Nasaw, David. 2003. *The Chief: The Life of William Randolph Hearst.* London: Gibson Square Books.

Negrine, Ralph M. 1996. *The Communication of Politics.* London; Thousand Oaks: Sage.

Neil, Andrew. 1996. *Full Disclosure.* London: Macmillan.

Neiva, Elizabeth MacIver. 1996. Chain building: The consolidation of the American newspaper industry, 1953–1980. *Business History Review* 70 (1):1–42.

Nelson, Teresa. 2003. The persistence of founder influence: Management, ownership, and performance effects at initial; public offering. *Strategic Management Journal* 24 (8):707–724.

Neuharth, Allen H. 1989. *Confessions of an S.O.B.* New York: Doubleday.

Nichols, John. 2007. Still a powerful voice. In *-30- The Collapse of the Great American Newspaper,* edited by C. M. Madigan. Chicago: Ivan R. Dee.

Niven, David. 2005. An economic theory of political journalism. *Journalism and Mass Communication Quarterly* 82 (2):247–263.

Noam, Eli M. 2005. Why the internet is bad for democracy. *Communication of the ACM* 48 (10):57–58.

Noam, Eli M. and Alex J. Wolfson. 1997. *Globalism and Localism in Telecommunications.* New York: Elsevier.

Nocera, Joseph. 1997. Heard on the street: Disgruntled heiress leads revolt at Dow Jones. *Fortune* 135 (2):72–81.

Nordberg, Donald. 2007. News and corporate governance: What Dow Jones and Reuters teach us about stewardship. *Journalism* 8 (6):718–735.

Nordenstreng, Kaarle and Herbert I. Schiller. 1979. *National Sovereignty and International Communication.* Norwood, NJ: Ablex Pub. Co.

Norris, Pippa. 2000. A Virtuous circle: Political communication in postindustrial societies. In *Communication, Society and Politics,* edited by L. B. R. Entman. Cambridge: Cambridge University Press.

North, Douglass. 1971. Institutional change and economic growth. *Journal of Economic History* 31 (1):118–125.

O'Brien, Mark. 2008. *The Irish Times: A History.* Dublin: Four Courts Press.

O'Clery, Conor. 2009. Keeping an eye on the world. *Irish Times* 150th anniversary supplement, 27 March 2009.

O'Malley, Pat. 1987. Regulating contradictions: The Australian Press Council and the "Dispersal of Social Control". *Law & Society Review* 21 (1):83–108.

O'Neill, Onora. 2002. *A Question of Trust: The BBC Reith Lectures 2002.* Cambridge: Cambridge University Press.

Oram, Hugh. 1983. *The Newspaper Book: A History of Newspapers in Ireland, 1649–1983.* Dublin: MO Books.

O'Toole, Fintan. 2009. A paper for all Ireland. *The Irish Times* 150, 27 March 2009:6–9.

Overholser, Geneva. 2001. Editor Inc. In *Leaving Readers Behind: The Age of Corporate Newspapering,* edited by G. Roberts, T. Kunkel, and C. Layton. Fayetteville: University of Arkansas Press.

Overholser, Geneva and Kathleen Hall Jamieson, eds. 2005. *The Press, Institutions of American Democracy.* New York: Oxford University Press.

Owen, David. 1964. *English Philanthropy.* Cambridge, MA: The Belknap Press of Harvard University Press.

Paisley, Robert. 1994. Economics of the media. *British Economy Survey* 24 (1):5(5).

Paterson, Chris. 2010. Changing times: The move online and the UK's Press Association. In *News Agencies in the Turbulent Era of the Internet,* edited by O. Boyd-Barrett. Barcelona: Government of Catalonia.

Patterson, Eugene. 1998. Nelson Poynter still lives through the newspaper he gave away. *St Petersburg Times* 15 June 1998.

Patterson, Thomas E. 1993. *Out of Order,* 1st ed. New York: A. Knopf.

———. 1998. Time and news: The media's limitations as an instrument of democracy. *International Political Science Review/Revue internationale de science politique* 19 (1):55–67.

———. 2003. The search for a standard: Markets and media. *Political Communication* 20 (April):139–143.

Pearson, Allison W., Jon C. Carr, and John C. Shaw. 2008. Toward a Theory of Familiness: A social capital perspective. *Entrepreneurship Theory and Practice* 32 (6):949–969.

Peel, Robert. 1977. *Mary Baker Eddy: The Years of Authority*. New York: Holt, Rinehart & Winston.

PEP. 1938. *The Report on the British Press: A Survey of Its Current Operations and Problems with Special Reference to National Newspapers and Their Part in Public Affairs April 1938*. London: Political and Economic Planning (PEP).

——.1959. *The Work of Newspaper Trusts*. PLANNING No. 435 August 1959. London: Political and Economic Planning (PEP).

Perez, Carlota. 2002. *Technological Revolutions and Financial Capital: The Dynamics of Bubbles and Golden Ages*. Cheltenham, UK: Edward Elgar.

Pérez-Peña, Richard. 2010. As shrinking newsrooms use upstarts' content, vetting questions arise. *New York Times* 18 January 2010:B6.

Perry, David K. 2002. *Theory and Research in Mass Communication: Contexts and Consequences*, 2nd ed., LEA's communication series. Mahwah, NJ: Erlbaum.

Peters, B. Guy. 1981. The problem of bureaucratic government. *The Journal of Politics* 43 (1):56–82.

Pew. 2012. How people get local news and information in different communities. *Pew Research Center* 26 September 2012.

Picard, Robert G. 1989. *Media Economics: Concepts and Issues*. Newbury Park, CA: Sage.

——. 2002a. *The Economics and Financing of Media Companies*, 1st ed., Business, economics, and legal studies series. New York: Fordham University Press.

——. 2002b. U.S. newspaper ad revenue shows consistent growth. *Newspaper Research Journal* 23 (4):21–33.

——. 2003. Cash cows or Entrecôte: Publishing companies and disruptive technologies. *Trends in Communication* 11 (2): 127–136.

Picard, Robert G. and Jeffrey H. Brody. 1997. *The Newspaper Publishing Industry*. Boston: Allyn and Bacon.

Picard, Robert G. and ebrary Inc. 2002. *Media Firms Structures, Operations, and Performance*. Mahwah, NJ: Erlbaum. http://site.ebrary.com/lib/auckland/Doc?id= 10084649

Picard, Robert G. and Aldo van Weezel. 2008. Capital and control: Consequences of different forms of newspaper ownership. *Journal of Media Management* 10 (1):22–31.

Pierce, Robert N. 1993. *A Sacred Trust: Nelson Poynter and the St Petersburg Times*. Gainsville, FL: University of Florida Press.

Plato, trans. Tredennick & Tarrant. 2003. *The Last Days of Socrates: Euthyphro, Apology, Crito, Phaedo*. London: Penguin.

Porter, Eduardo. 2007. Mexico's plutocracy thrives on robber-baron concessions. *New York Times* 27 August 2007.

Postman, Neil. 1986. *Amusing Ourselves to Death*. Harmondsworth UK: Penguin.

Potter, Elaine. 1975. *The Press as Opposition: The Political Role of South African Newspapers*. London: Chatto and Windus.

Powell, Walter W. and Paul J. DiMaggio, eds. 1991. *The New Institutionalism in Organizational Analysis*. Chicago: University of Chicago Press.

Price, Vincent and John Zaller. 1993. Who gets the news? Alternative measures of news reception and their implications for research. *The Public Opinion Quarterly* 57 (2):133–164.

Prior, Markus. 2005. News vs. entertainment: How increasing media choice widens gaps in political knowledge and turnout. *American Journal of Political Science* 49 (3):577–592.

Project for Excellence in Journalism. 2007. *Publisher Murdoch's U.S. Track Record: A PEJ Backgrounder* [web page]. Project for Excellence in Journalism 2007 [cited 28 September 2007]. Available from http://www.journalism.org/node/6757

Putnam, Robert. 2000. *Bowling Alone: The Collapse and Revival of American Community*. New York: Simon & Schuster.

Read, Donald. 1992. *The Power of News: The History of Reuters*. Oxford: Oxford University Press.

Reeves, Thomas C. 2000. *Twentieth-Century America: A Brief History*. Oxford: Oxford University Press.

Ricchiardi, Sherry. 2009. A dubious benefactor. *American Journalism Review* 31 (2): 48–53.

Rierden, Andi. 1998. New London's Feisty Newspaper, The Day. *New York Times* 20 December 1998.

Roberts, Gene. 1996. Corporate journalism and community service. *Media Studies Journal* 10 (2–3):103(5).

Roberts, Gene, Thomas Kunkel, and Charles Layton, ed. 2001. *Leaving Readers Behind: The Age of Corporate Newspapering*. Fayetteville, ARK: University of Arkansas Press.

Rockwell, Harold E. 1928. "Going to Press". *American Speech* 4 (2):134–136.

Roe, Mark J. 2000. Political preconditions to separating ownership from corporate control. *Stanford Law Review* 53 (3):539–606.

Rogers, Madeline. 1996. Moguls past and present. *Media Studies Journal* 10 (2–3): 49(6).

Roper, Dean. 2010. *"First of all I don't think U.S newspapers have lost anything completely": Interview with John Morton, Morton Research* [Web page]. WAN/IFRA 2010 [cited 15 March 2010]. Available from http://www.ifra.net/wiki/first-of-all-i-don%E2%80%99t-think-us-newspapers-have-lost-anything-completely

Rotman, Leonard Ian. 1996. *Parallel Paths: Fiduciary Doctrine and the Crown-Native Relationship in Canada*. Toronto: University of Toronto Press.

Rowlinson, Michael. 1997. *Organisations and Institutions*. Basingstoke: Macmillan Business.

Royal Commission. 1949. Royal Commission on the Press 1947–1949 Report. HMSO.

———. 1977. Royal Commission on the Press 1974–1977: Final Report. HMSO.

Rudd, Chris and Janine Hayward. 2005. Media takeover or media intrusion? Modernisation, the media and political communications in New Zealand. *Political Science* 57 (2):7–16.

Rugman, Alan. 2005. *The Regional Multinationals: MNEs and "Global" Strategic Management*. Cambridge: Cambridge University Press.

Russell, Nick. 2006. *Morals and the Media: Ethics in Canadian Journalism*. Vancouver: University of British Columbia Press.

Ryan, Mike and Jordan Sandman Were. 1995. *Telecom Corporation of New Zealand Limited, New Zealand Research Report*. Auckland [NZ]: Jordan Sandman Were.

Ryfe, David Michael. 2006. Guest editor's introduction: New institutionalism and the news. *Political Communication* 23 (2):135–144.

Sadler, Roger L. 2005. *Electronic Media Law*. Thousand Oaks, CA: Sage.

Scannell, Paddy. 1989. Public service broadcasting and modern public life. *Media Culture & Society* 11 (1989):135–166.

Scharpf, Fritz W. 1997. *Games Real Actors Play*. Boulder, CO: Westview.

———. 2000. Institutions in comparative policy research. *Comparative Political Studies* 33 (6/7 August/September 2000):762–790.

Schejter, Amit M. and Roei Davidson. 2008. "…and money is the answer to everything": The News Corp.-Dow Jones merger and the separation of editorial and business practices. *International Journal of Communication* 2 (2008):515–542.

Scherer, Michael. 2002. The Post Company's new profile. *Columbia Journalism Review* XLI (3):44–45.

Schiller, Dan. 1988. How to think about information. In *The Political Economy of Information*, edited by V. Masco and J. Wasko. Madison, WI: University of Wisconsin Press.

Schiller, Herbert. 1974. Waiting for orders: Some current trends in mass communications research in the United States. *International Communications Gazette* 20 (11):11–21.

Schlesinger, Philip. 1977. Newsmen and their time-machine. *The British Journal of Sociology* 28 (3):336–350.

——. 1986. The other way to own a newspaper. *The Guardian* 23 June 1986:13.

Schmalbeck, Richard. 2010. Financing the American newspaper in the twenty-first century. *Vermont Law Review* 35 (1):251–271.

Scholefield, Guy H. 1958. *Newspapers in New Zealand*. Wellington, NZ: A.H. & A.W. Reed.

Schramm, Wilbur. 1960. Who is responsible for the quality of mass communications? In *Mass Communications*, edited by W. Schramm. Urbana, IL: University of Illinois Press.

Schudson, Michael. 1978. *Discovering the News: A Social History of American Newspapers*. New York: Basic Books.

——. 1995. *The Power of News*. Cambridge, MA: Harvard University Press.

——. 1998. *The Good Citizen: A History of American Civic Life*. New York: Free Press.

——. 2002. The news media as political institutions. *Annual Review of Political Science* 5:249–269.

——. 2003. *The Sociology of News, Contemporary Societies*. New York: Norton.

——. 2005. Orientations: The press and democracy in time and space. In *The Press*, edited by G. Overholser & K. H. Jamieson. Oxford: Oxford University Press.

Schudson, Michael and Susan E. Tifft. 2005. American journalism in historical perspective. In *The Press*, edited by G. Overholser & K. H. Jamieson. New York: Oxford University Press.

Schultz, Julianne. 1998. *Reviving the Fourth Estate: Democracy, accountability and the media* Cambridge: Cambridge University Press.

Schultz, Julianne and Ideas for Australia Program. 1994. *Not Just Another Business: Journalists, Citizens and the Media*. Sydney: Pluto Press in association with Ideas for Australia, National Centre for Australian Studies, Monash University.

Schulze, William S, Michael H. Lubatkin, and Richard N. Dino. 2002. Altruism, agency, and the competitiveness of family firms. *Managerial and Decision Economics* 23 (4/5):247–259.

Scott, A. W. and W. F. Frater. 1987. *The Law of Trusts*, 4th ed., 1 vols. Boston: Little Brown.

Scott, George. 1968. *Reporter Anonymous: The Story of the Press Association*. London: Hutchinson & Co.

Scott, W. Richard. 2005. Institutional theory. In *Encyclopedia of Social Theory*, edited by G. Ritzer. Thousand Oaks, CA: Sage.

Scott, W. Richard and John W. Meyer, eds. 1994. *Institutional Environments and Organizations: Structural Complexity and Individualism*. Thousand Oaks, CA: Sage.

Scruton, Roger. 2007. *The Palgrave Macmillan dictionary of political thought*. Basingstoke: Palgrave Macmillan.

Seale, Clive, ed. 2004. *Researching Society and Culture*, 2nd ed. London: Sage.

Searle, John R. 2005. What is an institution? *Journal of Institutional Economics* 1 (1):1–22.

Shapiro, Ian. 2003. *The State of Democratic Theory*, 1st ed. Princeton, NJ: Princeton University Press.

Shawcross, William. 1992. *Rupert Murduch.* London: Chatto & Windus.
Shaw, Gerald. 1999. *The Cape Times: An Informal History.* Cape Town: David Philip Publishers.
Shepard Alicia, C. 2000. Get BIG or Get OUT. *American Journalism Review* 22 (2):22–29.
Sherman, Gabriel. 2010. Post Apocalypse: Inside the messy collapse of a great newspaper. *The New Republic* 241 (1):16–21.
Sherman, Scott. 2002. Stability: Donald Graham's Washington Post. *Columbia Journalism Review* XLI (3):40–49.
Shmanske, Stephen. 1986. News as a public good: Cooperative ownership, price commitments, and the success of the associated press. *The Business History Review* 60 (1):55–80.
Shubik, Martin. 1959. *Strategy and Market Structure: Competition, Oligopoly, and the Theory of Games.* New York: John Wiley & Sons.
Siebert, Fred S. 1963. The social responsibility theory of the press. In *Four Theories of the Press,* edited by Fred S. Siebert, Theodore Peterson and Wilbur Schramm. Urbana, IL: University of Illinois Press.
Sigelman, Lee. 1973. Reporting the news: An organizational analysis. *The American Journal of Sociology* 79 (1):132–151.
Simon, John G. 1995. The regulation of American foundations: Looking backward at the Tax Reform Act of 1969. *Voluntas* 6 (3):243–254.
Simons, Margaret. 2007. *The Content Makers: Understanding the Media in Australia.* Melbourne: Penguin.
Sinclair, Upton. 1919. *The Brass Check: A Study of American Journalism.* Pasadena, CA: Author.
Singer, Jane. 2006. The socially responsible existentialist: A normative emphasis for journalists in a new media environment. *Journalism Studies* 7 (1):2–18.
Snoddy, Raymond. 2004. Viscount Rothermere: The Lord of Middle England. *The Independent* 27 September 2004.
Soderlund, Walter C. and Kai Hildebrandt, eds. 2005. *Canadian Newspaper Ownership in the Era of Convergence: Rediscovering Social Responsibility,* 1st ed. Edmonton, Alberta: University of Alberta Press.
Soderlund, Walter C, Ronald H Wagenberg, Kai Hildebrandt, and Walter I Romanow. 2005. Ownership rights Vs. social responsibility: Defining an appropriate role for newspaper owners. In *Canadian Newspaper Ownership in the Era of Convergence: Rediscovering Social Responsibility,* edited by W. Sonderlund and K. Hildebrandt. Edmonton: University of Alberta Press.
Sparrow, Bartholomew H. 1999. *Uncertain Guardians: The News Media as a Political Institution.* Baltimore: Johns Hopkins University Press.
——. 2006. A research agenda for an institutional media. *Political Communication* 23:145–157.
Stark, David. 1992. From system identity to organizational diversity: Analyzing social change in Eastern Europe. *Contemporary Sociology* 21 (3):299–304.
——. 2009. *The Sense of Dissonance: Accounts of Worth in Economic Life.* Princeton: Princeton University Press.
Starr, Paul. 2004. *The Creation of the Media: Political Origins of Modern Communications.* New York: Basic Books.
Steed, Henry Wickham. 1938. *The Press.* Harmondsworth, Middlesex: Penguin.
Stephens, Mitchell. 1998. *History of News: From the Drum to the Satellite.* New York: Viking (Penguin).
Stepp, Carl Sessions. 1990. Access in a post-social responsibility age. In *Democrat and the Mass Media,* edited by J. Lichtenberg. Cambridge: Cambridge University Press.

———. 2004. Journalism without profit margins. *American Journalism Review* (October/November 2004):36–43.

Stern, Eddie. 1990. Crusader vs. Raider in St. Pete. *Columbia Journalism Review* 29 (1):8–13.

Stewart, Potter. 1975. "Or of the Press". *Hastings Law Journal* 26 (January 1975):631–637.

Stone, Gregory N. 2000. *The Day Paper: The Story of One of America's Last Independent Newspapers*. New London: Day Publishing Company.

Stonham, Paul. 1993a. The wellcome share offering: Part one: Strategy. *European Management Journal* 11 (2):158–168.

———. 1993b. The wellcome share offering: Part two: Technical execution. *European Management Journal* 11 (3):291–303.

Strömbäck, Jesper. 2005. In search of a standard: Four models of democracy and their normative implications for journalism. *Journalism Studies* 6 (3):331–345.

Sunstein, Cass R. 2007. *Republic.com 2.0*. Princeton: Princeton University Press.

Sussman, Leonard R. 1979. Mass media: Opportunities and threats. *Annals of the American Academy of Political and Social Science* 442:77–83.

Tash, Paul. 2009. Top 10 reasons the Tampa Bay Times reached its 125th anniversary. *St Petersburg Times* 19 July 2009.

Taylor, Geoffrey. 1993. *Changing Faces: A History of The Guardian 1956–88*. London: Fourth Estate Limited.

———. 1999. Alastair Hetherington. *Guardian* 4 October 1999.

Taylor, S. J. 2002. *Vere Rothermere and How the* Daily Mail *was Saved*. London: Weidenfeld & Nicolson.

Temple, Mick. 2008. *The British Press*. Maidenhead, UK: Open University Press McGraw Hill.

Thelen, Kathleen. 1999. Historical institutionalism in comparative politics. *Annual Review of Political Science* 2:369–404.

———. 2003. How institutions evolve: Insights from comparative historical analysis. In *Comparative Historical Analysis in the Social Sciences*, edited by J. Mahoney and D. Rueschmeyer. Cambridge: Cambridge University Press.

Thomas, Pradip and Zaharom Nain. 2004. *Who Owns the Media?: Global Trends and Local Resistances*. London: Zed Books.

Thompson, John B. 1995. *The Media and Modernity: A Social Theory of the Media*. Cambridge, UK: Polity Press.

Tifft, Susan E. and Alex S. Jones. 1999. *The Trust: The Private and Powerful Family behind the New York Times*. Boston: Little, Brown and Company.

Times. 1952. *The History of the Times: Vol. IV the 150th Anniversary and Beyond 1912–1948 Part II: 1921–1948*. London: The Times.

Tuccille, Jerome. 1989. *Murdoch: A Biography*. London: Judy Piatkus.

Tucher, Andie. 1997. The real dangers of conglomerate control. *Columbia Journalism Review* 35 (6):46–51.

Tuchman, Gaye. 1978. *Making News: A Study in the Construction of Reality*. New York: Free Press.

———. 2002. The production of news. In *A Handbook of Media and Communication Research: Qualitative and Quantitative Methodologies*, edited by K. B. Jansen. London: Routledge.

Tunstall, Jeremy. 1970. *Media Sociology: A Reader*. London: Constable.

———. 1977. *The Media Are American*. New York: Columbia University Press.

———. 1983. *The Media in Britain*. New York: Columbia University Press.

——. 1996. *Newspaper Power: The New National Press in Britain.* Oxford; New York: Clarendon Press; Oxford University Press.

——. 2001. *Media Occupations and Professions: A Reader, Oxford Readers in Media and Communication.* Oxford, UK; New York: Oxford University Press.

——. 2008. *The Media were American: US Mass Media in Decline.* New York: Oxford University Press.

Tunstall, Jeremy, Michael Palmer, and ebrary Inc. 1991. *Media Moguls.* London; New York: Routledge. http://site.ebrary.com/lib/auckland/Doc?id=5003751

Underwood, Doug. 1995. *When MBAs Rule the Newsroom: How the Marketers and Managers are Reshaping Today's Media.* New York: Columbia University Press.

United Kingdom. 2005. *Review of the BBC's Royal Charter: A Strong BBC, Independent of Government,* Department for Culture, Media and Sport. London: DCMS.

Ursi, Marco. 2006. In your face. *Ryerson Review of Journalism* (Spring 2006).

van der Wurff, Richard, Piet Bakker, and Robert G. Picard. 2008. Economic growth and advertising expenditures in different media in different countries. *Journal of Media Economics* 21 (1):28–52.

Veljanovski, Cento. 1990. Market driven broadcasting: Not myth but reality. *Intermedia* 18 (6):17–21.

Villalonga, Belén and Raphael Amit. 2009. How are U.S. family firms controlled? *Review of Financial Studies* 22 (8):3047–3091.

Villalonga, Belén and Christopher Hartman. 2008. *The New York Times Co.* Boston: Harvard Business School.

Villard, Oswald Garrison. 1944. *The Disappearing Daily.* New York: Alfred A. Knopf.

Vines, Stephen. 1996. A very hard market. *Media Studies Journal* 10 (2–3):131(8).

Walker, R. B. 1980. *Yesterday's News: A History of the Newspaper Press in New South Wales from 1920 to 1945.* Sydney: Sydney University Press.

Wallsten, Kevin. 2005. *Political Blogs and the Bloggers Who Blog Them: Is the Political Blogosphere an Echo Chamber?* Paper Presented at the American Political Science Association Annual Meeting Washington, D.C. September 2005.

Weaver, R. Kent and Bert A. Rockman, eds. 1993. *Do Institutions Matter? Government Capabilities in the United States and Abroad.* Washington, DC: Brookings Institute.

Wiklund, Johan. 2006. Commentary: Family firms and social responsibility: Preliminary evidence from the S&P 500. *Entrepreneurship Theory and Practice* 30 (6):803–808.

Williams, Peter. 2010. *The Story of the Wellcome Trust: Unlocking Sir Henry's Legacy to Medical Research.* Hindrigham, Norfolk, UK: JJG Publishing.

Williams, Raymond. 1966. *Communications.* London: Chatto & Windus.

Williamson, Oliver E. and Sidney G. Winter, eds. 1993. *The Nature of the Firm: Origins, Evolution, and Development.* New York: Oxford University Press.

Windschuttle, Keith. 1988. *The Media: A New Analysis of the Press, Television, Radio and Advertising in Australia.* New ed. Ringwood, VIC: Penguin.

Wolfe, Alan. 2004. The new pamphleteers. *New York Times* 11 July 2004.

Wolff, Michael. 2008. *The Man Who Owns the News.* Sydney: Random House (Knopf Book).

Wolzien, Tom. 1996. The big news-big business bargain. *Media Studies Journal* 10 (2–3):109(6).

Wright, Alex. 2007. *Glut: Mastering Information through the Ages.* Washington DC: Joseph Henry Press (National Academies Press).

Wright, Lawrence. 2009. Slim's time: Who is Carlos Slim, and does he want the paper of record? *New Yorker* 1 June 2009.

Yazdifar, Hassan. 2007. The value of integration: Old institutional economics and new institutional sociology. In *Economics of the Firm: Analysis, Evolution, History*, edited by M. Dietrich. London: Routledge.

Young, Hugo. 1996. Responses. *New Statesman* 9 (412):32–33.

Younger, R. M. 2003. *Keith Murdoch: Founder of a Media Empire*. Sydney: HarperCollins.

Zahra, Shaker A., James C. Hayton, Donald O. Neubaum, Clay Dibrell, and Justin Craig. 2008. Culture of family commitment and strategic flexibility: The moderating effect of stewardship. *Entrepreneurship Theory and Practice* 32 (6):1035–1054.

Zaller, John. 2003. A new standard of news quality: Burglar alarms for the Monitorial Citizen. *Political Communication* 20:109–130.

Zelizer, Barbie. 2004. *Taking Journalism Seriously*. Thousand Oaks, CA: Sage.

Zook, Chris and James Allen. 2001. *Profit from the Core: Growth Strategies in an Era of Turbulence*. Boston: Harvard Business School Press.

Zucker, Lynne G. 1977. The role of institutionalization in cultural persistence. *American Sociological Review* 42 (October):726–743.

———. 1991. The role of institutionalization in cultural persistence. In *The New Institutionalism in Organizational Analysis*, edited by W. W. Powell and P. J. DiMaggio. Chicago: University of Chicago Press.

Index

Note: Locators in italic with n refer to note number.

Printed and bound by CPI Group (UK) Ltd, Croydon, CR0 4YY

.